Ohio

D1239062

Rhineland Emigrants

Lists of German Settlers
in Colonial America

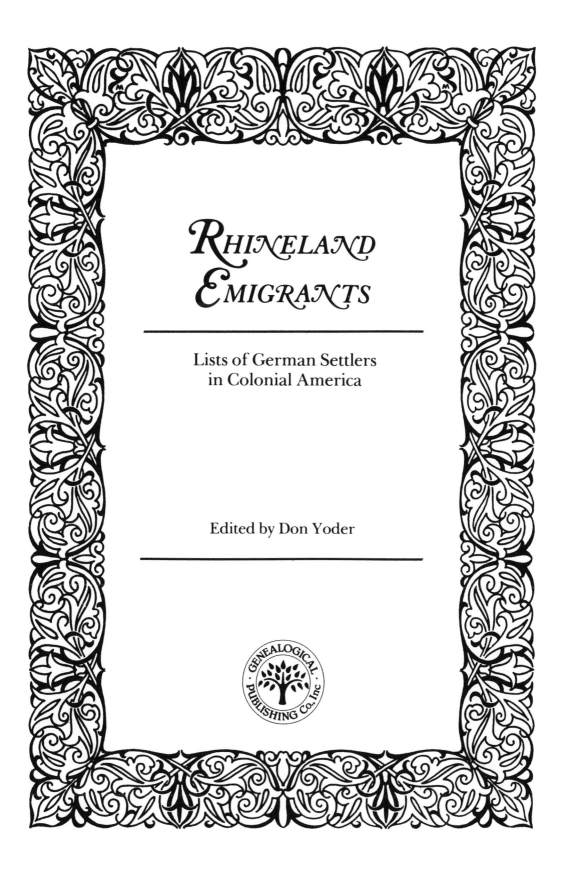

RHINELAND EMIGRANTS

Lists of German Settlers in Colonial America

Edited by Don Yoder

GENEALOGICAL PUBLISHING Co., Inc.

Excerpted and reprinted from *Pennsylvania Folklife*
by arrangement with the Pennsylvania Folklife Society
With a new Introduction and Indexes

Copyright © 1981 by
Genealogical Publishing Co., Inc.
1001 N. Calvert St., Baltimore, Maryland 21202
All Rights Reserved. No part of this publication
may be reproduced, in any form or by any means,
including electronic reproduction or reproduction
via the Internet, except by permission of the publisher.

First printing 1981
Second printing 1985
Third printing 1998

Library of Congress Catalogue Card Number 80-85116
International Standard Book Number 0-8063-0934-2
Made in the United States of America

CONTENTS

Introduction vii

1. Palatine Emigration Materials from the Neckar Valley, 1726-1766, by Friedrich Krebs, tr. and ed. by Don Yoder, from Vol. XXIII:4 (Summer 1975), 15-44 1

2. The Eighteenth-Century Emigration from the Palatinate: New Documentation, by Fritz Braun, tr. and ed. by Don Yoder, from Vol. XV:3 (Spring 1966), 40-48 32

3. New Materials on the 18th-Century Emigration from the Speyer State Archives, by Friedrich Krebs, tr. and ed. by Don Yoder, from Vol. XVI:1 (Autumn 1966), 40-41 41

4. New Materials on 18th-Century Emigration from Württemberg, by Friedrich Krebs, tr. and ed. by Don Yoder, from Vol. XVI:2 (Winter 1966-1967), 22-23 43

5. Eighteenth-Century Emigration from the Duchy of Zweibrücken, by Friedrich Krebs, tr. and ed. by Don Yoder, from Vol. XVII:1 (Autumn 1967), 42-48 45

6. Eighteenth-Century Emigrants to America from the Duchy of Zweibrücken and the Germersheim District, by Friedrich Krebs, tr. and ed. by Don Yoder, from Vol. XVIII:3 (Spring 1969), 44-48 52

7. Notes on Eighteenth-Century Emigration to the British Colonies, by Friedrich Krebs, tr. and ed. by Don Yoder, from Vol. XIX:2 (Winter 1969-1970), 44 57

8. A Siegerland Emigrant List of 1738, by Otto Baeumer, tr. and ed. by Don Yoder, from Vol. XIX:2 (Winter 1969-1970), 46 and inside rear cover 58

9. Palatine Emigrants of the 18th Century, by Friedrich Krebs, tr. and ed. by Don Yoder, from Vol. XXI:2 (Winter 1971-1972), 30-33 60

10. Emigrants from Dossenheim (Baden) in the 18th Century, by Gabriel Hartmann, tr. and ed. by Don Yoder, from Vol. XXI:2 (Winter 1971-1972), 46-48 63

11. 18th-Century Emigrants from the Palatinate, Lower Alsace, and Rheinhessen, by Friedrich Krebs, tr. and ed. by Don Yoder, from Vol. XXI:3 (Spring 1972), 46-48 66

12. American Emigrants from the Territories of the Bishopric of Speyer, by Werner Hacker, tr. and ed. by Don Yoder, from Vol. XXI:4 (Summer 1972), 43-45 69

13. Emigrants to America from the Duchy of Zweibrücken, by Friedrich Krebs, tr. and ed. by Don Yoder, from Vol. XXI:4 (Summer 1972), 46-48 72

14. Palatine Emigrants to America from the Oppenheim Area, 1742-1749, by Friedrich Krebs, tr. and ed. by Don Yoder, from Vol. XXII:1 (Autumn 1972), 46-48 76

15. Emigrants of the 18th Century from the Northern Palatinate, by Friedrich Krebs, tr. and ed. by Don Yoder, from Vol. XXII:2 (Winter 1972-1973), 46-48 80

16. American Emigration from Baden-Durlach in the Years 1749-1751, by Friedrich Krebs, tr. and ed. by Don Yoder, from Vol. XXII:3 (Spring 1973), 41-46 83

17. Pennsylvania Emigrants from Friedrichstal, by Don Yoder, from Vol. XXII:3 (Spring 1973), inside rear cover 89

18. American Emigration Materials from Pfeddersheim, by Albert Cappel, tr. and ed. by Don Yoder, from Vol. XXII:4 (Summer 1973), 43-48 91

19. Emigration Materials from Lambsheim in the Palatinate, by Heinrich Rembe, tr. and ed. by Don Yoder, from Vol. XXIII:2 (Winter 1973-1974), 40-48 97

20. Notes and Documents: I. A Letter to Germany (1806), ed. by Don Yoder, from Vol. XVI:1 (Autumn 1966), 44-45 106

21. The Old Goschenhoppen Burial Register, 1752-1772, tr. by Claude Unger, from Vol. XVII:2 (Winter 1967-1968), 32-34 109

22. Personalia from the "Amerikanischer Correspondent," 1826-1828, ed. by Don Yoder, from Vol. XVII:2 (Winter 1967-1968), 36-41 112

23. Notes and Documents: Eighteenth-Century Letters from Germany, ed. by Don Yoder, from Vol. XIX:3 (Spring 1970), 30-33 118

24. Swiss Mennonite Family Names: An Annotated Checklist, by Leo Schelbert and Sandra Luebking, from Vol. XXVI:5 (Summer 1977), 2-24 122

Index to Personal Names 145

Index to Ships 169

INTRODUCTION

1.

his book grew out of my first visit to the Palatinate. This took place in 1950, when, fresh out of graduate school, I decided it was time to investigate the archives of West Germany and Switzerland. On that first visit I had the good fortune to have as my host Dr. Fritz Braun, Director of the Heimatstelle Pfalz in Kaiserslautern, the principal West German center for emigration studies. In drives over the hills and valleys of this *gemütlich* little state Fritz Braun introduced me to the cultural and historical profile of the Palatine culture which has had so much influence upon Pennsylvania. He took me to villages where Pennsylvania families had originated. We visited the churches where they were baptized, we searched out archival records dealing with their emigration. We talked—in *Pfälzisch* and Pennsylvania German—with descendants of the emigrant families who had remained in the homeland. I met distant cousins who took me to their homes and hearts. We visited farms which had been in the same families since the late seventeenth century; we partook of meals at the farmers' tables.

During the same summer I also paid my first visit of genealogical and historical discovery to Württemberg, Franconia, and Switzerland, in each area meeting emigration scholars, familiarizing myself with the regional and community archive systems, and in general surveying the field of colonial emigration history.

On later visits to the Palatinate I had the good fortune to meet Dr. Friedrich Krebs, archivist at the Palatine State Archives at Speyer, who singlehandedly published more eighteenth-century Atlantic emigration data than any other individual scholar. At the time I was co-editor of the periodical entitled *The Pennsylvania Dutchman*, later to become *Pennsylvania Folklife*, of which I was Editor from 1961/2 to 1978. Among the many departments of which I was in charge was genealogy. In that area my principal interest was emigration history. I began then to translate, edit, and republish emigrant lists from archival sources in Europe, with the blessing of Fritz Braun and Friedrich Krebs, who were pleased to see their work in print in America where it would continue to benefit the descendants of emigrants working on family history.

Out of this extensive body of work I have chosen twenty-four articles dealing with German-speaking emigrants of the eighteenth century who crossed the Atlantic to find homes in the British colonies. These appeared in *Pennsylvania Folklife* from 1966 to 1977. (Fifteen earlier articles, including several by Fritz Braun and Friedrich Krebs, which I published in the years 1949 to 1957, during my editorship of *The Pennsylvania Dutchman*, have recently appeared in *New World Immigrants: A Consolidation of Ship Passenger Lists and Associated Data from Periodical Literature* [Baltimore: Genealogical Publishing Co., Inc., 1979], Volume II.)

2.

What is the value of the lists presented in this volume? First of all, they provide American genealogists with unique materials which not only identify the European birthplaces of their emigrant ancestors, but also enable researchers to trace ancestral families further back into European history. Where possible I have included the archival references to individual items. For example, in the many Palatine lists, one has archival references which can be ordered *in toto* from the relevant archive at Speyer or Karlsruhe. These can involve a page from a protocol book or an entire dossier, complete with letters, affidavits, and seals. Since the community from which the ancestor emigrated is also indicated, one can hire a local genealogist to check village church registers and other archives for the ancestry of the emigrant. In the case of the Palatinate, over 90% of the village registers are now centralized in the Provincial Church Archive (*Landeskirchliches Archiv*) in Speyer. There are also equivalent archives for parts of Baden and Württemberg. The non-centralized records, a minority in the case of the Palatinate, are customarily found in local town archives, although in other states the local pastors may still have charge of them. For American researchers who can read German script of the seventeenth and eighteenth centuries, it should be noted that the registers in the centralized church archive of the Palatinate have been filmed by the Mormons. Film copies of these records can be borrowed from the Genealogical Society of Utah in Salt Lake City to be used at the various Mormon research centers throughout the country.

As in the case of my earlier works on the Atlantic migration, I have tried valiantly to identify the emigrants in their American contexts, locating as many as possible in ecclesiastical and land records. Faced as I was with the exigencies of editing a quarterly periodical, some lists were more fully annotated than others. One of the model lists in this present collection, as far as annotation goes, is List 1. These Neckar Valley emigrants I searched in at least eighteen basic Pennsylvania sources (church records, tax lists, county histories, etc.), all listed in the introduction to the article. Most of the lists were collated with the emigration registers of the Port of Philadelphia as published in the Strassburger-Hinke *Pennsylvania German Pioneers*. Since I was unable to identify the American place of settlement of every emigrant in the lists, I cordially offer my readers the opportunity to notify me if they have made additional identifications.

The second basic value of the lists in this volume is that they provide a well-rounded picture of the eighteenth-century emigrant in his European setting. This is more complex than it would seem at first glance. Once we have established the European birthplace of an emigrant forefather the focus often shifts, and we learn that his forefathers may have migrated into the Rhineland from elsewhere in Europe. Hence in tracing one's transatlantic roots it is important to know the basic outline of Europe's seventeenth-century refugee problem which followed upon the Protestant Reformation and the Catholic Counter-Reformation, as well as the connection of intra-European migration with the economic disaster brought on by the Thirty Years War (1618-1648). One also has to be aware of the confessional patterns which existed in the Rhineland at the time of the emigration. The majority of the emigrants in these lists belonged to the state churches of Germany, the Lutheran and Reformed confessions, which therefore were in the majority among the Pennsylvania German population on this side of the Atlantic. It is important to know to what church the emigrant ancestor belonged. If he was Lutheran, he could come from Württemberg, which was officially Lutheran; from Alsace or Franconia; or from Hannover, Saxony, or elsewhere in the largely Lutheran area of North and East Germany. If he was Reformed, he could come from the Electoral Palatinate, Switzerland, or a smaller Reformed state in the Rhineland. Sometimes Protestants lived under predominantly Catholic rule, as in the case of the Bishopric of Speyer (List 12), and by the eighteenth century Catholics were tolerated in such states as the Palatinate. The picture is extremely complex for American genealogists. And added to this complexity is the existence within the Rhineland states of innumerable Swiss families, Reformed or Anabaptist, and a significant number of French and Belgian Protestant refugees, the so-called Huguenots and Walloons.

In the Palatinate the ranks of the Reformed Church were swelled by thousands of members of Swiss Reformed Churches who settled in Palatine villages after the Thirty Years War. They were free to move, and anxious to move to better their lot, and were often invited to settle in the Rhenish states by the authorities to rebuild the villages and the economy devastated by the war. There are many examples of Swiss Reformed families in the lists in this volume, not all of them noted in the text. Names like *Hungerbieler* (List 10) and *Götzendanner* (List 12) are traced to specific Swiss locations so that American genealogists can follow the lineage there. The *Diebendörffers* of Schriesheim (List 1), who became *Diffenderffers* in Pennsylvania,

viii

trace their name to the village of Dübendorf in Canton Zurich, Switzerland. The *Spengler* (*Spangler*) families (List 1) from the Kraichgau in Baden, prominent settlers of York and other Pennsylvania counties, had emigrated to Germany from Schöftland in what is now Canton Aargau, Switzerland. And the *Rudis*, also in List 1, trace their roots to Canton Basel.

The Huguenot contingent—Protestant refugees from France after the revocation of the Edict of Nantes in 1685—also swelled the ranks of the Rhineland Reformed churches. Examples are scattered throughout the lists, but the largest concentration came from the town of Friedrichstal in Baden, a planned Huguenot settlement founded in 1700 near Karlsruhe. These included, in addition to the *Goranflo* clan, with its unusual name (List 16), families named *Bouquet, leRoy, Bonnet,* and *Corbeau* (List 17). The individual case of *Daniel Jouis* (*Schui, Jue*) of the Münchhof at Dannstadt is typical (List 3). He emigrated in 1732, but returned after his father's death to settle property affairs in 1748. He was the grandson of *David Jouy* of the town of Grigy, near Metz, who had settled as a refugee in the Palatinate. The American emigrant took up land in what is now Lebanon County, Pennsylvania, founding there the widespread Pennsylvania German family of *Shuey.*

Along with the French Huguenot element in the Palatinate there were also some French Swiss families, who may or may not qualify, strictly speaking, as Huguenots (i.e., refugees from France into Switzerland). Examples of these are the *Salathe* family (List 6), now spelled *Solliday* and other ways in Pennsylvania; and the *Bertolets* of Canton Vaud, Switzerland (List 20), who settled for a time at Minfeld in the Palatinate before coming to Pennsylvania in 1726 where they became a leading Pennsylvania German family in the Oley Valley of Berks County. It is important to note that in most cases these French-speaking families, whether from France or Switzerland, had settled in German-speaking areas for a generation or two before proceeding across the Atlantic, and were already Germanized in culture when they arrived in the New World.

In addition to the state church emigrants—Lutherans and Reformed—who were to make up the majority of the Pennsylvania German population, there were also representatives of the sectarian wings of the Reformation. In our lists these were the *Täufer,* or Anabaptists, called Mennonites today. These were mostly of Swiss origin. Driven by persecution from their homelands (mostly Cantons Zurich and Bern), they found toleration and economic opportunity in the Rhenish states. Many were willing to become halfway citizens of the Palatinate, living on the *Höfe* (outlying farms) apart from the villages, or running the gristmills along the Palatine streams. Some actually became citizens (see List 19), others hereditary lessees (*Erbbeständer*) of their farm or mill properties. While tolerated by the government of the Palatinate, they were not encouraged to expand. In fact there appears to have been a *numerus clausus* for Mennonites there, a number beyond which they were not to expand. Hence at various times the Palatine authorities prepared a census of Mennonites in the territories of the Elector. These begin in 1664 and are on file in the Baden State Archives at Karlsruhe. (See Harold S. Bender, ed., "Palatinate Mennonite Census Lists, 1664 to 1774," *The Mennonite Quarterly Review,* XIV:1 (January 1940), 5-40; XIV:2 (April 1940), 67-89; XIV:3 (July 1940), 170-186; XIV:4 (October 1940), 224-248; and XV (January 1941), 46-63.)

When Pennsylvania was established, with promise of cheap land and full toleration, Rhineland Mennonites again pulled up stakes and thronged across the Atlantic. Among the Mennonites whose names appear in the lists in this volume are the following: *Johannes Musselmann,* 1753 (List 1); *Jacob Horsch,* 1766 (List 1); *Nicolaus Oehlenberger* (*Ellenberger*), 1739 (List 3); *Abraham Cetti* (*Zety*), 1752 (List 7); *Rudolph Landes,* 1749 (List 23); *Ulrich Jordan* (*Jordte*), 1749 (List 14); *Johannes Künzi,* 1772 (List 15); *Jacob Krebühl,* 1729 (List 15); *Peter Krebühl,* 1735 (List 15); *Ullrich* and *Peter Ellenberger,* 1749 (List 15); and *Georg Adam Hochermuth,* 1709 (List 19). Of course the entire List 24, the Schelbert-Luebking opus on "Swiss Mennonite Family Names: An Annotated Checklist," contains emigration citations for all of the 153 entries, from A to Z (*Ackermann* to *Zurflueh*).

The third value of the lists is that they provide the researcher with information for understanding the emigration process that our forefathers went through on leaving their homeland and transferring their lives and work to America. In leaving his homeland the emigrant of the eighteenth century was required by the authorities under which he lived to take official leave of the government of the state. If he owned property, he sold it and paid ten percent of its value to the state treasury, the so-called *Zehntpfennig* or tithe mentioned in many of the lists. In those areas where the individual still lived under vestiges of vassalage, he had to apply for manumission as well as permission to emigrate. Those, often single men, who "absconded" to America, leaving under cover of night, without applying for permission to emigrate, forfeited their rights to their parental property when it fell to them at the death of their parents. In some cases the parents aided or abetted the "absconding" of their unmarried sons. A case in point dates from Oberingelheim in 1742 (List 14), when four parents are accused of having "sent their grown sons to the New Land, a few weeks ago, and with the knowledge of the entire village gave each one of them 100 florins and various victuals for the trip." The emigrants were described as "still subject to vassal duties and were even incorporated into the last conscription of young men." For such clandestine emigrants the machinery set up to reclaim their forfeited property was intricate. In some cases such an emigrant had to go through the laborious process of returning to Europe himself or sending a power of attorney with someone who was returning. A few of the America letters included with these lists go into property matters of this sort.

Once they had fulfilled the governmental requirements, the typical emigrant and his wife and children often attended a church service in their home parish, for the last time, to bid their community farewell. Usually several families from a village or region left together, proceeding by boat down the Rhine, paying toll at many borders, to Rotterdam, where they struck a contract with a ship's captain to transport them to the "new land." Once arrived at the port of Philadelphia, they were required to take an oath of allegiance to the King of England and the colonial government, and then proceeded to take up land. Those who were unable to pay their passage worked it off by hiring themselves out as indentured servants.

Not only did groups of emigrants band together to get to the coast, and sail on the same ships, but they also often settled in the same communities in America. The best example appears in List 1 where some nine families—all from the village of Weiler am Steinsberg, near Sinsheim in the Kraichgau, now part of Baden but then part of the Electoral Palatinate— took ship at Rotterdam in the *William and Sarah,* arriving at Philadelphia on 18 September 1727. These were *Philipp Ziegler, Caspar Spengler, Tobias Frey, Johann Georg Ziegler, Adam Miller, Jr., Rudolf Wilcke, Philip Rudisille, Jerg Peter,* and *Ernst Rudi.* Of these, the Zieglers, Freys, and Spenglers pioneered in the settlement of York County, Pennsylvania. In addition to the Weiler crowd, there were on the same ship other emigrants from nearby villages, some of whom settled together in Pennsylvania with their compatriots from Weiler. They had been neighbors in the old world, they became neighbors in the new.

Finally, the lists treat us to a glimpse of our emigrant forefathers as seen by the authorities; they provide good social history as well as genealogical fact. The lists include all classes of people, from the humblest village characters who were not even citizens of the community, through the solidly settled citizens and craftsmen and farmers, to the educated and professional classes. Take the case of the *Wister* (*Wistar*) family of Germantown (List 1). They were public officials in Germany as well as public spirits here, founding, for example, the now extensive glass manufacturing industry of New Jersey. The *Helffrichs* and *Helfensteins,* also in List 1, were ministerial families from the Palatinate who continue to furnish distinguished clergymen to the Reformed Church in Pennsylvania to the present day. Among the emigrants there were town-planners as well as agriculturists. Examples in the present lists are the *Schaeffers* of Schaefferstown in Lebanon County (List 1); the *Hellers* of Hellerstown in

Northampton County (List 18); and the *Irions,* who planned a settlement of German crafts-men in Virginia (List 2). At the other end of the scale was an individual like poor *Adam Pfisterer* of Bauschlott (List 16), with a wife and five children and very little property. When ·he applied for release from vassalage in 1750, the government clerk described him as "in the category of those whom we can well do without." But the majority of the emigrants in these lists were relatively solid citizens, geared into community, state, and church. The men, if not farmers, had gone through the apprentice and guild system and were master bakers, coopers, blacksmiths, cabinetmakers, barbers, stonemasons, millers, and sawmillers—a whole range of indispensable trades. They brought these skills to Penn's Woods and elsewhere in colonial America, and with them helped to build our new world.

The majority of the articles in this collection are emigrant lists from archival sources in Europe. Most of them deal with emigration from the present state of the Palatinate in West Germany, or its predecessor, the Electoral Palatinate, which was dismembered in 1806, the areas on the right bank of the Rhine being at that time assigned to Baden. Other areas repre-sented are Württemberg (List 4), Siegerland in Westphalia (List 8), Alsace (Lists 6, 11, and 23), Baden-Durlach (Lists 16 and 17), and Switzerland (List 24). Not all of the articles are emigrant lists, properly speaking, but all of them contain emigrant data. For example, Lists 21 and 22 are based on emigration materials in church registers and German-American news-papers. Lists 20 and 23 are essentially letters of the emigrant generation, revealing the continu-ing ties between relatives on either side of the Atlantic.

There are other letters scattered through the collection. One of my favorites is the one sent by *Hans Adam Klein* from Conestoga in 1743 to his brother at Bubach in the Duchy of Zwei-brücken (List 5). He had left for America in 1709, and it was not until thirty-three years later that the first news arrived from his old home, brought in person by "Cousin Ludwig." The letter he sent in response presents a kind of Rip van Winkle scenario, for he has learned that only one brother is alive out of his entire family. The writer had settled near Albany, New York, where he married and raised a family. He is now up in years and hard of hearing and he could use some of the property that still belongs to him in Germany. Hence he made the 400-mile trip to Lancaster County, Pennsylvania, to "Cousin Henrich," who is planning a return trip to Germany. When he left, the good cousin agreed to bring back his relative's inheritance for him, which he accomplished. The letter is full of reminiscences of his leavetak-ing from the village in 1709. He recalls affectionately how his brother walked with him to Duntzweiler and Schellweiler for a last farewell chat before turning back. "I am now old," he writes, "and weary of life and almost long for death. Sixty-three years have gone by in my lifetime. I don't know how long the dear God may still let me live, yet I hope to see yet another letter from you." He closes by commending his "dear brother, nephews and nieces, friends, relations and acquaintances, into the protection of the Most High," cordially greeting them "many thousand times" and remaining "till death your faithful brother, cousin and friend *Hans Adam Klein* from Bubach."

3.

A final word is necessary here on the contributors. Dr. Fritz Braun, founder and longtime Director of the Heimatstelle Pfalz in Kaiserslautern, was born in 1905 in Metz, grew up in Saarbrücken, and was educated at the Universities of Heidelberg, Munich, and Bonn. In 1936 he founded the Heimatstelle as a research institute for the study of the Palatine population, its history and culture, as well as immigration into the Palatinate and emigration from it. The emi-gration materials which he gathered were largely destroyed during the war, but he reassembled the data and expanded it after the war. By 1970 his emigration index contained 100,000 cards with at least half a million individual emigrant items. His collecting of source materials and his many monographs spurred on the publication of Palatine family history, settlement history, and town chronicles after the second world war. His numerous genealogical articles, and the lengthy monograph series which he edited also helped in spurring on emigration history in West Germany. His constant help to American scholars, and his visits to Palatine communities in the United States, will long be remembered. He was, in a sense, an unofficial ambassador of the Palatinate. He was at home in the world wherever the Palatine dialect was spoken, above all in Pennsylvania. I here formally and gratefully acknowledge his generous and thoughtful help to me in the earlier stages of my academic career.

I owe Friedrich Krebs a word of gratitude also. When I met him in Speyer many years ago he generously allowed me to translate, edit, and republish his emigration articles for the American world. He was born at Karlbach in the Palatinate in 1908, and died at Speyer in 1978. He was a graduate of the University of Erlangen, and spent most of his career as an archivist in the Palatine State Archives at Speyer. He was a solitary figure, a social and academic loner, working on the eighteenth-century emigration from Germany across the Atlantic. I suspect that he got into this area of research out of boredom with the daily routine of archival work, but whatever route took him there he enjoyed it. In the Speyer Archives he had opportunity to work in the rich veins of emigrant documentation. For pastime he even occasionally took an archivist's holiday to Karlsruhe and Ludwigsburg to dig out similar materials. During my visits to Speyer I had many pleasant luncheons with him, mostly at the Domnapf in the shadow of the cathedral, discussing emigration source materials over huge Palatine meals.

One time he showed me the church registers in the Speyer State Archives which had been deposited there in the Napoleonic era. In going over one of them I found an emigrant that he had missed when he was going through it for an article. "Another emigrant redeemed!" he said with a laugh. It was true, but he had "redeemed" a great many himself, for which Pennsylvania genealogists will always remain in his debt.

The other contributors whose emigration materials have been translated and edited for this volume are Otto Baeumer (List 8), a local historian from Freudenberg in Westphalia; Gabriel Hartmann (List 10) of Heidelberg; Werner Hacker (List 12) of Frankfurt, retired director of the German Federal Railways, who has published several important areal surveys of emigration from Germany, although his specialty is German emigration to Eastern Europe; Albert Cappel (List 18) of Offenbach on the Main, a government official in Hesse; Heinrich Rembe (List 19), teacher, school administrator, and later archivist at Lambsheim; Claude W. Unger (List 21) of Pottsville, Pennsylvania, antiquary, genealogist, and local historian; Leo Schelbert (List 24), professor at the University of Illinois, Chicago Circle, and author of several volumes on the Swiss immigration to North America; and Sandra Luebking (List 24) of Chicago, teacher and genealogist. Not all of these are now in the land of the living, but to all of them, in memory or in actuality, I express my appreciation for their irreplaceable contribution to emigration studies.

To Karl Scherer, successor of Fritz Braun as Director of the Heimatstelle Pfalz, my thanks for generous help along the way, and for permission to republish materials which appeared in the many publications sponsored by his institution.

Finally, I wish to express my thanks to Dr. Richard P. Richter, President of Ursinus College, Collegeville, Pennsylvania, president of the board of trustees of the Pennsylvania Folklife Society, and to Dr. William T. Parsons, present editor of *Pennsylvania Folklife,* for permission to republish these twenty-four articles from *Pennsylvania Folklife.* May they be of continuing use to American genealogists and social historians concerned with emigration history and ethnic studies.

DON YODER

University of Pennsylvania
18 December 1980

RHINELAND EMIGRANTS

Lists of German Settlers
in Colonial America

Palatine Emigration Materials from the Neckar Valley, 1726-1766

By FRIEDRICH KREBS

Translated and Edited by Don Yoder

The present state of the Palatinate (now Rheinland-Pfalz) in West Germany lies entirely west of the Rhine. In the 18th Century, when the Palatine emigration to the New World was heavy, portions of territories east of the Rhine were also included in the Electoral Palatinate (Kurpfalz). Among these was the lower valley of the Neckar River, which included the two administrative districts *(Oberämter)* of Heidelberg and Mosbach.[1] Since this area is now part of the West German state of Baden-Württemberg, the records are housed in

[1]The upper valley of the Neckar belonged principally to Württemberg and those records are found in the Ludwigsburg Archives. For emigrants from the Württemberg territories of the Neckarthal, see Don Yoder, translator and editor, "Emigrants from Württemberg: The Adolf Gerber Lists," *The Pennsylvania German Folklore Society*, X (1945), 103-237.

the Baden State Archives at Karlsruhe *(Generallandesarchiv Karlsruhe).*

The present emigrant list, giving details on 141 individual emigrants, is composed of several lists published in Germany plus some newly discovered materials that are published here for the first time. The sources for the information are as follows: (1) Nos. 1-14 (emigrants of 1726-1727) come from the Protocols of the Electoral Palatine District of Heidelberg *(Protokolle des kurpfälzischen Oberamtes Heidelberg)* in the Baden State archives, and appeared in print in the article, "Zur Frühauswanderung aus dem kurpfälzischen Oberamt Heidelberg nach Amerika (1726-27)," in the *Südwestdeutsche Blätter für Familien- und Wappenkunde*, Jg. 10 Heft 2 (June 1958), 512. (2)

Map showing Neckar Valley, from Merian's Topographia Germaniae.

1

Nos. 15-32 (emigrants of 1727 and 1732) come from a protocol of the town of Weiler am Steinsberg bei Sinsheim (*Generallandesarchiv Karlsruhe,* Abt. 61, No. 13154) and have not previously been published. (3) Nos. 33-37 (emigrants of 1737-1738), Nos. 99-119 (emigrants of 1751), Nos. 124-125 (emigrants of 1753), and Nos. 126-134 (emigrants of 1754) are also drawn from the Protocols of the Electoral Palatine District of Heidelberg in the Baden State Archives at Karlsruhe, and appeared in the article "Die Amerikaauswanderung aus dem kurpfälzischen Oberamt Heidelberg in den Jahren 1737, 1738, 1751, 1753 und 1754," in *Badische Heimat,* Bd. 38 (1958), 303-304. (4) Nos. 39-67 (emigrants of 1741, 1742, 1743, 1744, and 1747) are from the article "Zur Amerikaauswanderung aus dem kurpfälzischen Oberamt Heidelberg 1741-1748," in *Zeitschrift für die Geschichte des Oberrheins,* Bd. 106 (1958), 485-486. (5) Nos. 73-89 (emigrants of 1749), and Nos. 90-97 (emigrants of 1750) are drawn from the Protocols of the Electoral Palatine Districts of Heidelberg and Mosbach in the Baden State Archives at Karlsruhe, and appeared in the article "Amerika-Auswanderer aus den kurpfälzischen Oberämtern Heidelberg und Mosbach für die Jahre 1749/50," in *Badische Heimat,* Bd. 33 (1953), 76-77. Finally, (6) Nos. 38 (1739), 68-71 (1747), 72 (1748), 98 (1750), 120-123 (1751), 135 (1754), 136 (1755), 137 (1764), 138-140 (1765), and 141 (1766) are drawn from the Protocols of the Districts of Heidelberg and Mosbach in the Baden State Archives. They appeared in the article, "Zur Amerikaauswanderung aus den kurpfälzischen Oberämtern Heidelberg (1764-66), und Mosbach (1739-55) und Baden-Durlach (1754)," *Zeitschrift für die Geschichte des Oberrheins,* Bd. 120 (1972), 493-495.[2]

Estimating four persons in each emigration party, the entire list must amount to about 550 persons in all. It is an extremely important emigrant list, not only for the genealogist but for the social historian as well, with references to trades and economic status of the emigrants, their religion, their family relationships, and other matters. The list has been collated with the Philadelphia ship lists, the Strassburger-Hinke *Pennsylvania German Pioneers,* 3 volumes (Pennsylvania German Society, 1934). Some of them may have entered the British colonies via other ports than Philadelphia, since some whose names do not appear in the ship lists turn up in other American source materials of the colonial period.

Particularly important are the materials on the emigrants who came over together on the first ship on the

[2]Preliminary versions of several of these lists of emigrants appeared in *The Pennsylvania Dutchman.* See Friedrich Krebs, "Pennsylvania Pioneers from the Neckar Valley, 1749-1750," V:2 (June 1953), 13; and "More 18th Century Emigrants from the Palatinate," V:13 (March 1, 1954), 12.

list, the *William and Sarah,* which arrived at Philadelphia September 18, 1727 (List 1 A-C). If we had no other proof of the fact, these data show us clearly that very often emigrants from the same area in Europe traveled to America together and frequently settled together in the new country. The long list of emigrants on the *William and Sarah,* many of them from the village of Weiler am Steinsberg, near Sinsheim, sheds light on the settlement of several Pennsylvania frontiers of the time—Goshenhoppen in what is now Montgomery County, the Conestoga area of what is now Lancaster County, the Maxatawny area of what is now Berks County, and the area across the Susquehanna that was in 1749 to become the County of York. These emigrants founded the churches, built schools, erected mills and shops. Their sons, some of them, became county officials, military officers of the Revolution, and served their adopted country in many ways. For the history of the Goshenhoppen settlement, and the founding of the Goshenhoppen Reformed Church in 1727 under George Michael Weiss, Reformed pastor who led the emigration party on the *William and Sarah,* see William J. Hinke, *A History of the Goshenhoppen Reformed Charge, Montgomery County, Pennsylvania (1727-1819)* (Lancaster, Pennsylvania: Pennsylvania German Society, 1920); also C. Z. Weiser, *A Monograph of the New Goschenhoppen and Great Swamp Reformed Charge, 1731-1881* (Reading, Pennsylvania: Daniel Miller, 1882).

Additional materials on the passengers of the *William and Sarah* can be found in Hannah Benner Roach, "Hans Georg Hertzel: Pioneer of Northampton County and His Family," in *The Pennsylvania Genealogical Magazine,* XXIV:3 (1966), 151-184. The Hertzel (Hirtzel) family was from Reihen on the Elsenz, a tributary of the Neckar. Like some other families in the vicinity, they had come originally from Switzerland. The Hirtzels were from Pfäffikon in Canton Zurich. Two brothers, *Hans Georg Hertzel* (born 1686) and *Hans Ulrich Hertzel* (1705-1771), emigrated from Reihen to Pennsylvania. They were the sons of *Clemens Hirtzel* (1659-1707) of Reihen and his wife *Anna,* daughter of *Hans* and *Margaretha (Mayer) Sinter.* *Ulrich Hirtzel* settled in Goshenhoppen with Pastor Weiss, *George Hertzel* settled in the Saucon area of what was to become Northampton County. The name has in more recent times become *Hartzell* in Pennsylvania.

The list could be enlarged from many other sources. For example, among the earliest emigrants to what is now the United States from the lower Neckar Valley were those who appear among the New York "Palatines" who were served by Joshua Kocherthal, Lutheran minister. Among the Neckarthalers whom he mentions in his church register—the earliest German church register in America—are the following: (1) *Johann Michael Wägelin,* of Bohnfeld in the Creichgau, 1710; (2) *Catharina,* daughter of *Johann Jacob Mussier,* of Steinsfurt in the Creichgau, 1710; (3) *Johann Paul Raitschaff,* from Dühren, but owing allegiance to the Durlach government, 1710; (4) *Susanna,* widow of *Johann Paul Clotter* of Berckenheim bei Weinheim in the Palatinate, 1710; (5) *Johann Adam Söllner (Söller),* from Eppingen in the Palatinate, 1710; (6) *Magdalena Schauer,* widow of *Michael Schauer* of Massenbach in the Creichgau, 1711; (7) *Elisabetha,* widow of *Jerg Humbel* of Mosbach in the Palatinate, 1711; (8) *Anna Maria Meyer,* daughter of *Johann Fridrich Meyer,* late of Rohrbach bei Sinsheim, in the Venningen government, 1715; and (9) *Andreas Ellich,* of Neckarburken, district of Mosbach in the Palatinate, 1715. For further details, see Otto Lohr, "Das älteste deutsch-amerikanische Kirchenbuch (1708-1719)," *Jahrbuch für auslanddeutsche Sippenkunde,* [I] (1936), 54-60.

Further searching in local records, particularly the church registers of the parishes of the lower Neckar Valley, will undoubtedly turn up additional names. We have added, in appendix I, brief sketches of four additional Neckarthal emigrants whose accomplishments in the new world are well known to our readers: (A) *Caspar Wistar* of Hilsbach, (B) *Alexander Schaeffer* of Schriesheim, and (C) *Johann Heinrich Helffrich* of Mosbach, and *Johann Conrad Albert Helffenstein* of Sinsheim, Reformed clergymen.

In editing the list, materials from American sources have been added in brackets to the basic European data. Identifying emigrants in American contexts is a difficult process. In some cases we have obviously been successful, in other cases we suggest difficulties involved, and call for help. Will readers who have information on where the unidentified emigrants settled, or who have additional information on those here identified, contact the American editor of the list. It is quite possible that some of the emigrants unidentified in Pennsylvania contexts will turn up in other colonies.

In locating individual emigrants in American sources, the editor has used the following sources, many of which are abbreviated in the text:

1. *Pennsylvania Archives,* Third Series, which include the 18th Century tax lists of the Pennsylvania counties.

2. Edward W. Hocker, *Genealogical Data Relating to the German Settlers of Pennsylvania and Adjacent Territory from Advertisements in German Newspapers Published in Philadelphia and Germantown, 1743-1800* (Germantown, Pa., 1935 (typescript). Retyped and published by Genealogical Publishing Co., Balto., 1980.)

3. *Abstracts of Wills,* Genealogical Society of Pennsylvania, Philadelphia, manuscript volumes for Philadelphia, Chester, Bucks, Northampton, Berks, Lancaster, York, and Cumberland Counties.

4. *The William J. Hinke Collection,* Schaff Library, Historical Society of the Evangelical and Reformed Church, Lancaster Theological Seminary, Lancaster, Pennsylvania. Bound volumes of 18th Century Reformed Church Registers for Pennsylvania and Maryland.

5. *Pennsylvania Church Register Collections,* Genealogical Society of Pennsylvania, Philadelphia; and State Library, Harrisburg.

6. *Proceedings of the Pennsylvania German Society,* particularly the earlier volumes of abstracts of church registers.

7. *The Pennsylvania German Magazine,* I-XVIII (1900-1918).

8. *Records of Rev. John Casper Stoever, Baptismal and Marriage, 1730-1779* (Harrisburg, Pennsylvania: Harrisburg Publishing Company, 1896).

9. *The Perkiomen Region,* first series, I-III (1894-1901; second series, I-IX (1921-1931).

10. *Publications of the Genealogical Society of Pennsylvania.*

11. Theodore W. Bean, *History of Montgomery County* (Philadelphia: Everts and Peck, 1884).

12. William Henry Egle, *History of the Counties of Dauphin and Lebanon in the Commonwealth of Pennsylvania* (Philadelphia: Everts and Peck, 1883), the two counties separately paginated.

13. John Gibson, *History of York County, Pa.* (Chicago: F. A. Battey Publishing Company, 1886).

14. Morton L. Montgomery, *History of Berks County in Pennsylvania* (Philadelphia: Everts, Peck and Richards, 1886).

15. J. Thomas Scharf, *History of Western Maryland,* 2 vols. (Philadelphia: Louis H. Everts, 1882).

16. Andrew S. Berky, translator and editor, *The Journals and Papers of David Schulze,* 2 vols. (Pennsburg, Pennsylvania: The Schwenkfelder Library, 1953).

17. Theodore G. Tappert and John W. Doberstein, translators and editors, *The Journals of Henry Melchior Muhlenberg,* 3 vols. (Philadelphia: The Muhlenberg Press, 1942-1958).

18. I. Daniel Rupp, *A Collection of Upwards of Thirty Thousand Names of German, Swiss, Dutch, French and Other Immigrants in Pennsylvania from 1727 to 1776* (Philadelphia: Ignatius Kohler, 1876), appendices.

To make the list more useful for genealogical purposes, we have prepared two indices, an Index of Places, including the names of the German villages and towns from which individual emigrants came (Appendix II); and an Index of Family Names (Appendix III). Spellings of proper names are given throughout as they appear in the source materials cited.

In conclusion, we wish to express our thanks for the basic materials of the article to Dr. Friedrich Krebs, Speyer, West Germany, retired archivist, who has contributed so much to our knowledge of the background of the 18th Century emigration to Pennsylvania; to the Generallandesarchiv, Karlsruhe, where the original emigrant protocols are preserved; to Dr. Karl Scherer, Director, and Dr. Fritz Braun, Director Emeritus, of the Heimatstelle Pfalz, Kaiserslautern, for materials useful in enlarging the data about certain emigrants; to Prof. Dr. Lau, for Weiler materials; and to Dr. Hermann Brunn, for Schriesheim materials. Other sources are noted in the text.—EDITOR.

EMIGRANTS OF THE YEAR 1726

1. JACOB KIESSINGER, "a poor non-citizen from Sandhofen" [*ein armer Beisass aus Sandhofen*], was permitted to go "to the island of Pennsylvania" [*in die Insul Pinsselvaniam*].

[According to the records of Trinity Lutheran Church, Reading, a *Michael Kissinger,* born on "Fastnacht Day," 1717, at "Sandhofen on the Rhine in the Palatinate," was buried at Reading, January 6, 1791. He had come to America as a child with his parents. He married *Catharina Ruland,* to whom he had four sons and five daughters.]

2. STEPHAN and JOHANN BRECHT. The widow of *Johann Brecht* of Schriesheim was permitted to go to Pennsylvania in 1726 with her two sons *Stephan* and *Johann Brecht.*

[The Brecht (Bright) family in Pennsylvania has important branches in Lebanon, Berks, and Northumberland Counties. *Stephan Brecht,* one of the emigrants of 1726, had children baptized in the Bern Reformed Church, Berks County (*Elizabeth,* 1738; *Anna Maria,* 1745) (Bern Church Records, 1738-1835, Hinke Collection).

Johann Michael Brecht, born May 30, 1706, at Schriesheim, married April 1728, in Heidelberg Township, Chester (now Lebanon) County, *Margaret Simone,* born 1708 in France, daughter of *Jacob Simone.* Margaret died March 21, 1778, in Heidelberg Township, Lancaster (now Lebanon) County. Johann Michael settled in Germantown in October, 1726, then came to the headwaters of the Millbach, Lebanon Valley, near what is now Schaefferstown. He moved to Reading in 1782, where his sons Michael and Peter were living. His son *Michael Brecht* (1732-1814) was County Commissioner of Berks County, 1774-1775, and Member of the Committee of Observation for Berks County, during the Revolution.

The Brechts and Schaeffers were connected in Pennsylvania through the marriage of *Margaretha Schaeffer,* daughter of *Alexander Schaeffer* (see Appendix), native of Schriesheim and founder of Schaefferstown, to *Johannes Brecht (Bright).*

In addition to the Brechts of Schaefferstown and Bern, one *Johannes Brecht* settled at Great Swamp in Bucks County. Schulze (Diary, I, 168) reports the death of his wife, February 13, 1756. Also one *David Brecht* was a taxpayer in Pine Grove Township, now Schuylkill County, 1772 (Montgomery, *Berks County,* p. 1192).

In the Heber Gossler Gearhart Collection at the Genealogical Society of Pennsylvania in Philadelphia are several volumes of typescripts on "The Bright Family of Pennsylvania," particularly those of Berks and Northumberland Counties. Heber Gearhart traced the family to *Johannes Brecht,* born at Schriesheim, October 12, 1662, married July 29, 1684, at Schriesheim, *Anna Catharina Hoffmann,* daughter of *Hans Jost Hoffmann.* Their children were (1) *Catharina,* born March 22, 1704, died July 24, 1794, married *John Dehuff,* saddler, October 1, 1727 (Burial Book of Moravian Church, Lancaster, *Publications of the Genealogical Society of Pennsylvania,* X:2 [March 1928], 155); and (2) *Johann Michael* (1706-1794), q.v. supra. *Johannes Brecht* (b. 1662) was the son of *Balthasar Brecht* (1636-1703), who married in 1658, at Schriesheim, *Anna Margaretha Christmann. Balthasar Brecht* was the son of *Christopher Brecht* (1591-1665), born at Neudorff in the Palatinate, died at Schriesheim.

For this family, see also Albert G. Green, "Historical Sketch of the Bright Family," *Transactions of the Historical Society of Berks County,* I (1898-1904).]

3. MICHAEL WEDEL. Michel Wedel from Dossenheim wanted to go to the New World, 1726.

[Other Wedels emigrated also from Dossenheim. *Anna Maria Wedel* of Dossenheim emigrated to Carolina, May 9, 1752. *Georg Wedel* of Dossenheim, who had married *Anna Barbara Schlepp* (born 1691), emigrated also to Carolina in 1752. On the Ship *Hero,* landing at Philadelphia October 27, 1764 (List 248C), appears another Wedel emigrant from Dossenheim, *Johann Peter Wedel,* Reformed, who married *Anna Sybilla Her,* and settled in Maryland. *Georg Albrecht Wedel* and wife *Eva Catharina,* born circa 1711, are said to have emigrated at the same time and also settled in Maryland. See Gabriel Hartmann, "Amerikafahrer aus Dossenheim im 18. Jahrhundert," *Mannheimer Geschichtsblätter,* XXVII (1926), cols. 55-58, republished in *Pennsylvania Folklife,* XXI:2 (Winter 1971-1972), 46-48.]

4. DANIEL LEVAN. *Daniel leVent (Levan)* of Hockenheim, wanted to go to the New World, 1726. *Daniel Levan* (party of 8 persons) arrived at Philadelphia, September 18, 1727, on the Ship *William and Sarah* (Strassburger-Hinke, *Pennsylvania German Pioneers,* List 1A).

[Daniel Levan was one of five sons of *Daniel Levan* of Amsterdam and his wife *Marie Beau,* Huguenot

4

refugees from Picardy in Northern France. The older sons, *Abraham, Isaac, Jacob,* and *Joseph,* are said to have emigrated to Pennsylvania circa 1715, Joseph dying at sea; Abraham settling in Oley; Isaac in Exeter; Jacob in Maxatawny, at Eaglepoint, Levan's Mill, which became an important stopover point for Moravian missionaries after 1740. *Daniel Levan* emigrated in 1727, settling near Jacob. A sister of the five Levan brothers, *Anna Elisabeth,* emigrated also and married *Sebastian Zimmermann* of Maxatawny.

Daniel Levan married *Susanna Siegfried,* daughter of *Johannes* and *Elisabeth Siegfried,* who were among the first settlers in the vicinity of Kutztown, where Siegfried's Dale is still on the map. *Daniel Levan* was an elder of the Maxatawny Reformed Church, and gave land for a church and school there. About 1740 he opened Levan's Tavern (now Kemp's), a mile east of Kutztown on the Easton Road. This was operated by him and after his death in 1777 by his son until 1788.

The children of *Daniel* and *Susanna (Siegfried) Levan* were the following: (1) *Peter,* (2) *Barbara (Reeser),* (3) *Catharine,* (4) *Mary (Siegfried),* (5) *Susanna (Kemp),* (6) *Magdalena,* (7) *Margaret,* and (8) *Daniel, Jr. Daniel Levan, Jr.,* was admitted to the Berks County bar in 1768, and was a prominent attorney. He became Judge of Berks County under the constitution of 1776, treasurer of the county, 1779-1789, sheriff, 1777-1779, prothonotary 1779-1789, 1791, and clerk of the quarter sessions, 1780-1791.

The Siegfrieds had settled first in Oley, in 1719, and came to Siegfried's Dale prior to 1732. Their home was a stopping place for Moravian missionaries. A son, *Joseph Siegfried* (born 1721), married *Anna Maria Romig,* born 1724 at Ittlingen near Heilbronn in the Palatinate. She came to Pennsylvania with her parents, *Johann Adam Romig* (born at Rüdenstein in the Palatinate) and his wife *Agnes Margaretha* nee *Bernhardt,* arriving at Philadelphia on the Ship *Dragon,* September 30, 1732 (List 26A-C). Joseph's son, *Colonel John Siegfried,* born at Siegfried's Dale, Maxatawny Township, in 1745, married *Mary Levan,* daughter of *Daniel Levan,* in 1769, and settled on the Lehigh River in Allen Township, Northampton County, in 1770, where he conducted a tavern and a ferry. He was a revolutionary hero, friend of Washington, and died 1793. For the Siegfrieds, see W. W. Deatrick, ed., *The Centennial History of Kutztown, Pennsylvania, Celebrating the Centennial of the Incorporation of the Borough 1815-1915* (Kutztown, Kutztown Publishing Co., 1915), pp. 21-24.

For the Levan Family see Warren Patten Coon, *Genealogical Record of the LeVan Family, Descendants of Daniel LeVan and Marie Beau (Huguenots), Natives of Picardy, France, Who Settled in Amsterdam, Holland, 1650 to 1927* (n.p., n.d.); Deatrick, pp. 26-30; and

P. C. Croll, *Annals of the Oley Valley in Berks County, Pa.* (Reading; Pennsylvania: Reading Eagle Press, 1926), pp. 65-68.]

EMIGRANTS OF THE YEAR 1727

5. MICHEL DIEL. *Michel Diel,* citizen, of Mannheim-Seckenheim, was permitted in 1727 to leave for the "New Land" (America). He had to pay 36 florins 55 kreuzer emigration tax. *Hans Michel Diel* took the oath of allegiance at Philadelphia, September 21, 1727, arriving September 18, 1727, on the Ship *William and Sarah* (List 1 A-B). See also No. 6, *Michel Bettle,* who came with him from the same town.

[One *Michael Diehl* was deacon in 1748, First Reformed Church, Philadelphia (Hinke Collection).

There were of course many Diehl families in Colonial America. To show the range of backgrounds, the following is the list of Diehl emigrants before 1808 available at the Heimatstelle Pfalz, Kaiserslautern, West Germany: (1) *Adam Diehl,* from Einöd (Homburg), 1737; (2) *Ananias Diehl,* mentioned in the Kocherthal Records, Colony of New York, 1714; (3) *Daniel Diehl,* from Oberweiler (Kusel), 1744; (4) *Jakob Diehl,* from Zweibrücken; 1803; (5) *Jacob Diehl,* from Thaleischweiler, 1741; (6) *Johannes Diehl,* from Zweibrücken; (7) *Johann Michael Diehl,* from Hengstbach, 1738; (8) *Johann Adam Diehl,* from Württemberg, 1731; (9) *Jost Diehl,* from Offenheim, 1739; (10) *Peter Diehl,* from Zweibrücken, 1749; (11) *Simon Jacob Diehl,* from Oberweiler, before 1757; (12) *Valentin Diehl,* from Niedermoschel, 1743; and (13) *Wilhelm* and *Jakob Diehl,* from Horschbach *(Kusel),* 1742.]

6. MICHEL BETTLE. *Michel Bettle,* of Mannheim-Seckenheim, was permitted to leave in 1727 for the New Land (America), with *Michel Diel,* No. 5, above. He had to pay 27 florins 48 kreuzer emigration tax. *Michel Bettle* took the oath of allegiance at Philadelphia, September 21, 1727, arriving September 18, 1727, on the Ship *William and Sarah* (List 1 A-B).

7. JACOB CUNZ. *Jacob Cunz* from Walldorf left for the "island of Pennsylvania" [*Insul Pensylvaniam*], with *Christian Müller,* No. 8, below. *Jacob Cuntz* appears among the passengers of the Ship *William and Sarah,* arriving at Philadelphia September 18, 1727 (List 1 A-B).

[One *Jacob Kuntz,* of Conewago (Hanover, Pennsylvania), had a son *John George,* born October 1735, baptized April 27, 1736; sponsors *John George Frosch* and wife (*Stoever Records,* p. 11). Additional Kuntz-Frosch items appear in the same source on p. 5.

There were of course other Kuntz (Koons, Coons) families in Pennsylvania. For the *George Michael Kuntz* who arrived at Philadelphia, September 24, 1727, see *The Perkiomen Region,* II (1923), 63-64. *John George Kuntz,* who arrived September 11, 1732, was one of the first settlers on the site of Hanover, and gave land for the first Lutheran Church there (Gibson, *York County*, p. 594).

Another *Jacob Kuntz,* of Lancaster Borough, made his will June 30, 1763, probated October 20, 1763. His executors were *William Bowsman* and *Casper Shaffner.* His wife's name was *Margaretta,* and his children were (1) *Elizabeth,* wife of *Casper Shaffner,* (2) *Margaretta,* wife of *Jacob Yeizer,* (3) *Catharina,* (4) *Anna,* (5) *Francis,* (6) *John,* (7) *Jacob,* and (8) *Christian.* A will of *Jacob Kuntz,* son of *Jacob,* was probated in 1778. *Jacob Kuntz, Sr.,* was also the executor of *Henry Walter* of Lancaster Borough, 1754-1755.

The *Jacob Kunz* who was buried at Lebanon, February 3, 1796, aged 77 years, 7 months, was a native of Alsace (Salem Lutheran Church Records, Lebanon, Pennsylvania).]

8. CHRISTIAN MUELLER. *Christian Müller* of Walldorf left in 1727 for the "island of Pennsylvania" [*Insul Pensylvaniam*] with *Jacob Cunz,* No. 7, above. He was either the *Christyan Miller* who arrived at Philadelphia on the Ship *Molly,* September 30, 1727 (List 3 A-B), or the *Christian Miller* who arrived on the Ship *James Goodwill,* September 27, 1727 (List 2A).

9. JOHANN ALEXANDER DIEBENDOERFFER. *Johann Alexander Diebendörffer,* of Schriesheim, emigrated in 1727.

[For the Diebendörffer (Diffenderffer) families in Pennsylvania, see Frank Ried Diffenderffer, *Some of the Descendants of John Michael Dübendorff 1695-1778, More Especially Those Directly Descended Through his Grandson David Diffenderffer, 1752-1846* (Lancaster, Pennsylvania: The New Era Printing Company, 1910). For the Maryland families, see "The Diffenderffers and Frieses," *Fifth Annual Report of the Society for the History of the Germans in Maryland,* 1891, pp. 91-95.

Frank Ried Diffenderffer, LL.D. (1837-1924), Lancaster journalist and historian and one of the principal founders of the Pennsylvania German Society in 1891, traced the family name from Dübendorf in Canton Zurich, Switzerland.

Alexander Dübendörffer (d. 1768) settled in Bucks County, on the present Lehigh County border, and was a member of the Great Swamp Reformed Church in 1736 (*New Goshenhoppen Reformed Records,* Pennsylvania German Society, XXVIII, 276). *Alexander Dieffendoerffer* married *Gertrude* [*Leidig?*], PGS, XXVIII and moved to Macungie Township, now Lehigh County. His widow, *Gertraut Diefenderfer,* made her will May 29, 1777, probated December 22, 1789 (Northampton County Will Book 2, p. 57).

The founder of the Lancaster County branch was *Michael Dübendörffer,* born at Neresheim in the Electoral Palatinate, near Heidelberg, January 10, 1695,

buried November 13, 1778, Zeltenreich's Church, Lancaster County, aged 83-10-2 (Hinke Collection). On January 21, 1721, he married *Barbara Hasen* or *Hesen.* They settled where New Holland, Lancaster County, now stands, and are believed to have been the first settlers there, and among the founders of Zeltenreich's Reformed Church.

For Frank Ried Diffenderffer, see PGS, XXXII (1924), 34-45.]

10. ANNA MARIA WILL, of Schriesheim, emigrated 1727.

[Among the early references to the Will family in Pennsylvania is the marriage of *Michael Will* and *Christina Puder* of Leacock in Lancaster County, June 2, 1735 (*Stoever Records,* p. 54). *Elizabeth Will,* widow of *Christian Will,* tinsmith, one mile from Schaefferstown or Heidelberg, Lancaster (now Lebanon) County, is mentioned in the *Staatsbote,* Philadelphia, May 26 and October 20, 1772 (Hocker, pp. 122, 126).]

11. JACOB MUELLER, from Mannheim-Neckerau, emigrated in 1727.

[One *Jacob Müller,* born at Kürnbach near Sinsheim in 1718, died November 21, 1776 and was buried on the 23rd at Reading, according to the records of Trinity Lutheran Church. He married *Mary Agatha,* widow of *Christian Kämmerer.* In the register the birthplace is given as "Hernbach in Bretten," which is obviously Kürnbach in the District of Sinsheim.]

12. ANDREAS ZIMMERMANN, from Meckesheim, wanted to go to Pennsylvania in 1727, with *Johann Andreas Hill* (No. 13, below).

[According to records in the Heimatstelle Pfalz, Kaiserslautern, *Andreas Zimmermann,* son of *Hans Georg Zimmermann,* married *Anna Elisabeth* [———]; they had the following children listed in the church registers of Meckesheim: (1) *Hans Michael,* born July 16, 1706; (2) *Hans Dietz,* born August 18, 1707; (3) *Margaretha,* born August 24, 1709; (4) *Anna Elisabetha,* born April 25, 1711; (5) *Johann Georg,* born March 6, 1714, married before 1740, *Anna Catharina* [———], to whom he had ten children; removed to Frederick, Maryland, after 1786; (6) *Anna Margaretha,* born January 13, 1716; and (7) *Amalia Maria Katharina,* born September 13, 1717. The emigration party included eight persons.

Andreas Zimmermann settled in Goshenhoppen, Montgomery County. See *The Zimmerman Family* (1955).]

13. JOHANN ANDREAS HILL, of Mannheim-Sandhofen, wanted to go to Pennsylvania in 1727, with *Andreas Zimmermann* (No. 12, above).

14. CHRISTOPH WALTER. In the case of *Christoph Walter,* of Dossenheim, who wanted to leave in 1727, the notation "America" is lacking in the protocols, but he is certainly identical with the *Christopher*

Walther who landed at Philadelphia on the Ship *William and Sarah,* September 18, 1727 (List 1 A-B).

15. PHILIPP ZIEGLER, citizen of Weiler, had to pay 24 florins, 19 kreuzer emigration tax, intending to go to Pennsylvania. He appears as *Philip Zigler* in the passenger lists of the *William and Sarah,* 1727.

[According to records in the Heimatstelle Pfalz, Kaiserslautern, *Georg Philipp Ziegler* was baptized Reformed, but was later Lutheran. He was baptized April 1, 1677, at Weiler am Steinsberg, Kreis Sinsheim, son of *Hans Georg Ziegler* (born 1622, buried February 22, 1685) and his wife *Sarah,* who died at Weiler December 18, 1689, aged 56 years. *Georg Philipp Ziegler* married (Lutheran) June 1702, at Weiler, *Anna Mayer,* born at Reihen (?), Kreis Sinsheim, daughter of *Jacob Mayer* of Reihen. The emigration party consisted of 5 ½ persons. The following children were born to *Georg Philipp Ziegler* (later referred to as *Johann Philipp Ziegler):*

1. *Johann Jacob,* born May 15, 1703, baptized May 17, at Weiler (Reformed Church Register, Hilsbach-Weiler). Confirmed 1717 Lutheran (Lutheran Church Register Sinsheim).
2. *Maria Catharina,* born March 1, 1705, died young?
3. *Barbara,* born July 25, 1707, died (?) Weiler August 11, 1707.
4. *Ludwig,* born October 22, 1708, died Weiler November 4, 1708.
5. *Hans Martin,* baptized March 12, 1710, died young?
6. *Johann Georg,* baptized February 2, 1712, confirmed 1726 (Lutheran).
7. *Johann Philipp,* born August 24, 1713, at Weiler (Lutheran Church Register, Sinsheim), confirmed 1726 (Lutheran).
8. *Anna Christine,* born December 15, 1715, Weiler (Lutheran Church Register, Sinsheim).

Possibly Nos. 1, 6, 7, and 8 emigrated with the parents. The emigration total is "5 ½" persons. The mother's name is given as *"Anna Martha"* 1705-1708, *"Anna Magdalena"* 1710-1713, and *"Anna"* 1715. Whether this is the same person is not certain. In Weiler however there is no further marriage of the father listed.

Philip Ziegler settled in Hellam Township, York County, where he petitioned about the land disputes in 1736, with *Tobias Frey* and other emigrants of 1727 (Gibson, *York County,* p. 602). *John Philip Ziegler,* [Jr.], of Codorus, had a daughter *Anna Christina,* baptized September 18, 1740; sponsors *Jacob Ziegler* and *Agnes Schmidt (Stoever Records,* p. 14). *Philip Ziegler, Jr.,* was sponsor at the baptism of a daughter of *Dietrich Mayer,* Codorus, 1740 (*Stoever Records,* p. 15).

Philipp Ziegeler, [Jr.], married *Margaretha Schmidt,* Codorus, November 21, 1737 (Stoever Records, p. 55). On the same day, *Christina Ziegeler* married *George Meyer,* Codorus (*Stoever Records,* p. 55).

Another *Philip Ziegler,* of Ridge Valley, Upper Salford Township, Philadelphia (now Montgomery) County, is mentioned in Sower's newspaper, February 16, 1750, and October 16, 1757 (Hocker, pp. 17, 36).]

16. CASPAR SPENGLER, citizen of Weiler, emigrant of 1727, had to pay 49 florins 5 kreuzer emigration tax.

[The great authority on the Spangler families of Pennsylvania is Edward W. Spangler, *The Annals of the Families of Caspar, Henry, Baltzer and George Spengler, who settled in York County Respectively in 1729, 1732, 1732 and 1751: With Biographical and Historical Sketches and Memorabilia of Contemporaneous Local Events* (York, Pennsylvania: The York Daily Publishing Co., 1896). While the name was originally "Spengler," the common spelling in 1896 was "Spangler," "except for one branch in Virginia" (pp. vii-viii). The family came from "Weyler under Steinsberg," according to the passport documents brought along on the emigration, and the Reformed pastor of Hilsbach-Weiler constructed a family tree which traced the family from Schöftland, Canton Aargau, Switzerland. *Hans Rudolf Spengler,* father of the emigrants, was the son of *Jacob Spengler of Schöftland,* and *Hans Rudolf* emigrated to Weiler, near Sinsheim, on the Elsenz, and married *Judith Haegis,* daughter of *Jacob Haegis.*

Of the emigrants to Pennsylvania, *Baltzer Spengler* was one of if not the first settler and one of the founders of York, Pennsylvania (Gibson, *York County,* p. 237). The Weiler emigrant families continued to intermarry in America. *Caspar Spengler's* daughter *Mary* married Colonel *Michael Swoope (Schwab),* who was Justice of the Peace, Judge, Member of the State Assembly 1768-1776, and Colonel in the Flying Camp during the Revolution. *Henry Spengler,* who emigrated in 1732, brought along a family Bible that he had purchased at the Frankfurt Fair for 4 florins, and when his first child was born in America, in 1732, the sponsors were *Rudolph Wilcke* (No. 20) and wife, both from Weiler.

Other Spangler families settled in the Schaefferstown area. *Michael Spangler* and wife *Elizabeth* and two sons emigrated from Heidelberg, Germany, in 1737, arriving at Philadelphia on the Ship *Samuel (The Spangler Family,* pp. 252-254). *Jacob* and *Adam Spangler* were residents of New Hanover Township (Falkner's Swamp), now Montgomery County, in 1741 (Bean, *Montgomery County,* p. 993); and *Stophel (Christopher) Spangler* was resident in Alsace Township, Berks County, 1759 (Montgomery, *Berks County,* p. 984). Other Spanglers settled in what is now Centre County, Pennsylvania, in the revolutionary era.

A distinguished descendant of the York County Spangler family was *Henry Wilson Spangler* (1858-

1912), engineer, educator, and author (*Dictionary of American Biography*, XVII, 429-430).]

17. TOBIAS FREY, citizen of Weiler, emigrant of 1727, had to pay 65 florins 18 kreuzer emigration tax. He appears in the passenger lists of the *William and Sarah*, 1727.

[According to records in the Heimatstelle Pfalz, Kaiserslautern, *Tobias Frey* was baptized June 1, 1684, at Weiler am Steinsberg bei Sinsheim (Reformed Church Register, Hilsbach-Weiler). He was the son of *Hans and Margaretha Frey* and was by trade a cartwright. He married (Reformed Church Register, Hilsbach-Weiler), July 17, 1709, at Weiler, *Anna Maria Peter*, from Eppingen. Their children, born before the emigration, were as follows:

1. *Conrad*, baptized at Weiler, March 10, 1715.
2. *Gottfried*, baptized at Weiler, August 4, 1721.
3. *Anna Maria*, baptized at Weiler, December 16, 1722.

Tobias Frey, with *Martin Frey* and *Philip Ziegler*, other emigrants of 1727, settled in York County, Pennsylvania, where they petitioned relative to the land disputes of 1736 (Gibson, *York County*, p. 602). *Martin Frey*, son of *Tobias Frey*, married *Maria Magdalena Willhaut*, daughter of *Frederick Willhaut*, from over the Susquehanna, on April 15, 1735 (Trinity Lutheran Church, Lancaster, Marriage Records, 1731-1850, State Library, Harrisburg).

Martin Frey (died 1739), who had settled on the northeastern section of what is now York, Pennsylvania, as early as 1734, also had a son *Tobias* (Gibson, *York County*, p. 514).

Frysville, Windsor Township, York County, is named for the family (Gibson, *York County*, p. 725).]

18. JOHANN GEORG ZIEGLER, cabinetmaker, citizen of Weiler, emigrant of 1727, had to pay 126 florins 25 kreuzer emigration tax. He appears as *Hans Georg Ziegler* in the passenger lists of the Ship *William and Sarah*, 1727.

[According to records in the Heimatstelle Pfalz, *Johann Georg (Hans Jerg) Ziegler*, was born 1697, either the son of *Hans Martin Ziegler* (July 28, 1697) or of *Christoph Ziegler* (May 18, 1697). He married 1720/21 *Anna Maria* [———]. The family was Lutheran. The emigration party numbered 3 persons. Children born before the emigration, as listed in the Lutheran Church Register, Sinsheim, are as follows:

1. *Anna Barbara*, born at Weiler July 28, 1722, baptized August 2.
2. *Elisabeth*, born at Weiler July 11, 1724, baptized July 13.
3. *Johann Ludwig*, born at Weiler December 15, 1726, baptized December 18.

John George Ziegler, emigrant of 1727, was a member of the Lutheran Church, York, Pennsylvania, 1733 (Gibson, *York County*, p. 525). *John George Ziegeler*

married *Margaretha Hamspacher*, Codorus, January 17, 1738 (*Stoever Records*, p. 55). *George Ziegler* was the first constable of Codorus Township, when York County was set up in 1749 (Gibson, *York County*, p. 492).]

19. ADAM MILLER, JR., citizen of Weiler, emigrant of 1727, paid 13 florins 2 kreuzer emigration tax. He appears as *Hans Adam Miller* in the passenger lists of the *William and Sarah*, 1727.

[According to the *William and Mary College Quarterly*, IX:2 (October 1900), reprinted in *The Pennsylvania-German*, IX (1908), 421, *Adam Miller* was naturalized in Virginia March 13, 1741-1742. In the naturalization paper, dated at Williamsburg and signed by Lieutenant Governor *William Gooch*, he is described as "Adam Miller born at Shresoin [Schriesheim] in Germany having Settled and Inhabited for fifteen years past on Shenandoa in this Colony". According to the commentary, the paper "proves beyond a doubt that Adam Miller was the first white man to build on this side of the Blue Ridge, as he came in 1726 [1727]. The Hites came to Winchester in 1732; the Lewises settled near Staunton also in 1732; so Adam Miller was the first white settler in the valley of the Shenandoah, as this old naturalization paper proves; and the land on which he located is still in possession of his descendants". The material was sent in by *Lizzie B. Miller*, Elkton, Virginia, copied from the original in her possession.

For Adam Miller, see also F. B. Kegley, *Kegley's Virginia Frontier: The Beginning of the Southwest; The Roanoke of Colonial Days, 1740-1783* (Roanoke, Virginia: The Southwest Virginia Historical Society, 1938), pp. 22-23.]

20. RUDOLF WILCKE, citizen of Weiler, emigrant of 1727, paid 57 florins 21 kreuzer emigration tax. His name appears as *Rutolff Wellecker* in the passenger lists of the *William and Sarah*, 1727.

[According to records in the Heimatstelle Pfalz, Kaiserslautern, *Rudolf Wilcke* was a baker and innkeeper, born about 1690. He was Reformed and married 1714/15 *Elisabetha* [———]. His emigration party consisted of three persons.

According to the Reformed Church Register of Hilsbach-Weiler, *Rudolph* and *Elisabeth Wilcke* had four children baptized at Weiler:

1. *Johann Georg*, baptized December 15, 1715; died.
2. *Anna Margaretha*, baptized October 27, 1718.
3. *Johann Gottfried*, baptized March 6, 1721.
4. *Johann Georg*, baptized July 29, 1723, died February 1, 1724 (?).

Rudolf Wilcke apparently joined other Weiler emigrants in settling in York County, Pennsylvania (see No. 16, above).]

21. PHILIP RUDISILLE. In the case of *Philip Rudisille,* citizen of Weiler, emigrant of 1727, it was noted that his father-in-law, *Georg Philipp Schopf,* had taken over for his own use what had been sold. The emigrant appears as *Philip Rutschly* in the passenger lists of the *William and Sarah,* 1727.

[According to records in the Heimatstelle Pfalz, Kaiserslautern, *Philipp Rudisille* was born in Michelfeld, Kreis Sinsheim, September 24, 1697, son of *Johann Jacob* and *Cleophe (Neff) Rudisille,* of Michelfeld. The family was originally from Switzerland, where the name was spelled *Rüdisühli. Philipp Rudisille* was a tailor by trade. On April 14, 1722, at Weiler am Steinsberg, he married *Anna Maria Schopf,* daughter of *Georg Philipp Schopf* and his second wife *Anna Maria.* Schopf was village mayor [*Schultheiss*] for the Venningen government, was baptized at Weiler October 15, 1656, and buried there March 29, 1742. *Anna Maria Schopf,* his daughter, was baptized (Reformed) November 3, 1702, and confirmed in 1715 (Lutheran Church Register, Sinsheim). The Lutheran Church Register of Sinsheim lists the following children born before the emigration:

1. *Georg Philipp,* born at Weiler March 30, 1723, baptized April 1, 1723.
2. *Georg Philipp,* born at Weiler, August 18, 1725, baptized August 19. Both of these appear to have died in infancy.

The Rudisills have proliferated through Lancaster, York, and Lebanon Counties, Pennsylvania, and Western Maryland.

Philipp Rudiesile married *Susanna Beyer,* of Conestoga, October 27, 1734 (*Stoever Records,* p. 54). *Philip Rudysil,* of Manheim Township, Lancaster County, made his will September 3, 1755, probated November 11, 1755. Executors were *Adam Simon Kuhn* and *Michael Immel.* His wife's name was *Susanna,* and his children were (1) *Michael,* (2) *Susanna,* and (3) *Catharine. Philip Rudesill* is also found in Lebanon Township, 1755 (Egle, *Lebanon County,* p. 130), and the records of the Hill Church, Lebanon County, list children of his baptized 1749-1756. Among the early members of the family in York County was *Weirich Rudiesiel,* of Codorus, whose daughter *Anna Johanna* was baptized May 17, 1741; sponsors *Jacob Ottinger* and *Ana Johanna Igsin* [Ickes?] (*Stoever Records,* p. 17). A descendant of the York County branch of the family, *Abraham Rudisill,* was responsible for one of the earliest printed Pennsylvania German genealogies, *Minutes of the Centennial Celebration, held by the descendants of the Elder Mathias Smyser, May 3rd, 1845, on the farm of Samuel Smyser, in West Manchester Township, York County, Pennsylvania* (Carlisle: Abraham Rudisill, 1852).

For additional materials on Philip Rudisill, with details on his children born in America, see Frederick Sheely Weiser, *The Tanger-Metzger Genealogy* (Gettysburg: Privately printed, 1955), pp. 8-9.]

22. JERG PETER, citizen of Weiler, emigrant of 1727, had to pay 27 florins, 34 kreuzer emigration tax. His name appears as *Jerg Petter* in the passenger lists of the *William and Sarah,* 1727.

[According to records of the Heimatstelle Pfalz, Kaiserslautern, *Hans Jerg Peter,* born circa 1690, Reformed, married (1) *Anna Barbara* [———], buried at Weiler, January 19, 1726, aged 32 years; (2) January 7, 1727, at Weiler am Steinsberg (Reformed Church Register, Hilsbach), *Margaretha Böhler (Büller, Biehler),* from Reihen, daughter of *Johann* and *Anna Barbara Böhler* of Reihen, baptized July 24, 1701 (Reformed) at Reihen, Kreis Sinsheim. The emigration party consisted of "2 ½" persons. Included was a son of the first marriage, *Rudolph,* baptized at Weiler (Reformed), October 25, 1722.]

23. ERNST RUDI, citizen of Weiler, emigrant of 1727, paid 18 florins 47 kreuzer emigration tax. His name appears as *Hans Ernst Rudi* in the passenger lists of the *William and Sarah,* 1727.

[According to records of the Heimatstelle Pfalz, Kaiserslautern, *Hans Ernst Rudi,* son of *Hans Conrad Rudi,* cooper, of Weiler, and his wife *Anna Maria,* nee *Schopf,* was baptized in Weiler February 5, 1682. He married, January 25, 1707, in Hilsbach (Reformed Church Register of Hilsbach-Weiler), *Anna Catharina Doll,* of Hilsbach, daughter of the Attorney Doll.

In the same ship lists appears the name of *Johann Dietrich Rudi,* born January 1, 1702, at Reihen, Kreis Sinsheim, son of *Sebastian* and *Anna Margaretha Rudi. Dietrich Rudi* settled first in Germantown, Pennsylvania, in 1737 was in Upper Salford, Philadelphia (now Montgomery) County, then to Rockhill, Bucks County, and finally settled at Indian Creek. See Price, *History of Christ Reformed Church at Indian Creek,* p. 67.

Other early Rudi emigrants included (1) *Bastian Rudi,* born at Reihen, Kreis Sinsheim, December 21, 1708, baptized the 23rd, son of *Dietrich* and *Anna (Schuch) Rudi,* arrived at Philadelphia on the Ship *Plaisance,* September 21, 1732; and (2) *Hans Conrad Rudi,* born August 5, 1683, at Dühren, son of *Hans Rudi* from Frenkendorf, Canton Basel, Switzerland, and his wife *Anna Dorothea Bender,* nee *Lang* (Heimatstelle Pfalz). According to the church registers of Dühren *Hans Conrad Rudi* went to the New Land before 1747 (Heimatstelle Pfalz).]

24. MICHAEL PFAUZ. An entry in the administrative protocols [*Amts- und Gerichtsprotocoll*] of Dühren (Generallandesarchiv Karlsruhe, Abt. 61, No. 5552) treats the handing over of a legacy of 549 florins 11 kreuzer, which *Michael Pfauz* of Rohrbach bei Dühren, "now in Pennsylvania" [*nunmehr in Pensilva-*

nien befindlich], had made to his deceased brother-in-law Jacob Mühlhauser in Steinsfurt, of which two relatives at Steinsfurt and at Rohrbach had each taken half into custody. Michael Pfauz desired that the legacy be transferred to his brother Andreas Pfauz. The Electoral Palatine Government directed that a relative, Martin Ludwig's widow at Steinsfurt, should transfer her share in the said legacy to Andreas Pfauz. The document is dated at Sinsheim, March 6, 1737.

Hans Michael Pfautz appears in the passenger lists of the Ship William and Sarah, 1727.

[According to records in the Heimatstelle Pfalz, Kaiserslautern, Hans Michael Pfautz, son of Hans Michael Pfautz, village mayor [Schultheiss], was born about 1680/1682, at Rohrbach, Kreis Sinsheim. He was the innkeeper of the Tree Inn [Baumwirt] at Rohrbach, and was married on February 10, 1702, at Steinsfurt, (Church Register, Rohrbach) to Ursula Mühlenhäuser of Steinsfurt, Reformed, daughter of Hans Jacob Mühlenhäuser of Steinsfurt. The emigration party consisted of five persons. On March 22, 1727, Michael Pfautz sold his property [Haus, Hof u. Acker] for 650 florins to the beerbrewer Hans Adam Tracken at Neckargemünd.

Hans Michael Pfautz settled in "Conestoga," i.e., Lancaster County, Pennsylvania. In 1737 his children numbered six: (1) Hans Michael, (2) Hans Jacob, (3) Johannes, (4) Andreas, (5) Anna Margaretha Wiederer, and (6) Anna Barbara Weller. Pfautz's Valley in Perry County, on the west side of the Susquehanna, is named for this family.

For the descendants of Michael Pfautz, see John Eby Pfautz, A Family Record of John Michael Pfautz, A Native of Switzerland, Europe, who emigrated from the Palatinate to America, about the year 1707 [sic] and His Posterity down to the year 1880 (Lancaster: John Baer's Sons, 1881). John Eby Pfautz was mistaken as to the date of his ancestor's emigration.

Other members of the family were found in Frederick Township, Philadelphia (now Montgomery) County, prior to 1734; Jacob Fauts, 100 acres, and Baltus Fauts, 100 acres (Rupp, p. 472). Anna Barbara Pfautz, of Leacock, married Jacob Heller, June 25, 1734 (Stoever Records, p. 54). David Pfautz was carpenter in Lancaster, 1761 (Hocker, p. 97). President Hoover's emigrant ancestor, Andreas Huber, married a Pfautz from Lancaster County. Andreas Huber, born January 23, 1723, at Ellerstadt in the Palatinate, from a family originally from Canton Aargau, Switzerland, came to Pennsylvania on the Ship Two Sisters, arriving at Philadelphia September 9, 1738. He settled in Lancaster County and married Margaret Pfautz circa 1745. Margaret Pfautz was said to be a daughter of Michael Pfautz, emigrant of 1727. In 1746 Andreas and Margaret Huber removed to Carroll County, Maryland,

near Little Pipe Creek, and in 1772 went on to North Carolina. Two brothers of Andreas preceded him to America, Johannes, on the Mortonhouse in 1728, and Christian, on the Dragon, 1732. For the Huber-Pfautz family, see Hulda Hoover McLean, Genealogy of the Herbert Hoover Family (Stanford, University: The Hoover Institute on War, Revolution and Peace, 1967), Hoover Institute Bibliographical Series, XXX. A daughter of Andrew Hoover, Elizabeth, born circa 1751, married David Fouts (Phouts) and emigrated to Ohio in 1801.]

25. JOHANN GEORG SCHWAB. According to family tradition, Johann Georg Schwab, emigrant of 1727, came from Wiesloch near Heidelberg, where he was a baker. His name also appears in the passenger lists of the William and Sarah, 1727.

[This emigrant, along with some of the Zieglers, Spanglers, and Rudisills, who arrived on the same ship, settled in York County, Pennsylvania (Gibson, York County, p. 525). He was one of the organizers of Christ Lutheran Church in York, 1733. He was named one of His Majesty's Justices of the Peace for the County of Lancaster, August 29, 1746, and reappointed in 1749 when York County was set off from Lancaster. He is described as a "principal inhabitant". He died in 1757.

Edwin Swope, Box 155, Mansfield, Missouri, USA 65704, is working on the Swope (Schwab, Schwob) family records in the Protestant church registers of Dühren (Baden) and Leimen/Walldorf (Baden). He has found that Hans Jörg Schwab was born July 19, 1682, at Dühren, son of Jost and Anna Catharina (Wolffhart) Schwab. Jost Schwab was the son of Georg Schwab, citizen of Sinsheim, and married Anna Catharina, daughter of Hans Jörg Wolffhart, of Dühren, May 17, 1681, at Dühren. Hans Georg Schwab had a son Johann Georg, born October 5, 1705, at Wiesloch, who died in America March 30, 1780, in Paradise Township, York County, Pennsylvania. Hans Georg Schwab, Sr., said to be one of the founders of the town of York, Pennsylvania, died there in 1759.

A recent volume on the Swope genealogy, Emily Swope Morse and Winfred Morse McLachlan, co-authors, The Swope Family Book of Remembrance: A History of the Origins of the First Schwab, Schwob,

Swope Families in Early Lancaster County, Pennsylvania, and Some of Their Descendants (Provo, Utah: J. Theron Smith, 1972), 2 volumes bound in one, besides being a model of genealogical research for one Pennsylvania German clan, contains all the basic Schwab-Schwob materials from the church registers of the Neckar Valley. Part I (1282 pages) deals with the descendants of *Jacob Schwob,* of Bennwil, Baselland, Switzerland, who settled in what is now Lebanon County in 1749. Volume II (pp. 1283-1397) presents material on *Jost Schwab* (1656-1727) of Leimen, who settled in Leacock Township, Chester (now Lancaster) County, in 1720. From this it appears that the *Johann Georg Schwab,* emigrant of 1727, was the oldest son of Jost Schwab. A daughter of Jost Schwab and sister of the 1727 emigrant, *Anna Elisabeth Schwab* (1692-1761), married in 1712 *Johann Eberhardt Riehm* (1687-1779), of Leimen, founder of Reamstown in Lancaster County. Another daughter of Jost, *Anna Maria Schwab* (born 1698), married in 1719 *Andreas Meixell,* widower of Leimen. The Meixells probably came to America with her parents in 1720. *Andreas Meixell* of Donegal Township, Lancaster County, made his will October 25, 1735, probated March 3, 1740.

The Morse-McLachlan volume contains full genealogical accounts of the German families that married into the Schwab-Schwob ancestry, particularly the *Wolfahrt-Wolfhardt* family of Waiblingen on the Neckar in Württemberg. An earlier genealogy, Gilbert Ernest Swope, *History of the Swope Family and their Connections, 1678-1896* (Lancaster, Pennsylvania: T.B. and H.B. Cochran, 1896) is still useful although superseded in many details by Morse-McLachlan.]

26. JOHANN FRIDERICH HILLIGASS. *Johann Friderich Hilligass,* emigrant of 1727, probably came from the city of Sinsheim, where the rather rare family name of Hilligass is to be found in the Protestant church registers.. He appears among the passenger lists of the *William and Sarah,* 1727.

[For *John Frederick Hillegass* (1685-1765), see *The Pennsylvania Magazine,* XVIII (1894), 85-89; and *The Perkiomen Region,* I (1895), 50-51. *Frederick Hillegass* and wife are mentioned as early as 1731 in the registers of the New Goshenhoppen Reformed Church, where they were sponsors to a daughter of *Philip Labaar* and a daughter of *Johann Michael Lutz* (PGS, XXVIII, 277). They had a daughter *Elisabetha Barbara,* baptized by *John Peter Miller,* June 4, 1732; sponsor, *Anna Barbara,* daughter of *Kaspar Kamm* (PGS, XVIII, 278); and a son *Georg Peter,* baptized May 9, 1736, by Pastor *Goetschy* (Ibid., p. 281). His residence was in Hanover Township, Philadelphia (now Montgomery) County. He built the oldest gristmill on the upper Perkiomen in 1739 (Bean, *Montgomery County,* p. 1105). Hillegassville in Upper Hanover Township is named for the family. A descendant founded the regional newspaper, *Town and Country,* in Pennsburg, in 1874.

A nephew of *Frederick Hillegass, Michael Hillegass* (1729-1804), was a distinguished Philadelphia merchant, revolutionary leader, and first Treasurer of the United States. For his career, see the *Dictionary of American Biography,* IX, 51-52; also Emma St. Clair Whitney, *Michael Hillegass and His Descendants* (Pottsville: M. E. Miller, 1891).

Frederick Hillegass died in 1759; his will is dated June 25, 1759. His widow, *Elizabeth Barbara,* died May 4, 1759 (Schulze, I, 237: "Old Hillegassin died on May 4th and was buried on the 6th".

Materials in the Dotterer Collection, Historical Society of Pennsylvania, Philadelphia, indicate that the "Hillengass" family was originally from "Schanheim am Eberbach" in Baden.]

EMIGRANTS OF THE YEAR 1732

27. CONRAD HILDENBRAND, JR., citizen of Weiler, was reported, with others, on May 7, 1732, as "intending to go to the island of Pennsylvania" [*in die Insulam Pensylvaniam zu ziehen gesonnen*]. He left after sale of property and payment of debts and the tithe *(10. Pfennig)* emigration taxes.

Conrad Hildenbrandt, with his family, arrived at Philadephia on the Ship *Pleasant,* October 11, 1732. He is listed as "sick," and his age is given as 34. With him in the ship lists were the *Spenglers* (Nos. 29, 32), *Johannes Keller* (see No. 28), and *Georg Michel Favian* (see Joseph Fabian, No. 41, below).

[According to records in the Heimatstelle Pfalz, Kaiserslautern, *Conrad Hildenbrand* was born February 12, 1699, at Weiler am Steinsberg, son of the shoemaker *Conrad Hildenbrandt,* who was born 1671 in Melsungen in Hessen and died at Weiler after 1740. *Conrad, Jr.,* was by trade a shoemaker, and married 1720/1721 *Susanna* [———].

Conrad Hildenbrandt, Sr., was married (1) circa 1698, to *Anna Elisabetha Barther,* baptized at Weiler July 11, 1660, died at Weiler September 9, 1701; (2) December 7, 1702 (Weiler, Reformed Church Register) *Anna Eva Brenneisen* (born at Heidelberg 1677, died at Weiler, June 13, 1740); and (3) October 18,

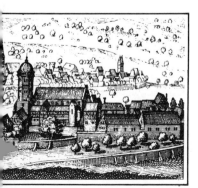

View of Sinsheim, from Merian's Topographia Germaniae.

11

1740 (Weiler, Reformed Church Register), *Francisca Catharina Sauter,* born at Schönau.

The emigrant, *Conrad Hildenbrandt, Jr.,* had the following children before emigration (Reformed Church Register, Weiler):

1. *Barbara,* baptized at Weiler, April 16, 1722.
2. *Georg Michael,* baptized at Weiler, October 1, 1724.
3. *Hans Georg,* baptized at Weiler, January 19, 1729.]

28. MARTIN KELLER'S WIDOW. The widow of *Martin Keller* is listed among other citizens of Weiler, in a document dated May 7, 1732, as "intending to go to the island of Pennsylvania" [*in die Insulam Pensylvaniam zu ziehen gesonnen*]. She left after sale of property and payment of debts and the tithe *(10. Pfennig)* emigration taxes.

[*Margaret Keller,* widow of *Martin Keller,* made a will dated August 4, 1737, probated October 14, 1737, at Lancaster. Executor was *Charles Keller,* and the children named were (1) *John,* (2) *Mary* wife of *George Sevic,* and (3) *Charles.* One *Martin Koeller* was married on April 19, 1737, to *Magdalena Leitner,* of Leacock (*Stoever Records,* p. 55).

Johannes Keller, aged 32, appears among the passengers of the Ship *Pleasant,* arriving at Philadelphia, October 11, 1732. (List 27 A-C), with the *Spenglers* (Nos. 29, 32) and *Conrad Hildenbrand* (No. 27), all of Weiler.]

29. HANS GEORG SPENGLER. *Hans Georg Spengler i*s listed with other citizens of Weiler in a document dated May 7, 1732, as "intending to go to the island of Pennsylvania" [*in die Insulam Pensylvaniam zu ziehen gesonnen*]. He left after sale of property and payment of debts and the tithe *(10. Pfennig)* emigration taxes.

Jerg Spengler, aged 31, arrived at Philadelphia on the Ship *Pleasant,* October 11, 1732 (List 27 A-C). With him were listed *Balzer Spengler* (No. 32, below), aged 24; *Henrich Spengler,* aged 26; and other Weiler names (see Nos. 27-28, above). For information on Jerg Spengler's family, see No. 16, above.

30. HANS PETER, JR. *Hans Peter, Jr.,* is listed with other citizens of Weiler in a document dated May 7, 1732, as "intending to go to the island of Pennsylvania" [*in die Insulam Pensylvaniam zu ziehen gesonnen*]. He left after sale of property and payment of debts and the tithe *(10. Pfennig)* emigration taxes.

31. BASTIAN KELLER'S WIDOW. *Bastian Keller's* widow is listed with other citizens of Weiler in a document dated May 7, 1732, as "intending to go to the island of Pennsylvania" [*in die Insulam Pensylvaniam zu ziehen gesonnen*]. She left after sale of property and payment of debts and the tithe *(10. Pfennig)* emigration taxes.

32. BALTZAR SPENGLER is listed with other citizens of Weiler in a document dated May 7, 1732, as "intending to go to the island of Pennsylvania" [*in die Insulam Pensylvaniam zu ziehen gesonnen*]. He left after sale of property and payment of debts and the tithe *(10. Pfennig)* emigration taxes..

Balzer Spengler, aged 24, arrived at Philadelphia on the Ship *Pleasant,* October 11, 1732 (List 27 A-C). With him were listed *Jerg Spengler,* aged 31, above); *Henrich Spengler,* aged 26; and other Weiler names (see Nos. 27-28, above). For information on Balzer Spengler's family, see No. 16, above.

EMIGRANTS OF THE YEAR 1737

33. CHRISTAN EWIG, of Wilhelmsfeld, was permitted in 1737, on payment of 50 florins manumission tax, to go with his wife and three children "to the island of Pennsylvania" [*in die Insul Pensilvaniam ziehen*] (Protocol 6183, pp. 462, 478, 527).

[*Christian Ewig* had 300 acres in Cumberland County, surveyed February 27, 1755 (*Pennsylvania Archives,* 3d Ser. XXIV, 669). On December 29, 1756, *Christian Ewig* was married to *Anna Magdalena Schmidt,* of Warwick, Lancaster County (*Stoever Records,* p. 66). A *Christian Ewy* is listed in Warwick Township, Lancaster County, 1756 (Hocker, p. 57), and a *George Ewy* in Bethel Township, Northampton County, 1757 (Hocker, p. 67). *Nicholas Ewig,* from Wächtersbach, aged 73, was buried by Michael Schlatter, March 29, 1748 (First Reformed Church, Philadelphia, Hinke Collection). Some confusion exists between the spelling "Ewy" and the Lancaster County Swiss-Mennonite name *Eby (Aebi),* which is a different name.]

34. CASPAR WEDEL, of Wieblingen (today Heidelberg-Wieblingen) was permitted in 1737 to emigrate to the New Land [*in das Neue Land*] on payment of an emigration tax of 9 florins, 54 kreuzer (Protocol 6183, p. 554). *Caspar Wedel* is probably identical with the *Caspar Wendell (Wendel, Wendle)* who was listed as sick on arrival at Philadelphia on the Billender *Townshend,* October 5, 1737 (List 48 A-C).

[For other Wedel emigrants, see No. 3 above.]

EMIGRANTS OF THE YEAR 1738

35. JOHANN GEORG ARNOLD. In 1738 *Johann Georg Arnold* of Zuzenhausen (Kreis Sinsheim) received permission to emigrate to America with his wife and children, on payment of 10 florins manumission tax *(Abkaufschilling)* (Protocol 6184, p. 366).

Johann Görg Arnold, aged 34, arrived at Philadelphia on the Ship *Elizabeth,* October 30, 1738 (List 64 A-C).

[*Johann Georg Arnold* was born September 4, 1712, at Zuzenhausen, Kreis Sinsheim, son of *Hans Adam* and *Maria Barbara Arnold.* He died 1768, in Frederick, Maryland. At the time of his death he owned eight farms in Western Maryland. His wives' names were *Anna Maria* and *Catharina*. A son, *Samuel,* born about 1734, settled in Hampshire County, [West] Virginia, in 1785 (Heimatstelle Pfalz).]

36. JOHANN LEONHARD NOTZ. In 1738 *Johann Leonhard Notz* of Zuzenhausen, was permitted to emigrate, on payment of 28 florins (Protocol 6184, p. 367). *Lenhart Notz,* aged 38, arrived at Philadelphia on the Ship *Two Sisters,* September 9, 1738, with wife *Catharina Notz,* aged 37, and daughter *Dorothy Notz,* aged 4 (List 54 A-C).

[*Leonard Notz,* of Lancaster Borough, wrote his will October 11, 1757, probated January 17, 1758. His wife's name was *Catharine.* His executors were *Caspar Shaffner* and *William Bowsman.* His children were (1) *Dorothea,* wife of *Christian Kinder,* (2) *Michael,* (3) *Margaret,* (4) *Leonard,* (5) *Jacob,* (6) *Elizabeth,* and (7) *John.*

In the Salem Lutheran Records, Lebanon (State Library) is the death record of *Anna Dorothea Günther* nee *Notz,* August 31, 1799, aged 65 years, 4 months, and 4 days. According to this she was born April 25, 1734, in the Durlach territory (now in Baden), and came with her parents, *Leonard Notz* and wife, to Pennsylvania in her fifth year. In 1752 she married *Christian Günther,* who died circa 1785. See also Egle, *Lebanon County,* p. 345.]

37. JOHANNES ROEHRER. In 1738 *Johannes Röhrer,* of Mauer (Kreis Heidelberg), was permitted to emigrate to America with wife and children, on payment of 10 florins (Protocol 6184, p. 403). *Johannes Röhrer* and *Johann Gottfried Röhrer* arrived at Philadelphia on the Ship *Robert and Alice,* September 11, 1738 (List 55 A-C).

[*Johannes Röhrer* was born about 1686, so that Gottfried was probably his son. *Gottfried Röhrer (Rehrer)* was born May 3, 1718, and died July 27, 1800, aged 82 years, 2 months. In 1745 he married *Magdalena Etschberger,* born September 18, 1724, died July 12, 1810, aged 85 years, 10 months, 6 days. They settled in Altalaha, Pennsylvania, now Rehrersburg. See Brossman, *Our Keystone Families,* Nos. 159/160, 161/162. For Gottfried Röhrer's children, see *Stoever Records,* p. 39.]

EMIGRANTS OF THE YEAR 1739

38. JOHANNES HOERPEL. In 1739 the Electoral Palatine Government allowed *Johannes Hörpel,* of Neckarelz, who had emigrated without permission, to transfer the properties he had received from his parents-in-law at Neckarelz to the church there, up to a small remainder of 100 florins, which he could apply to his return journey. The properties of the emigrant himself, because of illegal emigration, had been confiscated by the treasury (Protocol 8095, p. 473).

This was possibly the *Johans Herbel,* who arrived at Philadelphia September 6, 1730, on the Ship *Alexander and Anne* (List 12 B-C). In addition a *Johann Peter Herbel* arrived in 1741, a *Johann Görg Hörpel* in 1749, and a *Jeremias Hörpell* in 1754.

[*Johannes Herpel* of the Trappe is mentioned in Sower's newspaper, December 16, 1754: "*Johannes Herpel,* Trappe, New Providence Township, Philadelphia (now Montgomery) County, advertises that his German servant, *Bernhard Zimmermann,* 17, ran away" (Hocker, p. 46). Other representatives of the name are *Johann Peter Herpel,* at Oley, 1752 (Hocker, p. 36), and *Peter* and *Ludwig Herbel,* St. Luke's Reformed Church, Trappe, 1761 (GSP). The name is spelled *Harpel* after 1800 in the New Hanover Lutheran Church Records (PGS, XX, 255).]

EMIGRANTS OF THE YEAR 1741

39. VALENTIN ZWEISIG (ZWEISSIG). *Valentin Zweisig* of Mauer (Kreis Heidelberg) was permitted in 1741 to emigrate to America with wife and four children, on payment of 3 florins 30 kreuzer (Protocol 6187, pp. 812, 813, 864). *Valdin Zweisig,* aged 49, arrived at Philadelphia on the Ship *Molly,* October 16, 1741 (List 87 A-C). He was accompanied by *Diterich Shweyzig,* aged 24, and *Bernhart Switzig,* aged 16. Other emigrants from Mauer arrived on the same ship (See Nos. 40 and 41, below).

[*Bernhard Zwitzig* is listed as resident of Longswamp Township, Berks County, in 1759 (Montgomery, *Berks County,* p. 1049). *Bernhard Zweitzig* and wife *Marcretha* are sponsors to *Bernhard Roemer,* baptized October 2, 1760 (Christ Church, Bieber Creek Church, near Dryville, Berks County, GSP). *Bernhardt (Bernard) Zweizig* (and other spellings) was listed as resident of Windsor Township, Berks County, 1767, 1779, 1780, 1781, 1784, 1785 (*Pennsylvania Archives,* 3d Ser. XVIII, 47, 298, 427, 555, 688, 814). See also Conrad Lang (No. 60), below.]

40. MICHAEL MILLER. In 1741 *Michael Miller,* of Mauer (Kreis Heidelberg), was permitted to emigrate to America with his wife and five children, on payment of 6 florins emigration tax (Protocol 6187, pp. 813, 814). *Michael Miller,* aged 60, arrived at Philadelphia on the Ship *Molly,* October 16, 1741 (List 87 A-C). He was the second to sign the emigrant list in Philadelphia, after *Joseph Fabion,* which may mean that he was one of the leaders of the emigration party. He was accompanied by others from Mauer, the *Zweizigs* (No. 39, above), and his son-in-law, *Joseph Fabian* (No. 41, below).

41. JOSEPH FABIAN. Of *Joseph Fabian* of Mauer (Kreis Heidelberg), there is in the protocols only a request for emigration indicated (Protocol 6187, p. 811), but he landed at Philadelphia as *Joseph Fabion,* aged 41, on the same ship with the Zweisigs (No. 39,

13

The Joseph Fabian house in Mauer. This is the dwelling left by the emigrant when he came to Pennsylvania in 1741.
Photograph by Monroe H. Fabian, 1971.

Inscription-stone above main door on Fabian house.
Monroe H. Fabian photograph, 1971

above) and *Michael Miller* (No. 40, above), both from Mauer. Since his name appears first on the list he may have been a leader of the group.

[*Hans Joseph Fabian* was born at Mauer, March 4, 1700, son of *Hans Jacob Fabian*. Sponsor at his baptism was *Joseph Ritss*, cooper, of Dielheim. On February 20, 1719, *Joseph Fabian* married *Maria Dorothea Müller*. Her father was probably the *Michael Müller* who seems to be the co-leader of the group that arrived aboard the *Molly* (No. 40, above). This *Michael Müller* was the son of *Dietrich Müller* who was born (or baptized) at Mauer, April 7, 1678. *Joseph Fabian* had at least one brother, *Hans Michael Fabian*, born at Mauer August 23, 1695, son of *Hans Jacob Fabian*.

Joseph and *Maria Dorothea (Müller) Fabian* had several children before emigration. The one surviving son appears to be *Johann Valentin*, preceded by two sons of the same name who died in infancy.

Joseph Fabion first appears in the Goshenhoppen Reformed records on September 4, 1742, when he was sponsor at the baptism of *Joseph*, son of *Georg Michael Kolb*.

Another *Joseph Fabian* is mentioned in Sower's newspaper, April 16, 1749: "*Joseph Fabian*, 15 years old, has been indentured to a trade three times by his guardian, *Georg Welcker*, Goshenhoppen [Montgomery County], but he ran away each time" (Hocker, p. 13).

Michael Fabian preceded Joseph in emigration, arriving as *Michael Favon*, sick, aged 30, or *Jarrick Michr Favon (Georg Michel Favian)*, aged 23, on the Ship *Pleasant*, October 11, 1732 (List 27 A-C). According to William John Hinke, *A History of the Goshenhoppen*

14

Reformed Charge, Montgomery County, Pennsylvania (1727-1819) (Lancaster, 1920), *Michael Fabion* was a member of the church under Pastor *John Henry Goetschy*. Three children are listed to *Michael* and *Dorothea Fabian:*

1. *Anna Catharina,* baptized by Goetschy June 20, 1736; sponsors: *Friedrich Nuz* and wife *Catharina.*
2. *Johan Caspar,* baptized by Goetschy August 21, 1737; sponsors: *Johan Caspar Grisemer* and his mother.
3. *Anna Margreth,* baptized by Goetschy September 24, 1740; sponsors: *Anna Margaretha Dankels.*

The oldest surviving church register for the Evangelical parish at Mauer contains the records of the death of a child of *Hans Fabian* on May 14, 1674. This is the earliest reference to the family in Mauer. There is also a death record for *Hanss Fabian,* aged 62, October 5, 1683. On May 6, 1698, the death of *Anna C. (Zimmer) Fabian,* wife of *Hanss Michel Fabian,* is recorded. They were married April 2, 1695.

The little volume edited by Albert Haaf, *Meine Heimat: Mauer a. d. Elsenz* (Heidelberg: Gutenberg Druckerei, for Gemeindeverwaltung Mauer, 1961), describes the burning of the entire village of Mauer and the adjoining villages in the French war on August 10, 1689, and its rebuilding. After 1689 new families settled here, Lutherans from Württemberg, Hohenlohe and Brandenburg, who took up citizenship. Later, in the 18th Century, Catholics settled in Mauer from the Aschaffenburg area in the Main Valley and from the Austrian province of Vorarlberg.

In Pennsylvania the Fabians are found principally in Montgomery and Bucks Counties. A descendant of *Joseph Fabian, Monroe H. Fabian* of Quakertown, now associate curator of the National Portrait Gallery, Smithsonian Institution, Washington, D.C., is historian of the family and has furnished most of the data given here.]

42. JACOB HEZEL, of Schatthausen, made application to go to America (Protocol 6187, p. 813), but his name does not appear in the ship lists, so that it remains uncertain whether he left his homeland.

[One *Jacob Hetzel* arrived at Philadelphia on the Ship *Neptune,* September 23, 1751 (List 171 C); another on the *Polly,* August 24, 1765 (List 253 C), with *Johann Georg Schneck,* of Schatthausen (No. 138, below).

A later *Jacob Hetzel* had children baptized at the Tohickon Lutheran Church (PGS, XXXI [1920], 385, 390). *Henry Hetzel* was schoolmaster at Muddy Creek, Lancaster County, in 1764.]

43. JACOB MUELLER, of Wiesloch, cooper, was permitted in 1741, with the recommendation of the Wiesloch city council, to go to the New Land (Protocol 6187, pp. 640, 700, 713, 722).

44. CHRISTOPH GEISTER (GEISER?). In the year 1742 *Christoph Geister (Geiser?)* of Eschelbronn was released from vassalage in order to emigrate to America (Protocol 6188, p. 560). As *Christof Geiser* he arrived at Philadelphia on the Ship *Francis and Elizabeth,* September 21, 1742 (List 94 B-C).

[One *Chris. Geiser* had land surveyed in 1769, in what is now Montgomery County (Schulze, II, 258), probably the *Christopher Geiser* listed as taxpayer in Marlborough Township, Philadelphia County, 1774 (*Pennsylvania Archives,* 3d Ser. XIV, 381).]

45. MICHAEL DANNER. *Michael* and *Dieter Danner,* of Walldorf, totally impoverished brothers, who wanted to go to the New World in 1742, landed in Philadelphia as *Michel Danner* and *Dietrich Danner* on the Ship *Robert and Alice,* and took the oath of allegiance there September 24, 1742 (List 95 C).

[There were several *Danner (Tanner)* families in Pennsylvania and Maryland, and it is difficult to sort them out without help from the genealogists of the family. Of the *Michael Danners,* there were (1) *Michael* and *Elisabeth Danner,* who had a daughter *Catharina,* baptized May 24, 1761 (Trinity Lutheran Church, Lancaster, PGS, III, 239); (2) *Michel Danner* and wife *Eva,* who had a son *Johannes,* baptized March 19, 1745; sponsors: *Johannes Kranester* and *Maria Barbara* (Lower Bermudian Church, Adams County, also York Reformed Records, Hinke Collection); and (3) *Michael Tanner,* whose will was probated 1777, in Frederick County, Maryland (Scharf, *Western Maryland,* I, 432).]

46. DIETER DANNER of Walldorf, was described in his application to emigrate, with his brother *Michael Danner* (No. 45, above) as "totally impoverished". He arrived at Philadelphia on the *Robert and Alice,* and took the oath of allegiance there September 25, 1742 (List 95 C).

[Of the *Dieter (Dietrich) Danners,* there were (1) *Dietrich Danner,* listed as a founder of the Dover (Strayer's) Church in Dover Township, York County (Gibson, *York County,* p. 675); (2) *Teter Danner,* whose will was probated in 1768 in Frederick County, Maryland (Scharf, *Western Maryland,* I, 431); and (3) the obviously younger *Dietrich Danner,* yeoman, of Macungie Township, Northampton County, whose will was probated in 1792 in Northampton County, but with children under the age of 15.]

47. CASPAR HAUCK. In the year 1743 *Caspar Hauck* of Helmstadt was permitted to leave for the "Island of Pennsylvania" [*Insul Pensilvanien*] (Protocol 6189, pp. 666, 781, 850).

48. DIETRICH MUELLER, of Zuzenhausen, baker,

was permitted in 1743 to emigrate with *Jacob Hoffmann* (No. 49, below), without payment of the usual taxes because of their poverty (Protocol 6189, pp. 484, 528, 591, 622).

49. JACOB HOFFMANN, shoemaker, of Zuzenhausen, was permitted to emigrate in 1743, along with *Dietrich Müller* (No. 48, above), without payment of the usual taxes because of their poverty (Protocol 6189, pp. 484, 528, 591, 622). Possibly the *Jacob Hoffman* who arrived at Philadelphia on the Ship *Rosannah,* taking the oath of allegiance September 26, 1743 (List 100 A-C).

50. ABRAHAM SCHWANN. In 1743 *Abraham Schwann* of Schriesheim wanted to go to Pennsylvania (Protocol 6189, p. 559). He did not appear in the ship lists. Did he come to America, perhaps arriving at another port than Philadelphia?

51. HIERONIMUS TRAUTMANN, of Schriesheim, received permission to emigrate in 1743 after payment of the tithe *(10. Pfennig)* on his property which he was taking out of the country (Protocol 6189, pp. 485, 511, 563, 585). In the same application were *Johannes Trautmann* (No. 52, below), *Bernhard Tübinger* (No. 53, below), and *Georg Hoffstätter* (No. 54, below), all of Schriesheim. *Hyronimus Trauttman,* aged 34, is listed with *Bernhart Dübinger,* arriving at Philadelphia on the Ship *St. Andrew,* October 7, 1743 (List 103 A-C).

[According to records in the Heimatstelle Pfalz, Kaiserslautern, *Hieronimus Trautmann,* widower, married *Anna Maria Schäffer,* November 24, 1737. She was born February 9, 1707, daughter of *Hans Heinrich Schäffer,* who was born at Schriesheim, September 17, 1673, Reformed, son of the single *Anna Margaretha Karg,* daughter of the citizen *Hans Michel Karg.* The father was *Hans Schäffer,* cooper's apprentice from Martin in Alsace. *Hans Heinrich Schäffer* died at Schriesheim, March 13, 1746. He was married at Schriesheim November 21, 1702, to *Anna Mayer,* daughter of *Hans Velten Mayer* of Hohensachsen. *Anna Mayer* was born at Hohensachsen July 12, 1681, and died at Schriesheim August 23, 1761.

Hieronimus Trautmann was born January 22, 1708, son of *Philipp Trautmann,* citizen of Schriesheim, and wife *Dorothea* nee *Buchacker.* He married (1) August 11, 1732, *Anna Margaretha Krüger,* daughter of *Jörg Nickel Krüger* of Weinheim. *Anna Margaretha (Krüger) Trautmann* died October 15, 1736, after the birth of her third child.

Hieronimus Trautmann is referred to in the Palatine records as "farmer and vinedresser, in poor circumstances" [*Bauer und Winzer in armen Verhältnissen*]. He and his brother *Johannes* (No. 52, below) sold their properties on May 1, 1743, and on May 10, 1743 their house, "resolved to go to the new land Pennsylvania"

SCHRIESHEIM
Town Hall, Constructed 1684–1687, and Market Place

[*entschlossen, in das neue Land Pennsylvanien zu ziehen*].

Hieronimus Trautmann settled in Heidelberg Township, Lancaster (now Lebanon) County, in the vicinity of what is now Schaefferstown, joining his compatriots from Schriesheim, the *Schaeffers, Brechts,* and *Besches.* He is listed as a resident of Heidelberg Township in 1752 (Egle, *Lebanon County,* p. 196). He was a member of the Reformed Church. He made his will October 10, 1774, probated 1775. His wife's name is given as *Anna Mary.* His executors were *John Shaffer* and *John Brecht.* His children were listed as *George* and *Ann* (Lancaster County, Book X No. 2, p. 50).

Details on the Trautmanns in Schriesheim have been furnished by *Dr. Hermann Brunn,* author of the new history of Schriesheim.]

52. JOHANNES TRAUTMANN, brother of *Hieronimus Trautmann* (No. 51, above) was born December 3, 1713. He married at Leutershausen, May 1, 1742, *Eva Elisabetha Bauer,* daughter of *Philipp Bauer,* of Leutershausen. Like his brother *Hieronimus,* he was a "farmer and vinedresser, in poor circumstances," and a member of the Reformed congregation of Schriesheim. The brothers and their families occupied one house. For details of the sale of property prior to emigration, see No. 51, above.

[*Johannes Trautmann* settled in Lebanon County, Pennsylvania, where on August 6, 1749, his daughter *Maria Elisabeth* was baptized at Millbach Reformed Church; sponsors were *Hieronimus Trautmann* and his wife *Anna Maria* (Hinke Collection). This Traut-man family also appears in the nearby Host Reformed Church, 1755-1757 (Hinke Collection).

The American historian of the Trautmann (Trout-man) family is *Schuyler C. Brossman, Box 43, Rehrers-burg, Pennsylvania, USA 19550.*]

53. BERNHARD TUEBINGER (TIEBINGER, IBINGER). *Bernhard Tübinger,* of Schriesheim, ap-plied for emigration in 1743 along with other citizens of Schriesheim, *Hieronimus Trautmann* (No. 51, above), *Johannes Trautmann* (No 52, above), and *Georg Hoffstätter* (No. 54, below). He was permitted to emigrate upon payment of the tithe *(10. Pfennig)* on the property that he took with him (Protocol 6189, pp. 485, 511, 563, 585). *Bernhart Dübinger,* aged 29, arrived at Philadelphia on the Ship *St. Andrew,* Octo-ber 7, 1743 (List 103 A-C).

[What relation was this emigrant to *Kilian Tübinger (Duvinger, Dueffinger, Dibbinger)* who arrived at Phil-adelphia on the Ship *Dragon,* September 26, 1749, set-tling in York, where he was a member of the Reformed Church, and resident of York Town, 1781-1783 (*Penn-sylvania Archives,* 3d Ser. XXI, 328, 645, 663), and storekeeper in York 1783 (Gibson, *York County,* p. 517).]

54. GEORG HOFFSTAETTER, of Schriesheim, ap-plied for emigration in 1743 along with other citizens of Schriesheim (Nos. 51, 52, and 53, above). He was permitted to emigrate upon payment of the tithe *(10. Pfennig)* on the property that he took with him (Pro-tocol 6189, pp. 485, 511, 563, 585).

[One *George Huffstitter* was a taxpayer in Lower Darby Township, Chester County, 1781 (*Pennsylvania Archives,* 3d Ser. XII, 645).]

55. MARTIN ZIEGLER, of Hilsbach, was permit-ted to emigrate to the new world in 1743 (Protocol 6189, pp. 490, 528, 591, 756), although his name does not appear in the Philadelphia ship lists. *Johann Wolff-gang Kellermann* (No. 56) of Hilsbach received per-mission at the same time.

[Another *Martin Ziegler,* from "Malsem," Württem-berg, is mentioned in the *Staatsbote,* Philadelphia, July 28, 1772 (Hocker, p. 124).]

56. JOHANN WOLFFGANG KELLERMANN, of Hilsbach, single, was permitted in 1743 (with *Martin Ziegler* of Hilsbach, No. 55, above) to emigrate to the New World, although his name does not appear in the Philadelphia Ship Lists. Did he emigrate?

EMIGRANTS OF THE YEAR 1744

57. JOHANN ESAIAS STEIN, of Zuzenhausen, was granted permission in 1744 to emigrate to America with his wife, a stepson, and three stepdaughters (Protocol 6190, pp. 355, 431, 444).

58. JOHANN ADAM KREHEBUEHL, of Bam-menthal, was permitted in 1744 to emigrate to America with his wife and three children (Protocol 6190, p. 439).

59. GEORG WELCKER, of Spechbach, was per-mitted in 1744 to emigrate to America, with his wife and two children.

[What relation was this emigrant to the *John George Welcker,* who was a resident in Hanover Township, Philadelphia (now Montgomery) County before 1734 (Rupp, p. 474), and member of the New Goshenhoppen Reformed Church in 1731 (Bean, *Montgomery County,* p. 1108), when he had a daughter baptized (PGS, XXVIII, 274)? The Schulze Diary gives us details of the death of this early emigrant and his wife, March 1782: "Old Mrs. Welker died on the 27th [of Febru-ary] and was buried on March 1st. She was nearly 78 years old, less one month". On March 6, Schulze "wrote old George Welker's will". And "Old Hans George Welker died at 3 o'clock in the afternoon on the 8th and was buried on the 10th. He was 85 years old (Schulze, II, 145-146).]

60. CONRAD LANG, of Spechbach, was permitted in 1744 to emigrate to America, with his wife and four children. See also *Georg Welcker* of Spechbach (No. 59, above).

[The name *Lang (Long)* is so common that it is almost impossible to identify this emigrant. However, it may be of value to note that *Cunradt Long* and wife were sponsors to *John Cunradt,* son of *Christian Zwey-sich,* of Northkill, now Berks County, on April 12, 1747 (*Stoever Records,* p. 30); and again, *Cunradt Lang* and wife *Barbara* were sponsors to *John Cunradt,* son of *John Jacob Soerer* of Atolhoe (Altalaha, i.e., Rehr-ersburg), February 8, 1756 (*Ibid.,* p. 33). *Conrad Lang* was from Spechbach and the *Zweysichs* and *Roe-hrers* were from the nearby town of Mauer.

Another *Conrad Lang (Lange),* emigrant from Ger-many to Pennsylvania, evidently settled in North Car-olina before the Revolution. See S. A. Ashe, ed., *Biographical History of North Carolina* (Greensboro, N. C., 1917), VIII, 286-291. A later *Conrad Long* of York County had children born 1771-1777 (William Gabriel Long, *History of the Long Family of Pennsyl-vania* [Huntington, West Virginia: Huntington Publish-ing Company, 1930], p. 317).]

61. ANNA MARIA (REGINA) HEYLMANN. In 1744 *Anna Maria (Regina) Heylmann,* single, of Zuzen-hausen, was permitted to emigrate to America. See also Nos. 62-65 (Protocol 6190, pp. 442, 477, 484, 538).

[Possibly she joined *John Adam Heilman* in Lebanon (later North Annville) Township, Lebanon County, Pennsylvania. He was one of the pioneers in the town-ship, and one of the founders of the Hill Church *(Berg-kirche),* where he was an elder as early as 1745. He was baptized February 24, 1715, at "Zutzenhausen," and died September 25, 1770, in Lebanon Township.

17

He was a son of *John Jacob Heilman* (d. 1753), of Zuzenhausen, who came to America in 1732, settling in what is now Lebanon County. *John Adam Heilman, Jr.*, married *Maria Catharina Steger* (1709-1787), daughter of *John Barnhard Steger*. For this family see Egle, *Lebanon County*, pp. 226, 242.]

62. GEORG KIRSCH, of Zuzenhausen, was permitted to emigrate to America in 1744, with his wife and two small children. See also Nos. 61, 63-65, also from Zuzenhausen (Protocol 6190, pp. 442, 477, 484, 538).

[A later *George Kirsch* had a daughter baptized at Trinity Lutheran Church, Lancaster, 1792 (PGS, V, 200).]

63. ANNA DOROTHEA LICHT(N)ER. In 1744 *Anna Dorothea*, widow of *Georg Licht(n)er*, of Zuzenhausen, was permitted to emigrate to America with her 16-year-old son. See also Nos. 61-62, 64-65, also from Zuzenhausen (Protocol 6190, pp. 442, 477, 484, 538).

[*Johann Georg Lechner* is listed as resident of Tulpehocken in the period 1743-1746 (Rupp, p. 466). *Georg Lechner* and wife were sponsors to *Anna Margaretha*, daughter of *Stephan Cunradt*, of Swatara, March 3, 1751 (*Stoever Records*, p. 27); and *George Lechner* and *Anna Margaretha Lay*, sponsors to *Georg Philipp*, son of *Stephan Cunradt* of Swatara, December 17, 1752 (*Stoever Records*, p. 27).]

64. JOHANN JACOB KIRSCH, of Zuzenhausen, was permitted to emigrate to America in 1744. At the same time *Georg Kirsch* and *Conrad Kirsch* received permission, as well as other Zuzenhausen residents (Nos. 61, 63) (Protocol 6190, pp. 442, 477, 484, 538).

[*Jacob Kirsh (Kersh)* was listed in Codorus Township, York County, Pennsylvania, 1779-1783 (*Pennsylvania Archives*, 3d Ser. XXI, 79, 251, 465, 545, 705), and in Shrewsbury Township, York County, 1780, 1782, 1783 (*Ibid.*, XXI, 271, 615, 709). *Jacob Karsh*, bookbinder, was listed in Hopewell Township, Cumberland County, Pennsylvania, in 1785 (*Pennsylvania Archives*, 3d Ser. XX, 725).]

65. CONRAD KIRSCH, of Zuzenhausen, single, received permission in 1744 to emigrate to America. At the same time permission was granted to *Georg* and *Johann Jacob Kirsch*, and other residents of Zuzenhausen (Protocol 6190, pp. 442, 477, 484, 538).

66. VEIT MEISTER, of Hoffenheim, received permission in 1744 to emigrate to America. He received manumission on payment of 3 florins, before his wedding in the Gemmingen territories at Hoffenheim bei Sinsheim (Protocol 6190, pp. 561, 621). He was born at Bargen, son of *Georg Bernhard Meister*. According to an advertisement of the Electoral Palatine District of Dilsberg, dated December 10, 1787, published in the *Frankfurter Kaiserliche Reichsoberamtspostzeitung*, February 8, 1788, republished in the *Philadelphische Correspondenz*, October 21, 1788 (Hocker, p. 195),

Veit Meister had emigrated to America from Hoffenheim in the year 1751, with wife and children. He appears as *Veit Meister*, arriving at Philadelphia on the Ship *Shirley*, September 5, 1751 (List 163 C).

[According to records in the Heimatstelle Pfalz, Kaiserslautern, *Vei[d]t Meister* married, July 7, 1744, at Hoffenheim (?), Kreis Sinsheim, *Anna Elisabeth Krafft*, Reformed, born May 20, 1724, at Hoffenheim, daughter of *Hans Georg Krafft (Crafft)*, born 1680. Their children were as follows:
1. *Georg Conrad*, born April 5, 1746, at Hoffenheim.
2. *Elisabetha Margaretha*, born October 1, 1748, at Hoffenheim.
3. *Johann Jürg*, born September 18, 1751, baptized September 21, 1751, St. Michael's and Zion's Lutheran Church, Philadelphia.

With the Meisters emigrated the wife's stepbrother, *Johann Friederich Kraft*, son of *Hans Georg* and *Anna Margaretha (Pfeil) Krafft*, born October 12, 1730, at Hoffenheim, Kreis Sinsheim. He was confirmed in 1747. His name appears also among the passengers on the Ship *Shirley*.]

EMIGRANTS OF THE YEAR 1747

67. CHRISTIAN RUPP, of Daudenzell, a citizen's son released from military service, was permitted in 1747 to emigrate "to the new land" on payment of the tithe amounting to 11 florins and in addition 2 florins 40 kreuzer emergency taxes (Protocol 6193, pp. 437, 464). *Christian Rupp* took the oath of allegiance at Philadelphia, arriving on the Ship *Restauration*, October 9, 1747 (List 114 C).

[Two individuals bearing the name *Christian Rupp (Roop)* appear in Pennsylvania records about the time of the Revolution. In Earl Township, Lancaster County, *Christian Rupp (Roop)* appears with *John Rupp*, 1773, 1779, 1782 (*Pennsylvania Archives*, 3d Ser. XVII, 449, 495, 887). Another appears in Hellam Township, York County, 1779-1783 (*Pennsylvania Archives*, 3d Ser. XXI, 57, 288, 491, 517, 693) and in York Town, York County, 1781 (*Ibid.*, XXI, 332).

The pioneer Pennsylvania German historian *Israel Daniel Rupp* has left an early genealogy of his emigrant ancestor, *John Jonas Rupp*, born 1729, who first settled at the Hill Church *(Bergkirche)* in Lebanon County and moved to Cumberland County in 1772. He was born in "the town of Reihen, in the bailiwick of Sinsheim, seven leagues from Heidelburg". See *A Brief Biographic Memorial of Joh. Jonas Rupp, and Complete Genealogical Family Register of his Lineal Descendants, From 1756 to 1875* (Philadelphia: S. P. Town, 1875). Some of the sketches had previously appeared in the *Reformed Church Messenger*.

Other distinguished members of the Rupp family in Pennsylvania include *William Rupp* (1839-1904), professor at the Theological Seminary in Lancaster

(*Dictionary of American Biography*, XVI, 226-227);
Henry Wilson Rupp (PGS, XXVII [1920], 51); and
the Reverend *William J. Rupp*, Reformed pastor, Pennsylvania German historian, and dialect columnist (*Der
Buschgnippel*, in the Pennsburg newspaper, *Town and
Country*).]

68. HANS GEORG DUERR, of Reihen, was permitted in 1747 to leave for Pennsylvania, along with
Johannes Knecht and *Hans Adam Kauffman*, both of
Reihen. Because of his propertyless status *(Ohnvermögenheit)*, Dürr had to pay nothing to the government
(Protocol 8101, pp. 350, 354, 407).

Hans George Törr arrived, with the two others listed
above, on the Ship *Restauration*, October 9, 1747 (List
114 C).

[One *John George Derr* of Hempfield Township,
Lancaster County, made his will September 11, 1754,
probated 1761. In it he names as his executors *Adam
Hambrecht* and *George Honey*. His wife's name was
Mary. His children were *Juliana, John, Mary, Leonard,
George,* and *Anna* wife of *Anthony Kneissley*. Other
George Doerrs lived in the Tulpehocken area, 1749;
and Heidelberg Township, Berks County, 1755-1757
(Hocker, pp. 14, 48, 63). An earlier *John Georg Doerr*
of Manheim, had three children baptized 1734-1738
(*Stoever Records*, p. 19).

Other references include the *George Terr* who had
land surveyed in Lancaster County, January 12, 1749
(*Pennsylvania Archives,* 3d Ser. XXIV, 546); *George
Terr,* land surveyed, Northampton County, April 21,
1753 (*Ibid.,* XXVI, 190); and the *George Derr* listed
as resident of Upper Salford Township, Philadelphia
County, 1769, and Upper Hanover Township, Philadelphia County, 1779 (*Pennsylvania Archives,* 3d Ser.
XIV, 54, 729).]

69. JOHANNES KNECHT, of Reihen, was permitted in 1747 to leave for Pennsylvania, along with *Hans
Georg Dürr* and *Hans Adam Kauffmann* of the same
place. Because of his propertyless status, Knecht had
to pay nothing to the government (Protocol 8101, pp.
350, 354, 407). *Johannes Knecht* arrived with the two
others listed above on October 9, 1747, on the Ship
Restauration (List 114 C).

[One *John Knecht* was a farmer in Bethlehem Township, Northampton County, 1772 (*Pennsylvania Archives,* 3d Ser. XIX, 24); also (with *Henry Knecht*)
in Lower Saucon Township, Northampton County,
1772 (*Ibid.,* XIX, 33).]

70. HANS ADAM KAUFFMANN, of Reihen, was
permitted in 1747 to leave for Pennsylvania, along with
Hans Georg Dürr and *Johannes Knecht,* both of Reihen.
He paid only the usual supplementary tax and the
emergency taxes. *Johann Adam Kauffman* arrived at
Philadelphia with the two others listed above on the
Ship *Restauration,* October 9, 1747 (List 114 C).

71. JOHANN ADAM STENGER, of Steinsfurt, was
permitted in 1747 to emigrate to Pennsylvania, on payment of 15 florins (Protocol 8101, p. 333).

[One *Adam Stenger, Sr.,* along with another *Adam
Stenger,* and *Jacob, Daniel, Christian, Salomon* and
another *Jacob Stenger* arrived at Philadelphia on the
Ship *Betsy,* October 26, 1768 (List 273 C). One of
these is probably the *Johann Adam Stenger* who with
his wife *Anna Catharina* had children baptized in 1770
and 1772 at the Heidelberg Church in what is now
Lehigh County, Pennsylvania (see Raymond E. Hollenbach, *Heidelberg Church History and Records, 1740-
1940* (n.p., n.d.), pp. 61, 62.]

72. TOBIAS SCHALL, of Mittelschefflenz, who had
asked in 1748 for permission to emigrate to Pennsylvania, was allowed to leave the country without paying
the usual emigration taxes (Protocol 8102, pp. 131,
231). *Tobias Schall,* aged 42, arrived at Philadelphia
on the Ship *Hampshire,* September 7, 1748 (List 118
A-C).

[*Tobias Schall* settled in the Oley Valley of Berks
County; see *The Perkiomen Region,* I (1895), 127-128.
In the records of Christ Lutheran Church, the "Bieber
Creek Church" near Dryville, Rockland Township,
Berks County, is the baptism of his daughter *Anna
Catharina,* October 5, 1750. *Tobias Schall's* wife's
name is given as *Anna Magdalena* nee *Bechtold.* The
sponsors at the baptism were *Peter Gerhard* and wife
Christina (GSP).]

73. JOHANNES EULER, citizen and master blacksmith at Hohensachsen (Kreis Mannheim) was manumitted on payment of 10 florins for the tithe *(10. Pfennig).* *Johannes Eulen (sic)* arrived at Philadelphia on
the Ship *Patience,* September 19, 1749 (List 134 C).

[One *John Eyler* was listed as taxpayer in Manheim Township, York County, Pennsylvania, 1779-1783
(*Pennsylvania Archives,* 3d Ser. XXI, 21, 212, 398,
594, 788).]

74. LEON(H)ARD EBERLE, of Eiterbach (Kreis
Heidelberg), was permitted by the electoral government in 1749 to go to the New Land with wife and
three children, on payment of 4 florins manumission
tax and 40 florins emigration tax.

[For *Johann Leonhard Eberle* of Eiterbach, see Heinz
F. Friederichs, *President Dwight D. Eisenhower's Ancestors and Relations* (Neustadt/Aisch, 1955), p. 103.]

75. JACOB GRAUSS (KRAUSS), inhabitant of
Daisbach (Kreis Heidelberg), was, on account of his
poverty and lack of property, manumitted gratis with
wife and children for emigration to the New Land.
Jacob Krauss, with *Joh. Georg Krauss,* arrived at Philadelphia on the Ship *Dragon,* September 26, 1749 (List
136 C).

76. PHILIPP GEORG MUELLER, of Meckesheim (Kreis Heidelberg), was permitted in 1749 to emigrate to the New Land with wife and two children, on payment of 10 florins emigration tax. Perhaps identical with the *Pips Gorg Müller* who arrived on the Ship *Chesterfield,* September 2, 1749 (List 126 C).

[One *Filip Gorg Müller* and wife *Barbara* had a son *Johann Jacob* baptized at the Egypt Reformed Church, March 6, 1754 (*Pennsylvania Archives,* 6th Ser. VI, 184).]

77. JOHANN MICHEL MUELLER, of Meckesheim (Kreis Heidelberg) was permitted in 1749, on payment of the tithe on his property, to emigrate to Pennsylvania "in hopes of better luck" [*in Hoffnung besseren Glücks*]. *Johann Michel Müller* arrived at Philadelphia on the Ship *Speedwell,* September 25, 1749 (List 135 C).

78. JACOB FREY, of Wieblingen (Kreis Heidelberg) was permitted in 1749 to emigrate gratis on payment of the tithe. *Jacob Frey* arrived at Philadelphia on the Ship *Dragon,* September 26, 1749 (List 136 C).

[Among the *Jacob Freys* in Pennsylvania is the *Jacob Frey* who in 1751 had a son *Johann Jacob* baptized at First Reformed Church, Reading; sponsor was *Hans Adam Tiefetörfer* (Hinke Collection). Other *Jacob Freys* lived at Perkasie, 1751; and between Philadelphia and Frankford, 1766 (Hocker, pp. 26, 35, 88).]

79. GEORG LINZ, of Asbach (Kreis Mosbach), received permission in 1749 to emigrate to the New Land on payment of the tithe. He had to pay in addition the sum of 10 florins to buy himself out of vassalage. With him in application and in the ship lists are Nos. 80 and 81, below. *Jerg Lintz* arrived at Philadelphia on the Ship *Patience,* September 19, 1749 (List 134 C).

[*George Lintz (Lins)* was resident of Heidelberg Township, Northampton (now Lehigh) County, in 1785 (with *John*), 1786 (with *Martin* and *John*), and 1788 (with *Martin* and *John*) (*Pennsylvania Archives,* 3d Ser. XIX, 122, 236, 327). Among the other bearers of the name before the Revolution were *Anna Lintz,* servant, New Hanover Township, Philadelphia (now Montgomery) County, who ran away in 1756 (Hocker, p. 59); and *Sebastian Lintz,* single, Longswamp Township, Berks County, 1759 (Montgomery, *Berks County,* p. 1049). A *George Lentz* (also spelled *Lantz*), which presumably is a different name, was found in Bethel Township, Lancaster County, Albany Township, Berks County, and East District Township, Berks County, in 1779.]

80. PHILIPP BRENNER, of Asbach (Kreis Mosbach) received permission in 1749 to emigrate to the New Land on payment of the tithe. He applied with *Georg Linz* (No. 79, above) and *Georg Kumpff* (No. 81, below), both of Asbach, and appears in the ship lists with them as *Hans Philipp Brenner* (with *Philip Adam Brenner*), arriving at Philadelphia on the Ship *Patience,* September 19, 1749 (List 134 C).

[Was this the *Philipp Brenner,* of Donegal Township, Lancaster County, whose will is dated July 29, 1783, and probated August 28, 1788? His wife was *Ann,* who with *Philip Brenner* [*Jr.*] was executor. Children were *Catharine* wife of *Jacob Young,* Ann wife *of Jacob Hoffman, Susanna, Philip,* and *Elizabeth* wife of *John Gorner.* A grandchild, *Elizabeth Gorner,* is listed also.

Other references include the birth of *Philip Adam Brenner,* son of *Philipp* and *Maria Catharina Brenner,* born January 8, baptized January 21, 1750 (Trinity Lutheran Church, Lancaster). *Philipp* and *Anna Catharina (Klein) Brenner* had a son *Johann Philipp,* born December 2, baptized December 10, 1752 (Trinity Lutheran Church, Lancaster). Another *Philipp Adam Brenner,* whose wife was *Anna Maria* nee *Rudesill,* had a child baptized December 10, 1752 (Trinity Lutheran Church, Lancaster). *Philipp Brenner* and wife were sponsors to *Philipp Jacob Ziegler,* son of *Jacob Ziegler, Jr.,* of Lebanon, and wife *Judith,* in 1767 (*Stoever Records,* p. 52).]

81. GEORG KUMPFF, of Asbach (Kreis Mosbach) received permission to emigrate to the New Land in 1749 on payment of the tithe. He applied with *Georg Linz* (No. 79, above) and *Philipp Brenner* (No. 80, above) and appears with them in the ship lists as *Hans Jörg Kamp* (with *Daniel Camp*), arriving at Philadelphia on the Ship *Patience,* September 19, 1749 (List 134 C).

[Another *Georg Gump,* born October 9, 1709, came to Pennsylvania from Hüffenhardt, two miles from Heilbronn, in the Palatinate. He was a Lutheran and settled first at Monocacy in Maryland and in 1762 removed to York, Pennsylvania. He had married (1) in Europe, July 24, 1731, *Rosina Mack* (died June 6, 1769, aged 64). See Records of the Moravian Church, York (*Publications of the Pennsylvania Genealogical Society,* IV [1909], 326-327).

John Georg Gump was sponsor to *Susanna Catarina,* daughter of *Heinrich Fortunee,* of Monocacy, 1738 (*Stoever Records,* p. 12).]

82. WILHELM BESCH, of Mittelschefflenz (Kreis Mosbach), was permitted to go to Pennsylvania in 1749. Undoubtedly the *Willhelm Bosch* who arrived at Philadelphia on the Ship *Patience,* September 19, 1749 (List 134 C). The original (see facsimile, II, 457) has been misread.

[*Wilhelm Besch* settled at Schaefferstown in what is now Lebanon County, in 1749, where he joined the *Schaeffers, Trautmanns, Brechts* and others from his neighborhood in the Neckar Valley. He was a member of St. Paul's Reformed Church there. In 1758 he is listed as a taxpayer in Heidelberg Township, Lancaster

County (Egle, *Lebanon County*, p. 196). On December 29, 1750 *John William Pesch* and *Anna Maria* had a son *John Andrew* baptized; sponsors were *John Andrew Peischlein* and *Elsa Rosina* (Millbach Reformed Records, Hinke Collection). See also *The History of St. Paul's United Church of Christ (Formerly St. Paul's Reformed) Schaefferstown, Pa.* (Myerstown, Pennsylvania: Church Center Press, 1965), p. 121.]

83. JACOB BEHR, of Eberbach (Kreis Mosbach), received permission to emigrate to "England," i.e. New England, on payment of the tithe. He applied with *Martin Treibel* (No. 84, below) of Eberbach, and appears in the ship lists with him as *Johann Jacob Ber*, arriving at Philadelphia on the Ship *Jacob*, October 2, 1749 (List 140 C).

[Other Bär emigrants left Dossenheim in 1749, 1752, and 1757, some of them for "Carolina". See Gabriel Hartmann, "Amerikafahrer von Dossenheim im 18. Jahrhundert," *Mannheimer Geschichtsblätter*, XXVII (1926), cols. 55-58, republished in *Pennsylvania Folklife*, XXI:2 (Winter 1971-1972), 46-48. For the Bähr families of Weinheim a.d.Bergstrasse, see *Pfälzische Familien- und Wappenkunde*, XVII Jg., Bd. 6, Heft 7 (1968), 221-222.]

84. MARTIN TREIBEL, of Eberbach (Kreis Mosbach) received permission to emigrate to "England," i.e., New England, on payment of the tithe. He applied with *Jacob Behr* (No. 83, above) of Eberbach, and appears in the ship lists with him as *Martin Treibel*, arriving at Philadelphia on the Ship *Jacob*, October 2, 1749) (List 140 C).

[*Martin Trible*, farmer, is listed as resident of Bethlehem Township, Northampton County, in 1772 (*Pennsylvania Archives*, 3d Ser. XIX, 26).]

85. PETER EHRET, of Mittelschefflenz (Kreis Mosbach), was permitted in 1749 to emigrate to "New England," on payment of the tithe.

[*Peter Ehret* first appears in Pennsylvania records in the Colebrookdale Township tax list, Berks County, 1752. In the records of the Oley Hills Church, Berks County, is the baptism of *John George Ehret*, May 26, 1754, son of *Peter "Erred"* and wife *Maria Christina*, both Reformed. Sponsors: *George Schall*, single son of *Tobias Schall*, and *Eva Barbara*, single daughter of *Stephan Hauck*. *Tobias Schall* (No. 72, above), also from Mittelschefflenz, had emigrated in 1748 and settled in the Dryville, Berks County, area, and appears in the Mertz's (Beaver Creek) church register.

The *Pennsylvanische Berichte* for April 1, 1758, contains a reference to *Peter Eret* of "Koolbruckdel," Berks County (Hocker, p. 72).

Peter Ehret moved to Northampton County, where he is listed in the Bethlehem Township tax lists for 1766. He died intestate in 1779. Letters of administration were granted to *George Ehret* and *John Ehret*

(1757-1838) of Bethlehem Township, August 12, 1779. Two other children are listed: *Margaret* who married *George Phile (Feil)* of North Carolina, and *Elizabeth* who married *John Philip Wolf*. In Northampton County the Ehrets were members of the Dryland Church at Hecktown. See "Ehret of Dryland," *The Pennsylvania Dutchman*, June 15, 1950.]

86. ADAM LUDWIG, of Burcken (=Neckarburken), received permission, with *Jacob Bender* (No. 87, below), to emigrate to New England. *Hans Adam Ludwig* arrived at Philadelphia on the Ship *Patience*, September 19, 1749 (List 134 C).

[A single *John Adam Ludwig* was confirmed October 19, 1768, son of *Philipp Ludwig* (Muhlenberg, Journal, II, 362). *Adam Ludwig*, single, stood sponsor at the baptism of a daughter of *Carl Sill*, October 20, 1776 (Muhlenberg, Journal, II, 750).]

87. JACOB BENDER, of Burcken (=Neckarburken), received permission, with *Adam Ludwig* (No. 86, above), to go to New England.

[Among the *Jacob Benders* in Pennsylvania were those in Bucks County, 1751, and Heidelberg Township, Northampton County, 1757 (Hocker, pp. 27, 64). One *Jacob Benter* and wife *Catharina* were sponsors at a *Filler* baptism at Heidelberg, November 13, 1752 (Records of Egypt Reformed Church, *Pennsylvania Archives*, 6th Ser. VI, 9). Another *Jacob Bender* and his wife *Susanna* had children baptized, 1771-1781, New Hanover Lutheran Church (PGS, XX, 207); and there was a *Jacob Bender* mentioned in Muhlenberg, Journal, III, 335 ff.]

88. PETER SPOHN, of Schollbrunn (Kreis Mosbach) was permitted to emigrate to New England on payment of 14 florins for manumission and 14 florins for the tithe. *Petter Spohn* arrived at Philadelphia on the Ship *Patience*, September 19, 1749 (List 134 C).

[*Peter Spohn (Spoon)* was a resident of Richmond Township, Berks County, 1768, 1779, 1784-1785 (*Pennsylvania Archives*, 3d Ser. XVIII, 147, 261, 671, 791). He also appears to have owned land in Ruscombmanor Township 1780-1781, 1784-1785 (*Ibid.*, XVIII, 408, 528, 665, 780) ¬and in Heidelberg Township, Berks County, 1785 (*Ibid.*, XVIII, 753).

Other representatives of the name were *George Spoon*, resident of Greenwich Township, Berks County, 1759 (Montgomery, *Berks County*, p. 1076); and *Henry* and *Adam Spohn*, Heidelberg Township, Berks County, 1759 (*Ibid.*, p. 1108). *Michael Spon*, of Maxatawny, had children baptized 1732 and 1736 (*Stoever Records*, p. 5).]

89. MICHEL ZILLING, of Mittelschefflenz (Kreis Mosbach), wanted in 1749 to emigrate to New England. *Michael Zilling* arrived at Philadelphia on the Ship *Patience*, September 19, 1749 (List 134C).

[*Georg Zilling* of Towamencin Township, son of

Michael Zilling, applied November 18, 1778, for publication of the banns to marry *Hannah Henrich,* of Towamencin Township (Muhlenberg, Journal, III, 194).]

EMIGRANTS OF THE YEAR 1750

90. JOHANN BATTENFELD, of Michelbach (Kreis Mosbach), received permission to go to the New Land with wife, two sons, and three daughters, on payment of the tithe, amounting to 30 florins. *Johannes Battefelt,* with *Philipp Bathenfeld* and *Hans Adam Battenfeld,* arrived at Philadelphia on the Ship *Two Brothers,* August 28, 1750 (List 153 C).

[According to the *Jacob Lischy* Records, 1744-1769 (Hinke Collection), *Adam* and *Elisabeth Battfeld* had a daughter *Catharine,* baptized November 26, 1758; sponsors were *Leonard* and *Catharine Sabel.* This was somewhere in the York-Adams County area, where Lischy was Reformed pastor. *Philip Batanfeld* is listed as taxpayer in Manheim Township, York County, in 1781 (*Pennsylvania Archives,* 3d Ser. XXI, 397). A possible misreading of the name involves the marriage of *Adam Brecht* and *Margaretha Battesteld (sic),* of Bethel Township, July 5, 1752 (*Stoever Records,* p. 63).]

91. JOHANN ADAM EBERLE, of Eiterbach (Kreis Heidelberg), was manumitted in 1750, on payment of 10 florins for manumission and 9 florins emigration tax. *Adam Eberle,* with *Conradt Israel Eberle,* arrived at Philadelphia on the Ship *Brothers,* August 24, 1750 (List 152 C).

[One *Adam Everly* was a taxpayer in Springhill Township, Westmoreland County, 1783 (*Pennsylvania Archives,* 3d. Ser. XXII, 422). An earlier *Adam Eberley* had land surveyed in Bucks County, 1746 (*Ibid.,* XXIV, 124).

For the Eberles of Eiterbach and the Neunhöfe, see Heinz F. Friederichs, *President Dwight D. Eisenhower's Ancestors and Relations* (Neustadt/Aisch, 1955), pp. 49, 103.]

92. JOHANN GEORG GANSSHORN, of Bammenthal (Kreis Heidelberg), baker, was permitted in 1750 to emigrate gratis. *Hans Görg Ganshorn* arrived at Philadelphia on the Ship *Brothers,* August 24, 1750 (List 152 C).

[According to records in the Heimatstelle Pfalz, Kaiserslautern, *Johann Georg Gantzhorn (Gansshorn)* was born March 17 or 19, 1725, at Bammenthal, Kreis Heidelberg, son of *Johann Philippus* and *Appolonia (Ziegler) Gansshorn.* He was a baker, and married January 5, 1746, *Susanna Elisabetha Bückle,* daughter of *Johann Adam* and *Veronica Maria (Wildt) Bückle,* born March 22, 1723, at Wiesenbach. See No. 101, below, *Adam Bückle.*

Children, born in Bammenthal before the emigration, include:

1. *Johann Bartholomäus,* born January 30, 1747.
2. *Maria Katharina,* born June 12, 1749, died in America or during the passage across the Atlantic.

Information from *Gerhard Wohlfahrt,* of Braunschweig, April 15, 1954.

Evidently the emigrant settled in York County, where three additional children of *Georg* and *Susanna Elisabeth Ganshorn* appear in the *Jacob Lischy* Record, 1744-1769 (Hinke Collection):

3. *Johann Jacob,* baptized March 1, 1752; sponsor: *Jacob Ottinger* and *Johanna.*
4. *Johann Georg,* baptized February 1, 1756; sponsors: *Nicholas Wild* and *Catharina.*
5. *Johann Philipp,* baptized June 25, 1758; sponsors: *Nicholas Wild* and *Catharina.*

Nicholas Wild was probably a relative of *Georg Ganshorn's* wife. One *Nicholas Wild* arrived at Philadelphia on the *Johnson Galley,* September 18 (O.S.), 1732 (List 21 A). With him was *Valentin Wild.* Both were over 16 years of age.

In addition there was a *Mateis (Matthias) Gantzhorn,* listed in the records of the York Reformed Church in 1754 (Hinke Collection).]

93. JOHANN MATHIAS GERNER, of Helmstadt (Kreis Heidelberg), wanted in 1750 to go to the so-called New Land. *Johan Matthes Gerner,* with *Hans Jorg Garner,* arrived at Philadelphia on the Ship *Two Brothers,* August 28, 1750 (List 153 C).

[*Mathias Gerner,* of Earl Township, Lancaster County, made his will December 5, 1786, probated April 27, 1787. Executors were *Benjamin Lessle* and *Bernard Geiger,* his son-in-law. His wife's name was *Maria* and his children were *Michael, Catharine, Susan, Eve, Anna,* and *Margaret.*]

94. JOHANN GEORG KOBERSTEIN, of Zuzenhausen (Kreis Heidelberg), applied in 1750, along with *Johann Georg Ludwig* (No. 95, below), of the same place, to go to the so-called New Land with his wife *Anna Catharina.* He had to pay 3 florins. *Hans Gorg Koberstein,* with Ludwig, arrived at Philadelphia on the Ship *Osgood,* September 29, 1750 (List 157 C).

95. JOHANN GEORG LUDWIG, of Zuzenhausen (Kreis Heidelberg), applied in 1750, along with *Johann Georg Koberstein* (No. 94, above), for permission to go to the so-called New Land with his wife *Maria Margaretha.* He paid 2 florins 30 kreuzer manumission tax. *Johan George Ludwig,* with Koberstein, arrived at Philadelphia on the Ship *Osgood,* September 29, 1750 (List 157 C).

[Several *George Ludwigs (Ludwicks)* were found in 18th Century Pennsylvania, in Tulpehocken and Bern Townships, Berks County, 1767, 1779-1781, 1784-1785 (*Pennsylvania Archives,* 3d Ser. XVIII, 76, 83, 202, 321, 450, 577, 708); and in Philadelphia, deceased, 1779 (*Ibid.,* XIV, 552, 829).]

96. JOHANN FRIEDRICH MUELLER, of Meck-

esheim (Kreis Heidelberg), was permitted in 1750 to go to the so-called New Land on payment of 2 florins on his property of 20 florins.

97. JOHANN ADAM WOLLFARTH, an orphaned citizen's son from Spechbach (Kreis Heidelberg), was released from vassalage in 1750, on payment of 20 florins, and received permission to emigrate on payment of 18 florins additional tax. *Johan Adam Wolfart* arrived at Philadelphia on the Ship *Brothers,* August 25, 1750 (List 152 C).

[The only reference I could locate to an *Adam Wollfarth* was *Adam Wolfart,* who had 110 acres surveyed in Bedford County, June 10, 1785, possibly a younger man (*Pennsylvania Archives,* 3d Ser. XXV, 657); on the same day a *Joseph Wolfart* had 100 acres surveyed (*Ibid.,* XXV, 657).

The name is unusual and perhaps a survey of other families of the name will be useful. For example, there was *Nicolaus Wolfart,* Reformed, member of the Old Goshenhoppen Church in Upper Salford Township, Montgomery County (Bean, *Montgomery County,* p. 1135). He and his wife *Catharina* were sponsors at a *Muck* baptism in 1760 (New Goshenhoppen Reformed Church, PGS, XVIII, 296). According to *The Perkiomen Region,* I:6 (1922), 108-110, *Nicholas Wohlfart* emigrated on the Snow *Charlotte,* arriving September 5, 1743. He made his will in Marlborough Township, Montgomery County, April 12, 1788. He died March 16, 1796, aged 78 years, 3 months, and 12 days. He is buried at Old Goshenhoppen. He was a member of the Reformed congregation, his wife was Lutheran.

Another emigrant was *Michael Wohlfahrt* of Tulpehocken Township, Berks County, 1759 (Hocker, p. 81). The Wohlfarts of Atolhoe (Rehrersburg) appear in the *Stoever Records.*

A third family appears to have settled in Lancaster County, in the Warwick and Whiteoak area. On February 25, 1755, *Ludwig Wohlfahrdt* and *Anna Margaretha Hoeg,* of Warwick, were married (*Stoever Records,* p. 65). *Conrad Wohlfart* is listed in "Weisseichenland" (Whiteoak) in 1755 (*Waldschmidt Records,* 1752-1786, Hinke Collection).]

98. JOHANN LEONHARD ZIEGLER, of Sinsheim, a blacksmith, wanted to go to Pennsylvania in 1750, but had his petition refused by the government (Protocol 8204, pp. 224, 247).

EMIGRANTS OF THE YEAR 1751

99. PETER BENNINGER, of Epfenbach (Kreis Sinsheim), was permitted to emigrate in 1751, with his wife and four children (Protocol 6197, p. 140).

100. HENRICH BECK, of Epfenbach (Kreis Sinsheim), with his wife *Anna Margaretha* and son *Johann Jörg,* was permitted in 1751 to emigrate on payment of 11 florins for manumission and 10 florins additional tax (Protocol 6197, pp. 359, 451).

101. ADAM BUECKLE (BICKLE), the Reformed schoolmaster from Spechbach (Kreis Heidelberg), was in 1751 permitted, on account of his poverty, to emigrate gratis with his wife and children (Protocol 6197, pp. 458, 495).

[According to the records of Trinity Lutheran Church, Reading, Pennsylvania, *Johann Adam Bückle,* son of *Johann Adam Bückle,* Reformed schoolmaster at Wiesenbach (Kreis Heidelberg), and his wife *Veronica,* was born at Wiesenbach, May 1, 1708. In 1729 he was installed as schoolmaster at "Spechtbach," serving there 22 years. He married (2) *Elisabeth Gernion,* of Germersheim, in 1741. He had four children, of whom one son survived him. He died in Reading November 3, 1783, and was buried in the Reformed churchyard. His sister married *Johann Georg Gansshorn,* of Bammenthal (No. 92, above).

Adam Bickle was taxpayer in Robeson Township, Berks County, 1759 (Montgomery, *Berks County,* p. 1149).

Adam Bickly, tailor, was taxpayer in Reading, Berks County, in 1780, also *Henry Beckly,* taylor (*Pennsylvania Archives,* 3d Ser. XVIII, 394).

Tobias Bickle was resident in Heidelberg Township, new Lebanon County, in 1752 (Egle, *Lebanon County,* p. 196). On October 22, 1764, *George Adam Bueckle* and *Maria Salome Huber,* of Reading and Derry, were married (*Stoever Records,* p. 70). *Adam* and *Maria Eva Bickel* had a son *Johann Adam,* baptized August 25, 1754 (New Hanover Lutheran Church, PGS, XX, 210). *Ludwig Adam Bickel,* Lutheran, was a member of the Old Goshenhoppen Church, Upper Salford Township (Bean, *Montgomery County,* p. 1135).]

102. JOHANN GEORG ERNST, of Lobenfeld (Kreis Heidelberg), was permitted to emigrate in 1751 (Protocol 6197, pp. 458, 495).

[One *Georg Ernst* and wife *Catharina* (Reformed), had a son *Johann Jürg,* baptized October 8, 1752; sponsors: *Michael Ege,* as proxy for his son and wife (St. Michael's and Zion's Lutheran Church, Philadelphia, PGS, VIII, 206).]

103. WIDOW BECKENBACH. The widow *Beckenbach* with her children, from Eiterbach, were permitted to emigrate in 1751 after lengthy negotiations and payment of 130 florins for manumission and 117 florins and 30 florins for the tithe *(10. Pfennig)* (Protocol 6197, pp. 330, 378, 429, 505, 536). This family probably includes the *Adam Beckebag, Caspar Beckebach, Geörg Adam Beckenbach, Johann Georg Beckenbach,* and *Georg Leonhardt Beckenbach* who arrived at Philadelphia on the Ship *Janet,* October 7, 1751 (List 175 C).

[*Anna Maria Beckenbach,* widow of *Johann Adam Beckenbach,* who was killed in 1747, was from Heiligkreuzsteinach-Eiterbach (Kreis Heidelberg). She emigrated with her children. *George Beckenbach* died before 1802, in Frederick, Maryland (Lutheran Church Register, Frederick, Md.) Heimatstelle Pfalz, Kaiserslautern.

The name came in some areas to be spelled *Peckinpah*.

Additional materials on the Beckenbach(er) families of the Odenwald can be found in Heinz F. Friederichs, *President Dwight D. Eisenhower's Ancestors and Relations* (Neustadt/Aisch, 1955), pp. 95, 100, 103, 158.]

104. ELISABETH HILD, citizen's daughter from Handschuhsheim (today Heidelberg-Handschuhsheim), was permitted to emigrate in 1751, on payment of 5 florins (Protocol 6197, pp. 501, 504).

105. JOHANNES SCHILLING, of Reichartshausen (Kreis Sinsheim), vassal, was permitted in 1751 to emigrate with his wife and children, on payment of 5 florins to buy themselves out of vassalage, and 13 florins for the tithe *(10. Pfennig)*. (Protocol 6197, pp. 428, 474). *Johannes Schilling* arrived at Philadelphia on the Ship *Phoenix* September 25, 1751 (List 173 C).

[One *Johannes Schilling* and wife *Anna Maria* had a son *Johann Conrad* baptized 1753 (The Trappe Records, PGS, VI, 213). A later *John Shilling*, single, was listed in Manheim Township, York County, in 1779 and 1780 (*Pennsylvania Archives*, 3d Ser. XXI, 27, 217).]

106. ANDREAS WETZSTEIN, of Gauangeloch (Kreis Heidelberg), was permitted in 1751 to emigrate with his wife and two chldren, on payment of 10 florins for manumission and 9 florins for the tithe *(10. Pfennig)* (Protocol 6197, p. 461).

[*Henrich Wetzstein* is listed in Maxatawny, Berks County, 1756 (Hocker, p. 60) and (=Wetstone), 1759 (Montgomery, *Berks County*, p. 1041). *Henry Wetstone* had "located lands," Longswamp Township, Berks County, 1759 (Montgomery, p. 1049).]

107. SAMUEL SCHWEIGERT (SCHWEIKERT), of Bargen (Kreis Sinsheim) was permitted to emigrate in 1751, on payment of 10 florins (Protocol 6197, pp. 480, 504). *Hans Samuel Shweyart* arrived at Philadelphia on the Ship *Shirley*, September 5, 1751 (List 163 C).

108. JOHANN LEONHARD SCHEID, of Schriesheim (Kreis Mannheim), was permitted to emigrate in 1751 (Protocol 6197, p. 533).

[Other Scheidts from various Pennsylvania records include *Carl Scheidt* who with his wife was sponsor to the son of *Nicholas Wolf*, of Bethel, in 1753 (*Stoever Records*, p. 42). Evidently from the same family is the marriage of *Catarina Scheidt* and *Wilhelm Stein*, of Atolhoe (=Altalaha, i.e., Rehrersburg), August 29, 1762 (*Stoever Records*, p. 69).]

109. ADAM HENRICH HOFFMANN, of Schries-

heim (Kreis Mannheim), who had already emigrated, was in 1751 retroactively manumitted (Protocol 6197, pp. 487, 525, 535).

110. NICKLAS REINHARD, day laborer from Wilhelmsfeld, was permitted in 1751, along with *Caspar Heckmann* (No. 111, below) and *Adam Eisenhauer* (No. 112, below), all from the same place, to emigrate on payment of the usual taxes (Protocol 6197, pp. 384, 395, 468, 534, 550, 762).

111. CASPAR HECKMANN, day laborer from Wilhelmsfeld, was permitted in 1751, along with *Nicklas Reinhard* (No. 110, above) and *Adam Eisenhauer* (No. 112, below), all from the same place, to emigrate on payment of the usual taxes (Protocol 6197, pp. 384, 395, 468, 534, 550, 762).

112. ADAM EISENHAUER, day laborer from Wilhelmsfeld, was permitted in 1751, along with *Nicklas Reinhard* (No. 110, above) and *Caspar Heckmann* (No. 111, above), all from the same place, to emigrate on payment of the usual taxes (Protocol 6197, pp. 384, 395, 468, 534, 550, 762).

[*Johann Adam Eisenhauer*, of Eiterbach, Reformed, was born circa 1697, lived after 1729 in Wilhelmsfeld, where he was overseer of the poor [*Almosenpfleger*] in 1733. In 1734 he was sponsor to the child of *Georg Pfeiffer*, Catholic, in Wilhelmsfeld. He married (1) before 1724 *Anna Elisabeth* [————], Reformed, born 1699, died at Wilhelmsfeld December 15, 1743, aged 44 years 10 weeks; (2) at Heiligkreuzsteinach, June 14, 1744, *Anna Margarethe Franck*, Reformed, widow of *Johann Adam Heeb* in Falkengesäss.

Johann Adam Eisenhauer was the son of *Hans Nicolaus Eisenhauer*, of Eiterbach, baptized at Waldmichelbach, October 11, 1674, Reformed, died between 1737-1745. He lived in the newly founded town of Wilhelmsfeld from about 1711. He married, circa 1696, *Susanna (Anna)* [————], Reformed, born circa 1672, died at Wilhelmsfeld, May 19, 1730, aged 58. Their daughter *Anna Elisabeth*, born circa 1698, Reformed, married *Johann Georg Pfeiffer*, Catholic, of Wilhelmsfeld.

The children of *Johann Adam Eisenhauer* of Eiterbach and Wilhelmsfeld were the following, all baptized at Heiligkreuzsteinach:

1. *Magdalena*, born August 17, 1724, Catholic.
2. *Johannes*, born 1728, confirmed March 22, 1742, Reformed.
3. *Magdalena*, baptized November 12, 1729, Reformed (sponsor: *Margaretha*, daughter of *Johann Leonhard Reinhardt*).
4. *Johann Georg*, baptized January 22, 1733, Reformed (sponsor: *Johann Georg*, son of *Johann Gärtner* in Wilhelmsfeld).
5. *Anna Elisabeth*, baptized November 24, 1735, Reformed (sponsor: *Anna Elisabeth*, wife of *George Pfeiffer*, nee *Eisenhauer*); died December 6, 1735.

6. *Johann Nicolaus,* baptized November 29, 1738, Reformed (sponsors: *Johann Nicolaus Biehler* in Wilhelmsfeld, Catholic, and his wife *Juliane,* Reformed); died 1739/1740.
7. *Johann Nicolaus,* baptized September 23, 1740, Reformed.
8. *Elisabeth,* baptized January 20, 1748, Reformed (sponsor: *Elisabeth Catharina,* wife of *Johann Theobald Schmidt* in Wilhelmsfeld).

For Adam Eisenhauer and his ancestry, see Heinz F. Friederichs, editor, *President Dwight D. Eisenhower's Ancestors and Relations: Genealogical, Historical and Sociological Studies on the Odenwald Emigration during the First Part of the Eighteenth Century* (Neustadt/Aisch: Verlag Degener & Co., Inhaber Gerhard Gessner, 1955), pp. 100-101, 104-105. Other members of the Eiterbach—Wilhelmsfeld branch of the Eisenhauer family emigrated in the 19th Century to Australia, Africa, and the United States [*Ibid.,* pp. 100-101).]

113. PETER LEYER, of Heiligkreuzsteinach, was permitted in 1751 to emigrate, along with *Niclas Zimmermann* of Altneudorf (No. 114, below) and *Jacob Reichert* of Heddesbach (No. 115, below) (Protocol 6197, pp. 384, 395, 468). It is not without interest that one of the wives of these emigrants, who was Catholic—which one is involved, is not indicated—did not receive the desired permission to emigrate, "because in the country to which they are going, the exercise of the Catholic religion has not been introduced" [*weilen in dem Land, wo sie hinziehen, das katholische Religionsexercitium nicht eingeführt*].

[There were other Leyer families in Pennsylvania: *Martin Leyer* was a member of Cacusi (Hain's) Reformed Church in Berks County in 1752 (Hinke Collection); and *Adam Layer* in 1768-1770. *Jacob Leier* is referred to in the New Hanover Lutheran Church Records, 1756, 1759; and *Michael Leier* in 1765 (PGS, XX, 279).]

114. NICLAS ZIMMERMANN, of Altneudorf, was permitted in 1751 to emigrate along with *Peter Leyer* (No. 113, above) and *Jacob Reichert* (No. 115, below) (Protocol 6197, pp. 384, 395, 468). See the note under No. 113, above, involving the Catholic wife of one of these three emigrants.

115. JACOB REICHERT, of Heddesbach (Kreis Heidelberg), was permitted to emigrate in 1751, along with *Peter Leyer* (No. 113, above) and *Niclas Zimmermann* (No. 114, above) (Protocol 6197, pp. 384, 395, 468). See the note under No. 113, above, involving the Catholic wife of one of these three emigrants.

[One *Jacob Reichert* was a taxpayer in Bern Township, Berks County, 1768 (*Pennsylvania Archives,* 3d Ser., XVIII, 111) and an early member of St. Michael's Church near Hamburg (Thomas S. Stein, *Centennial History of Lebanon Classis* [Lebanon, Pennsylvania: Sowers Printing Company, 1920], p. 298).]

116. BALTHASAR KOENIG, citizen of Schönau (Kreis Heidelberg) was permitted in 1751 to emigrate taxfree on account of poverty. Included in the permission were *Jörg Happes* (No. 117), *Johannes Wagner* (No. 118), and *Jörg Lücker* (No. 119), all of Schönau. Although in their application no goal of emigration is indicated (Protocol 6197, p. 505), they are obviously the *George Licker, Balzar Konig, Johannes Wagner* and *George Happes* who arrived at Philadelphia on the Ship *Queen of Denmark,* October 4, 1751 (List 174 C).

[*Baltzar Kenig* had land surveyed in Berks County, 1754 (*Pennsylvania Archives,* 3d Ser. XXVI, 278). A *Baltzer King* was a taxpayer in Cumru Township, Berks County, 1767 (*Ibid.,* XVIII, 73); another in Heidelberg Township, York County, 1783 (*Ibid.,* XXI, 751).]

117. JOERG HAPPES, citizen of Schönau (Kreis Heidelberg) was permitted in 1751 to emigrate taxfree of account of poverty (Protocol 6197, p. 505). Included in the permission were Nos. 116, 118-119, all of Schönau. The four arrived at Philadelphia on the Ship *Queen of Denmark,* October 4, 1751 (List 174 C).

[According to H. N. Hoppes, Gaithersburg, Maryland, *Jörg Happes* settled in North Carolina, where he died after 1790. His children were named *George, Johannes,* and *Daniel.* According to the same source, his brother *Johann Michael Happes,* son of *Johann Michael Happes* (1688-1750) of Hirschhorn (Odenwald) settled in Pennsylvania. His children were named *Michael, Jr., Hans Adam, Jacob, Heinrich,* and *Johannes* (Heimatstelle Pfalz).]

118. JOHANNES WAGNER, citizen of Schönau (Kreis Heidelberg), was permitted in 1751 to emigrate taxfree on account of poverty (Protocol 6197, p. 505). Included in the permission were Nos. 116-117, and 119, all of Schönau. *Johannes Wagner* arrived with these other three countrymen on the Ship *Queen of Denmark,* October 4, 1751 (List 174 C).

119. JOERG LUECKER, citizen of Schönau (Kreis Heidelberg), was permitted in 1751 to emigrate taxfree on account of poverty (Protocol 6197, p. 505). Included in the permission were Nos. 116-118, all of Schönau. *George Licker* arrived with them on the Ship *Queen of Denmark,* October 4, 1751 (List 174 C).

[On November 27, 1753, *Anna Johanna Luecker,* of Warwick, in Lancaster County, married *John Peter Dinnies* (*Stoever Records,* p. 64).]

120. JACOB STAHL, of Neckarelz, wanted to leave for Pennsylvania in 1751 (Protocol 8105, p. 124). He is perhaps identical with the *Jacob Stahl* who arrived in Philadelphia on the Ship *St. Andrew,* September 14, 1751 (List 165 C).

[For an earlier *Jacob Stahl,* from Lambsheim, who arrived at Philadelphia on the Ship *Winter Galley,* September 5, 1738 (List 52 A-C), see Heinrich Rembe, *Lambsheim* (Kaiserslautern, 1971), p. 224, noted in

Pennsylvania Folklife, XXIII:2 (Winter 1973-1974), 47-48. Still another *Jacob Stahl* arrived in 1739 (List 73 A-C).]

121. MARTIN DIETZ, of Mosbach, wanted to go to Pennsylvania in 1751. The government had no objection to his emigration. *Martin Dietz* arrived at Philadelphia on the Ship *St. Andrew,* September 14. 1751 (List 165 C).

122. JOHANN HENRICH SEYDENBENDER, possibly of Mosbach, wanted to go to Pennsylvania in 1751. The government had no objection to his emigration. "Such people of common rank remain here among us only as a nuisance, since they are incapable of paying the seigneurial duties, hence let there be no scruples in speeding them on their way most graciously" *[dergleicher Leut gemeiner Statt nur zum Ueberlass sich hier aufhalten, auch die herrschafftliche Beschwerden zu entrichten ausserstand, also finde man keine Bedenklichkeit wann in dem Gesuch gnädigst willfahret werde]* (Protocol 8105, p. 102). *Hennrich Seydenbender* arrived at Philadelphia on the Ship *St. Andrew,* September 14, 1751 (List 165 C).

[*Henry Seidebender* is listed as resident of Brecknock Township, Berks County, in 1759 (Montgomery, *Berks County,* p. 1182). In the Waldschmidt Records, 1752-1786, is the marriage of *George Seidenbender,* son of the late *Henry Seidenbaender,* to *Susanna Brendel,* daughter of *Philip Brendel,* February 16, 1784 (Hinke Collection).]

123. MARTIN SCHUCK, of Reihen, was permitted in 1751 to emigrate to America on payment of 4 florins for manumission and 3 florins emigration tax (Protocol 8105, p. 172). *Martin Schuch* arrived in Philadelphia on the Ship *Edinburgh,* September 16, 1751 (List 167 C). *Johann Petter Schuch* accompanied him.

[One *Martin Schuck,* of Rapho Township, Lancaster County, made his will January 26, 1801, probated November 11, 1801. His wife's name is not given. His executors were *John* and *Joseph Schuck.* His children were (1) *John,* (2) *Susanna* married *John Rubert,* (3) *Joseph,* (4) *Esther* married *Joseph Gengrich,* (5) *Abraham,* and (6) *Salome. Martin Schuck* is mentioned in Sower's newspaper, February 29, 1760, as living in Hempfield Township, Lancaster County; his wife's name is given as *Anna Maria* (Hocker, p. 87).]

EMIGRANTS OF THE YEAR 1753

124. JOHANNES MUSSELMANN. In 1753 the Mennonite *Johannes Musselmann* of Zuzenhausen received permission to marry the daughter of the Mennonite *Samuel Petzer* of Meckesheim and permission to emigrate to America (Protocol 6199, pp. 663, 678). *Hans Musselmann,* aged 22, arrived at Philadelphia on the Ship *Patience,* September 17, 1753 (List 200 A-B).

[According to H. Frank Eshleman, *Historic Background and Annals of the Swiss and German Pioneer Settlers of South Eastern Pennsylvania* (Lancaster, Pennsylvania, 1917), p. 238, *Hans Musselman* belonged to the Mennonite congregation in Meckesheim, two hours southward from "Neckarsmond" (=Neckargemünd). The congregation included the Mennonites at Zuzenhausen, Daisbach, and Langzael.

For the *Johannes Musselman* of Great Swamp (1750) and Upper Saucon (1759), see Schulze, I, 110, 213, 260. *John Musselman* of Upper Saucon, Northampton County, made his will January 4, 1773, probated March 29, 1773. The will names his wife *Elisabeth,* the following children: *Jacob* (a minor), *Veronica, Catharina,* and *Elisabetha.* Executors were *Jacob Yoder,* and *John Newcomer, Jr.*

Another *John Musselman,* of Warwick Township, Lancaster County, made his will August 20, 1793, probated November 18, 1797. It names his wife *Christina,* and the following children: *Christian, Abraham, Jacob, Barbara, John, Margaret,* and *Christina.* Executors were *Christian Frantz* and *Christian Hostetter.*]

125. GEORG MARTIN, of Neunkirchen (Kreis Mosbach) received permission in 1753 to emigrate with his wife and three children (Protocol 6199, p. 637). *Joerg Marthin* arrived on the Ship *Edinburg,* September 14, 1753 (List 199 B-C).

EMIGRANTS OF THE YEAR 1754

126. JOSEPH BUBIGKOFFER, Reformed, noncitizen *[Beisass],* on the Rohrhof near Brühl (Kreis Mannheim), was, on account of poverty, manumitted gratis and permitted in 1753 to emigrate (Protocol 6200, p. 520). *Joseph Bubikofer,* aged 30, arrived at Philadelphia on the Ship *Brothers,* September 30, 1754 (List 219 A-C).

["Bibikhoffer" families appear in the records of First Reformed Church, Lancaster (PGS, IV). For example, *John Bibikhoffer,* son of *Nicholas* and *Anna Delia Bibikhoffer,* was born April 1, baptized April 13, 1740 (p. 254). In the Waldschmidt Records, 1752-1786 (Hinke Collection), appears the marriage, on August 1, 1756, of *Joseph Buby-Kofer,* son of the late *Frantz Buby-Kofer,* to *Anna Maria Ulrich,* daughter of the late *John Jacob Ulrich* (p. 59). *Joseph* and *Ann Maria Bibickhoffer* had a son *John Jacob,* born August 27, baptized September 7, 1758 (First Reformed Church, Lancaster, PGS, IV, 273).]

127. NICOLAUS FEDEROLFF, of Dossenheim (Kreis Heidelberg), who wanted to go to South Carolina with his wife and three children, was permitted to emigrate in 1753 (Protocol 6200, p. 631).

[Among the Federolff families of Pennsylvania, who may or may not have been related to *Nicolaus Federolff,* are the Württemberg family headed by *Peter Feterholf,* born at Wachbach,, Württemberg, March 20, 1699, who married *Anna Maria Rothermel,* born February,

1712, at Wachbach, daughter of *John* and *Sybilla (Zimmermann) Rothermel,* of Wachbach. They settled in Macungie Township, Lehigh County, where the emigrant died August 15, 1784. See Abraham H. Rothermel, "The Pioneer Rothermel Family of Berks County," in *Transactions of the Historical Society of Berks County,* III (1923), 134-143; also *Penn Germania,* XIII, 204-207. A *Johannes Federwolf (sic),* with wife *Anna Catharina* and three daughters, left Dossenheim for Carolina in 1752. See Hartman, "Amerikafahrer von Dossenheim im 18. Jahrhundert," *Mannheimer Geschichtsblätter,* XXVII (1926), cols. 55-58, republished in *Pennsylvania Folklife,* XXI:2 (Winter 1971-1972), 46-48].

128. JOHANN MICHAEL ROESCH, day laborer from the Bruchhäuserhof (today Bruchhausen, Gemeinde Sandhausen, Kreis Heidelberg), was permitted in 1754, along with *Johannes Krauss* of the same place (No. 129, below) to emigrate taxfree with his wife and children (Protocol 6200, pp. 648, 659). *Michael Räsh (Rich, Rust)* arrived at Philadelphia on the Ship *Brothers,* September 30, 1754 (List 219 A-C).

[One *Michael Resch* and wife *Anna* had a child baptized July 6, 1761, by the Reverend *George Michael Weiss* (Goshenhoppen Records, PGS, XXVIII, 300). A *Michael Rosch* was among the elders and deacons of the Reading Lutheran congregation in 1777 (Muhlenberg, Journal, III, 45).]

129. JOHANNES KRAUSS, day laborer, of the Bruchhäuserhof (today Bruchhausen, Gemeinde Sandhausen, Kreis Heidelberg) was permitted in 1754, along with *Johann Michael Rösch* of the same place (No. 128, above), to emigrate taxfree with his wife and children (Protocol 6200, pp. 648, 659).

[This relatively common name is difficult to sort out. One Palatine *John Krause* settled in what is now Lebanon County, where his son Captain *David Krause,* born circa 1750, in Lebanon Township, achieved fame in the Revolution and served as member of the Assembly from Dauphin County, 1785, Associate Judge of Lebanon County and other offices (Egle, *Lebanon County,* p. 277).

Another *Johannes Krauss* settled in Heidelberg Township, Lehigh County; for a sketch of his descendants, see *The Pennsylvania German,* VII (1906), 298-301.

Still another *John Krauss* married in 1753 and was a member of Zeltenreich's Reformed Church, Lancaster County, in 1754 (Waldschmidt Records, 1752-1786, Hinke Collection). Another *Johannes Krauss,* with his wife *Catharina,* appears in the New Hanover Lutheran Church, 1770 (PGS, XX, 273). And of course the Krauss families of Montgomery County include the Schwenkfelder Krausses from Silesia, emigrants of the 1730's.]

130. PHILIPP LEYER, widower, of Aglasterhausen (Kreis Mosbach), was permitted in 1754, with his six children, to emigrate gratis on account of their propertyless status (Protocol 6200, pp. 421, 452).

131. DAVID MUELLER, of Altneudorf (Kreis Heidelberg), was permitted to emigrate taxfree in 1754 (Protocol 6200, p. 634).

132. JACOB SCHIFFERDECKER, of Neunkirchen (Kreis Mosbach), was permitted in 1754 to emigrate on payment of the usual taxes (Protocol 6200, pp. 385, 426). *Jacob Schifferdecker* arrived at Philadelphia on the Ship *Henrietta,* October 22, 1754 (List 226 A-C).

[*Jacob Shiffendecker (sic)* settled in or near Lancaster, Pennsylvania, where he appears in the records of First Reformed Church (Hinke Collection), where his name is spelled *Shiffendecker.* His wife's name is given variously as *Maria Catharina* and *Catharina.* They had a son *Jacob* born February 27, 1756, baptized March 3, 1756 (PGS, IV, 268); a daughter *Margaret,* born October 13, 1757, baptized November 23, 1757 (PGS, IV, 272); and a daughter *Anna Maria,* born August 28, 1759, baptized September 28, 1759 (PGS, IV, 276). A *George Shifferdecker* is listed as an inmate in Warwick Township, Lancaster County, in 1779 and 1782 (*Pennsylvania Archives,* 3d Ser. XVII, 507, 781).]

133. CATHARINA ZIMMERMANN, of Moosbrunn (Kreis Heidelberg), received permission to marry in 1754 and at the same time permission to emigrate (Protocol 6200, pp. 932, 946).

134. JOHANN STEPHAN MARTIN, citizen's son, of Neckarkatzbach (Kreis Mosbach), who had already emigrated to Pennsylvania, was granted manumission in 1754 (Protocol 6200, pp. 440, 464). *Hans Steffan Marthin* arrived at Philadelphia on the Ship *Shirley,* September 5, 1751 (List 163 C).

[One *Stephen Martin* was a resident and tavernkeeper in Lancaster Borough, Lancaster County, 1771-1773, 1779, 1782 (*Pennsylvania Archives,* 3d Ser. XVII, 10, 296, 461, 611, 760). *Stephen Martin* married *Catharine Weidler,* daughter of *Michael Weidler* of Manheim Township, Lancaster County, who died in 1770. *Stephen Martin* was executor of *Elizabeth Weidler,* of Manheim Township, his mother-in-law, in 1783; he was also executor of the estate of *Leonard Klein,* of Lancaster, probated 1793.]

135. JOHANN MICHEL WAGNER, of Sinsheim, was permitted to go to the New Land in 1754 (Protocol 8107, pp. 250, 325).

EMIGRANTS OF THE YEAR 1755

136. MICHAEL WEIS, of Waldkatzenbach, was permitted in 1755 to emigrate to America, on payment of 30 florins for the tithe *(10. Pfennig)* (Protocol 8108, p. 335). *Johan Michael Weiss* arrived in Philadelphia on the Ship *Neptune,* with *Mathias Weiss,* on October 7, 1755 (List 234 A-C).

27

EMIGRANTS OF THE YEAR 1764

137. GEORG PFRANG, SR., of Weinheim, cooper, who wanted in 1764 to go to Virginia or New England, was permitted to leave for Philadelphia with his wife and four children, but because his property ran to the sum of 458 florins and 26 kreuzer, he had to pay a tithe of 48 florins (Protocol 6210, pp. 473, 479, 482, 603, 620).

[*George Prong* was resident in Augusta Township, Northumberland County, 1778-1784 (*Pennsylvania Archives*, 3d Ser. XIX, 409, 444, 527, 547); and in Catawissa Township, Northumberland County, in 1787 (*Ibid.*, XIX, 732).

Earlier references to the family include the marriage of *Johann Michael Pfrang* (emigrant of 1749?) to Mrs. *Anna Rosina Lerch,* April 21, 1750 (New Hanover Lutheran Church, PGS, XX, 408).

Other Pfrangs were located in Lebanon County. *John Michael Pfrang* was married to *Anna Catarina Gring* of Lebanon, July 6, 1756 (*Stoever Records,* p. 65); *Anna Maria Pfrang,* of Lebanon, to *Johannes Kuemmerling,* May 31, 1757 (*Ibid.,* p. 66); *Maria Agnes Pfrang,* of Lebanon, to *Adam Stephan,* December 20, 1757 (*Ibid.,* p. 66). Johann Adam *Steffen,* who had come to Pennsylvania in 1750 in the Ship *Bennet Galley,* moved to Northumberland County, Pennsylvania. His son, *Frederick Steffy,* removed to Jefferson County, Ohio, circa 1801 (*The Genealogical Helper,* November 1974, p. 622). *Maria Eva Pfrang* was married to *Christian Friedrich Wegman,* of Lebanon, in 1764 (*Stoever Records,* p. 70).

One *Jacob Prank* had a son *Johann Georg* baptized 1750 (First Reformed Church, Philadelphia, Hinke Collection).

Johann Michael and *Matthäus Pfrang, Sr.,* of Grötzingen in Württemberg, arrived at Philadelphia on the Ship *Chesterfield,* September 2, 1749 (PGFS, X, 200).]

EMIGRANTS OF THE YEAR 1765

138. JOHANN GEORG SCHNECK, of Schatthausen, was permitted in 1765 to emigrate to America with his two children, without paying the usual fees; presumably he was manumitted gratis on account of poverty (Protocol 6211, pp. 528, 687). *Hans Georg Schneck* arrived at Philadelphia on the Ship *Polly,* August 24, 1765 (List 253 C). With him is listed a second *Hans Georg Schneck* and a *Jacob Schneck,* and a *Jacob Hetzel* (see No. 42, above).

[An earlier emigrant, *Hans Jurg Snek,* with *Peter Lish* (Reformed), was witness to the wedding of *Gerhard Mühlefeld* (Reformed) and *Cathrin Roht* (Lutheran), January 1, 1756, St. Michael's and Zion's Lutheran Church, Philadelphia (PGS, XIV, 52). *Georg Schneck,* with *Johannes Bender* and others, was witness to the marriage of *Gerhart Mühlefeld* and *Anna Catharina Boettinger,* February 17, 1761, same church (PGS, XIV,

106); and with others, he was witness to the marriage of *Johann Friederich Mühlefeld* and *Catharina Margretha Stein,* January 18, 1763 (same church, PGS, XIV, 127).]

139. ANNA MARIA HOFFMANN, citizen's daughter of Zuzenhausen, petitioned in 1765 for permission to emigrate, but was refused by the government, because a general prohibition on emigration was involved (Protocol 6211, pp. 458, 575, 622).

140. GEORG ADAM MARTIN, of Neckar-Katzenbach, petitioned for permission to emigrate in 1765, but was refused by the government, because a general prohibition on emigration was involved (Protocol 6211, pp. 458, 575, 622).

EMIGRANTS OF THE YEAR 1766

141. JACOB HORSCH, of Mauer (Kreis Heidelberg), Mennonite and non-hereditary tenant [*Temporalbeständer*], received permission from the electoral government in 1766 to emigrate to Pennsylvania, upon payment of the sum of 50 florins for the tithe *(10. Pfennig)* (Protocol 6212, pp. 419, 498). He arrived in Philadelphia on the Ship *Minerva,* October 29, 1767 (List 267 C). The name appears incorrectly in the ship list transcripts as *Gorsch;* in the original document (facsimile, II, 827), the name is *Horsch.*

[In a German history of the Horsch family by Paula Petri, of Aschaffenburg (n.p., 1939), deposited in the Heimatstelle Pfalz, it appears that *Jacob Horsch* was the son of *Joseph* and *Barbara Horsch,* listed in the Mennonite Census Lists in the Baden State Archives as residents of Mauer, 1739 ff. After Joseph Horsch's death, circa 1763, his two eldest sons, *Peter* and *Jacob Horsch,* with *Johann Steiner* and a second *Jacob Horsch* (possibly Joseph's brother, of Schatthausen), all Mennonites, renewed the lease on December 6, 1763. Jacob Horsch's application for emigration, published in the above history, is dated May 13, 1766. In the application he is described as single, and 32 years of age.]

APPENDIX I

A. THE WISTAR-WISTER FAMILY

Among the most distinguished of all Pennsylvania German families, from their varied contributions to the economic and cultural history of the United States, were the Wistars (Wisters), descendants of Caspar Wistar (1696-1752), a native of Wald-Hilsbach near Heidelberg. The name was spelled *Wüster* in Germany. The emigrant's father, *Johann Caspar Wüster* (1671-1727), was a *Jäger* or forester in the service of the Elector Palatine. Caspar Wistar, founder of the American family, arrived at Philadelphia September 16, 1717, his property consisting, according to family tradition, of his clothing, a pistareen (9 pence), and "a double-barreled gun of curious construction". In 1739 he began a glass furnace at Wistarburg, near Alloway and Salem, New Jersey, the first successful glass business in this country. Among his children were his eldest son *Richard Wistar* (1727-1781), who continued the glass business. His grandson, *Dr. Caspar Wistar* (1761-1818), was professor of anatomy at the University of Pennsylvania and founder of the Wistar Institute (1808), the oldest medical research institution in the United States. Other Wistars came to America from Hilsbach in 1727, including the emigrant's brother John and a sister Catharine who married a Hiester in the Tulpehocken Valley and became the ancestress of Governor Joseph Hiester. Finally, a niece of Caspar Wistar married *Heinrich Keppele* (1716-1797), Philadelphia merchant and founder of the German Society of Pennsylvania in 1764.

For the Wistar Family and its significance in the new world, see Caspar Wistar Haines, *Some Notes Concerning Caspar Wistar (Immigrant) and on the Origin of the Wistar and Wister Families* (Philadelphia: The Wistar Institute Press, 1926); Milton Rubincam, "The Wistar-Wister Family: A Pennsylvania Family's Contributions Toward American Cultural Development," *Pennsylvania History,* April 1953, 142-164; and William S. Middleton, "Caspar Wistar, Junior," *Annals of Medical History,* IV (1922), 64-76. In the *Dictionary of American Biography,* see the articles "Caspar Wistar (1696-1752)," XX, 432-433; "Caspar Wistar (1761-1818)," XX, 433-434; and "Sarah Wister (1761-1804)," XX, 434-435.

B. THE SCHAEFFERS OF SCHAEFFERSTOWN

Alexander Schaeffer is remembered in Pennsylvania as the founder of Heidelberg, now Schaefferstown, in Heidelberg Township, Lebanon County. He was a native of Schriesheim, born January 8, 1712, and died April 10, 1786. With his wife, *Anna Engle,* and three children, he came to America in 1738, landing in Philadelphia on the Ship *Robert and Alice,* September 11, 1738 (List 55 A-C), with emigrants by the name of *Röhrer* and *Trautmann* (q.v.). He brought with him a *Taufschein* dated at Schriesheim May 7, 1738, which is still in existence. His business interests included the King George Inn (in more recent times the Franklin House) which he built about 1746, and a general store. He was a large landowner in Heidelberg Township and in 1758 laid out the town of Schaefferstown. In 1765 he gave land for the Reformed church, of which he was a leading member, and the cemetery. In 1758 he purchased the property later known as the Brendle farm, which now forms the nucleus of the Historic Schaefferstown open air museum. Alexander Schaeffer made his will April 28, 1784, probated April 17, 1786. His executor was *Henry Schaeffer* of Heidelberg Township. His wife was *Catharine* (his second wife, as *Anna Engle* had died in 1772, aged 64), and his children were named (1) *Henry;* (2) *Sabina,* wife of *Michael Hake;* (3) *Anna,* wife of *Christian Meyer;* (4) *Catharine,* wife of *John Meyer;* (5) *John;* and (6) *Margaret,* wife of *John Bright.* For the last-named, see the Brecht family, No. 2, above. For Alexander Schaeffer's town-planning activities, see Charles H. Huber, compiler, *Schaefferstown, Pennsylvania, 1763-1963* (Myerstown, Pennsylvania: Church Center Press, for the Schaefferstown Bicentennial Committee, 1963), pp. 17-23, 24-39.

Henry Schaeffer (1749-1803) inherited the Brendle farm from his father, where he operated a tile factory for roofing and floor tiles, and a distillery, where he made apple-brandy or applejack. In the community he was a Justice of the Peace and a penman or scrivener. He organized a company of volunteers during the Revolution and became their captain. After the Revolution he served as Associate Judge of Dauphin County.

C. THE HELFFRICHS AND HELFFENSTEINS

From the Mosbach area in the lower Neckar Valley there came to Pennsylvania the two distinguished clerical families of *Helffrich* and *Helffenstein,* who served the Reformed Church through many generations. *Johann Heinrich Helffrich* was born at Mosbach, October 22, 1739, son of *Johann Peter Helffrich,* burgomaster of Mosbach, and his wife, *Anna Margaretha Dietz.* His father dying soon after the birth of this his only child, the widow married the Reverend *Peter Helffenstein,* of Sinsheim, who was superintendent (inspector) of the Reformed Churches for the Palatine government. The Helffensteins had three children: (1) *Johann Albert Conrad,* who came to America and became minister of the Reformed Church of Germantown and elsewhere, (2) *Johann Heinrich,* pastor of the Reformed church in Sinsheim, and (3) *Dorothea Margaretha,* who married the Reverend *D. M. Helffenstein,* pastor at Schönau.

Johann Heinrich Helffrich was reared by the Helffensteins, studied theology at the University of Heidelberg, and came to America in 1771 with his half-brother, *Johann Albert Conrad Helffenstein* (1748-1790), as Reformed missionaries to Pennsylvania. After an almost disastrous sea voyage of over four months in the Fall and Winter of 1771-1772, they arrived in New York in January, 1772, and came on to Pennsylvania. Helffrich was installed in the Reformed parish that covered Western Lehigh and Eastern Berks Counties—with the churches of Maxatawny, Delongs, Lowhill, Weissenburg, and Heidelberg. Other congregations were added during the

course of his ministry: Longswamp, Ziegels, Upper Milford, Trexlertown, Moselem, and Towamensing. He died December 5, 1810, having served the Reformed Church 50 years, 11 in Europe and 38 in Pennsylvania. In his ministerial career in America he baptized 5830 and confirmed about 3000 individuals.

Pastor Helffrich's descendants have been important also in the history of the Reformed Church in Pennsylvania. His son *Johannes Helffrich* (1795-1852) succeeded him in his charge, and likewise his grandson, *William A. Helffrich* (1837-1894). The line continues in the grandsons of the latter, the Reverend *Reginald Helffrich,* an official of the World Council of Churches, and Dr. *Donald L. Helffrich,* who for many years was president of Ursinus College at Collegeville, Pennsylvania. For details on the Helffrichs, see William A. Helffrich, *Lebensbild aus dem Pennsylvanisch-Deutschen Predigerstand: Oder Wahrheit in Licht und Schatten,* edited by N. W. A. and W. U. Helffrich (Allentown, Pennsylvania, 1906); and *Geschichte verschiedener Gemeinden in Lecha und Berks Counties, wie auch Nachricht über die sie bedienenden Prediger, vornehmlich aus der Familie Helffrich, deren Ursprung und Ausbreitung in Europa, nach authentischen Quellen, und deren Immigration und Verbreitung in Amerika, nebst einem Rückblick in das kirchliche Leben Ostpennsylvaniens* (Allentown, Pennsylvania: Trexler and Hartzell, 1891), particularly pp. 71-104, "Nachrichten über die Familie Helffrich". For both the Helffrich and Helffenstein families, see Henry Harbaugh, *The Fathers of the German Reformed Church in Europe and in America,* Vols. II-IV (Lancaster, Pennsylvania, 1857-1872); and William J. Hinke, *Ministers of the German Reformed Congregations in Pennsylvania and Other Colonies in the Eighteenth Century,* edited by George W. Richards (Lancaster, Pennsylvania: Historical Commission of the Evangelical and Reformed Church, 1951).

APPENDIX II
INDEX OF PLACES

To give our readers some idea of the geographical extent of the area involved in this emigration, as well as to provide help on possible family relationships between emigrants from the same village, we add the list of the German towns and villages involved and the list numbers of individual emigrants from each place. In addition, the following place-names appear in the introduction but not in the emigrant list—Berckenheim, Bohnfeld, Dühren, Eppingen, and Massenbach.

1. Aglasterhausen (No. 130).
2. Altneudorf (Nos. 114, 131).
3. Asbach (Nos. 79, 80, 81).
4. Bammenthal (Nos. 58, 92).
5. Bargen (No. 107).
6. Bruchhäuserhof (Bruchhausen) (Nos. 128, 129).
7. Burcken (Neckarburken) (Nos. 86, 87, Introduction).
8. Daisbach (No. 75).
9. Daudenzell (No. 67).
10. Dossenheim (Nos. 3, 14, 127).
11. Eberbach (Nos. 83, 84).
12. Eiterbach (Nos. 74, 91, 103).
13. Epfenbach (Nos. 99, 100).
14. Eschelbronn (No. 44).
15. Gauangeloch (No. 106).
16. Handschuhsheim (Heidelberg-Handschuhsheim) (No. 104).
17. Heddesbach (No. 115).
18. Heiligkreuzsteinach (No. 133).
19. Helmstadt (Nos. 47, 93).
20. Hilsbach (Nos. 55, 56, Appendix I-A).
21. Hockenheim (No. 4).
22. Hoffenheim (No. 66).
23. Hohensachsen (No. 73).
24. Lobenfeld (No. 102).
25. Mannheim-Neckerau (No. 11).
26. Mannheim-Sandhofen (No. 13).
27. Mannheim-Seckenheim (Nos. 5, 6).
28. Mauer (Nos. 37, 39, 40, 41, 141).
29. Meckesheim (Nos. 12, 76, 77, 96).
30. Michelbach (No. 90).
31. Mittelschefflenz (Nos. 72, 82, 85, 89).
32. Moosbrunn (No. 133).
33. Mosbach (Nos. 121, 122, Introduction, Appendix I-C).
34. Neckarkatz(en)bach (Nos. 134, 140).
35. Neunkirchen (Nos. 125, 132).
36. Neckarelz (Nos. 38, 120).
37. Reichartshausen (No. 105).

29

38. Reihen (Nos. 68, 69, 70, 123, Introduction).
39. Rohrbach bei Dühren (No. 24, Introduction).
40. Rohrhof bei Brühl (No. 126).
41. Sandhofen (No. 1).
42. Schatthausen (Nos. 42, 138).
43. Schollbrunn (No. 88).
44. Schönau (Nos. 116, 117, 118, 119, Appendix 1-C).
45. Schriesheim (Nos. 2, 9, 10, 50, 51, 52, 53, 54, 108, 109, Appendix I-B).
46. Sinsheim (Nos. 26, 98, 135, Appendix I-C).
47. Spechbach (Nos. 59, 60, 97, 101).
48. Steinsfurt (No. 71, Introduction).
49. Waldkatzenbach (No. 136).
50. Walldorf (Nos. 7, 8, 45, 46).
51. Weiler am Steinsberg (Nos. 15, 16, 17, 18, 19, 20, 21, 22, 23, 27, 28, 29, 30, 31, 32).
52. Weinheim (No. 137).
53. Wieblingen (Heidelberg-Wieblingen) (Nos. 34, 78).
54. Wiesloch (Nos. 25, 43).
55. Wilhelmsfeld (Nos. 33, 110, 111, 112).
56. Zuzenhausen (Nos. 35, 36, 48, 49, 57, 61, 62, 63, 64, 65, 94, 95, 124, 139).

APPENDIX III
INDEX OF EMIGRANTS

Because of the wealth of material presented in this list, and since it is not alphabetized, a cross-index of family names has been prepared. The numbers refer to numbers of individual emigrants in the list (Nos. 1-141). Family names mentioned in the Introduction and Appendices are included.

Arnold—35
Barther—27
Battenfeld—90
Bauer—52
Beau—4
Bechtold—72
Beck—100
Beckenbach—103
Behr (Bär)—83
Bender—23, 87, 138
Benninger—99
Bernhardt—4
Besch—82
Bettle—6
Beyer—21
Boettinger—138
Böhler (Büller, Biehler) —22, 112
Bowsman—7, 36
Brecht (Bright)—2, 51, Appendix I - B
Brendel—122
Brenneisen—27
Brenner—80
Bubigkoffer—126
Buchacker—51
Bückle (Bickle)—92, 101
Christmann—2
Clotter—Introduction
Cunradt—63
Cunz (Kunz)—7
Dankels—41
Danner—45, 46
Dehuff—2
Diebendörffer (Diffenderffer)—9, 78
Diehl (Diel)—5
Dietz—121, Appendix I - C
Dinnies—119
Doll—23
Dürr—68
Eberle—74, 91
Ege—102
Ehret—85
Eisenhauer—112
Ellich—Introduction
Engle—Appendix I - B
Ernst—102
Etschberger—37
Euler—73
Ewig—33

Fabian—41
Federolff—127
Feil (Phile)—85
Filler—87
Fortunee—81
Franck—112
Frantz—124
Frey—17, 78
Frosch—7
Gansshorn—92, 101
Gärtner—112
Geiger—93
Geis(t)er—44
Gengrich—123
Gerhard—72
Gerner—93
Gernion—101
Gorner—80
Grauss (Krauss)—75
Griesemer—41
Gring—137
Gump—81
Günther (36)
Haegis—16
Hake—Appendix I - B
Hambrecht—68
Hamspacher—18
Happes—117
Hasen (Hesen)—9
Hauck—47, 85
Heckmann—111
Heeb—112
Helffrich—Appendix I - C
Helffenstein—Appendix I - C
Heller—24
Henrich—89
Her—3
Hertzel (Hirtzel)— Introduction
Heylmann—61
Hezel—41
Hiester—Appendix I - A
Hild—104
Hildenbrand—27
Hill—13
Hilligass—26
Hoeg—97
Hoffman—2, 49, 80, 109, 139
Hoffstätter—54
Honey—68
Hörpel—38

Horsch—141
Hostetter—124
Huber—24, 101
Humbel—Introduction
Igsin (Ickes?)—21
Immel—21
Kamm—26
Kämmerer—11
Karg—51
Kauffman—70
Keller—28, 31
Kellermann—56
Kemp—4
Keppele—Appendix I - A
Ki(e)ssinger—1
Kinder (Günther)—36
Kirsch—62, 64, 65
Klein—80
Knecht—69
Kneissley—68
Koberstein—94
Kolb—41
König—116
Krafft—66
Kranester—45
Krauss—129
Krehebühl—58
Krüger—51
Kuhn—21
Kümmerling—137
Kumpff—81
Labaar—26
Lang—23, 60
Lay—63
Leidig—9
Leitner—28
Lerch—137
Lessle—93
Levan—4
Leyer—113, 130
Licht(n)er—63
Linz—79
Lish—138
Lücker—119
Ludwig—24, 86, 95
Lutz—26
Mack—81
Martin—125, 134, 140
Mayer-Meyer—15, 51, Introduction
Meister—66
Meixell—25
Meyer—Appendix I - B
Muck—97
Mühlefeld—138
Mühlhäuser (Mühlenhäuser)—24
Müller (Miller)—8, 11, 19, 26, 40, 41, 43, 48, 76, 77, 96, 131
Musselmann—124
Mussier—Introduction
Neff—21
Newcomer—124
Notz—36
Nuz—41
Ottinger—21, 92
Peischlein—82
Peter—17, 22, 30
Petzer—124
Pfauz—24
Pfeiffer—112
Pfeil—66
Pfrang—137
Puder—110
Raitschaff—Introduction
Reeser—4
Reichert—115
Reinhard—110, 112
Riehm—25
Ritss—41
Roemer—39
Roesch—128

Röhrer—37
Roht—138
Romig—4
Rothermel—127
Rubert—123
Rudi—23
Rudisille—21, 80
Ruland—1
Rupp—67
Sabel—90
Sauter—27
Schaeffer—2, 51, Appendix I - B
Schaffner—7, 36
Schall—72, 85
Schauer—Introduction
Scheid—108
Schifferdecker—132
Schilling—105
Schlepp—3
Schmidt—15, 33, 112
Schneck—138
Schopf—21, 23
Schuch—23
Schuck—123
Schwab (Schwob)—16, 25
Schwann—50
Schweigert (Schweikert) —107
Sevic—28
Seydenbender—122
Siegfried—4
Sill—86
Simone—2
Sinter—Introduction
Smyser—21
Soerer—60
Söller—Introduction
Söllner—Introduction
Spengler—16, 29, 32
Spohn—88
Stahl—120
Steger—61
Stein—57, 108, 138
Stenger—71
Stephan—137
Tracken—24
Trautmann—51, 52
Treibel—84
Tübinger (Tiebinger, Ibinger)—53
Ulrich—126
Wägelin—Introduction
Wagner—118, 135
Walter—7, 14
Wedel—3, 34
Wegman—137
Weidler—134
Weis—136
Welcker—59
Weller—24
Wiederer—24
Wilcke—16, 20
Wild(t)—92
Will—10
Willhaut—17
Wistar-Wister (Wüster) —Appendix I - A
Wolf—85
Wolffhart (Wolfhardt, Wolfahrt)—25
Wollfarth—97
Yeizer—7
Yoder—124
Young—80
Ziegler—15, 18, 55, 80, 92, 98
Zilling—89
Zimmer—41
Zimmermann—4, 12, 38, 114, 127, 133
Zweis(s)ig—39, 60

The Eighteenth-Century Emigration

Photograph by Alf Rapp, Landau.

Half-timbered and stone farmhouses on main street of Kallstadt, wine-village in the Palatinate.

·om the Palatinate:
New Documentation

By FRITZ BRAUN

Translated and Edited by Don Yoder

Again we offer our readers a valuable new emigrant list from 18th Century German archival sources, valuable especially for the social history materials it provides about the emigrants and their lives in Germany and in the "New Land."

Our list is abstracted from Fritz Braun, *Auswanderer aus Kaiserslautern im 18. Jahrhundert* (Kaiserslautern, 1965), No. 17 in the Series: *Schriften zur Wanderungsgeschichte der Pfälzer*, published by the Heimatstelle Pfalz, Kaiserslautern. This is a pamphlet of 32 pages, reprinted from the Braun-Rink *Bürgerbuch der Stadt Kaiserslautern 1597-1800.* We have included only the 18th Century materials involving emigrants to the American colonies. The pamphlet includes additional 19th Century American emigration materals, and valuable 18th Century data relating to the Palatine colonies in Pomerania, Brandenburg, Hungary, Galicia, the Batschka, and the Banat.

Of particular value is. the long *Amerikabrief* of Philipp Jacob Irion, sent from Virginia to relatives in the Palatine in 1766, which gives us a glimpse into the life of a well-educated, public-spirited emigrant concerned with American agriculture and trade, the Newlander and redemptioner systems, as well as with, as is the case with so many of the 18th Century letters from America, the problems of getting his inheritance to the new world. The letter is in the florid literary style that was in fashion in 18th Century Germany, full of baroque clichés and French expressions, very different from the peasant-level missives of most of the emigrants.

Equally important for social history is the Moravian *Lebenslauf* of Peter Pfaff (1727-1804) which describes his boyhood and education in Germany, his emigration to Pennsylvania, and his further trek to the Moravian settlements of North Carolina. This document sheds great light on the appeal that the Moravian gospel had for the emigrant generation, and the description of his last years, added by the hand of a Moravian scribe, gives a revealing glimpse into Moravian attitudes toward life and death.

This article is one of a long series of American editions of German articles on the 18th Century emigration which we have had the pleasure of publishing for American readers, genealogists and social historians, in the columns of *Pennsylvania Folklife* and its predecessor, *The Pennsylvania Dutchman.* For the complete list of our earlier articles on this subject, see Harold A. Lancour, comp., *A Bibliography of Ship Passenger Lists, 1538-1825: Being a Guide to Published Lists of Early Immigrants to North America, Third Edition,* Revised and Enlarged by Richard J. Wolfe (New York: The New York Public Library, 1963).

Our thanks in connection with the present article, to Dr. Fritz Braun, Director, Heimatstelle Pfalz, Kaiserslautern; and Dr. Fredrich Krebs, Speyer State Archives, Speyer-am-Rhein —— EDITOR.

1. *FRIEDRICH LUDWIG HENNOP* (HENOP in the United States), Reformed minister, born at Kaiserslautern, November 7, 1740, student of theology in Heidelberg, 1758-1761, son of the Rector of the Latin School in Kaiserslautern, *Lucas Hennop* and his wife *Johanna Maria Schäfer.* Applying for the parish ministry in America, he was examined March 27, 1765, by representatives of the Synod of the Reformed Church in Holland, and after ordination emigrated to America. He arrived at Philadelphia in October, 1765, after a passage of 15 weeks. His first regular parish was Easton, Pennsylvania, 1766-1770, with outlying churches of Plainfield and Dryland in Pennsylvania and Greenwich in New Jersey. He served the Frederick parish in Maryland, including Walkersville and Middletown, for 14 years, 1770-1784. Many Palatines resided in Frederick and among them the Reformed schoolmaster *John Thomas Schley*, from Mörzheim near Landau, founder of the town of Frederick. From Frederick Pastor Henop made periodical visitations of Virginia. He died in Frederick, October 30, 1784, a respected and beloved minister.

Sources: Heimatstelle Pfalz, Kaiserslautern, Auswanderer-kartei und Familienarchiv; Reformed Church Registers, Kaiserslautern. For full details of his biography, see William J. Hinke, *Ministers of the German Reformed Congregations in Pennsylvania and Other Colonies in the Eighteenth Century* (Philadelphia, 1954); also *A History of the Evangelical Reformed Church, Frederick, Maryland* (Frederick, Md., 1964).

·rea of heavy 18th-Century emigration to the New World.

2. *PHILIPP JACOB IRION* , died (Culpepper County, Virginia?) before 1784, commerce-secretary for the Baden-Durlach government, resident in Eselsfürth, married *Regina Heiler (Heyler)* who died in Kaiserslautern-Eselsfürth, August 7, 1765 (in her death-entry the name of her husband is given as *Johann Philipp Irion*). Philipp Jacob Irion emigrated ostensibly in 1764 with his two eldest sons to Culpepper County, Virginia. However, he is mentioned there in a will already in the year 1759, before the birth of his last daughter, Katharine Regina, in Kaiserslautern. Also in 1774 he was living in Culpepper County, Virginia. His residence he named "Jacobs-Vale" (Jacobs Valley?). One of his letters from the year 1766 was published by Dr. Friedrich Krebs in *Pfälzer Heimat,* 1951, No. 1.

There are not too many letters from emigrants, which like this one are written from the viewpoint of a critical and farseeing man, who was obviously provided with good knowledge. Placed only a few years in a new environment, he gives an excellent picture of the colonization system with its sunny and shady sides, he shows the great possibilities for the economic advance of the new world, to which he commits himself without reserve, and he reveals his unlimited love for the old homeland, for family relations and for his friends. Therefore we have included this letter, in slightly abridged form, within the framework of this article on emigration.[1]

Jacobs-Vale, May 9, 1766
My very dear and very esteemed brother!

Since I have been delighted with four letters from you, namely, December 6, 1764, February 11, 1765, April 30, 1765, and May 6, 1765, and each one of them has a separate purport, I will answer them consecutively.

For the gracious act of taking care of those letters which I have taken the liberty of including with this, I thank you most dutifully, and am sorry for the pains I have caused you, but very much more in fact for your long and severe illness. I hope and wish that a long-lasting health may make you forget the misery you had.

To the Court Riflemaker Hess in Zweibrücken I owed 22 florins, which I sent there through Schmoll a few days before my departure. But (as Schmoll now says) he forgot to pay it and out of fear, failed to acknowledge his blunder to me. You will oblige me very much accordingly if you will pay this honest man the 22 florins in question, explaining the situation to him.

My dear brother, you demand again and again a true, candid, and veracious report of Van Stampel in particular and of this country in general. I wish to be acquainted quite sufficiently with both matters, to be able to give you satisfaction, however, I will do herein what is in my power and thereby take the aforesaid faithfulness, sincerity, and reliability—in short, my conscience—as my guide.

In the last war Van Stampel as a colonel with the Hannover troops; conducted himself in such a way that the King made him a present of 20,000 *morgen* of land in North America, in order to plant the same. Stampel did not have means enough to do this, so he formed a company with some

merchants in London and these made an immediate advancement of 20,000 pounds sterling, to bring people from Germany to the land in question. Stampel brought nearly 5000 persons to London and not until he had received the charter for his land from the King did he notice that his land would be given him in the province of North Carolina, and not, as the company believed, in Virginia. This error made the merchants so indignant that they immediately dissolved the company, which made it necessary for Stampel to take flight, leaving the poor Germans to their fate in London, where they had to endure much misery and certainly would have been ruined if the charity of different Englishmen had not taken them up and had them transported free of charge to South Carolina and other provinces.

On the one hand, I praise the warnings put out in Germany by the authorities, since very seldom does a so-called Newlander appear who does not seek to feather his nest at the expense of these poor emigrants, through which circumstance their serving time is much protracted. Our laws order that whoever brings anyone at his expense across the

Pfälzischer Verkehrsverband

Winter foodstuffs dry under the barn roof in a South Palatine "Hof" while casks are readied for the autumn vintage.

---

[1] This letter is of great interest from the linguistic standpoint. First of all, it is dated, addressed, and concluded in French: "Jacobs-Vale, le 9e May 1766"; "Monsieur, très-honoré et très cher frère!"; . . . "Monsieur, très-honoré et très cher frère / votre très humble et très obéissant serviteur / J. Irion." Similar American-German examples of the use of French in correspondence can be found in the letters of the 18th Century Reformed minister, Abraham Blumer, of Allentown. Irion also uses several English words in the body of his letter: *charter, county, credit,* and *duti* (duty).

Vine-covered farmhouses in a Palatine Wine-village.   Photograph by Alf Rapp, Landau.

ocean into this province, to him such emigrants shall be bound to serve for four years without wages. In this time the master must provide board, lodging, and clothing, also he must after the passage of four years give a new suit of clothes or as much as 30 florins on dismissal. Now the Newlanders commonly keep for themselves with the ship captains for each head a certain sum or bring out free a certain number of people whom they then sell here. For this reason the cost of passage comes for the most part one half higher than it rightly should, so emigrants can never be careful enough.

On the other hand, I wish that my good fellow-countrymen would have more freedom to come here, but also at the same time, that such an arrangement might be made which protected them sufficiently from the more than too manifold treacheries of the Newlanders, since this country wants for nothing but sufficient inhabitants in order to attain such a high level of prosperity compared with which no other

35

Pfälzischer Verkehrsverband ph

Gimmeldingen's red tile roofs rise along the Haardt Mountains in the Rhine-Palatinate.

could make a show. The soil is rich and produces rich harvests. The waters are full of fish, the forests full of game, the mountains full of rich ores, the air pure and healthy and everyone enjoys such great freedoms, the like of which are to be found nowhere else.

I find nothing to find fault with, except that there are not a thousand times more inhabitants here, which, if it could be, must be nothing but Germans. Since these have the reputation for industry and hard work, while others yield to laziness, do nothing but promenade and ride and plant just as little as is necessary for their housekeeping. Hence probably the proverb which has arisen here—that a German can support himself on a ´rock. One can ride for half a day in different places, before one gets a single house to see, although there are many inhabitants in this province. Virginia is the largest among all others, Pennsylvania is much more heavily populated, likewise Maryland, yet it is impossible to seek anyone out if one does not know precisely the province and the county in which the person lives.

We still have at this time no further trade than with Old England, the English West Indian islands, and Portugal.[2] The first takes our tobacco and furs, and we get in return all kinds of linen, woolen, and silk fabrics, hardware, glass, etc. The West Indies get wheat, flour, smoked and salt fish, barrel staves and hoops, we from them sugar, molasses, and rum. Portugal takes wheat, flour, and meat, and sends us wine, lemons, oranges, and salt. Now isn't it an eternal shame, that we have to sacrifice our goods for such things instead of for cash, which things could be made better and

more cheaply in this country, if we had the necessary artisans? Many kinds of artisans, if they are equipped and are pretty familiar with the country, earn so much that a good industrious worker can earn 500 to 600 florins. Because with the exception of foodstuffs we get everything that we need from far across the ocean, everything is uncommonly dear, particularly clothing and especially linen, which is five or six times more expensive than in Germany.

Of the demise of our late mother-in-law I could in fact not read without being touched, all the more because this brought me to consider that I must be prepared for a similar parting from all those whom I esteem higher than the treasures of this world, before I once again will have been able to enjoy the inestimable pleasure of seeing you. I confess that the many calamities with which my entire life is entwined, have oftentimes made me weary of life, yet never so much as now, when I must live in the midst of strangers in an unknown land, very far removed from my friends, whose counsel and help I could console myself with, were I with them. It is a great consolation to me that my most highly esteemed brothers, namely you and our brother the revenue official, want graciously to trouble themselves about me and my children. It gives me hope for a help which I never supposed I would need. I have so conducted myself that I have gained not only the confidence of our company but also of different other respectable merchants and through this I had credit enough to begin something whereby I could not only live but also lay by money.

A theft in my house necessitated me to take my two children again, since I am no longer in position to devote to them the necessary costs for having them educated in a city. Yet I will do everything that is in my power. They have

2 On the triangular trade, which Irion describes so carefully in this letter, see the recent book by Arthur L. Jensen, *The Maritime Commerce of Colonial Philadelphia* (Madison, Wisconsin, 1963).

already come pretty far in the English language, and the German has been carried on without intermission. They give good promise of themselves and I hope that God's blessing will in one way or another again place me in position not to leave their good gifts without exercise.

Very dear brother, if my dear mother should ask you for money, please help her out, since if I can otherwise practicably work it out, I propose to have nothing of the inheritance brought here, and if our brother the revenue official (as I do not doubt at all) wants charitably to take further care of my dear Franz, then half interest is to be applied to my dear mother and Catharina Regina. This is simply and solely what I have to ask. Everything else I leave to your and our brother the revenue official's proven loyalty to me, without proposing a further word about it, except to ask for a report as soon as possible.

Letters, and whatever is to be sent to me in future, must be sent to Mr. Zacharias Mayer, wine-merchant in Rotterdam, as he has my address and will continue to look out for my interests, yet over and above this I enclose my own address. If you should find safe opportunity to send letters here without sending them via Mr. Mayer, then please place my address on them, as I send it, then make a cover for them and put on it the other address, to Messrs. Scott and Lenox, so that when the letters are in America they can go with the post. Please be so good as to forward the enclosed letters, and pardon the trouble occasioned, but count up the postage costs. The place where I now live, I have named Jacobs-Vale. I have made Mr. Lay a commission, if he needs your help, then please support him, since it is of unusually great consequence to me.

Hearty thanks to Mr. Heidweiler for his good wishes, somewhat jokingly written, with regard to the materials. I hope the richness of this country over here will indeed not exclude me from a share in its fruitfulness, although for the above-mentioned reason all remaining enterprises and businesses must languish.

I sympathize quite deeply with the painful condition of your dear Wilhelmine and hope that her health has already for a long time been restored, and that all the rest of your most estimable family [are] still in just as good comfort, at this time, as they were then. God grant a long continuance [to it]!

It is quite a pleasant satisfaction to me, to hear so much good of my little Franz. God continue to be with him and bless our brother the revenue official's further exertions, for which I cannot thank him enough.

I should really be ashamed of myself, my very dear brother, to make for you in regard to these previously mentioned things still more burden and trouble, but since my circumstances are so constituted that I must seek to help myself in divers ways, I hope and pray that you will also pardon me this time, when I request you to send to me, at good opportunity via Mr. Mayer in Rotterdam, everything that will be sent you by my dear mother. And if, as I suppose, our late mother's household linen is distributed, then please also send along the portion that is coming to me, but including nothing among it that is not first sewn up and washed, since whole linen cloth is confiscated. I am writing to Mr. Zacharias Mayer that he is to provide for an opportunity to get it here and then send you word of it, which pray wait for before you send anything. Perhaps you have a friend in Mannheim, who can send it by water to Rotterdam. The safest and best way would be, if it could be sent along with an honest man who is going to Virginia, Maryland, or Pennsylvania, who must pass it as for his own, when the ship, as is customary, is visited, since each one is allowed to bring along as much as he wants of used linen for his own use.

From the kind remembrance of your brother and the house of Rebell I thank you most warmly and offer them and other good friends my hearty compliments, and assure Mr. Horn the Government Councilor herewith that the tobacco is by no means forgotten. I already would have sent it long ago, if I had had good opportunity, but since no ship may go elsewhere in Europe except direct to England and there the tobacco is not only unpacked, but also six times as much duty as the purchase price must be paid, I do not know how to set about it.

I cannot possibly live without seeing Germany once again and this must happen, just as soon as it ever can be possible.

The love for my friends is much greater than all danger or inconvenience of the ocean [voyage]. Nothing but death shall keep me from seeing you again. But meanwhile give my kindest regards and those of my family (who thank God are quite well) to my friends in constant affection and friendship, assuring them that I shall be and remain, with regard and devotion, Sir, very esteemed and very dear brother, your very humble and very obedient servant,

J. IRION

It remains to be clarified why the emigrant did not bring his wife along to America; with great concern he remembers the two children left behind, who after the death of their mother were attended to by one of his brothers [-in-law].

According to notes of Klaus G. Wust, Arlington, Virginia, Philipp Jacob Irion married in Culpepper County, Virginia, August 12, 1765(?), *Sarah Poindexter*, who was born about 1744 and died October 27, 1814. The emigrant left behind a large family, which today is predominantly resident in Louisiana.

Sources: Heimatstelle Pfalz, Kaiserslautern, Auswandererkartei und Familienarchiv; Culpepper County, Virginia, Will Book A, 1749-1770, p. 490; Lutheran Church Registers, Kaiserslautern; *Pfälzer Heimat*, 1951 and 1957.

3. *PETER PFAFF,* born at Kaiserslautern, June 24, 1727, died at Bethania, North Carolina, January 22, 1804, son of the citizen *Johann Daniel Pfaff,* miller of the Hospital Mill [*Spittelmüller*], emigrated to America in 1749. The birthdate of Peter Pfaff is no longer proveable in Kaiserslautern, because the Lutheran church register in question has been lost. Through correspondence with R. A. Poff,[3] Roanoke, Virginia, the editor came into possession of an autobiography of the emigrant himself, which reads as follows:

"I was born June 24, 1727, in the Electoral Palatinate, in the district capital of Kaiserslautern, at which place my father Johann Daniel Pfaff was citizen and master-miller. My mother was Anna Barbara *nee* Hartung. When I was five years old, my father, who had the character of an awakened and peace-loving man, died the death of a Christian, and what my mother later told me about him, I bore well in mind. My mother however, after some time married again, [to] a miller [named] Jacob Bart. This my stepfather

[3] The name "Poff" is of course an American form of the family-name *Pfaff.* As I have pointed out in another connection, this change represents not so much an Americanizing as a dialecting of it, i.e., spelling it as it was pronounced in the dialect. Other examples: *Pfaffenmeier* became *Puffenmoyer,* even *Buffamoyer* (Dauphin County, Pennsylvania); *Pfaffenberger* became *Poffenberger* (Juniata County, Pennsylvania). See "Dutchified Surnames," *'S Pennsylvaanisch Deitsch Eck, The Morning Call,* Allentown, Pennsylvania, September 21, 1946.

took upon himself the oversight of my education and sent me diligently to school. When my schooldays were over, I hired out with various people as driver [*Fuhrmann*], until I went to Pennsylvania in the year 1749.

"I first went to Yorktown and worked there at the blacksmith trade. Quite soon I had opportunity to hear the Brethren [Moravians] preach. Their confident testimony that nothing is effectual before God but grace in the blood of Jesus, was joyous tidings to me, and I was convinced in my heart that this was the true ground of salvation. In 1750 I married Anna Walburga Kerber and soon went with her to my land that I had bought, 15 miles from Yorktown. Since we both loved the Brethren, we agreed to attach ourselves to them; therefore [we] sold this land and moved again to the neighborhood of Yorktown. We soon had the joy, too, to be numbered among their Society [*Societät*]. This made me so very happy that I wished some time afterwards to be united still more closely, through admission into the Moravian Congregation [*Brüder-Gemeine*]. When I spoke with my wife about this, she spoke to this effect, that she did not yet feel this way, but that she would not hinder me. For that reason therefore I came forward and on April 4, 1756, it fell to my happy lot to be able to regard myself, through admission, as a member of the Moravian Congregation.

"On November 4, 1759, my wife and I had the favor to partake of the Holy Communion with the congregation, which brought blessing to our hearts.

"In 1771, with the blessing of the congregation in Yorktown, we left for North Carolina and settled in the Friedberg settlement. Soon after my arrival there, I was named as vestry-man[4] in the Moravian parish, which office I occupied for four years. Also I was charged with the office of steward of the Friedberg Congregation, which was at that time still very small. When I entered into this office, I spoke simply with the dear Savior about it, entreating Him to stand by me in it with His grace, and to oversee me with His eyes, for otherwise I could not succeed; and that indeed He did the 13 years of my service in that place. The brethren and sisters loved me, and I them; and whatever I had to propose to them in my office, they were always willing to accept. But before the dear Savior I have nothing further to exhibit than His grace and remain His poor sinner."

A scribe of the Moravian Congregation has added the following lines to his autobiography:

"On the 9th of November, 1774, his beloved wife went happily to her Savior. His 24-year marriage had been blessed by God with six children, four sons and two daughters, of whom one daughter preceded him into eternity. From these his children he lived to see 30 grandchildren, of whom 20 are still alive (i.e., in the year 1804). After the death of his wife his children took him into their especial care and managed his farm in the Friedberg settlement for nearly 12 years, until in the year 1786, he with his children, our Brother and Sister Isaac Pfaff, moved hither to the vicinity of Bethania. Here he lived in retirement, had further no particular employment, but helped his son on the farm as much as he could and as his strength permitted, which after some years seemed to decline quite sharply. In 1793 there overtook him suddenly, while he was riding to Bethabara, such a powerful dizzy spell, that

Tile-roofed stairway to ornate second-floor landing, Dörrenbach on the Weinstrasse.

he fell from his horse and could not help himself, but had to be brought home by his son Isaac. From that time on he was markedly weaker, all the more so [as] similar attacks returned from time to time. With all this he came here, as much as his circumstances permitted, to meeting and to the Holy Communion, until some years ago his bodily weakness as well as the gradual decline of his understanding hindered him from it. Then he spent his time at home reading our denominational writings [*Gemeinschriften*],[5] until finally in the last years his reason so entirely declined that he was no longer able to do even this. For that reason he was a quite special object of our sympathy and supplication to the Savior, in His mercy soon to make an end to his misery.

"Concerning the progress of his heart, there is—especially of the last years—little or nothing to say, because he was seldom so in control of his wits that one could have been able to talk with him properly about these matters. Yet he

4 The document uses a few English words: *Vestry-Mann*, *steward* (in the combination *Steward-Amt*) and *parish* (in the combination *Brüder Parish*); several of these would seem to have been taken over from the vocabulary of the Church of England.

5 On the place devotional reading held in the lives of the sectarians, cf. the description, by a 19th Century German emigrant, of Uncle Jacob Mellinger, aged 78, of Lancaster County, Pennsylvania, 1833: "In a nice little room, which is prettily furnished, he sits the livelong day at his books, reading and praying" ("From the Palatinate to Frontier Ohio: The Risser Letters [1832–1833]," *The Mennonite Quarterly Review*, XXX [1956], 52).

testified last summer, when he was visited at one time, and was somewhat serene in spirit, that he had many reasons both for heartily thanking the Savior for His grace and mercy that He showed him, and for being ashamed before Him for his mistakes and oversights, and to appear before Him as sinner, from which we could conclude that in his solitude he was indeed thinking more about himself than he had made manifest through utterances about himself.

"His children testify that they had in him a faithful father, for whom it was very important to train them up in discipline and admonition before the Lord; therefore also he held with them, in their younger years, daily morning and evening prayers [Morgen- und Abendsegen]; so that he generally was very much concerned over their outward and inward well-being. Often he had testified to them himself of his own joy and thankfulness over the fact that the Savior had brought them all into His congregation, and until then had preserved his dear ones in the same, and added his wish, that his beloved grandchildren might also enjoy the same happiness in the future, therefore he oftentimes had admonished the latter to love the Savior and to consecrate themselves to Him as His sole possession.

Half-timbered farmhouse, Southern Palatinate.

"On January 4th of this year 1804 such a weak spell overtook him suddenly that his death was hourly expected. He was therefore given, on the request of his children, the benediction for his departure, after he had previously been heartily commended unto the Savior for grace and attainment. His end however was protracted longer than had been expected, and he had to endure yet many difficult things, yet about which—since he was seldom conscious—he did not complain, but mostly lay quite still and quiet. Some days before his end he testified himself, that he would go on this occasion to his Savior. When on the 21st, toward evening, he again became very weak, his children assembled around his bed and sang some verses on death [Heimgangs-Verse]. But his departure was further delayed until the following morning, the 22d, toward 4 a.m., when amidst the singing of his children, he went out quietly like a candle, and was released from all his misery and suffering.

"He had brought his age to 76 years, 7 months, less 2 days."

The children of Peter Pfaff, Nos. 1–5 born at York, Pennsylvania, No. 6 at Friedberg, North Carolina, were the following:

1. *Isaac,* born April 25, 1755.
2. *Anna Barbara,* born February 23, 1758.
3. *Anna Maria,* born May 5, 1762.
4. *Samuel,* born August 14, 1764.
5. *Joseph,* born September 28, 1768.
6. *Peter, Jr.,* born January 27, 1773.

From the personal notes of the emigrant we can gather that his mother was Anna Barbara, *nee* Hartung. In actuality Anna Barbara was not the mother, but the stepmother of Peter Pfaff. He himself evidently did not know that she was the second wife of the hospital-miller Johann Daniel Pfaff, who was admitted as citizen of the City of Kaiserslautern on August 23, 1726, and was married first to Maria Magdalena [——]. Up to now only the two following children of this first marriage are known:

1. *Maria Juliana Wilhelmine Pfaff,* born in Kaiserslautern, died in Pomerania, married at Enkenbach, April 4, 1741, *Johann Conrad Eberle.*[6]
2. *Peter Pfaff* (1727–1804), the emigrant.

The father Johann Daniel Pfaff married as his second wife, at Münchweiler an der Alsenz, February 11, 1729, *Anna Barbara* nee *Hartung.* A child of this second marriage, *Theobald Pfaff,* born (at Kaiserslautern?) 1729, died at Hochspeyer, April 15, 1748, single.

Peter Pfaff reports that his mother (i.e., stepmother) Anna Barbara Hartung, soon after the death of his father, married another miller named Jacob Bart. This concerns *Jakob Barth,* born 1683 and died July 5, 1749, in Hochspeyer, a tenant farmer [Hofmann] of the ducal house of Leiningen, who was situated as tenant [Beständer] on the Mühlhof at Hochspeyer and had three sons to his first marriage (with *Maria Catharina* [——]): *Peter, Georg,* and *Heinrich Barth,*

[6] Johann Conrad Eberle, tailor, member of the Reformed Church, was the son of Johann Görg Ludwig Eberle and his wife Anna Margaretha Schreiner. He was baptized at Kaiserslautern, December 27, 1716, and married at Enkenbach, April 4, 1741, Maria Juliana Wilhelmina Pfaff. The Eberle family emigrated in 1747 to Pomerania, settling in the new Palatine colony of Augustwalde, named for Duke August of Braunschweig-Beveren, then Governor of Stettin. Johann Conrad Eberle appears in the list of Palatine farm-owners at Augustwalde 1775, but not in the list of 1800. For Eberle, see also Fritz Braun, *Auswanderer aus Enkenbach seit Beginn des 18. Jahrhunderts* (Kaiserslautern, n.d.), Schriften zur Wanderungsgeschichte der Pfälzer, No. 11. This item is of interest since it accents the complex character of the 18th Century German emigration. Many American colonial German emigrants must have had relatives, as did Peter Pfaff, in the other German settlements of Europe as well as other American colonies.

who were all three of them older than Peter Pfaff. It remains only to add that Anna Barbara Barth died March 26, 1746, in Hochspeyer, and that after her death Jakob Barth, on September 7, 1747, entered into a third marriage, with *Maria Ziegler,* daughter of the oil-miller [*Ölschläger*] from Guntersblum.

What had happened before Peter Pfaff in 1749 made his way to America? His beloved stepmother, whom he had taken for his rightful mother, was already dead three years, his sister Maria Juliana Wilhelmina was married to Johann Conrad Eberle and had been in Pomerania for two years, his stepbrother Theobald had died a year previously and his stepfather was already married for two years to his third wife. Since the exact time of his emigration in the year 1749 is not known, it cannot be said whether Peter Pfaff had lived to see the death of his stepfather on July 5, 1749. At any rate it is not difficult to gain a picture of the young man's frame of mind from the circumstances and occurrences cited. These sensations are clearly to be deduced from the first sentences of his autobiography, even if these were written from the perspective of a mature man. So too it can be understood that Peter Pfaff felt himself appealed to in a peculiar degree by the comforting confession of Moravianism.

In North Carolina the memory of the emigrant Peter Pfaff from Kaiserslautern is preserved in the place-name "Pfafftown." There is therefore in America, now for nearly 200 years, a parallel with the name "Pfaffstadt," a very recent nickname for Kaiserslautern, from the location there of the great Pfaff Sewing-Machine Factories. Actually the forefathers of the emigrant and those of the founder of the Pfaffwerke are the same family.

Sources: Heimatstelle Pfalz, Kaiserslautern, Auswandererkartei und Familienarchiv; Lutheran Church Registers, Kaiserslautern; Reformed Church Registers, Kaiserslautern; Ludt, *Hochspeyer: Die Geschichte eines Dorfes* (Otterbach, 1959).

4. *CARL PHILIPP PLANNET,* born at Kaiserslautern, October 6, 1757, son of the button-maker *Johann Anton Planet,* born in Treysa in Hesse, and his wife *Maria Philippina Dieterich,* arrived in Philadelphia as emigrant on the ship *Adolph* and took his oath of allegiance immediately after his arrival on August 27, 1785. The *Philadelphische Correspondenz* of May 9, 1786, announces that the button-maker C. Philipp Plannet, born in Kaiserslautern, has run away from his employer, *Joseph Muszi,* in Philadelphia. Plannet obviously did not last very long in America, for on October 19, 1794, his marriage is recorded in the Reformed Church Register of Kaiserslautern, to *Salome Compter,* born at Kaiserslautern, April 20, 1770, daughter of the master tawer [*Weissgerbermeister*] *Adam Compter.* Carl Philipp Plannet (Planet) died at Kaiserslautern February 3, 1804.

Sources: Heimatstelle Pfalz, Kaiserslautern, Auswandererkartei und Familienarchiv; Reformed Church Registers, Kaiserslautern; Strassburger and Hinke, *Pennsylvania German Pioneers* (Norristown, Pennsylvania, 1934), III, 5.

5. *JOHANN HENRICH SCHAFER (SCHEFFER),* from Rutsweiler, citizen and linenweaver; married *Anna Magdalena* [——]. In the Protocols of the City Council of Kaiserslautern, May 11, 1744, it is reported that Heinrich Schäfer is on the point of transferring his residence "into the so-called New Land or Pennsylvania." Since "this emigrating Heinrich Schäfer and his son find themselves with meager means, the tithe of both, in consideration of this fact and on behalf of the Council, was reduced to 13 florins." Henrich Scheffer can be identified as passenger of the ship *Friendship,* which arrived at Philadelphia, November 2, 1744.

Children, No. 1 born presumably at Rutsweiler, Nos. 2–4 at Kaiserslautern:

1. *Henrich, Jr.,* married *Elisabetha Catharina* [——]; their daughter *Catharina* was born at Kaiserslautern, March 2, 1738.
2. *Anna Margretha,* born September 5, 1723, twin.
3. *Maria Salomea,* born September 5, 1723, twin.
4. *Susanna,* born August 2, 1727.

Sources: Reformed Church Registers, Kaiserslautern; Council Minutes [*Ratsprotokoll*], Kaiserslautern, May 11, 1744; Strassburger and Hinke, *Pennsylvania German Pioneers* (Norristown, Pennsylvania, 1934), I, 357.

6. *JOHANN JACOB SCHLOSSER,* born at Kaiserslautern, October 8, 1732, master locksmith [*Schlossermeister*], son of *Johann Peter Schlosser* and wife *Anna Margaretha;* married at Kaiserslautern, February 15, 1759, to *Maria Catharina Brauns,* daughter of *Leonhard Brauns* and wife *Anna Catharina Wagner.* He emigrated without his wife and children to America and was in 1766 in Jacobs-Vale, Virginia, with Philipp Jacob Irion (q.v.), who had made possible his passage. Because of bad conduct to his benefactor, he had to leave Jacobs-Vale.

Son, born at Kaiserslautern, *Johann Mathias,* born January 23, 1760.

Sources: Heimatstelle Pfalz, Kaiserslautern, Auswandererkartei und Familienarchiv; Reformed Church Registers, Kaiserslautern; *Pfälzer Heimat,* 1951 and 1957.

7. *JOHANNES WEBERLING (WEBERLIN),* master weaver, Lutheran, son of the citizen and weaver at Kaiserslautern, *Peter Weberlin;* married, secondly, at Kaiserslautern, August 26, 1750, to *Maria Salome Edelmann,* daughter of the deceased master-baker at Katzweiler, *Johann Peter Melchior Edelmann* and his wife *Anna Margaretha Schremm.* The couple emigrated to America in 1751. After the baptismal entry in the church register, May 23, 1751, is the notation: "Went to the New Land Tuesday after the baptism," i.e., on May 25, 1751.

This Johannes Weberling (Weberlin) could be identical with Johannes Weber, who took his oath of allegiance at Philadelphia on September 5, 1751. It is not uncommon for emigrants to change or shorten their names. Worthy of note in this connection is the fact that after him in the oath-list one *Johannes Lindöhmer* has entered his name. Might this not be *"Lindemer"* from the village of Bann? That would be quite possible. Since at that time people from the same area of origin decided on joint emigration, it might be possible to identify "Weber" here as "Weberling." This case can only be cleared up if among the settlers in America a Johannes Weberling or a Johannes Weber is discovered, who had a wife Maria Salome Edelmann and a daughter Margaretha.

Son of the first marriage of Johannes Weberling, married at Kaiserslautern, January 22, 1737, to *Anna Ottilia* [———], widow of *Ludwig Schaffer,* born at Kaiserslautern: *Johann Ludwig,* born September 5, 1738.

Daughter of the second marriage, born at Kaiserslautern, *Margaretha,* born May 22, 1751.

Sources: Heimatstelle Pfalz, Kaiserslautern, Auswandererkartei und Familienarchiv; Lutheran Church Registers, Kaiserslautern; Strassburger and Hinke, *Pennsylvania German Pioneers* (Norristown, Pennsylvania, 1934), I, 452.

New Materials on the
18TH CENTURY EMIGRATION
from The Speyer State Archives

By FRIEDRICH KREBS

Dr. Friedrich Krebs, of the Speyer State Archives, Speyer, Germany, who has furnished us with many articles in the past dealing with the genealogy and social history of the emigrant generations of the 18th Century, here presents some new materials which he has unearthed in the Speyer Archives. They appeared in Germany in the article "Amerika auswanderer des 18. Jahrhunderts aus den Akten des Staatsarchivs Speyer," in *Pfälzische Familien – und Wappenkunde* (Ludwigshafen/Rh.), XIII. Jahrgang (1964), Band 5, Heft 4, 125-127, in the section of the journal edited by Dr. Fritz Braun and entitled "Mitteilungen zur Wanderungsgeschichte der Pfälzer." *Pennsylvania Folklife* is happy to make this article, as translated by the editor, available to American readers. It presents much valuable social history about a selected number of emigrants of the 18th Century, and is particularly good for the new light it sheds on the relation that the emigrants had to the tenant-farm system in the Rhineland after the Thirty Years' War. For Dr. Krebs' earlier articles on the 18th Century emigration, see Harold Lancour, *A Bibliography of Ship Passenger Lists, 1538-1825: Being a Guide to Published Lists of Early Immigrants to North America*, Third Edition, Revised and Enlarged by Richard J. Wolfe (New York: The New York Public Library,1963),Nos.17, 132, 139-141,150-152,156,159,162-163, 167-172, 174-178, 181-182. Many of these lists appeared in *Pennsylvania Folklife* or its predecessor, *The Pennsylvania Dutchman.*—EDITOR.

1. In the year 1727 *Johann Jacob Stutzmann*, journeyman tailor, left Gönnheim for America. He was born January 1, 1706, on the Weilacher Hof, near Hardenberg, son of the tenant-farmer (*Hofmann*) on the Weilacher Hof, *Johann Jacob Stutzmann (Stotzmann)* and his first wife, *Regina Elisabetha* (Entry in Lutheran Church Register of Kallstadt, according to certified transcript in *Akt Kurpfalz Nr. 1064*). Johann Jacob Stutzmann landed at the port of Philadelphia in 1727 as passenger on the Ship "Adventure" and took his oath on October 2, 1727. His property in Gönnheim, administered for him under care of a guardian, was in 1773 surrendered to the relatives on security. The accounts in the documents are contradictory as to whether he was already married at the time of his departure or not. To be sure, according to an attestation of *Michael Kröbiel (Krebiel)* in Eisenberg, dated December 10, 1768, but available only in transcript form, his brother *Heinrich Krebiel* is said to have written him from the New Land (America) that their brother-in-law Stutzmann, married to a sister of the Krebiels in America, had died without issue. His wife was also dead. Since this attestation exists only in transcript, its contents are not fully conclusive. Source: *Staatsarchiv Speyer, Akt Kurpfalz Nr. 1064*.

2. In the year 1738 *Johann Gerhard Dinges*, hereditary lessee of the Daimbacher Hof property (i.e., Daimbacherhof near Mörsfeld in the District of Kirchheimbolanden), which belonged to the University of Heidelberg, surrendered his 2/6 share of the Hof property to his son *Johann Philipp Dinges* and to his son-in-law *Johann Nickel Herbst*. According to the contents of the documents Johann Gerhard Dinges died March 5, 1743. In 1748 (Johann) Philipp Dinges, as co-tenant at Daimbach, sought for permission to sell or to alienate his 1/6 share in the Hof property, in order to be able to go to the New Land (America). Permission was granted by the University of Heidelberg. Johann Philipp Dinges is said to have left April 15, 1749. We find him as "Filipp Dinges" among the passengers of the Ship "Edinburgh," which landed at Philadelphia in 1749. The taking of the oath took place on September 15, 1749, in Philadelphia (Strassburger-Hinke, *Pennsylvania German Pioneers*, List 132 C). Source: *Staatsarchiv Speyer, Akt Universität Heidelberg Nr. 7*.

3. In the year 1739 the Mennonite *Nicolaus Oehlenberger (Ellenberger)* at Gönnheim, who wanted to go to the New Land (America), sold, with the approval of the University of Heidelberg to whom the property belonged, the Fasseichergültgut at Gönnheim, to *Jacob Stutzmann*. He was an inhabitant at Gönnheim and former tenant (*Hofmann*) on the Weilacherhof and may be identical with the "Niclaus Ellenberger" who landed at Philadelphia in 1739

Gönnheim in the Rhine-Palatinate, 1941. From tile-roofed villages such as Gönnheim, set in the midst of vineyards, came farmers and craftsmen who populated Pennsylvania's Dutch Country. Courtesy Heimatstelle Pfalz

41

The Münchhof near Dannstadt in the Rhine-Palatinate, 1965. From such farms, tenanted by one or more families, came many of the 18th Century Palatine emigrants to Pennsylvania and other British colonies. From this particular "Hof," the Huguenot emigré family of Shuey (Jouis) came to Pennsylvania in 1732. Courtesy Dr. Friedrich Krebs

on the Ship "Robert and Alice." The taking of the oath of the passengers took place on September 3, 1739 (Strassburger-Hinke, *Pennsylvania German Pioneers*, List 71 A and C).

4. In the year 1748 *Daniel Jouis (Schui, Jue)*, who had returned from America, sold, as lessee, 1/4 of the Münch property (Münchhof) at Dannstadt, belonging to the University of Heidelberg, to *Theobald Koob* of Weisenheim am Sand, for 3350 or 3325 florins. According to the contents of the documents he had "already sixteen years ago, with wife and children, betaken himself to the New Land," and had there taken up residence. He must therefore have emigrated about 1732. His father *Daniel Jouy,* tenant of the *Universitätshof (Münchhof)* at Dannstadt, had died on August 22, 1737, and was buried on August 24, 1737, at Dannstadt. This *Daniel Jouy* was in turn the son of *David Jouy* of "Grissy (Grichy) near Metz" (i.e., Grigy, southeast of Metz), who is designated in the church register as a refugee. After the death of his father the share of Daniel Jouis in the Münch property at Dannstadt was administered through a guardian. We find the name of the emigrant badly distorted and scarcely recognizable as "Daniel Schwe" among the passengers of the Ship "Johnson" on September 18, 1732, in Philadelphia. In the oath list of the passengers of the same ship, dated September 19, 1732 (List 21 B), the name is written "Daniel Schew," in an additional oath list of September 19, 1732, as "Daniel Schuhl" (Strassburger-Hinke, *Pennsylvania German Pioneers*, Lists 21 A, B, and C).

Daniel Juy had married, at Dannstadt on October 16, 1725, *Maria Martha Schilling*, who came from Dannstadt. Three children were born to this marriage, all born on the Münchhof at Dannstadt and baptized in Dannstadt: (1) *Ludwig Heinrich*, born October 15, 1726; (2) *Anna Margaretha*, born February 15, 1729; and (3) *Johannes*, born

November 24, 1730, died November 28, 1730.

The List 21 A of September 18, 1732, names also the name of the wife of Daniel Juy (Jouy) "Maria Schwe" and likewise the names of the children "Lodawick Schwe" and "Margaretta Schwe," both under 16 years of age. From these references it is evident that this was unequivocally the emigrant Daniel Jouy (Jouis). The pronunciation of the name is, corresponding to the French origin of the family, also French, as indeed Daniel wrote his name "Schui" in the documents. Source: *Staatsarchiv Speyer, Universität Heidelberg Akt Nr. 14;* Reformed Church Register of Dannstadt .

5. Through decree of the Zweibrücken government of May 7, 1767, the property of *Johann Michael Decker*, who had gone to America 15 years previously, was confiscated. He was son of *Heinrich Decker*, a member of the community of Hirstein (today in the District of St. Wendel). The remainder of his credit, a sum of 347 florins, was to be confiscated according to a further decree of the government dated June 6, 1767. This sum was to be raised for the government by the two brothers of the emigrant, who had taken over house and properties. Michael Decker was sick on arrival in Philadelphia on the Ship "Edinburgh"; he took the oath on September 14, 1753 (Strassburger-Hinke, Lists 199 B and C).

6. Through a further decree of the Zweibrücken government dated November 29, 1768, the property of *Wendel Decker* of Hirstein was confiscated for the Treasury, a sum of 12 florins, 3 batzen and 12 pfennig. He had gone secretly with his family out of the country, without manumission, and had, according to report, gone to the New Land. Wendel Decker arrived in Philadelphia on the Ship "Minerva"; he took the oath on December 12, 1768 (Strassburger-Hinke, List No. 271 C).

New Materials on 18th Century Emigration from Württemberg

By FRIEDRICH KREBS

Translated and Edited by Don Yoder

Again we present archival material on the 18th Century emigration to Pennsylvania. The emigrants in this list are from two areas: (1) the town of Lienzingen, in Northern Württemberg, and (2) the city and district of Freudenstadt in the Black Forest in Southern Württemberg. Württemberg, in the 18th Century the Grand Duchy of Württemberg, in the 19th Century the Kingdom of Württemberg, and now part of the West German state of Baden-Württemberg with its capital at Stuttgart, was one of the sources of the strong Lutheran contingent among the Pennsylvania Germans. The dates of emigration in this case are 1751 and 1752, which were near the high point of the 18th Century German migration, with some 16 ships landing at the port of Philadelphia in 1751, and 19 in 1752.

For similar materials on the economic necessity which drove these people to emigration, see "Emigrants from Württemberg: The Adolf Gerber Lists," in *The Pennsylvania German Folklore Society*, X (1945), 103-237.

The list will be of value to social historians as well as genealogists, from the valuable insights into the reasons for emigration, and the description of arrangements made when property was inherited after emigration. Also of interest are the names of the emigrant generation—with the heavy incidence of names such as Sophia, Jacobina, Tobias, Ludwig, Rosina, Bernhard, Immanuel, Juliana, etc.—names which were not common after the settlement in America.

We are grateful to Dr. Friedrich Krebs, of the Speyer State Archives, Speyer, West Germany, for permission to translate and republish his article, which first appeared as "Beiträge zur Amerikaauswanderung des 18. Jahrhunderts aus Altwürttemberg," in *Südwestdeutsche Blätter für Familien- und Wappenkunde* (Stuttgart), Vol. XI No. 8 (November 1961), 186-189.—EDITOR.

EMIGRATION FROM LIENZINGEN

According to an official document dating from about 1775, *Jacob Geigle,* son of *Johann Jacob Geigle* of Lienzingen, District of Maulbronn (today Lienzingen, District of Vaihingen/Enz), had emigrated to Pennsylvania from his native village as a single fellow about 24 years previously, accompanied by the maid of the keeper of the Stag Inn [*Hirschwirt*] of Lienzingen, one *Anna Juditha Drexler,* to whom he got married on the way.

At home he is said to have got with child the unmarried daughter of a citizen named *Stumpf,* for which he was sentenced to prison. Actually Jacob Geigle landed at the port of Philadelphia on the ship *Phoenix* in the year 1751 and there took the oath of allegiance to the British government on 25 September 1751. When later (around 1775) the emigrant, through an attorney, demanded the delivery of his share of his parents' property, his brothers-in-law, *Conrad Munzinger* of Lienzingen and *Friedrich Link* of Schmie, who had till then been administrators of the inheritance, refused its passage to America, because the legacy (about 1000 florins) was too large and the power of attorney had passed through several hands. Also they were afraid that since America was already in a state of war, the money could fall into enemy hands. As a matter of fact the Württemberg government arrested the issuance of the property until a later time. From the official documents it is unfortunately not clear whether the emigrant finally came into his rights or not. According to the evidence in the official document in the case (Staatsfilialarchiv Ludwigsburg A 213, B 320) Jacob Geigle was living in Middletown Township, Cumberland County, Pennsylvania.

EMIGRATION FROM FREUDENSTADT

A mass emigration to Pennsylvania from the city and district of Freudenstadt in the year 1752 is implied in an official document of the Staatsfilialarchiv Ludwigsburg (A 343/344 B14), for on 7 May 1752 Bailiff [*Vogt*] Brastberger of Freudenstadt reported to the Württemberg authorities that in the city and district over which he had been given authority, 18 households with all their members had "resolved" to leave their fatherland to go away to Pennsylvania. The number of emigrants involved was given as 111, the property that they wanted to take along was declared at 2180 florins.

Specifically the following persons wanted to leave for Pennsylvania.

FROM THE CITY OF FREUDENSTADT

1. *Ludwig Uber,* butcher, aged 30, with his wife Margaretha Barbara, aged 30, and three children: Johann David (7), Johannes (5), and Johannes Ludwig (3).

2. *Johann Philipp Artz (Artzt),* aged 29, nailsmith by trade, with wife Maria Barbara, aged 26, and children: Sophia Dorothea and Catharina Christina (4 weeks old).

3. *Tobias Finckbeiner,* aged 30, day laborer, and wife Esther, aged 46, and four children from the wife's first marriage: Maria Agnes (14), Anna Maria (11), Philipp Andreas (7), and Ludwig Heinrich (5).

4. *Jacob Bosch,* aged 46, carpenter, with wife Barbara, aged 37, and children: Johann Jacob (15), Johannes (10), Anna Maria (6), Joseph (4), and Johann Friedrich.

5. *Johann Georg Ott,* aged 32, bookbinder, a convert [i.e., from Roman Catholicism], with wife Anna Maria, aged 26, and children: Rosina Barbara (2) and Johannes (six months).

6. *Eva,* widow of *Jerg Schmätzlen,* aged 49, with children: Barbara (19), Simon (14), and Agatha (11).

7. *Andreas Schneider,* aged 53, gatekeeper [Obertorwart] and shoemaker, with wife Anna, aged 51, and child: Anna Elisabetha (18).

8. *Tobias Bub,* aged 42, joiner, with wife Barbara, aged 40, and children: Jerg Friedrich (7), Tobias (5), Johannes (3), and Sophia Dorothea (1).

9. *Georg Ziegler,* aged 43, weaver, with wife Jacobina, aged 42, and six children: Anna Maria (15), Georg Jacob (11), Christiana Margaretha (7), Agnes Catharina (5), Magdalena (3), and Georg Bernhard (six months).

10. *Jacob Bernhard Schwab,* aged 52, baker, with wife Elisabeth, aged 45, and 6 children: Christina Barbara (22), Johann Adam (20), Johann Friedrich (18), Jacob Bernhard (16), Dorothea (14), and Elisabetha Catharina (8).

11. *Emanuel Friedrich Weckerlen,* aged 24, tinsmith by trade, with wife Maria Elisabetha, aged 32, and 3 children: Sabina Margaretha (4), Jeremias Friedrich (3), and Juliana Dorothea (six months).

12. *Anna Barbara Heinzelmann,* aged 24, single, sister of the wife of No. 11, above, wanted also to go along.

13. *Georg Christoph Westlen,* of Freudenstadt, aged 42, who with his wife Rosina Margaretha also wanted to go along, remained at home.

FROM THE DISTRICT OF FREUDENSTADT

A. From Neuneck (Wüerttemberg, Kreis Freudenstadt).

14. *Bernhard Kauffmann,* aged 40, with wife Agatha, aged 32, and children: Johannes (13), Bernhard (8), and Johanna (3).

15. *Johannes Flait,* aged 32, day laborer, with wife Margaretha, aged 30. Flait also wanted to take along a relative named Anna, aged 10, who was feeble and mentally retarded. In addition there were in this party Flait's single brother-in-law, *Johann Friedrich Pfefferlen,* tailor; and still another relative of Flait's by the name of Anna Maria, aged 16.

16. *Hanss Jerg Lockmayer,* aged 52, with wife Magdalena, aged 50, and children: Christina (25), Hanss Michel (22), and Johannes (16).

17. *Hannss Jerg Geyser,* aged 51, and wife Barbara, aged 50, with the twins: Anna Maria and Johannes, both 18.

B. From Unteriflingen

18. *Hanss Martin Schwarz,* aged 40, stonemason, with wife Catharina, aged 40, and children: Agnes (9), Elisabetha (4), and Maria. Also Schwarz's brother, *Jacob Schwarz,* wanted to go along.

19. *Mattheus Brechtlen,* assessor [Beisitzer], aged 38, with wife Elisabetha, aged 32, and child: Barbara (10).

20. *Michel Bach (Baach),* single, with his fiancée *Anna Kauffmann,* aged 28.

21. *Elisabeth Frick,* aged 26, who wanted to marry *Michel Marquart* of Dornstetten.

C. From Böeffingen (Wüerttemberg, Kreis Freudenstadt)

22. *Hanns Jerg Späth,* aged 56, day laborer, with wife Barbara, aged 50, and children: Eva Margaretha (26), Anna (22), Catharina (20), Magdalena (18), Hannss Jacob (17), Christian (14), Hannss Jerg (12), and Hannss Martin (7).

D. From Rodt Bei Lossburg (Wüerttemberg, Kreis Freudenstadt)

23. *Franz Anton Sinn,* aged 50, day laborer, with wife Christina, aged 46, and children of the first marriage: Catharina (23), Anna Maria (22), Eva (19); and of the second marriage: Elisabetha (15), Jacob (14), Michel (10), Hannss Jerg (6), and Barbara (2).

The Württemberg government had little objection to make to the emigration of the persons concerned. All were permitted to leave after giving notice of their rights of citizen and subject for themselves and their children, although the return to the homeland (*regressus in patriam*) was no longer permitted (Decree of 13.5.1752). Only in the case of the children of the first marriage of *Tobias Finckbeiner* was the restriction decreed that in case they possessed a considerable property, this could not be taken along except by special permission; and in the case of *Johannes Flait,* that he had better provide otherwise for his mentally retarded relation Anna than to take her along on the journey to America.

In the ship lists of the port of Philadelphia we find a large part of those who had signified their desire to emigrate, as passengers on the ship *Duke of Wirtenburg,* which landed in the year 1752 (Hinke-Strassburger, *Pennsylvania German Pioneers,* List 190 C), namely: *Johann Ludwig Uber, Jacob Bosch, Johann Georg Ott, Georg Ziegler, Jacob Bernhard Schwab, Johann Adam Schwab, Immanuel Friderich Weckerlin, Tobias Baub* (obviously *Bub*), *Johannes Flait, Johann Lockmir* (for *Lockmayer*), *Johann Georg Jayser,* and *Michel Bach.* The others on the Freudenstadt List, if they did not die on the Atlantic passage, may have landed at other American ports, for which no ship lists are in existence.

The cause of the emigration is almost always economic necessity and overpopulation of the country; so says the document in the case literally: "They [the emigrants] are mostly poor people who in the present hard and moneyless times were forced to earn a very scanty living, people who indeed—what with raised taxes and investments of much ducal money and all sorts of other difficulties—scarcely knew how to maintain their domestic honor, which they then also gave as the reason for their emigration" [*Sie seynd mehist arme Leuthe, welche bey gegenwärttigen hardten und geldlosen Zeiten sich sehr kümerlich nähren müssten, ja bey erhöheten Steuern u. Anlagen vilen herrsch. Gelder, auch sonst allerhand Beschwehrden, bey hausslichen Ehrn sich fast nicht mehr conserviren wusten, welches Sie auch vor die Ursach ihrer emigration angeben."*]

Bernhard Kaufmann, the baker from Neuneck, gave as his reason for emigration that there were too many bakers in Neuneck, who just could not "carry on" their trade alongside each other. He had no real estate, also he was not a day laborer, so that he did not know how he could maintain and support himself, wife and child. The nailsmith *Johann Philipp Artzt* gave as his reason that it was impossible to support oneself in Freudenstadt, since iron and coal were getting more expensive every year, and he could not compete with the foreign artisans of his trade, who as a consequence of cheaper raw materials (iron and coal) could produce more cheaply and underbid the native nailsmiths out in the country and in the market towns. A similar complaint was expressed by *Georg Christoph Westlen,* who however remained at home, that the gravest necessity was driving him to emigration, since he could find neither work nor livelihood in his trade of baker.

Eighteenth-Century Emigration From the Duchy of Zweibrücken

By FRIEDRICH KREBS

Translated and Edited By Don Yoder

[1] According to an extract of the Law-Court Protocols of the Superior Bailiwick of Zweibrücken, dated July 14, 1781, *Philipp Buchmann* of Nünschweiler had—according to information furnished by the Orphan Registry—"gone to America sixteen years ago." His property which was under guardianship was confiscated November 13, 1781, by the District of Zweibrücken. *Philipp Buchmann* reached Philadelphia on October 13, 1766, on board the Ship "Betsy" (Hinke-Strassburger, *Pennsylvania German Pioneers* [Norristown, Pennsylvania, 1934], List 259 C).

[2] In the year 1761 the property of *Johannes Göltzer* from Mimbach was confiscated for the treasury, because he had emigrated from Webenheim to America without manumission. The usufruct of a piece of pasture land was turned over to his mother as long as she lived, after that it passed to a member of the family. On October 2, 1761, *Johannes Göltzer*, who had returned from America, was given permission by government decree to stay with his relatives in Mimbach until the following Spring; but if he should mislead people into emigration, he was at once to be put under arrest.

[3] *Friedrich Hilspach*, son of the citizen and master shoemaker at Zweibrücken, *Georg Friedrich Hilspach*, died in 1757 in Surinam (Dutch Guiana), according to a document in the archives. The confiscation decreed for his property in the homeland was lifted by decree on October 22, 1767,

Pfälzischer Verkehrsverband

Zweibrücken landscape viewed from the Potzberg. This is "Musikantenland" —land of music-makers.

45

Dörrenbach on the Weinstrasse. Pfälzischer Verkehrsverband

and the inheritance awarded to the heirs, in case they could furnish proof that their relative had died without heirs abroad.

[4] *Peter, Jacob,* and *Conrad Klee* of Steinberg in the District of Nohfelden (today Steinberg-Deckenhardt in the District of St. Wendel), sons of *Peter Klee* of Steinberg, asked in an official petition for the issue of the property of their brother *Michael Klee* who had left for foreign parts eleven years previously. He had gone away in order to improve himself in the tailor trade and is said to have reached America in 1749. The property which the emigrant left behind

amounted to 131 florins, 8 batzen, and 3 pfennig. It was finally given up to the petitioners on payment of interest and instalment payment of the capital. *Michael Klee* arrived in Philadelphia on October 7, 1749, on the Ship "Leslie" (Hinke-Strassburger, *Pennsylvania German Pioneers,* List 141 C).

[5] 'On resolution of the Zweibrücken Government of March 30, 1771, the petition of *Abraham Roland* from Lamsborn, who had emigrated to America and was living in Lebanon (now county-seat of the county of the same name) in Pennsylvania, to let him have his parental inheritance, was

Harvest-time in the Rhine Palatinate.

dismissed and the property declared fallen to the treasury, because he had emigrated to America without official permission. However the government, in decrees dated February 10, 1781, and April 3, 1781, granted the emigrant's sister, *Maria Elisabeth,* wife of *Simon Alt* at Einöd, the usufruct of the confiscated property of her brother. *Abraham Roland* is identical with the emigrant who has signed the oath of allegiance of August 11, 1750, as *"Aberham Roland."* In Strassburger-Hinke, List 146 C, the name appears as *"Aberham Reiland."* He arrived in Philadelphia on the Ship "Patience."

[6] By decree of the Zweibrücken Government of April 13, 1790, the petition of *Jakob Schamar* of Brenschelbach, to grant him and his brothers and sisters the property of their brother *Peter Schamar* who had emigrated to America, and to lift the confiscation—was dismissed once for all. Possibly identical with *Peter Schowmacker, Shamar, Shammer,* in Hinke-Strassburger, List 221 A–C. The spelling *Schowmacker* in List A suggests *"Schuhmacher,"* but the names in the A-Lists are frequently very much garbled [since they were written by scribes rather than the individuals themselves]. The emigrant did not, however, actually sign Lists B and C, but rather used his mark.

[7] *Georg Jacob, Peter,* and *Magdalena Schirmer,* children of *Jacob Schirmer* from Winden, had emigrated to America in the years 1750 and 1751. In 1770 the inheritance of the emigrants was publicly confiscated by the state on account of

illegal emigration. Also in the same year the petition of their brother, *Anton Schirmer,* who had remained behind, and his sister, the wife of *Ludwig Schmitt* at Weingarten, to turn over the emigrants' portion to them, was dismissed, yet *Anton Schirmer* was permitted to keep back 60 florins each year from the bulk of the estate for the board and lodging of his father. About 1770 the confiscated property was put up for sale. *Anton Schirmer* acquired the greatest part of it; he was later, finally, in 1783, granted the payment of the auction fees [*Steigschilling*] in installments. *Peter Schirmer* landed at the port of Philadelphia on the Ship "Phoenix" on August 28, 1750 (Hinke-Strassburger, List 154 C); *Georg Jacob Schirmer* on the Ship "Janet" in 1751, taking the oath of allegiance on October 7, 1751 (Hinke-Strassburger, List 175 C). *Peter Schirmer* was baptized at Winden, January 10, 1723, son of *Jacob Schirmer* and *Anna Catharina. Georg Jacob Schirmer* was born at Winden of the same parents, March 3, 1730, and baptized there March 7, 1730. The parents, *Johann Jacob Schirmer,* son of the deceased *Sebastian Schirmer,* citizen at Winden, and his wife *Anna Catharina,* who came from Höfen near Kandel, had married November 22, 1718, at Winden. On February 17, 1750, *Peter Schirmer* was married at Winden to *Magdalena,* daughter of *Andreas Wendel* from Gleiszellen; to this couple was born, at Winden, on May 7, 1750, before the emigration, another daughter, *Maria Barbara.* Entries about a *Magdalena Schirmer,* sister of the emigrants, were not to be found in the Reformed Church Register of Winden. Possibly there is involved here a confusion with *Magdalena,* wife of *Peter Schirmer.* Source: Documents in the Speyer State Archives; Reformed Church Register of Winden.

[8] According to an extract of the Law-Court Protocols of the High Bailiwick of Bergzabern, dated December 18, 1772, the inheritance of *Barbara Schober,* nee *Wüst,* which had fallen to her share from her deceased father, *Georg Wüst* of Winden, was confiscated for the treasury, because she had gone to America in the year 1750 with her husband and children, without payment of the emigration tax. The last will of her father, made out in his daughter's favor, was annulled. According to the Reformed Church Register of Winden, *Simon Schober,* son of *Hans Peter Schober* of Erlenbach near Kandel, was married, on January 12, 1740, to *Maria Barbara,* daughter of *Georg Wüst* of Winden. On May 28, 1719, the parents, *Georg Wüst, Jr.,* and *Anna Maria,* had a daughter, *Anna Barbara,* baptized at Winden. *Johann Simon Schober* landed at Philadelphia on the Ship "Janet" and took the oath of allegiance on October 7, 1751 (Hinke-Strassburger, List 175 C).

Children, born and baptized in Winden:

1. *Isaac,* born November 23, 1740, baptized November 27, 1740.
2. *Maria,* born November 26, 1741, baptized December 3, 1741.
3. *Johann Adam,* born October 15, 1743, baptized October 23, 1743.
4. *Georg Peter,* born December 12, 1745, baptized December 19, 1745.
5. *Sophia,* born February 24, 1749, baptized March 2, 1749, died at Winden, April 21, 1750, at the age of one year and eight weeks.

[9] According to an entry in the Lutheran Church Register at Annweiler, *Johann Georg Süss* was born at Rinnthal, January 25, 1734, son of *Johann Philipp Süss* and *Maria Catharina,* and baptized (presumably at Annweiler), January 31, 1734. In connection with this entry there is a marginal notation: "became a pilgrim to America" [*ward ein Pilgrim nach Amerika*]. He is presumably identical with the *Gorg Jacob Süss* who landed at Philadelphia on the Ship "Hamilton" in the year 1767 and took the oath of allegiance

Theisbergstegen with view of the Remigiusberg — mountain of St. Remigius.

Heimatstelle Pfalz

there November 9, 1767 (Hinke-Strassburger, List 265 C). In favor of this identity is the fact that there is in the same church register a further notation, "Extract, the 5th of May, 1767," which leads us to conclude that on this day a birth certificate was prepared for the emigrant.

[10] Through resolution of the Zweibrücken Government, November 29, 1764, the property of the citizen and master locksmith *Carl Philipp Witz* of Annweiler was confiscated and declared fallen to the treasury, because this person had gone to America clandestinely 24 years previously. The emigrant arrived at Philadelphia on the Ship "St. Andrew," October 2, 1741. His age is given as 28 years. (Hinke-Strassburger, List 85 A–C).

According to records of the Heimatstelle Pfalz, *Carl Philipp Witz* was in 1792 a member of the Falkner Swamp Reformed Church in Pennsylvania. He had married in 1764, as his second wife, *Margaret,* widow of *Karl Neuman(n)*. A *Carl Neumann* from Callbach in the District of Rokkenhausen emigrated to Pennsylvania in 1738; he was 26 years old when he arrived in Philadelphia on board the sailing vessel "Glasgow," September 9, 1738.

The children of his first marriage, born in Pennsylvania, were as follows:

1. *Johannes,* born March 15, 1752.
2. *Georg Michael,* born June 26, 1755.
3. *Margaretha,* born July 29, 1757.

[11] *Hans Adam Klein,* born March 7, 1680, according to an entry in the Reformed Church Register of Niederkirchen in the Ostertal, was born at Bubach, son of *Johannes Klein* (died March 22, 1709, at Bubach) and *Anna* (died February 24, 1701, at Bubach), emigrated to America in 1709 as a cartwright. He lived last in the State of New York, in Mohawk County, near Albany. In 1748 there appeared in the Duchy of Zweibrücken, as deputy for *Johann Adam Klein,* a relative of his named *Henrich Klein,* who lived in Lancaster in Pennsylvania, to reclaim the paternal inheritance of his client, which the latter at the time of his departure in 1709 had pledged in the sum of 70 gulden to his brother *Wendel Klein.* Since the power of attorney was found wanting, and the children of *Wendel Klein* made difficulties in the issuance of the legacy, a legal battle ensued, which finally in 1748 under mediation of the Zweibrücken authorities was settled through a compromise, whereby the attorney was paid out 275 guldens for his client in America, promising to produce a better power of attorney, to provide surety, and to pay the official state emigration taxes for his client. The appended letter was directed to *Adam Klein's* brother *Jacob* and played a role as evidence in the legal contest. It reports nothing of the circumstances in America, but only of family matters, yet it is despite this of great interest.

Johann Henrich Klein from Kusel is presumably identical with *Johann Henrich Klein,* who landed in Philadelphia on the Ship "Samuel" in 1737. He had married a daughter of *Daniel Grimm* from Kusel and at the time was schoolteacher [*Schuldiener*] at Wolfersweiler. According to notes of the Heimatstelle Pfalz the 1709 emigrant *Johann Adam Klein*

Contemporary Zweibrücken — the Rose Garden.

49

The past in the present — village fountain and watering trough (1584), Leinsweiler on the Weinstrasse.

Pfälzischer Verkehrsverband

was manumitted in 1748. He was part of the group of emigrants who arrived at St.Catharine's, England, June 11, 1709, coming from Holland, and [in the lists he is described as] aged 28, Reformed, and without family. In the New York Lists of the years 1710 and 1712 he is described as unmarried and childless. On September 2, 1715, *Adam Klein* and *Anna Catharina* had a daughter *Anna Clara* born to them—see the Kocherthal Church Register in West Camp, New York. In the so-called "Simmendinger Register" the emigrant appears with his wife *Catharina* and two children, at New Heidelberg in the colony of New York.

LETTER OF HANS ADAM KLEIN, CONESTOGA, 1743

The grace of our dear Lord Jesus Christ, which is better than life, inhabit and preserve, move, enliven and inspirit all of our hearts, Amen.

The great joy which I had on receipt of your letter, which Cousin Ludwig brought over to this country, cannot sufficiently be expressed, especially since I had had no word from you in 33 years. Now I have found from your letter that you alone of all my brothers and sisters, are still living. I wish you and your children further good health and good fortune.

50

As for me, after I left you in 1709 I finally arrived in England, and at that time with still more of our countrymen [was sent] by Queen Anne over the sea to America, and finally arrived in *Georgin* [York, i.e., New York?], where I stayed as a single man some three years in the same neighborhood. Afterwards I was married according to God's will to a widow who was without children. She is a native of the Hundsrück, from the village of Kellwiler; her maiden name was Han and she has brothers living in Gettebach and Oberweiler on the Glan. We had then during our marriage four children, i.e., one son and three daughters, of whom two daughters are still living and are both married. We live in *Albanien* [Albany] and my children near me. I have worked at my trade the entire time.

If otherwise I have been well, yet I have had to undergo many sicknesses, which also deprived me completely of my hearing, so that I hear quite laboriously. Yet I have, thank God, never suffered much want. But now since I and my wife on account of old age and inconvenience cannot earn much anymore and I now have, through my Cousin Johann Henrich Klein, heard the first news of you, but now learn from your letter how my inheritance still stands among my late brother Wendel's heirs, but in my old age I am in very great need of what is mine, so along with my son-in-law I have taken upon myself the far journey of 400 American miles, in order to go to our cousin, from whom I have learned that he might make a trip to Germany, so I knew no other way of executing my business than to give Cousin Henrich full power of attorney, to look up my properties and to deal with them as if I myself were present, as you will see from the power of attorney, which has been prepared by a county judge and justice of the peace here and which I and my son-in-law have both signed in our own hand. Now will you, dear Brother Jacob, do so much for me and be helpful in all parts to Cousin Henrich, so that he can bring over what belongs to me.

When I left, our deceased Brother Wendel gave me 70 florins for the journey, for which he was to make use of my properties, on condition, to be sure, that if I should return in three or four years, I should give him, Brother Wendel, the 70 florins back. At that time he should place my property in my hands again without attachment. But if I should stay away a longer time, then he should use the property in return for the above-mentioned 70 florins, besides paying the government and give back the property into my hands without attachment and minus the 70 florins. Now I believe they will be in accord with this agreement, since they have used it now for 33 years, and faithfully and fraternally place in my hand, through Cousin Henrich, what is mine from God and the law. Sontag of Albessen wrote down our agreement, which will surely still be at hand.

Among the 70 florins which the deceased Wendel gave me, were two ducats which were gilded but were of copper, which I had to throw away here in this country. My share of our late father's house I received, namely half from Hanss Adam Seyler, the other half from Hanss Müller of Selchenbach, who has written it up, I for my part don't know any more how much it was. Lastly this is my will, that if, after giving for it what it is worth, my property remains among you, then each shall have a share of it like the other, you as as well as Brother Wendel and our late Sister Catharina's surviving children.

Moreover I should wish that before my death I might yet see one of my relationship here in this country, then I would be ready to part from the world more peacefully, since I am

now old and weary of life and almost long for death. Sixty-three years have gone by in my lifetime, I don't know how long the dear God may still let me live, yet I hope to see yet another letter from you. I could indeed have wished that one of my sons-in-law had been able to travel to you, but because they are natives of this country and have no knowledge of such a troublesome journey, also can scarcely leave their own properties, since they are both young beginners, also the travel costs on this account would be too heavy, so that they would bring back little of the capital. So I hope Cousin Henrich Klein will be received and recognized in our place.

We have stayed four days at Cousin Henrich's, during which at first I had great joy, but also at times have had to shed tears, since I learned from him and Cousin Ludwig that not only my Brother Wendel and Sister Catharina besides their husband and wife, also many friends have parted from this world. May the Lord give us who are still living, to consider that we must die, so that we become prudent and may prepare ourselves well and in a Christian manner for a blessed hour of death.

It would not really be necessary to write much to you of the state of this country. Cousin Henrich, if God lets him come safe and sound to you, will report everything in detail and with all faithfulness to you.

Also Cousin Henrich will tell you how at the time of my departure Brother Jacob brought me on the road, where then Old Benners who was called Magdalena, went down a piece of the way to the Griesswald, but my brother accompanied me to Duntzweiler, where I had left 200 birchen felloes, which he purchased from me and gave me a doubloon for them, which doubloon I put in his presence between the soles of my shoe, so that I should not lose it. From there we went to Schellweiler, where he turned back. Also, dear brother, you will still remember how Schäfer stole your new blue camisole from you, when we were learning the cartwright trade at Wendel Lang's. I should have liked to report still other memories, but don't think it necessary.

Lastly, I commend you, dear brother, nephews and nieces, friends, relations and acquaintances, into the protection of the Most High and, cordially greeting you many thousand times, I am and remain till death

Your faithful brother, cousin and friend
Hans Adam Klein from Bubbach

N.B. My family, i.e., my wife and daughters, sons-in-law, and four grandchildren, send you hearty greetings. Adieu. *Conastocke* [Conestoga], August 22, 1743.

[Of the places named in the Hans Adam Klein letter, Dr. Krebs suggests in his footnotes that *Kellweiler* is perhaps Gehlweiler (Simmern); *Gettebach* is Jettenbach (Kusel); *Oberweiler* is Oberweiler im Tal (Kusel), which however is not on the Glan but at some distance from it; and *Albessen* is also in the Kusel area. *Conestoga* was of course in Lancaster County, Pennsylvania. For additional background on the 18th Century emigration from the Duchy of Zweibrücken and its dependencies, see William John Hinke and John Baer Stoudt, "A List of German Immigrants to the American Colonies from Zweibruecken in the Palatinate, 1728–1749," in *The Pennsylvania German Folklore Society*, I (1936), 101–124; also Dr. Friedrich Krebs, "A List of German Immigrants to the American Colonies from Zweibruecken in the Palatinate, 1750–1771," *The Pennsylvania German Folklore Society*, XVI (1951), 171–183.—EDITOR.]

Eighteenth-Century Emigrants to America From the Duchy of Zweibrücken and the Germersheim District

By FRIEDRICH KREBS

Translated and Edited by DON YODER

[The many articles on the 18th Century emigration by Dr. Friedrich Krebs of the State Archives, Speyer, West Germany, provide invaluable information for Pennsylvania social historians, folklife scholars, and genealogists. The present article, entitled in German "Auswanderer nach Amerika im 18. Jahrhundert aus dem ehemaligen Herzogtum Zweibrücken und dem kurpfälzischen Oberamt Germersheim," appeared in *Pfälzische Familien -und Wappenkunde* (Ludwigshafen/Rh.), XVI. Jahrgang (1967), Band 6, Heft 3, 89-95, in the section of the journal edited by Dr. Fritz Braun and entitled "Mitteilungen zur Wanderungsgeschichte der Pfälzer."

Additional information on several of the emigrants listed (Clementz, Sonntag) can be found in (1) William John Hinke and John Baer Stoudt, "A List of German Immigrants to the American Colonies from Zweibruecken in the Palatinate, 1728-1749," *The Pennsylvania German Folklore Society*, I (1936), 101-124; and (2) Friedrich Krebs, "A List of German Immigrants to the American Colonies from Zweibrücken in the Palatinate, 1750-1771," *The Pennsylvania German Folklore Society*, XVI (1951), 171-183.— EDITOR.]

1. *Berckmann-Gaul.* On September 7, 1792, *Johannes Berckman(n)*, resident and tanner at Maxatawny, Berks County, Pennsylvania, native of the Zweibrücken Superior Bailiwick of Lichtenberg, son of *Hermann Christoph Berckmann*, clerk to the petty sessions of Lichtenberg and his wife *Johanna Henrietta Philippina Goldner*, made out, at Philadelphia, to *Martin Gaul*, merchant and businessman in the city of Philadelphia, a power of attorney for the reception of his parental property. From this power of attorney we understand that *Martin Gaul* had recently been resident of Otterberg in the Electoral Palatinate. He may be identical with the *Johann Marthin Gaul* who arrived in Philadelphia, October 29, 1770, on the ship "Sally" (Strassburger-Hinke, *Pennsylvania German Pioneers*, List 283).

2. *Clemenz-Säger.* In the Protocol of the Superior Bailiwick of Bergzabern for 1761 there is found a reference to *Jakob Clemenz* who had emigrated in the year 1753 from Ilbesheim, District of Landau, whose attorney, one *Gabriel Säger,* had emigrated to America seven years previously (i.e., in 1754), and was born in Allertshofen, District of Darmstadt, son of *Johann Balthasar Seeger (Säger),* who was later schoolmaster in Kleinbieberau, District of Dieburg, and his wife *Anna Elisabetha.* In 1761 *Gabriel Säger* appeared and reclaimed the outstanding property of *Jakob Clemenz.* He produced a power of attorney dated at· Philadelphia, November 1, 1760, according to which *Jakob Clemenz* lived at Bedminster in Bucks County, Penn-

Baroque-spired village church at Göllheim in the Palatinate.

sylvania, and *Gabriel Säger* in Rockhill in the same county. But in the entry in the Bergzabern protocols, Skippack, now in Montgomery County, Pennsylvania, is given as the residence of *Gabriel Säger*. *Gabriel Seeger* is one of the passengers of the ship "Nancy," who as new arrivals took their oath of allegiance on September 14, 1754, at Philadelphia (Strassburger-Hinke, List 215).

Village Street in Hassloch. Farmers live in Palatine villages, drive out of town to farm. Note huge farmhouses (center) with arched wagon gates to enclosed farmyards.

According to records at the Heimatstelle Pfalz *Jacob Clemens* had married on January 16, 1753, at Mörzheim, District of Landau, *Anna Margaretha Schwartz,* who was born there March 27, 1733, daughter of *Georg Schwartz.* The Clemenses emigrated to America in the same year. *Gabriel Säger (Seeger)* was born at Allertshofen, July 24, 1734; his mother's maiden name was *Keller.* He died January 31, 1816, in Bristol Township, Trumbull County, Ohio. Through his marriage on April 8, 1762, to *Margareta Delp* (born September 26, 1737, in Kleinbieberau), *Gabriel Säger* became a Mennonite. *Margaretha Säger* died August 20, 1822.

3. *Diehl.* By ordinance of the Zweibrücken Government of March 25, 1777, it was decided that the present as well as the future property of *Johannes Diehl* should be seized for the treasury and that the 300 florins which his father *Jacob Diehl* had, against regulations, sent to his son in America, should, after the father's death, likewise fall to the treasury out of his estate. *Johannes Diehl,* who had already "gone to America" illegally some years previously and "is actually there now," was the son of the Zweibrücken citizen and tanner *Jacob Diehl.* A further governmental decision of January 27, 1789, further declared that the maternal inheritance of *Johannes Diehl* (who had died at Reading in Pennsylvania) be seized for the treasury, but that the paternal legacy, until the minor son of *Johannes*

Photographs by H. Ullmann, from A. Pfeiffer, *Pfälzische Dorfbilder,* an album of Palatine village views published in Munich about half a century ago.

Diehl in Reading achieved his majority, should be administered by a guardian in the homeland; however, the interest should be turned over to the son. But as for the remainder, *Johannes Diehl's* co-heirs and brothers and sisters, 5/6 of the 300 florins which *Jacob Diehl* already had sent on earlier to America and which had already been seized for the treasury, should be made good out of the inheritance of *Johannes Diehl,* so that they would be held indemnified for the "forbidden emigration of their brother." The emigration cannot for the present be traced further, since there are several emigrants by this name.

4. *Gentes (Jentes)-Herzel-Neu.* According to a report of the burgomaster's office of Webenheim of June 13, 1788, the following persons from Breitfurt had "some years ago left for America," and "their property confiscated presumably on account of illegal emigration:

a. *Juliana Margaretha Gentes (Jentes),* wife of the former chairmaker *Andreas Herzel* of Zweibrücken.

b. *Georg Elias Gentes (Jentes).*

c. *Jacob Neu.*

d. *Magdalena Neu.*

The request of *Christian Vogelgesang* of Mittelbach, a stepbrother of *Juliana Margaretha Jentes* of Breitfurt, for delivery of the legacy of the emigrated persons, was denied by order of the Zweibrücken Government, October 24 1788, because the petitioner was "a bad manager." The real estate of *Georg Elias Jentes* in Breitfurt was sold at auction on September 19, 1788, for which 110 florins and 45 kreuzer were realized. *Georg Elias Jentes* is surely identical with the *Elias Jentes* who landed at Philadelphia in 1754 on the ship "Phoenix" and took the oath of allegiance there on October 1, 1754 (Strassburger-Hinke, List 222). As

Quiet reigns in Scheibenhardt. Note half-timbered houses, also pent roofs to protect walls and window frames from weathering—the continental root of Pennsylvania's "Germantown Pent Roof"

proof of the correctness of the identity the fact should be considered that other emigrants from the Zweibrücken area were on the same ship.

There are additional emigrants by the name of *Neu* known to have come from Breitfurt: *Joseph Neu,* son of *Georg Neu* of Breitfurt, and *Christina Margaretha Gentes,* emigrated in 1740 to America. His brother *Peter Neu* followed in 1753. *Johann Otto Neu,* son of *Wilhelm Neu* of Breitfurt and wife *Anna Margaretha,* and his brother *Johann Simon Neu* were living in America in May, 1767.

5. *Jopp (Job).* In the Germersheim Documents (Ausfautheiakten[1] No.100) in the State Archives at Speyer there is found under date of April 4, 1754, the inventory of one *Michael Jopp (Job)* of Ottersheim, District of Germersheim, of whom it is said that he died some time ago, but his wife *Anna Maria* had died six or seven years ago. According to an entry in the Reformed Church Register of Ottersheim *Michael Job* was buried on March 9, 1754, at Ottersheim, at the age of about 90 years. Of the children of *Michael Jop* the daughter *Margaretha* (who had married *Thomas Kern* of Freisbach, District of Germersheim) had emigrated to America. *Nikolaus Jop,* son of *Georg* and grandson of *Michael Jop,* is described in the same family

1 I prefer to leave this word in the original since there is no precise equivalent in English. "Ausfautheiakten" are 18th Century inheritance and guardianship records. The curious word, not in most German dictionaries, comes from the name of the official of the Electoral Palatinate who produced the records, the "Ausfauth." This word in turn is related to "Fauth" (Vogt). The nearest English equivalent would be something between notary and clerk of the orphans court.—EDITOR.

register in which the daughter *Margaretha* appears, as "in the New Land." According to this the father of *Nikolaus Jop* had emigrated, and is surely identical with *George Job* who landed in Philadelphia in 1738 on the ship "Davy" and took the oath of allegiance there October 25, 1738 (Strassburger-Hinke, List 61).

From *Nikolaus Job* in Lancaster, the capital of the county of the same name in Pennsylvania, three letters were sent to his relative *Johannes Ludwig* in Ottersheim, who was married to Job's aunt *Appollonia.* The letters are dated December 8, 1755; February 7, 1762; and August 11, 1763. They all have to do with the reclamation of the paternal inheritance. *Georg Job* cannot be identified with certainty in the Reformed Church Register of Ottersheim, since there was a *Hanss Görg Job* confirmed there on Easter of 1711, aged 16, and in 1715 a *Georg Job* confirmed at 15, [both of] whom appear from 1715 to 1723 as godfathers at various baptismal entries.

From the standpoint of its contents the most interesting of the three emigrant letters is that of December 8, 1755, given here:

This letter is to come to Johannes Ludwig in Ottersheim near Lantdau.

God greet you, Dear Cousins and Aunt!

If these few lines will find you well, we shall be greatly pleased. As for us, we are, thank God, still all active and well. As for further matters, we received your letter all right and note therein that you want to send me my property that is coming to me from Grandfather's estate, by a trusty man named Jacob Henning, resident in Lancaster [*Lenckester*] with his wife and child. I trust this man as if I myself were among you. So I will leave it up to you. I hope you will know best what it is worth, since it would not pay me to go there and fetch it myself. But as for the rest I hope that you will indeed send me, with this man, what is coming to me. You yourself are well aware that my father, viz., Georg Jopp, had received little or nothing, so I leave it up to you, to your good opinion and conscience. Deal with me whatever you think is right on both sides, for I do not demand more than what belongs to me. You can leave it up to this man, for he is a propertied man by the name of Jacob Henning, resident in Lancaster, for I will perhaps not have such an opportunity soon again. Further as to Cousin Thomas Kern, they live a day's journey from us, but as we have heard, they are still well.

Further than that I know nothing to write, except that I Nicklaus Jopp do send my Aunt Apolonia Ludwig a silver finger-ring as a remembrance.

Remain your true friend Nicklaus Jopp.

Written, the 8th of December, 1755, Lancaster in Pennsylvania [*Lenckester in Bintzelfania*].

In the later letters it is reported that *Nikolaus Jopp* received 100 florins of his paternal inheritance, through his attorney *Matheis Rost*, and that his relative *Thomas Kern* had died in 1761, leaving behind a widow, who was living with her son.

6. *Reb.* In the document collection of the municipal archives of Ilbesheim, District of·Landau, there is a "Speci-

The journey home in vintage time —along the Haardt at Neustadt.

fication of those who have gone to the New Land." In it was reported:

In 1749 the Reformed school porter [*Schuldiener*] *Reb* from here allowed his son to go there—*Jacob* by name, single, who was subject to no vassalage, had according to the deposition of his father taken along not more than 8 florins in cash and sundry household goods estimated at 16 florins, 8 batzen, 8 pfennig. In 1753 the abovementioned *Reb* allowed a daughter to emigrate, named *Linora (Eleonore),* single, subject to no vassalage, who received to take along on her journey 52 florins, 7 batzen, 8 pfennig, and sundry household goods and other victuals estimated at 42 florins.

According to an entry in the Reformed Church Register of Ilbesheim and Leinsweiler, District of Landau, *Jacob Reb* was confirmed in 1747, *Eleonore* in 1748. The birth entry of both is not to be found in that church register. Up to 1733 the *Schuldiener* named in the said church book is *Johann Peter Regula.* According to this the family of *Jacob Reb* must have removed there later. *Jacob Reb* reached Philadelphia on the ship "Phoenix" and took the oath of allegiance on August 28, 1750 (Strassburger-Hinke, List 154).

7. *Reich (Reicher).* On order of the Zweibrücken authorities, dated February 25, 1758, the property of *Georg Reich* of Mittelbach, who had emigrated "about five years ago to America," was confiscated for the treasury in accordance with the edict of May 9, 1739. Through a later decision of the Zweibrücken authorities of April 11, 1758, this confiscation of property was again annulled.

According to the family register of Mittelbach-Hengstbach, the *Johann Georg Reich* must be meant here, who was born April 27, 1733, Reformed, at Mittelbach, son of *Johann Reich(er)*—who had originally come from Reichenbach in the district of Berne in Switzerland—and his wife (of the second marriage), *Elisabeth Klein.*

8. *Riess.* An edict of the Zweibrücken Government of October 21, 1790, states that the parental property fallen to the brothers *Christian* and *Georg Riess* of Mauschbach, who had gone to America, is seized for the treasury on account of this emigration, and is to be awarded as a gift of the government to *Ludwig Riess* of Mauschbach, who is serving in the Ducal Body-Guard Regiment. A *Johann Georg Riess* was on the ship "Halifax" in 1754 (Strassburger-Hinke, List 227) and a *Christian Rietz* in the same year on the ship "Neptune" (Strassburger-Hinke, List 221). According to records of the Heimatstelle Pfalz a *Melchior Riess* of Mauschbach had emigrated to America by 1749, with wife and four children.

9. *Salathe.* According to an entry in the Protocol of the Superior Bailiwick of Bergzabern for the year 1771, dated February 6, 1771 (State Archives, Speyer, Souveränitätslande[2] Akt No.1037), *Sophia Vierling,* who was not a native of the Palatinate, widow of the cowherd *Philipp Jacob Salathe* of Bergzabern, left to each of her three then absent sons, who as appears from the text of the entry were in America, *Niklaus Salathe, Michael Salathe,* and *Johannes Salathe,* a legacy of 5 gulden. The entry in the protocol of the superior bailiwick refers to a will of the testatrix dated January 1, 1771.

[2] "Souveränitätslande" were the territories between the rivers Weislauter and Queich in the Southeastern Palatinate, to which France claimed sovereignty according to the Treaty of Westphalia in 1648. Some German states, such as the Duchy of Zweibrücken, acknowledged the French claims.—EDITOR.

Nikolaus Salathe landed in 1752 on the ship "Snow Ketty" in the port of Philadelphia and there took the oath of allegiance on October 16, 1752 (Strassburger-Hinke, List 189). *Johannes Salade* and *Migel Salade* landed in 1764 on the ship "King of Prussia" and likewise took the oath of allegiance in Philadelphia on October 13, 1764 (Strassburger-Hinke, List 264).

The family of *Salathe* is surely of Swiss origin. According to the records of the Heimatstelle Pfalz one *Johann Georg Salathee* from Canton Basel in Switzerland was in 1662 Reformed pastor in Marnheim, District of Kirchheimbolanden. *Barbara Salathe* from Arisdorf, Canton Basel, died in 1694 at Oberhoffen, Alsace.

10. *Scheidt.* According to an entry in the Court Protocol of the Superior Bailiwick of Bergzabern dated 1786, pages 677-679 (State Archives, Speyer, Souveränitätslande Akt No. 1056), the portion of the inheritance of the deceased parents of *Georg Scheidt* and *Heinrich Scheidt* of Hergersweiler, who had emigrated to America in the years 1748 and 1749, had been openly confiscated for the treasury on account of illegal emigration. The portion of *Georg Scheid(t)* amounted to 5 florins, 9 batzen, and 1 pfennig, the portion of *Heinrich Scheid(t)* to 35 florins, 9 batzen, and 1 pfennig, which *Heinrich Scheid's* inlaws at Hergersweiler had to pay—altogether 41 florins, 3 batzen, and 2 pfennig.

In the oath list, which was subscribed by the passengers on the ship "Dragon" at Philadelphia on October 17, 1749, there appear, one after the other, the names of *Conrad, Georg,* and *Georg Henry "Shyd".* These three emigrants did not personally sign the list, but used only a mark. The family name was entered by the clerk in the above-named form, which certainly must be read as *Scheidt.* According to this *Conrad Scheidt* must have been a close relative of *Georg* and *Georg Henry* (Strassburger-Hinke, List 143).

11. *Sonntag.* A letter from *Adam Sonntag* from Selchenbach, living in Pennsylvania, to his brother *Nikolaus Sonntag:*

> Esteemed brother Nicklas Sonntag! We have sent you a deed of gift in which we have made over to you everything which is to be found in the Duchy, for Cousin Brill of Pfeffelbach told me everything, he knew everything, as it stands among you, and also said I should remember you, for you are an honest man. You will also not be unfair to me, for we have suffered and endured much with the war. He also said how clever you are at clockmaking, and in your trade; if you are as expert as Cousin Brill has told me, if you came among us you could earn much money and live quite richly and perfectly. To write to you of this country is not necessary—Brill will have told you everything. Send me a large Bible and a dozen hymnbooks, even though it be very [—]; they must be Zweibrücken hymnals. And send me too a shipment of iron rods, a horse must be able to work in a horse-collar, and they must be eight feet long. There are three letters in addition to the deed of gift. This letter you must show to no one. You will have a brotherly love, for I also have it toward you and yours. A greeting, esteemed brother Nicklas Sonntag in the Duchy of Zweibrücken, District of Lichtenberg.
>
> Done at Tulpehocken *{Tulbenhacken},* Berks *{Bercks}* County, on the 29th of June, 1768.
> *Adam Sontag*
> *Anna Elisabetha Sonntag's* mark.

This letter and a second one are preserved in Akt Zweibrücken I No. 1332/2, in the State Archives at Speyer. As *Hann Adam Sonntag* he had signed the oath of allegiance at Philadelphia on October 26, 1741, with the passengers who had arrived in the ship "Snow Molly" (Strassburger-Hinke, List 88).

According to records of the Heimatstelle Pfalz *Hans Adam Sonntag* was born about 1714. In a list of emigrants to America from the Zweibrücken area from an American source, Pfeffelbach, District of Birkenfeld, was given as the place of the emigrant's origin.

12. *Waldmann.* In the Rent Accounts of Ingenheim for 1780-1781 (State Archives, Speyer, Souveränitätslande Akt No. 1253) under the rubric "Money Outstanding," Folio 103, it appears that "*Immanuel Waldmann,* formerly resident at Appenhoofen, now in America, is in arrears of 6 florins 21 kreuzer capital the interest with annually 19 kreuzer from the year 1767 to 1780, 13 years . . . 4 florins 8 kreuzer."

Immanuel Waldmann was citizen, local collector of taxes for the Electoral Palatinate, and church elder at Appenhofen. He was married to *Margaretha Beuerle.* On October 26, 1768, *Emanuel Waltmann* and his eldest son *Görg Jacob* inscribed their names on the oath of allegiance with the other passengers of the ship "Crawford" in the court house at Philadelphia (Strassburger-Hinke, List 272).

Children, born at Appenhofen, are listed as follows in the Church Register of Billigheim:

a. *Georg Jacob,* born December 12, baptized 15, 1745.
b. *Johann David,* born August 21, baptized 25, 1748, died at Appenhofen, January 23, 1749.
c. *Johann Nicolaus,* born December 12, baptized 14, 1749, died at Appenhofen, March 9, 1751.
d. *Johann Wilhelm,* born April 7, baptized 9, 1752.
e. *Marianna,* born June 9, baptized 12, 1755.
f. *Georg Michael,* born April 20, baptized 23, 1758.
g. *Georg Friedrich Sam(uel),* born March 12, baptized 15, 1761.
h. *Johann Michael,* born March 27, baptized 27, 1763, died at Appenhofen, October 29, 1763.

13. *Theobald-Jung-Kuntz-Anthess.* A decision of the Zweibrücken Government, November 11, 1758, under reference to a report of the Palatine Antskeller[3] Hautt of Nohfelden, concerns resolutions about "different district bondsmen at that place, who went to America without being manumitted." The property of *Friedrich Theobald* of Wolfersweiler had already been confiscated by rescript of March 11, 1755, and there the matter should end. Because *Michael Theobald* had not reported to the District before his departure, so also his property was to be attached and shortly seized.

The property of *Johannes Jung,* son of *Friedrich Jung* of Wolfersweiler, remains confiscated; likewise that of his sister *Elisabeth Barbara Jung* is to be seized, because she had not reported to the district office before departure. The two last confiscations were still of concern to the Zweibrücken Government in the year 1774.

Also the property of *Johann Nickel Kuntz* of Achtelsbach was to be seized for failing to give notice before emigration; on similar grounds also the property of *Friedrich Anthess* of Ellweiler and *Franz Anthess* of Ellweiler (Source: State Archives, Speyer, Act No. 1838 I of Archive Division Zweibrücken III).

Friedrich Theobald appears in Strassburger-Hinke, List 231 A-C; *Johann Michel Theobalt,* List 141 C; *Nick Cuntz,* List 141 C; and *Johann Friedrich Antes,* List 117 C.

[3] "Amtskeller" was an official who had charge of the administration of taxes and the natural revenues of the state (wine, corn, etc.). There seems to be no 20th Century equivalent in either the German or the American governmental systems.—EDITOR.

Notes on Eighteenth-Century Emigration To the British Colonies

By FRIEDRICH KREBS   Translated and Edited by DON YODER

[The following emigrant list appeared in *Pfälzische Familien- und Wappenkunde,* XVII. Jahrgang, 1968, Band 6, Heft 7, 225-226, under the title of "Amerika-auswanderer des 18. Jahrhunderts aus verschiedenen Kirchenbüchern und anderen Quellen." It comes from the researches of Dr. Friedrich Krebs of the Palatine State Archives at Speyer-am-Rhein, whose articles on 18th Century emigration we have published in translation, a long and distinguished series from the old *Pennsylvania Dutchman* days through all the years of *Pennsylvania Folklife.* The article appears in the special section of the journal, edited by Dr. Fritz Braun of the Heimatstelle Pfalz, Kaiserslautern, dedicated to the emigration history of the Palatine population, and entitled in German, *Mitteilungen zur Wanderungs-geschichte der Pfälzer.* We are grateful to both Dr. Braun and Dr. Krebs for the opportunity to share these new materials with our readers. — EDITOR.]

FROM THE LUTHERAN CHURCH REGISTER OF GLANMUENCHWEILER

1. *Johann Nickel Ohr,* master tailor at Nanzweiler, son of *Henrich Ohr of Linden,* married November 23, 1779, *Maria Margretha Kiefer,* born at Nanzweiler, July 22, 1754, daughter of *Andreas Kiefer* and wife *Elisabetha Margaretha,* "went to America in the year 1784."

Children, born at Nanzweiler and baptized at Glanmünchweiler: (1) *Johann Philipp Ohr,* born November 26, 1780; (2) *Maria Elisabeth Ohr,* born March 2, 1782.

FROM THE REFORMED CHURCH REGISTER OF GROSSBOCKENHEIM

2. *Johann Peter Gutmann,* born August 15, 1718, son of the master tailor *Rudolph Gutmann* and wife *Anna Elisabetha,* married April 14, 1741, *(Maria) Christina Eichelberger (Euchenberger),* born April 29, 1713, daughter of *Rudolph Eichelberger.* In the Church Register there is among the baptisms for the time from about March to July 1742 the baptismal entry for a child of Johann Peter Gutmann with the following notation: "went away from here to Pennsylvania without indicating his child's name and godparents" *(von hier weg in Pensylvaniam gezogen ohne seines Kindes Nahmen und Taufzeugen anzuzeigen).*

Peter *Guthman* appears among the passengers on the Ship *Robert and Alice,* and took his Oath of Allegiance at Philadelphia September 30, 1743 (Strassburger-Hinke, List 102 C).

3. *Johann Henrich Frey,* linenweaver, married November 27, 1729, *Maria Margaretha Wolf,* baptized November 19, 1702, daughter of *Johannes Wolf* and wife *Christina.*

Children, born at Grossbockenheim: (1) *Johann Caspar Frey,* born September 26, 1730, died August 29, 1732; (2) *Anna Catharina Frey,* born December 18, 1732; (3) *Catharina Philippina Frey,* baptized January 14, 1735; (4) *Margaretha Dorothea Frey,* born November 30, 1737; (5) *Anna Margretha Frey,* born November 11, 1739; and (6) an unnamed child, born September 21, 1742.

The notation in the Church Register reads, "Left here for Pennsylvania without rectifying his child's name" *(Von hier weggezogen in Pensylvaniam ohne seines Kindes Nahmen zu rectificiren).*

Henrich Frey appears among the passengers on the Ship *Lydia,* and took the Oath of Allegiance at Philadelphia, September 20, 1743 (Strassburger-Hinke, List 99. A-C).

FROM THE REFORMED CHURCH REGISTER OF KRIEGSFELD

4. *Anna Margretha Hardong,* born October 21, 1725, daughter of *Johannes Hardong* and wife *Maria Apollonia,* "to the New Land in the year 1754" *(ins Neue Land anno 1754).*

5. *Anna Sara Helbig,* born March 19, 1725, daughter of *Andreas Helbig* and wife *Anna Elisabetha,* "to the New Land in the year 1754."

6. *Johannes Maurer,* born July 8, 1740, son of the pastor *Friedrich Magnus Maurer* and wife *Maria Philippina,* "died September 5, 1777, in New York in America" *(starb 1777 den 5. September in Neyorck in America).*

FROM THE RECORDS OF THE DISTRICT OF HEIDELBERG, 1752

7. *Abraham Cetti,* Mennonite, farm tenant on the Rohrhof *(Hofbeständer auf dem Rohrhof)* in the parish of Brühl (Schwetzingen), on payment of 32 florins for the tithe, receives permission to go to the New Land.

Abraham *Zety* appears among the passengers of the Ship *St. Andrew,* and took the Oath of Allegiance at Philadelphia, September 23, 1752 (Strassburger-Hinke, List 181 C).

8. *Peter Brauss,* citizen of Waldwimmersbach, whose wife and three little sons, a daughter, and a married son by the name of *Andreas Brauss,* have permission to leave for the New Land, for which Peter Brauss must pay 20 florins tithe and the married son 15 florins.

Andreas Brauss appears among the passengers on the Ship *Rawley,* and took the Oath of Allegiance at Philadelphia, October 23, 1752 (Strassburger-Hinke, List 191 C).

A Siegerland Emigrant List of 1738

By OTTO BAEUMER
Translated and Edited by DON YODER

[The following emigrant list dates from the year 1738 and was located in the Siegerland of Westphalia. It comes from the research of Otto Bäumer of Freudenberg, and appeared in the periodical *Heimatland: Beilage zur Siegener Zeitung,* Zweiter Jahrgang, Nr. 10, 1927, 148-149. The emigrants, who came from the towns of Freudenberg, Plittershagen, Böschen, and Anstoss, in the Siegen area, are said to have gone to the new British colony of Georgia, which had been opened up for settlement in 1732 and had attracted the emigration of Salzburgers and Moravians in the interim.

However, one of the emigrants, Tillmanus Hirnschal (see No. 16) had been in Pennsylvania and returned, and it is possible that some of the other families or individuals may have come to Pennsylvania or other colonies instead of Georgia. Will readers who identify any of the emigrants as Pennsylvania settlers please notify the Editor.

The evidence for the prior emigration of "Tielman Hirnschael," aged 55, appears in Strassburger-Hinke, List 42 A: Ship *Princess Augusta,* qualified at Philadelphia, September 16, 1736. The name is spelled "Thielman Hirnschall" in Lists 42 B and 42 C.

Further research into emigrant backgrounds will probably reveal more emigration from the Freudenberg area in the Siegerland directly to Pennsylvania. For example, on the Ship *Nancy,* whose passengers took the Oath of Allegiance at Philadelphia, August 31, 1750 (Strassburger-Hinke, List 155 C), there are listed one following the other, as if traveling together, *Johann Peter Gutelius* and *Tilman Creutz.* There is also a *Johan Thiel [mann?] Selbach* listed on the Ship *Aurora,* qualified at Philadelphia, October 8, 1744 (Strassburger-Hinke, List 105 C).

From the same general area in Westphalia there had come to the Germanna Colony in Virginia in 1714 the families of *Fishback* and *Kemper,* and later additional families came to the Tohickon and Lower Saucon Reformed settlements in Pennsylvania. For this evidence, which we intend to republish in a larger article on Westphalian Emigration to the British Colonies in the 18th Century, see the journal *Siegerland: Blätter des Vereins für Heimatkunde und Heimatschutz im Siegerlande samt Nachbargebieten,* 10. Band, 1. Heft (January-March 1928), 27-29. — EDITOR.]

Emigrants from the Parish
of Freudenberg, Siegerland

A memorandum by the Protestant Pastor Göbel in an old parish register of the year 1738 gives explanation about the emigrations which were taking place at that time from the Freudenberg region to America. Many of the names are still to be found here, without their present bearers knowing that relatives once left their homeland and ventured into unknown distant parts. The memorandum, which was entered in the Burial Register, reads as follows:

As information I wished to write down on these pages that today, the 13th of March, 1738, there left for Georgia, the new island [sic] under the protection of His Majesty the King of England, out of this land and parish, with the knowledge and consent of the authorities of this our land, the following named persons, some of them householders with wife and children, others single male persons, namely:

FREUDENBERG

1. *Tillmanus Seelbach* with his wife *Anna Beata,* also his son-in-law and daughter.

2. *Gerlach Waffenschmidt* and his wife *Anna Maria* with four children.

3. *Henrich Ernstorf* and his wife *Anna Catharin* with three children.

4. *Her[mann]. Bach* and his wife *Anna Margreth* with one child.

5. *Joh[ann]. Friedrich Müller* and his wife *Anna Maria* with one child.

6. *Hymenäus Creutz* and his wife *Elisabeth.*

7. *Georg Weidman,* single status, *Henrich Weidman's* orphaned son.

8. *Tillmanus Steinseiffer, Joh[ann]. Henrich Steinseiffer's* orphaned son.

9. *Johannes Hoffman* from Dirlenbach, *Johannes Hoffman's* son.

10. *Johann Henrich Schmidt, Christian Schmidt's* son.

11. *Johannes Klappert,* son of the former villagemayor in the prince's government, *Joh[annes]. Klappert.*

12. *Tillmany Gudelius, Christophel Gudelius'* son.

13. *Hermanus Müller,* son of the village justice, *Hermanus Müller.*

PLITTERSHAGEN

14. *Johannes Halm* and his wife *Anna Cath[a]rin* with two children.

BOESCHEN

15. *Johann Henrich Schneider* and his wife *Maria Catharin* with two children.

16. *Johann Georg Hirnschal* and his wife *Anna Catharin* with one child; whose father, *Tilmanus Hirnschal,* had left for America two years ago and just now returned and has gone back along with the others.

ANSTOSS

17. *Henrich Schneider* and his wife *Anna Margreth* with two children.

18. *Hanna Schneider, Joh[annes]. Schneider's* widow, with her son *Johannes Schneider* and his wife, born in the Hadamar country, with four children.

Title page of Siegerland, *local history periodical in which*
Otto Bäumer's article originally appeared. The cut shows
a view of the old section of the town of Siegen.

View of the ancient college buildings at H e r b o r n,
drawn from a photograph taken in the 1930s.

Siegen in the 17th
Century, showing
walls and towers of
what was then still
essentially a medie-
val town. After an
engraving in Sieger-
land, XVI: 4 (Octo -
ber-December 1934).

Herborn in the 17th Century.
From Herborn came Philipp
Wilhelm Otterbein, Pietist
Reformed pastor who was
one of the founders of the
first native American
denomination, the United
Brethren in Christ.

Palatine Emigrants of the 18th Century

By FRIEDRICH KREBS

Translated and Edited by DON YODER

I. ODERNHEIM ON THE GLAN

[The following article by Dr. Krebs, entitled in German "Einige Amerikaauswanderer des 18. Jahrhunderts aus Odernheim am Glan," appeared in the *Nordpfälzer Geschichtsverein: Beiträge zur Heimatgeschichte*, Volume 49, Number 1 (March 1969), 20-21. The periodical is published at Rockenhausen in the Palatinate. The village of Odernheim can be located on the map in the vicinity of Kreuznach, directly north of Kaiserslautern.—EDITOR.]

1. In the guardianship accounts of the community archives of Odernheim emigration to Pennsylvania before the year 1757 is documented for one *Johann Henrich Wölffling*, son of *David Wölffling*, citizen and master tailor at Odernheim. In 1757 there appeared at Odernheim *Henrich Messemer (Misemer, Miesemer)*, formerly of Mandel bei Kreuznach, who was a merchant in Philadelphia, with power of attorney from the emigrant Wölffling, who is said to have been a master shoemaker in the city of Philadelphia, for the purpose of collecting his inheritance for him. Messemer received from the curators for delivery to his client, after deduction of the sextile tax, 210 florins 5 batzen and 10 pennies. Heinrich Wölffling landed in Philadelphia on the Ship *John & Elizabeth* in 1754 as *Henry Welfling (Wilflinger)* and took the oath of allegiance there on November 7, 1754 (Strassburger-Hinke, *Pennsylvania German Pioneers*, List 231 A-C).

2. In an inventory dated August 23, 1769, of the estate of the citizen and master shoemaker *Valentin Scheib* of Odernheim, who is said to have died "about

four weeks ago," therefore probably in July 1769, a son of the first marriage is listed named *Christian Scheib*, of whom it is said that he was married and living in America, whither he had emigrated 23 years previously as a single man. The emigrant may be identical with the *Christian Scheib* who landed in Philadelphia in 1751 on the Ship *Edinburgh* and took the oath of allegiance there on September 16, 1751 (Strassburger-Hinke, List 167 C).

3. In a release of the citizen *Leonhard Weydner* of Odernheim and his wife *Susanna Margaretha*, dated January 29, 1763, it is said of the son *Leonhard Weydner, Jr.*, that he went to America at the end of April 1741 and is 53 years old. Of *Johann Henrich Weydner*, a son of the first marriage to *Anna Margaretha Hofmann*, it is said that he was a shoemaker *(Schuhknecht)*, emigrated to America in 1734, and is 44 years old. To increase the confusion it is stated that several children of Leonhard Weydner's wife, to her first marriage with *Valentin Graf*, have moved to Pomerania. From a document dated January 24, 1768, we can gather that Leonhard Weydner, Sr., died about 1765 and that the two emigrants to America, Henrich and Leonhard Weydner, Jr., who emigrated in 1734 and 1741, still had claims on 365 florins and 3 batzen as their inheritance after deduction of the sextile tax. In a letter of May 14, 1765, Johann Henrich Weydner of Odernheim inquired of his brother, *Philipp Conrad Weydner*, citizen, master cabinetmaker and glazier of Germantown near Philadelphia, for the address of the emigrants for the purpose of settling their inheritance. Later, in

Bergzabern in the Palatinate — engraving by Matthaeus Merian, from the Topographia Germaniae *(1672).*

1767-1768, there appeared as attorney for both brothers *Philipp Odenwälder,* who had emigrated to America and hailed from Weinheim on the Bergstrasse, to whom, according to an agreement to bring over the inheritance to his clients, there was finally turned over the sum of 339 florins 2 batzen and 8 pennies (August 22, 1768). The information on the emigration year of both Weydners is not free of contradictions. But that they were certainly in America is proved by a letter of both dated October 19, 1767, which is addressed to *Friedrich Graf* or *Nicolaus Weidner* in Odernheim, in which reference is made to the regulation of the inheritance business and the sending over of Philipp Odenwälder. *Leonhard (Lenert) Weydner* lived at that time at Easton in Northampton County, Pennsylvania, *Henrich Weydner* in Oxford (?) in Sussex County, New Jersey.

II. FRANKENTHAL

[Frankenthal in the Palatinate can be located on the map between Worms and Ludwigshafen, a few miles northwest of Mannheim. In the 17th Century it received many Huguenot refugees after the revocation of the Edict of Nantes in 1685. This article listing seven emigrants of the 18th Century from Frankenthal is translated from Friedrich Krebs, "Amerikaauswanderer des 18. Jahrhunderts aus der Stadt Frankenthal," *Mitteilungen der Westdeutschen Gesellschaft für Familienkunde,* XIX (1959), columns 577-580.—EDITOR.]

The few following names of emigrants were taken from the *Ausfautheiakten*[1] (inventories, lists of property, and wills) of the City Archives of Frankenthal. As far as possible they have been supplemented through genealogical data from the church registers. As far as the arrival of the said emigrants in the port of Philadelphia can be documented in the published ship lists (Strassburger-Hinke, *Pennsylvania German Pioneers*), this information is given in parentheses. The list makes no claim of comprehensiveness.

1. *Henrich Basler,* son of *Andreas Basler,* citizen and master cartwright at Frankenthal and his wife *Anna Catharina Schubard (Schuppert),* "at this time gone to Pennsylvania and resident there" [*dermahlen in die Böhnsylvaniam gereisst und sesshaften allda*] (Inventory No. 62, dated December 17, 1735). According to data in this inventory Andreas Basler must have died about 1730.

2. *Johann Heinrich Chembenois*—son of the Frankenthal citizen *Jacob Chembenois* (who died probably in 1767) and his wife *Catharina Götz*—"who is at this time in the New Land in America and is 18 years old"

[*welcher dermahlen im Neuen Landt in América und 18 Jahr alt ist*] (Inventory of Jacob Chembenois, No. 239, dated October 16, 1767). The family name was also written *Chesnebenoist.* A letter from the emigrant from the year 1779 has been published in the *Monatsschrift des Frankenthaler Altertumsvereins,* I:3 (1893), according to which he had settled in Lancaster County, Pennsylvania, not far from the county seat of Lancaster.

3. *Johann Christoph Hartmann,* born August 30, 1744, at Frankenthal, son of *Valentin Hartmann* and his wife *Elisabetha Catharin Bayer,* married at Frankenthal April 23, 1767, *Maria Susanna Böhmer* from Baumholder. He is described as "married and living in the New Land" [*verheurathet und in dem neuen Landt wohnhafft*] (Inventory No. 545, of Valentin Hartmann, dated October 15, 1767). Strassburger-Hinke, List 265 C: *Christoph Hartmann.*

4. *Juliana Krick,* daughter of the citizen and invalid *Wilhelm Krick,* who must have died at Frankenthal in 1782, was, according to data in his inventory (No. 768, dated January 31, 1782), married to the master baker *Konrad Böhm* and living in North America. A brother of Juliana Krick, *Jeremias Krick,* is, according to data in the inventory, said to have died in Batavia.

5. *Johann Wilhelm Lotschberg,* born at Frankenthal December 23, 1740, son of the master tailor *Johann Conrad Lotschberg (Lotspeich)* and his wife *Catharina Elisabetha Wilhelmina Ladenberger* (both married at Frankenthal, June 3, 1739), had settled in Virginia and married there, according to data in the inventory of Conrad Lotschberg (No. 879, dated October 24, 1778). Conrad Lotschberg died September 30, 1778, at Frankenthal. But according to data from the above source there had also emigrated to Virginia *Johanna Friderica Lotschberg* (born at Frankenthal March 25, 1744) and *Johann Christoph Lotschberg* (born at Frankenthal July 11, 1750), sister and brother of Johann Wilhelm Lotschberg. In any case it is documented of *Johann Christoph Lotspeich* that he landed at the port of Philadelphia in 1772 (Strassburger-Hinke, List 297 C). The family name is written sometimes *Lotschberg,* sometimes *Lotspeich.* Johann Conrad Lotschberg, the emigrant's father, was the son of Johann Conrad Lotschberg, master shoemaker from the district of Mahlberg in Baden-Baden, and therefore the first of the name in Frankenthal. The family is of the Lutheran confession. Perhaps in the case of this family, "Pennsylvania" is meant for "Virginia," since the references to place in the 18th Century documents are not always reliable.[2]

[2]Evidently they did settle in Virginia, where some of them were converted to Methodism. An early historian of Methodism tells us of "William Lotspeich, a German, born in Virginia, who, without extraordinary abilities, was a sound, studious, and useful preacher, and, from 1803 to 1813, traveled in Tennessee, Kentucky, and Ohio, and died in the latter year, saying, 'Tell my old friends all is well, all is well'" (Abel Stevens, *History of the Methodist Episcopal Church in the United States of America,* IV, 434.—EDITOR.

[1]*Ausfautheiakten* (there is no English equivalent for this word) are inheritance and guardianship records. For the etymology of the word, see footnote 1 in Friedrich Krebs, "Eighteenth-Century Emigrants to America from the Duchy of Zweibrücken and the Germersheim District," *Pennsylvania Folklife,* XVIII:3 (Spring 1969), 46.

6. *Johanna Petri,* daughter of *Johannes Petri* and his wife *Anna Weber,* "who has already been absent 19 years and from what we hear, is said to be in the New Land" [*welche bereits 19 Jahr abwesend und dem Vernehmen nach sich in dem neuen Land befinden soll*] (Inventory No. 1070, of Johannes Petri, dated January 24, 1782). It is likely that other Petri families from Frankenthal also emigrated to America.

7. *Johann Nicolaus Römer,* son of the deceased citizen and master locksmith *Wilhelm Römer* (who died at Frankenthal February 26, 1740) and his wife *Barbara.* He is described as "gone to Pennsylvania" [*in Pensylvanien gezogen*] (Inventory No. 1147, of Wilhelm Römer, dated April 20, 1758). Johann Nicolaus Römer landed at the port of Philadelphia in 1732 on the Ship *Loyal Judith* (Strassburger-Hinke, List 24 A-C).

III. District of Wegelnburg, Duchy of Zweibruecken

[The villages referred to in this emigrant list can be located on the Southern border of the Palatinate, South of Bergzabern and very near Weissenburg, across the border in Alsace. The original article by Dr. Krebs is entitled "Amerikaauswanderer des 18. Jahrhunderts aus dem Gebiet des zweibrückischen Amts Wegelnburg," and appeared in the *Mitteilungen der Westdeutschen Gesellschaft für Familienkunde,* XXIII (1968), columns 283-284.—EDITOR.]

The District of Wegelnburg in the former Duchy of Zweibrücken consisted of the villages of Schönau, Hirschtal, Nothweiler and Rumbach, along with several outlying farms. The source for the following emigrants' names was the Accounts of the Prefecture *(Vogtei)* of Wegelnburg, also Akt Zweibrücken III Nr. 1838/II in the Palatine State Archives at Speyer. The year of the accounts, in which the emigrants are mentioned, should almost always be identical with the year of emigration. As far as the said emigrants' names could be located in the published ship lists (Strassburger-Hinke, *Pennsylvania German Pioneers),* this has been noted.

In 1737 the following villagers went to Pennsylvania: *Georg Kern* of Rumbach; *Friedrich Neuhard* of Rumbach; *Michael Neuhard,* a tailor, of Rumbach; *Hans Georg Neuhard,* single, of Rumbach; *Christoph Schwenck* of Rumbach; and finally *Georg Hefft* of Nothweiler. As date of emigration, May, 1737, is indicated almost throughout. We find Georg Hefft, Christoph Schwenck, George Kern, Michel Neuhard (Neihart), Georg Neuhard (Neihart), and also Friedrich Neuhard (Jerg Friedrich Neihart) listed as passengers on the Ship *St. Andrew Galley* which landed at Philadelphia in September, 1737, where they all took the oath of allegiance on September 26, 1737

(Strassburger-Hinke, List 47 A-C).

In 1738 *Ulrich Stöckel* of Hirschtal; *Johannes Weinmüller,* single, of Rumbach; and lastly *Elisabeth Neuhard,* daughter of *Christoph Neuhard* of Rumbach, likewise were permitted to go to Pennsylvania with official license. Of these only Johannes Weinmüller could be located in the ship lists. He landed at Philadelphia on the Ship *Thistle* in 1738 (Strassburger-Hinke, List 57 A-C).

In 1751 *Nicolaus Wolff* of Hirschtal was permitted to emigrate to America. This could be either *Nickolas Wolff* (Strassburger-Hinke, List 164 C), or *Jo. Nicklas Wolff* (List 175 C).

In 1753 *Martin Schneider, Georg Friedrich Schneider, Maria Elisabeth Schneider* and *Heinrich Balthasar Schneider,* and *Johann Adam Bley,* all of Rumbach, likewise *Magdalena Weber* from Schönau, were permitted to emigrate to America. *Martin Schneider,* aged 26, arrived at Philadelphia September 24, 1753 (Strassburger-Hinke, List 204 A). Likewise in 1755 *Jacob Schneider* from Nothweiler received permission to emigrate.

On June 1, 1786, the Zweibrücken Government decreed that the property of *Michael* and of *Jacob Schneider* of Rumbach, who had "already gone to America 20 years ago" [*bereits vor 20 Jahren in Americam gezogen*], as far as the same had been derived from what their parents had acquired, should be handed over to their brothers and sisters. But that part of the legacy which had come from the yielded property of the parents, was to be collected for the treasury.

By decree of April 23, 1765, the property of the brothers *Wendel* and *Peter Scheid, Adam Neuhard, Jacob Schneider (Heinrich Schneider's* son), *Henrich Schaub, Georg Bley* and *Catharina Bley* (children of the deceased shepherd, *Christoph Bley),* all of Rumbach, also that of *Catharina Imhoff* (daughter of *Hans Imhoff* of Hirschtal), who was serving in Rumbach as a hired girl, was to be collected for the treasury, since in the past year they had left Rumbach and had evidently gone to the "New Land" without governmental permission. Of these only *Henrich Schaub* can be identified, as *Joha. Henrich Schaub,* passenger on the ship *Sarah,* which landed at Philadelphia in September, 1764 (Strassburger-Hinke, List 244 C). A decree of the government dated June 29, 1769, instructed the prefect *(Vogt)* at Schönau again to confiscate the property of the following who had secretly emigrated to America: *Jacob Neuhard, Henrich* and *Michael Schneider* (sons of *Heinrich Schneider), Georg Bley* and *Catharina Bley* (children of *Christoph Bley),* and *Henrich Schaub* (son of *Balthasar Schaub),* all of Rumbach. Since in the years 1763-1764 there was emigration from the Palatinate to Cayenne (French Guiana in South America), that country could possibly be intended in the documents when "America" is referred to.

Emigrants from Dossenheim (Baden) In the 18th Century

By GABRIEL HARTMANN

Translated and Edited by DON YODER

[The following emigrant list, with its intriguing title, "Amerikafahrer von Dossenheim im 18. Jahrhundert," by Gabriel Hartmann of Heidelberg, was published in the series *Mannheimer Geschichtsblätter,* XXVII (1926), columns 55-58. The materials were extracted from the Family Register of the Reformed congregation of Dossenheim. Dossenheim, Handschuhsheim, and Schriesheim belonged in the 18th Century to the Electoral Palatinate. They are located today in Baden, in the West German state of Baden-Württemberg, and can be found on the map a few miles West of Mannheim and directly north of Heidelberg.—EDITOR.]

In 1761, when the Reformed pastor Kaiser[1] of Handschuhsheim and Dossenheim on the Bergstrasse changed his residence, he wrote the following into the Dossenheim Church Register:

> Just as this Dossenheim congregation during my almost 30 year service here has sharply diminished due to raging illnesses and especially the removal of many families to America and Jutland, so may the dear Lord through his grace increase it again in true members in the love of Jesus Christ [*Gleich wie diese Dossenheimer Gemeind seit meiner fast 30 jährigen Bedienung wegen grassierender Krankheiten und besonders Wegziehung vieler Familien nach Amerika und Jüttland sehr vermindert worden, so wolle der liebe Gott durch seine Gnade sie wieder vermehren an wahren Gliedern in der Liebe Jesu Christi*].

These anxious words of the departing minister had an only too serious and tragic background. Mysterious sicknesses had cut very deeply into the core of the congregation. Beginning with the year 1732[*] and in accordance with a governmental decree, the sicknesses of the deceased were listed, and the designations consumption *(Abzehrung)*, fever *(hitzige Krankheit)*, dysentery and diarrhoea *(rote und weisse Ruhr)*, and purples *(weisse Frieseln)* appear very frequently here. Along with this came bad crop years and a monstrous tax levy. The Electoral Court[2] engaged in all sorts of unprofitable fiscal experiments, like the raising of angora goats, for which honor Dossenheim was chosen. These animals had so to speak a free passport, could gad about at will to feed, wherever it suited them. Naturally through all this great damage was done to fields and vineyards, against which the peasants were unable to protect themselves. All of this turned a great part of the villagers against the homeland government. With sadness many must perhaps have remembered the tales

of their parents and grandparents from the times under Karl Ludwig, when work was plentiful and people were happy. Then life still seemed to be worth living. The despair crept through the poverty-stricken huts of the village and many a one told himself: better an end to fear than fear without end.

Away, away from this hard-hearted abode, which to most had become a hell, was the watchword of many. For there was nothing left anymore to life, except hard compulsory labor. The tax vultures indeed took away everything.

It is characteristic of the conditions of that time and place, that the emigration involved not only the young people. There were old people involved too, who had long since passed the zenith of their life. These preferred to die abroad in an unknown land rather than in Karl Theodor's "paradise," and willingly lent their ear to the agents for the "New Land".

The first report of Dossenheim emigrants to America comes to us from the year 1749. Then came the notorious "Black Monday" of May 7, 1752, and the emigration of 1757; the last group of emigrants is mentioned in 1764.

It can be assumed as self understood that these unfortunate lower class farmers of a village that was at that time small, realized but little for their modest properties at the time of this mass flight, and the little that was left could scarcely reach farther than Southampton. There they at once got into a new slavery—the debt slavery of the shipping entrepreneur. The ships would certainly, according to our present day standards, have been the worst type of soul-destroyer, for on them only a very questionable maintenance was allotted to the redemptioners on their long voyage. The ship's sicknesses from that time speak on this question a very eloquent language.

The shipping entrepreneurs, despite their great intimacy with the Bible, were very smart business men, who did not want to take over too much risk with the freighting of their debt slaves.

According to the data from the aforementioned Fam-

[1]Everywhere that Pastor Kaiser was active, for example also Schriesheim, he started family registers and left instructions on how they were to be continued. These are very carefully set up and give immediate information on when a family first appears at the place concerned and on its further development.
[2]From a lecture on local history given at Dossenheim, in January 1924, by the schoolmaster, Peter Reinhard. See also *Mannheimer Geschichtsblätter,* XXVI (1925), column 8.

The Town Hall of Otterberg in the Palatinate. Photograph by Erich Schneider, Otterberg, from the Otterberger Kalender of 1955.

ily Register of Dossenheim, we gather that these emigrants all arrived safely in the New World. There are even indications at hand that they were soon relieved of their debts. Of one it is reported that he went to Carolina in 1752, but came back. The year of his return is not indicated, but from this fact we can conclude that he came into some means, and he perhaps brought some along in order to manage, otherwise he would not have been able to pay his ship's debts and the return journey.

The following are the names of these emigrants to America from Dossenheim, as they are to be found in the documentary source listed above:

1749.

1. *Johann Bär, Johann Georg Bär* and his wife *Anna Catharina*, May 1749, went to the New Land, three persons.

2. [..............................] *Reinsperger*, born 1718, and his wife *Anna Catharina*, left May 16, 1749, for Pennsylvania or St. Mary's Land, two persons.

1752.

3. *Johann Georg Bär*, born 1706, and [his wife?] *Eva Catharina Wedel*, born 1706, left May 9, 1752, for Carolina, two persons.

4. *Johann Michael Casper*, born 1708, went to Carolina in 1752 without his wife and children, but came back, one person.

5. *Johannes Fontius*, born 1700, and his wife *Anna Catharina*, went with all eight children, with the exception of the oldest, *Johann Georg*, to Carolina, May 9, 1752, ten persons.

6. *Johannes Federwolf* and his wife *Anna Catharina* and three girls, went to the New Land circa 1752, five persons.

7. *Johann Valentin Herder* and his wife *Anna Elisabeth* and three children, to Carolina, May 9, 1752, five persons.

8. *Johann Conrad Hungerbieler* and his wife *Maria Elisabeth* and five children, to Carolina, May 9, 1752, seven persons. (The Hungerbielers had gone to the Electoral Palatinate from Thurgau in the second half of the 17th Century, settling in Schriesheim and Dossenheim.)

9. *Johann Valentin Möll*, born 1731, to Carolina, May 9, 1752, one person.

10. *Johann Heinrich Möll* and his wife Maria *Catharina* née *Wedel*, born 1711, with three daughters, to Carolina, May 9, 1752, five persons. (The Mölls, also

*The Marketplace of Otterberg in the Palatinate.
Photograph from the* Otterberger Kalender.

spelled Möhl, still represented today in Dossenheim, settled in Dossenheim at the end of the 17th Century, stemming from Brüsswihl in Canton St. Gall.)

11. *Johann Michael Klein* and his wife *Susanna* née *Oberle,* to Carolina, May 9, 1752, two persons.

12. *Johann Heinrich Scholl,* born 1718, and his sister *Maria Barbara Scholl,* born 1721, to Carolina, two persons.

13. *Anna Margaretha Stief,* born 1715, *Anna Clara Stief,* born 1718, and *Anna Christine Stief,* born 1726, to Carolina, May 9, 1752, three persons.

14. *Anna Maria Wedel* with her child, to Carolina, May 9, 1752, two persons.

15. *Georg Wedel* and his wife *Anna Barbara* née *Schlepp,* born 1691, with two children, to Carolina, May 9, 1752, four persons.

16. *Johannes Werner,* born 1702, and his wife *Anna Elisabeth* née *Impfinger,* with seven children, to Carolina, May 9, 1752, nine persons.

1757.

17. *Johann Georg Bär,* with wife and five children, to Carolina, seven persons.

1764.

18. *Johannes Dreher,* born 1722, and his wife *Anna* Margaretha, with five children, went to America 1764 (in another citation: "to Philadelphia in the English territories" [*ins Engländische nach Philadelphia*], seven persons. [*Johannes Trehr* arrived at Philadelphia in October, 1764 on the Ship *Hero* (Strassburger-Hinke, *Pennsylvania German Pioneers,* List 248 C).]

19. *Petronella Dreher,* born 1697, née *Loscher,* to Philadelphia 1764 (apparently the mother of Johannes Dreher), one person.

20. *Georg Albrecht Wedel* and *Eva Catharina,* born 1711, two persons.

21. *Johann Peter Wedel* and his wife *Anna Sybilla,* née *Her,* went to the New Land, to Maryland, May 7, 1764, two persons, [*Petter Wedel,* with *Johannes Trehr* (No. 18, above) arrived at Philadelphia on the Ship *Hero* in October 1764 (Strassburger-Hinke, List 248 C).]

(WITHOUT DATE.)

22. Mayor [*Bürgermeister*] *Valentin* and his wife *Susanna Elisabeth* and seven children, to America, nine persons.

Total = 84 persons.

Now what became of these 84 homeland-weary emigrants on the other side of the big water? No "song, no heroes' book" reports of them. Not even an "Astor" appears to have arisen from among them.[3] But perhaps somewhere in South Carolina or Pennsylvania the young lads still hold the mock court in the village meadow [Bannweidbubengericht] before the village festivals, where they sit in judgment, tongue in cheek, over every sinner who has transgressed the field rules, and consider the atonement money that they rake in as a highly welcome contribution to the common festival celebration. Or somewhere in the United States perhaps the youth still practice the crabapple dance [Holzapfeltanz], and no one remembers anymore that these amusements were brought along from Dossenheim, where they are still practiced.[4]

In the year 1762 the Reformed pastor Johann Jakob Waltz from Handschuhsheim assumed the Dossenheim congregation also. As answer, so to speak, to those melancholy words of the departing clergyman Kaiser, cited above, he wrote the following in the church register:

Jehovah grant that as this Dossenheim congregation has hitherto decreased, it may henceforth again increase and reveal itself indeed as true members of the congregation of Jesus Christ.

The increase of the congregation had to wait, though, almost a century. New storms of war, new heavy emigrations to the Crimea (or, as it stands in the registers, the "Island of Crimea" [*Insul Grimm*]), and to Russian Poland, did not let the congregation prosper.

In conclusion I wish to express my thanks to Church Councilman Kappler of Dossenheim for his friendly kindness in making the church registers available.

---

[3]John Jacob Astor was born in the nearby village of Walldorf, south of Heidelberg, in 1763. He founded the Astor dynasty in the United States and Britain. The name of his home village was preserved for many years in New York's Waldorf-Astoria Hotel, and has come into international cuisine in the form of Waldorf Salad.—EDITOR.
[4]The author was a bit too optimistic about the transplantation of specific cultural forms from the small village cultures of Europe to the new world setting. Since the village concept and its culture was in most cases not transplanted with the 18th Century emigrants, there was little or no transplantation of the village festivals that are so much a part of European village life.—EDITOR.

18th-Century Emigrants from the Palatinate, Lower Alsace, and Rheinhessen

By FRIEDRICH KREBS

Translated and Edited by DON YODER

[We present here two articles on the 18th Century emigration to the American colonies by Dr. Friedrich Krebs of the Speyer State Archives in West Germany. The first is entitled "Amerika-Auswanderer des 18. Jahrhunderts aus dem Gebiet der Pfalz und dem ehemals pfälzischen Unterelsass," and appeared in *Genealogie*, 1970, No. 7, 175-176. The second appeared under the title, "Einige Amerika-Auswanderer des 18. Jahrhunderts aus Rheinhessen," in *Genealogie*, 1970, No. 12, 337-338. Additional names of emigrants from the Districts of Kleeburg and Katharinenburg referred to in footnote 2 in the first article given here can be found in William John Hinke and John Baer Stoudt, editors, "A List of German Immigrants to the American Colonies from Zweibruecken in the Palatinate, 1728-1749," *The Pennsylvania German Folklore Society*, I (1936), 101-124; and Friedrich Krebs, "A List of German Immigrants to the American Colonies from Zweibruecken in the Palatinate, 1750-1771," *The Pennsylvania German Folklore Society*, XVI (1951), 171-183.—EDITOR.

I.

1. *Johann Theobald Grub* was born July 14, 1718, in Glanmünchweiler, a town in the Palatinate South of Kusel and West of Kaiserslautern. He was the son of *Johann Henrich Grub,* grocer in Glanmünchweiler and his wife *Anna Catharina,* and married November 28, 1741, *Anna Elisabeth Margretha Weber,* born October 10, 1723, in Haschbach, a small village near Glanmünchweiler, daughter of *Johann Michael Weber* and his wife *Maria Margaretha.* Children, born in Glanmünchweiler: (1) *Johann Theobald,* born April 4, 1743, (2) *Eva Catharina,* born September 23, 1745, (3) *Johann Michael,* born February 15, 1748, died November 24, 1750, in Glanmünchweiler at the age of 2 years, 9 months and 9 days, (4) *Johann Jacob,* born February 17, 1750, and (5) *Maria Johannetta,* born April 29, 1752. "These people went to America" [*Diese Leuthe sind in Americam gezogen*]—Lutheran Church Register of Glanmünchweiler. *Debalt Grub* arrived at Philadelphia on the Ship *Richard and Mary,* September 1752 (Strassburger-Hinke, *Pennsylvania German Pioneers,* List 183 C).

2. According to a ruling of the Zweibrücken Government dated May 8, 1760 (Staatsarchiv Speyer, Akt Zweibrücken No. 4297), the property of *Philipp Edinger* of Bledesbach, near Kusel, who having emigrated before the edict of 1739 which threatened illicit emigration with confiscation of property, was free of such confiscation; but after the death of the emigrant's father one-fifth of the emigrant's property was to be collected as emigration tax [*censu emigrationis*], likewise the tenth part of the property which the emigrant took abroad. *Johann Philipp Edinger* took the oath of allegiance at Philadelphia, September 27, 1737 (Strassburger-Hinke, List 47 A-C).

3. By decree of June 17, 1760, the property of *Johann Jacob Simon* of Birlenbach, Lower Alsace, was confiscated on account of illicit emigration. According to a report by the district bailiff *Keller* of Kleeburg' Simon "had gone to America some nine years ago, after he

had secretly married in the Dürckheim village of Leinenhaussen" [bereits vor 9 Jahren, nachdeme er sich zuvor in der Dürckheimischen Ortschaft Leinenhaussen heimlich verheurathet, nach Americam gezogen]. Presumably the emigrant was *Jacob Simon,* who arrived on the Ship *Sandwich* and took the oath of allegiance at Philadelphia, November 30, 1750 (Strassburger-Hinke, List 160 C).

4. The property left behind by *Salome Neufer,* who had gone to America from Hofen, Lower Alsace, was confiscated for the treasury by decree of the Zweibrücken Government dated July 14, 1778. At the same time the request of her brothers and sisters for the release of the property was denied.

5. According to a decree of the Zweibrücken Government dated December 18, 1762, the paternal inheritance of *Johann Jacob Heinel,* "who had gone away to America in the year 1733" [*welcher in anno 1733 in Americam abgegangen*]

[1]Staatsarchiv Speyer, Akt Zweibrücken No. 2022, "Vermögenskonfiskation in den Aemtern Klee und Katherinenburg 1756-1784". The Zweibrücken District of Kleeburg embraced Schloss Kleeburg and Kleeburg village and the villages of Rott, Steinselz, Oberhofen, Ingolsheim, Hunspach, and Hofen; the District of Katherinenburg included the villages of Birlenbach, Keffenach, half of the village of Schöneberg, the Wernershäuser Mill and the Welchen Mill near Memmelshofen. All of these villages are in Lower Alsace, South of Wissembourg. Up to this time only the permitted emigration from the Districts of Kleeburg and Katherinenburg to America in the 18th Century has been treated in publications. The items in this short list are of persons whose emigration was not permitted by the government.

], was delivered without security to the children of his father *Simon Heinel* of Kleeburg, Lower Alsace, although 24 florins still had to be deducted from the said inheritance for his manumission. Probably the *Jacob Hainel (Hennel),* aged 20, who arrived at Philadelphia on the Brigantine *Richard and Elizabeth,* September 28, 1733 (Strassburger-Hinke, List 33 A-C).

6. By decree of the Zweibrücken Government dated July 12, 1764, the property of *Jacob Weimer* of Hundsbach, Lower Alsace, "who is at this time in America" [*welcher dermahlen sich in America befindet*], was declared fallen to the treasury on account of illicit emigration. He had requested the delivery of his property left behind in his home village to the sum of 254 florins, 11 batzen, and 3 shillings. Likewise by decree of February 1, 1759, it was ordered by the Zweibrücken Government that the property of *Jacob Weimer* of Hofen, Lower Alsace, who had "gone to America" [*in Americam gezogen*], be collected for the treasury. Both of these emigrants appear to have arrived at Philadelphia on the Ship *Janet,* taking the oath of allegiance on October 7, 1751, the one signing his name, the other making his mark (Strassburger-Hinke, List 175 C). The signer is identified by Editor Hinke in a footnote as the Reformed minister discussed in James I. Good, *History of the German Reformed Church in the U.S., 1725-1792,* p. 568, but without further information it is impossible at this time to state whether the minister

ey in the Palatinate, from Merian's Topographia Germaniae *(1672).*

67

was the Jacob Weimer from Hundsbach or the Jacob Weimer from Hofen.[2]

II.

The following short list of emigrants is derived from the Inventory Protocols of the City of Alzey as well as from the numerous inventories available in the community archive of Guntersblum, both dating from the 18th Century. In view of the relative scarcity of documentation on emigration to America in the 18th Century, even the publication of a few names seemed of importance to me. The protocols of the Electoral Palatine Oberamt Alzey, which undoubtedly would have been an important source for emigration research, are unfortunately—except for scanty remnants in the State Archives of Darmstadt—no longer preserved. The protocols of the Electoral Palatine Oberamt Oppenheim in the city archive there had a better fate. They owe their preservation to being stored in a city archive and list a series of emigrants to America for the period 1740-1749.

CITY OF ALZEY

1. Alzey, March 7, 1763: "Whereas *Conrad Pillanus,* cititzen and master baker here, recently deceased, has besides his widow *Margaretha Gertrutis* née *Carbach,* left a [son] living in Philadelphia named *Simon Pillanus* and two little grandchildren, *Anna Catharina* and *Maria Margaretha Schuhler* from his deceased daughter (from his first marriage), *Maria Margaretha,* who was married to the Reformed schoolmaster at Sprendlingen, *Johann Michel Schuhler* [*Nachdem der dahiesige Bürger und Beckermeister Conrad Pillanus ohnlängst Todes verfahren und nebst der Witwen Margaretha Gertrutis gebohrne Carbachin einen in Philadelphia wohnenden (Sohn) Simonn Pillanus und aus seiner verstorbenen Tochter erster Ehe Maria Margaretha, so an den reformierten Schulmeister zu Sprendlingen Johann Michel Schuhler verheurathet gewesen, 2 Enckelger Annam Catharinam und Mariam Margaretham im Leben nach sich zurückgelassen . . .*]

According to an entry in the Reformed church register at Alzey *Simon Pelanus (Pilanus)* was born at Alzey October 15, 1718, son of *Johann Conrad Pelanus* and his wife *Catharina,* and baptized there on October 19, 1718, in the Reformed faith. *Conrad Pilanus,* citizen and baker at Alzey, was buried at Alzey January 31, 1763, at the age of 78 years. His first wife *Catharina* died at Alzey December 6, 1723, at the age of 27 years, and was buried there December 8, 1723. The widower

[2]William J. Hinke's last book, the posthumous work edited by George W. Richards, *Ministers of the German Reformed Congregations in Pennsylvania and Other Colonies in the Eighteenth Century* (Lancaster, Pennsylvania: Historical Commission of the Evangelical and Reformed Church, 1951), contains a biography of Jacob Weymer (Weimer), pp. 152-155. According to this Weimer was born in 1734 and served as Reformed schoolmaster in Pennsylvania, at Longswamp, for 17 years until 1768-1769 when he entered the Reformed ministry. He served several churches in Berks and Lehigh Counties before his removal to Western Maryland in 1770, where his parish centered around Hagerstown. He died at Hagerstown, Maryland, in 1790.—EDITOR.

had married at Alzey on November 12, 1736, as his second wife *Maria Gertruda,* daughter of *Adam Carbach.* *Simon Pilanus* arrived on the Ship *Edinburgh* and took the oath of allegiance at Philadelphia September 5, 1748 (Strassburger-Hinke, List 117 C).

2. Alzey, July 29, 1758: "Whereas the widow of *Casper Weisskopf,* citizen and master baker here, has recently died leaving two children from her first marriage, i.e., *Joh[ann]. Erdmann Dory,* who is at this time in Pennsylvania, and *Dorothea Dory,* married to the tinsmith *Benjamin Haass,* as well as a child of the last marriage named *Carl Weisskopf,* aged 21 . . . [*Nachdeme des dahiesigen Bürgers und Beckermeisters Caspar Weisskopfs nachgelassene Wittib kurtzhin Todes verblichen und 2 Kinder erster Ehe benanntl. Joh. Erdmann Dory, so sich dermahlen in Pennsylvanien befindet, und Dorotheam Dorijn an den Spengler Benjamin Haass verheurathet sodann ein Kind letzter Ehe nahmens Carl Weisskopf von 21 Jahren im Leben nach sich und zurückgelassen . . .*]

According to an entry in the Lutheran church register of Alzey, *Gerhard Johann Thori* had a son named *Johann Erdmann Thori,* born May 20 and baptized May 21, 1723, in the Lutheran faith. The wife of *Gerhard Johann Thori,* citizen and master sackmaker at Alzey, was *Anna Felicitas,* who after his death married as her second husband, at Alzey on June 12, 1736, the master baker at Alzey, *Johann Caspar Weisskopf.*

GUNTERSBLUM

1. According to the inventory of *Georg Heimlich* dated at Guntersblum, December 20, 1782, the decedent had died in May 1782 and his wife *Anna Margaretha* "four weeks ago" [*vor 4 Wochen*]. He left behind a son *Andreas Heimlich,* 34 years old, absent in America. *Andreas Heimlich* arrived at Philadelphia on the Ship *Delphin* and took the oath of allegiance on May 31, 1773 (Strassburger-Hinke, List 304 C).

2. Guntersblum, June 28, 1762: "Whereas *Elisabetha Gertraudta,* wife of *Dietrich Jäger,* departed this life on Lätare of this year, and after her *Dietrich Jäger,* she left behind from her first marriage with *Johannes Tesch* of Guntersblum three children, namely, (1) *Catharina,* wife of *Philipp Schmit,* of Guntersblum, (2) *Elisabetha,* wife of *Jacob Wagner* of Dolgesheim, and (3) *Wilhelm Henrich Tesch,* who is dwelling on the Island of South Carolina . . ." [*Nachdem Elisabetha Gertraudta, Dietrich Jägers Ehefrau auf Lätare h(uius). a(nni). mit dem Tod abgegangen und nach sich Dietrich Jäger und aus 1. Ehe von dem Johannes Teschen (aus Guntersblum) 3 Kinder, namens Catharina, Philipp Schmits Ehefrau dahier, Elisabetha Jacob Wagners Ehefrau von Dolgesheim und Wilhelm Henrich Tesch, welcher sich auf der Insul Sudcarolina aufhältet . . . . hinterlassen . . .*] On this emigrant there was nothing more here to document; perhaps American scholars will succeed in identifying him.

American Emigrants from the Territories of the Bishopric of Speyer

By WERNER HACKER

Translated and Edited by DON YODER

[The basis of this article is the American emigration section (pp. 121-140) in Werner Hacker, *Auswanderungen aus dem früheren Hochstift Speyer nach Südosteuropa und Uebersee im XVIII. Jahrhundert* (Kaiserslautern, 1969), in the series *Schriften zur Wanderungsgeschichte der Pfälzer,* No. 28. The book provides valluable documentation on and analysis of the emigration from one relatively small government in the Rhineland—the territories which were formerly under the secular jurisdiction of the Bishop of Speyer *(Hochstift Speyer).* The diocese of Speyer, which involved ecclesiastical jurisdiction over churches and parishes, was not identical to this secular wing of the bishop's authority. The territories of the *Hochstift* embraced 119 separate localities (cities, villages, hamlets, and single estates) which were immediately under the bishop in his secular administration. These localities were scattered on the left and right banks of the Rhine in the present-day states of Baden, the Palatinate, and Alsace.

The emigration from this territory—which was not a continuous, united geographical area but was made up of enclaves scattered through other jurisdictions—was thus subject to the same economic and social motives for emigration as the rest of the Rhineland in the 18th Century. The poverty years, the lack of land for expansion, and the devastation and disruption caused by the wars all contributed to the appeal of emigration to Southeastern Europe as well as the "New Land" that beckoned across the Atlantic. The book includes details on some 1600 families or single persons who left for the German settlements of Hungary and other areas of Southeastern Europe (pp. 35-120), and on about 400 familes and single emigrants who went "overseas," which in the 18th Century meant America. Of these the majority left in 1763-1764 for the French settlement of Cayenne (French Guiana), called sometimes in the records, the "island" of Cayenne. The North American destinations involved Pennsylvania, New England, Canada, and Mississippi (Louisiana).

The documents on which Werner Hacker based his emigrant book are found in the Karlsruhe State Archives *(Generallandesarchiv Karlsruhe),* covering the Speyer territories on the right bank of the Rhine which were ceded to Baden in 1803. Not included are those Speyer territories on the left side of the river, the documents for which are located in the Speyer State Archives, nor for the Alsatian villages formerly under Speyer, the records for which are deposited in French archives.

The list is valuable for the historian and sociologist as well as the genealogist, for it gives details about occupation, property, and family, personal reasons for emigration, the procedure of emigration, etc. Particularly useful are the introductory sections (pp. 9-33) which provide the reader with a clear and detailed account of what vassalage *(Leibeigenschaft)* meant in the 18th Century, a relationship to the state very different from the current connotation of citizenship, and how one was released through it by manumission. The introduction includes also details on the system used in taxing emigrant property, and descriptions of the fate of those manumitted emigrants who changed their minds and decided to stay, not all of whom were graciously readmitted.

We are indebted to Werner Hacker, to Dr. Fritz Braun, Director emeritus, and Dr. Karl Scherer, Director, Heimatstelle Pfalz, Kaiserslautern, West Germany, for the privilege of republishing for our readers this important list of emigrants to North America.—EDITOR.]

1. *Jacob Böhler,* of Freimersheim, with wife and 5 children, property of 65 florins, manumitted, to New England, 1766.

2. *Josef Brunner,* of Klein-Schifferstadt, Reformed, with wife and 3 children *(Maria Catharina* 19, *Johannes* 18, and *Heinrich Elias* 6), property of 422 florins, manumitted April 26, 1729. Arrived at Philadelphia, September 11, 1729, on the Ship *Allen* with *Christian Götz(endanner)* (q.v.) and *Johann Waydmann* (q.v.). All three took the oath of allegiance on September 15, 1729 (Strassburger-Hinke, *Pennsylvania German Pioneers,* List 10A,B,C). In the ship lists the name is spelled "Bruner" and "Prunder". The wife, *Catharina Elisabeth,* is listed among the women, the son *"John Henderick"* among the boys under 15 years of age, and the son *Johannes* is listed with the men, with the notation "sick". Missing is the daughter's name, *Maria Catharina.* According to the records, the wife's maiden name was *Thomas.*

3. *Appolonia Dreher,* wife of *Martin Dreher,* of Balzfeld, applied for emigration to America with her four daughters and was manumitted, March 1764. Her

69

husband had wilfully deserted her during the war, is living in Saxony and is said to be Lutheran. An *Andreas Dreher* from Balzfeld, with wife *Maria Anna* and 4 children *(Appolonia, Maria Eva, Catharina,* and *Johann Peter)* appears in the same list as destined for Cayenne. Could he be identical with the *Andreas Dreher* who arrived at Philadelphia on the Ship *Hamilton* in 1767 (Strassburger-Hinke, List 265 C)?

4. *Michael Franckh,* of Rohrbach (Sinsheim). Received manumission to emigrate to Mississippi, 1723, but wants to stay. Is ordered to purchase his citizenship anew, or leave, "since the episcopal villages (i.e., of the Bishopric of Speyer) are not to be considered a dovecote" [*da man die Stiftsflecken als vor keinen Taubenschlag gehalten haben will*].

5. *Christian Götz (Götzendanner),* of Schifferstadt, Reformed, property of 65 florins, was manumitted to emigrate to Pennsylvania, April 26, 1729, with wife and son (aged 6) and daughter (aged 5). It appears that this emigrant was *Christian Götzendanner,* from the Swiss family of *Giezendanner* which had emigrated into the Palatinate. The name is spelled in the ship lists *Kitsintander, Kitsenlander,* and *Kilsenlander* (Strassburger-Hinke, List 10A,B,C). He arrived at Philadelphia on the Ship *Allen,* September 11, 1729, and took the oath of allegiance on September 15th with his fellow countrymen *Josef Brunner* (q.v.) and *Johann Waydmann* (q.v.). Brunner and Götz(endanner) had been

manumitted on the same day and it is known from the archives that Christian Götzendanner of Klein-Schifferstadt had married *Anna Barbara Brunner,* daughter of *Josef Brunner.*

6. *Hans Georg Gobel,* of "Hofheim in the Austrian territories" [*Hofheim im Oesterreichischen*], citizen, vassal of the bishop of Speyer, by bad luck overloaded with debts (wife and children, free of vassalage), had property of 160 florins, was manumitted to go to his relatives in Pennsylvania [*zu Verwandten in Pennsylvanien*], April 24, 1733. Arrived at Philadelphia on the Ship *Hope,* August 28, 1733. In the ship list the name is spelled "Gobel," "Gabel," and "Gobl" (Strassburger-Hinke, List 31A). The father's age is given as 40, the wife *Barbara* (38), and five children are listed *(Antoni* 12, *Anna Maria* 10, *Magdalena* 8, *Jerg Adam* (5), and *Hans Jerg* (3 ½)).

A letter to the Editor from Dr. Fritz Braun, Director, Heimatstelle Pfalz, Kaiserslautern, dated February 24, 1970, furnishes additional data on this family. The town of origin is now Hoffenheim near Sinsheim in Baden. From the church registers of Hoffenheim it appears that there were eleven children in all: (1) *Antonius,* born August 24, 1717; (2) *Carl Antony,* born October 21, 1718, died August 26, 1720; (3) *Maria Elisabetha,* born September 3, 1720, died October 2, 1720; (4) *Anna Maria,* born August 14, 1721; (5) *Georg Balthasar,* born March 3, 1723, died August 23, 1724;

Speyer on the Rhine, from Merian's Topographia Germaniae *(1672).*

(6) *Maria Magdalena,* born January 1, 1725; (7) *Anna Margaretha,* born March 23, 1726, died February 28, 1728; (8) *Georg Adam,* born April 13, 1727; (9) *Hanss Georg,* born September 12, 1728; (10) *Anna Catharina,* born February 28, 1730, died February 24, 1733; and (11) *Maria Dorothea,* born April 13, 1732.

7. *Johann Peter Hauck,* of Rot, with wife *Barbara* and 5 children *(Georg Peter, Wilhelm, Caspar Anton, Maria Susanna,* and *Nicolaus),* to America 1764. Could this have been the *Johan Petter Hauck* who arrived at Philadelphia on the Ship *Chance,* November 1, 1763 (Strassburger-Hinke, List 239 C)? On the same ship, listed separately, was *Johann Valatin Hauck.*

8. *Gertrud Kammer,* of Kronau, single, went "to the New Land" [*ins neue Land*], 1763. Her property amounted to 27 florins 35 kreuzer. The accounts were settled in 1774.

9. *Andreas Kolb,* of Dielheim, with his family "to the new island" [*in die neue Insul*], 1763. The record, however, gives "America" rather than Cayenne as goal of emigration. One *Johann Andreas Kolb* arrived at Philadelphia on the Ship *Richmond* and signed the oath of allegiance, October 20, 1764 (Strassburger-Hinke, List 247).

10. *Johann* and *Julius Meyer,* brothers, of Oberhausen, property 90 florins, manumitted March 21, 1764, to emigrate, presumably to America.

11. *Peter Meickhart,* of Tiefenbach, with his family, manumitted to emigrate to Mississippi, about 1724. Was readmitted.

12. *Johann Caspar Michenfelder,* of Zeutern, married 5 years ago in Lancaster [Pennsylvania]. His property amounted to 2156 florins; received manumission. Since the document is dated 1773, the marriage must have taken place in 1768.

13. *Johann Milch,* of Wiesenthal, 28 years old, property of 460 florins, wants to settle in Philadelphia, 1808. One *Johann Millich* had arrived at Philadelphia on the Ship *Little Cherub* on October 18, 1805 (Strassburger-Hinke, List 488).

14. *Daniel Müller,* of Freimersheim, resident and citizen, Lutheran, with wife and 6 children, property of 40 florins, paid 2 florins manumission tax to go "to the New Land" [*ins Neue Land*], April 1, 1751. One *Daniel Miller* arrived at Philadelphia on the Ship *Elizabeth,* taking the oath of allegiance September 5, 1751 (Strassburger-Hinke, List 162 C).

15. *Catharina Schäfer,* nee *Maurer,* of Zeutern, her husband from Odenheim, 4 children, property of 32 florins 56 kreuzer, manumitted 1764 to go "elsewhere" [*anderwärts*]. America was intended.

16. *Jacob Schweickard,* of Freimersheim, Catholic, property of 26 florins, paid 3 florins manumission tax, March 8, 1741. "To the New Land, which according to him is Pennsylvania" [*ins neue Land, welches seiner Meinung nach Pennsylvanien sein solle*].

17. *Michael Thomas,* of Klein-Schifferstadt, with wife and 7 children, property of 555 florins and 23 kreuzer, manumitted to go to Pennsylvania, July 1, 1729. Arrived on the Ship *Thistle of Glasgow,* taking the oath of allegiance August 29, 1730 (Strassburger-Hinke, List 11A,B). In list A the emigrant is listed as "sick".

18. *Johann Ulm,* of Kronau, citizen and baker, with wife and 5 children, property of 224 florins, manumitted in the second quarter of 1737, to go "to relatives in Mississippi" [*zu Verwandten nach Mississippi*].

19. *Martin Ulm, Margarete Ulm,* and *Catharina Ulm,* of Kronau, brother and sisters (guardian: *Valentin Knöller*), manumitted to go to Pennsylvania, March 23, 1752.

20. *Conrad Waldhuber,* of Zeutern, with wife and 5 children *(Juliana 15, Johann 12, Maria Eva 8, Jacob 6,* and *Michael 1 ½),* manumitted to emigrate to Canada, 1763.

21. *Johann Waydmann,* of Marientraut, with wife and 3 children (daughter 8, little daughter, and baby son), 51 florins property, manumitted to go to America, July 1, 1729. Appears in the same ship list (Strassburger-Hinke, List 10A,B,C) as *Josef Brunner* (q.v.) and *Christian Götz(endanner)* (q.v.). All three took the oath of allegiance on September 15, 1729.

22. *Michael Weber,* of Freimersheim, with wife and 3 children, property of 36 florins, to New England, 1766.

FLUVIUS

nes 9. Iesuiter Coll. 10. Die Domkirch. 11. Des Bischoffhofe.

71

Emigrants to America
from the Duchy of Zweibrücken

By FRIEDRICH KREBS

Translated and Edited by DON YODER

[The following list of 18th Century emigrants, mostly to Pennsylvania, appeared in the article, "Amerika-Auswanderer des 18. Jahrhunderts aus dem Gebiet des Herzogtums Zweibrücken," in *Genealogie,* II (1970), 50-53. The data was extracted from documents in the Palatine State Archives at Speyer, West Germany. Additional materials on some of these emigrants can be found in William John Hinke and John Baer Stoudt, editors, "A List of German Immigrants to the American Colonies from Zweibruecken in the Palatinate, 1728-1749," *The Pennsylvania German Folklore Society,* I (1936), 101-124; and Friedrich Krebs, "A List of German Immigrants to the American Colonies from Zweibruecken in the Palatinate, 1750-1771," *The Pennsylvania German Folklore Society,* XVI (1951), 171-183.— EDITOR.]

1. On May 3, 1741, *Theobald Braucheller (Bräucheler)* of Schellweiler asked officially for permission to go to America with his brother-in-law *Peter Burgey.* This permission was granted by decree of the Zweibrücken Government the very next day, on May 4, 1741, at which time the Oberamt Lichtenberg received the order to prepare the manumission certificate for him upon payment of the manumission tax of 10 batzen. *Theobald Brauchler* landed at Philadelphia in 1741 on the Ship *Snow Molly* and took the oath of allegiance there on October 26, 1741 (Strassburger-Hinke, *Pennsylvania German Pioneers,* List 88 A-C).

2. From a document of *Jacob Jost,* son of *Daniel Jost* of Baumholder, dated May 2, 1739, it appears that about eleven years previously he had set out upon the journey "to Pennsylvania" [*nacher Pensylvaniam*] in company with some people, and married after his arrival there. On account of the inheritance of his wife, a native of Fussgönheim in the Palatinate, he had returned to the homeland and received 300 florins paid out by the brothers and sisters from the paternal estate, of which he then paid back 40 florins. Of the remaining 260 florins he wanted to pay the tithe (tenth penny) tax. However, the Zweibrücken Government decided on May 14, 1739, that Jacob Jost of Baumholder would have to pay the sixth penny (i.e., the sixth part) on the entire 300 florins. *Jacob Jost* landed at Philadelphia in August 1728 and took the oath of allegiance there on August 24, 1728 (Strassburger-Hinke, List 6A,B).

3. By decree of the Zweibrücken Government dated April 18, 1741, permission to emigrate to America was granted to *Anna Elisabetha Kuhn,* widow of *Abraham Kuhn* of Baumholder, upon payment of 106 florins, 6 batzen, and 11 pennies. In the permission to emigrate were included her two sons *Johannes Kuhn,* 23 years old, and *Johann Wilhelm Kuhn,* 13 years old. In her petition of February 21, 1741, the widow cites the fact that she was very poor and always has been; she has incurred many debts during her married life, so that nothing remained anymore for her support. Besides, on account of her advanced age, a second marriage was not to be considered. As goal of emigration she indicated Carolina. Possibly *Johannes Kuhn,* who landed at Philadelphia on the Ship *Marlborough* in September 1741 (Strassburger-Hinke, List 82 A-C).

4. By decree of the Zweibrücken Government dated March 24, 1781, the property of *Anna Ottilia Arnold* of Leinsweiler was confiscated for the treasury. She had been married to *Daniel Berger* of Breitfurt "about 40 years ago" (according to other documents, in 1733 or 1734) and after the death of her husband in 1754 had gone away with several children, secretly and without permission, from Breitfurt to America. During her absence the property had devolved upon a cousin and was then left in part to a soldier named *Arnold.* The marriage entry Berger-Arnold was nowhere to be found, although in the Reformed Church Register of Walsheim on the Blies there were found the birth entries of several children of the couple: 1. *Wilhelm,* born September 1738, 2. *Johannes,* born July 29, 1736, died April 19, 1738, 3. *Johann Georg,* baptized September 3, 1741, 4. *Maria Catharina,* born March 15, 1745, and 5. *Johannes,* born October 28, 1751. *Daniel Berger,* inhabitant and linenweaver at Breitfurt, died March 5, 1754, at Breitfurt and was buried there on March 7, 1754, at the age of 43 years.

5. *Nickel Hundsicker,* son of the deceased inhabitant [*Gemeindsmann*] *Jacob Hundsicker* of Breitfurt, had emigrated in the year 1753 "to the American islands" [*in die amerikanische Insuln*] without previous manumission and permission of the government. Because of this his property was confiscated for the treasury. The Freifrau von Schorrenburg was notified that his property, which his brothers *Elias* and *Daniel Hundsicker* still possessed, also what he was to inherit from his mother (who was still living) was to be put into arrest, and if such had devolved upon him, it should be conveyed to the proper land office after deduction of the manumission and other taxes. (Decree of the Zweibrücken Government, September 1, 1767).

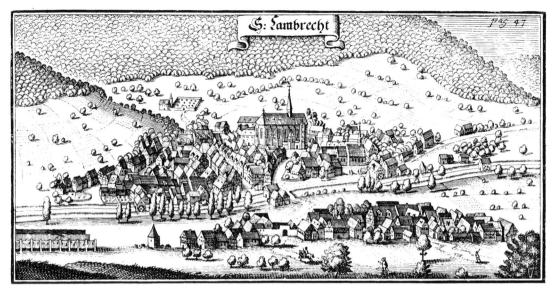

St. Lambrecht in the Palatinate. From Merian, Topographia Germaniae *(1672).*

6. An inheritance of 3 florins, 8 batzen and 8 pennies, which had fallen to *Philipp Frey,* native of Hornbach, was confiscated, since he had gone to America. It was finally awarded to the emigrant's brother, *Paul Frey* of Böckweiler, on account of a claim of 17 florins on the emigrant (Document of the Zweibrücken Government, August 26, 1778). Possibly the *Philipp Frey* who arrived at Philadelphia in 1754 (Strassburger-Hinke, List 221 A-C).

7. The property of *Christian Scherrer,* formerly the winter schoolmaster at Frohnhofen, who had "absconded" to America, was declared forfeited to the treasury (Document of the Zweibrücken Government, May 28, 1765).

8. The Zweibrücken Government decreed on October 15, 1776, that the property of *Johannes Keller* of Böckweiler, who had gone to America, was to be collected for the treasury. At the same time the petition from a married couple at Waldmohr, that it be granted to them, was rejected. Since a great number of persons bearing the name *Johannes Keller* emigrated before 1776, it is impossible to identify this particular emigrant in the ship lists.

9. By decree of the Zweibrücken Government of October 18, 1768, the present and future property of *Elisabeth Meyer,* daughter of *Hans Georg Michel* of Dellfeld, was declared forfeited to the treasury. The reason given was that she had gone away "to America" [*in Americam*] about 16 or 17 years ago with *Georg Meyer* of Kleinsteinhausen, whom she had married in the year 1751, without previous permission and payment of emigration tax. Possibly *Georg Meyer,* listed twice, arriving at Philadelphia October 4, 1752 (Strassburger-Hinke, List 187 C).

10. The property of *Hans Georg Schwartz* of Contwig, who had gone away to America [*nacher America*]

about the year 1752 without previous manumission, was exempted from the property confiscation, but on the said property 7 florins hd to be paid for manumission and the tithe (tenth penny) paid on the exported property (which had amounted to 21 florins). Possibly *Hans Jerg Schwartz,* arriving at Philadelphia September 23, 1752 (Strassburger-Hinke, List 182 C).

11. The Zweibrücken Collection Office announced in a document dated July 13, 1762, that because of the confiscation of the property of *Jakob Simon* of Pfeffelbach, who had gone to America, the appropriate sealed document would be delivered in duplicate to the authorities. Since before 1762 at least three different persons bearing the name of *Jacob Simon* appear in the ship lists of the port of Philadelphia, the arrival of this particular emigrant is at the present time impossible to establish clearly.

12. The heirs of *Wilhelm Müller* of Konken petitioned in 1779 for the release of his confiscated property. *Wilhelm Müller,* a son of the inhabitant [*Gemeindsmann*] *Adam Müller* at Konken and of his wife *Anna Margaretha Jung,* had according to the documents gone to Pennsylvania about 1747-1748. His share of the property in an inheritance amounting to 219 florins, 13 batzen and 2 1/6 pence had been turned over to a guardian for administration. In 1782 the government was informed by the Collection Office that this confiscated property would be turned over at the assessed price on assurance of the taxes to the point of canceling the capital. The government thereupon, by decree of May 23, 1782, released to the brothers and sisters *Jacob, Nickel,* and *Maria Magdalena Müller* the properties belonging to their absent brother at the assessed price.

13. According to a report of the Village Mayor at Kübelberg and the opinion expressed by the Oberamt

73

Lautern, January 14, 1772, *Peter Molter* (subject of Dittweiler) and his wife *Margaretha Catharina Clos* of Miesau, both vassals of the Electoral Palatinate, had gone on April 15, 1766, to "the New Land or Pennsylvania" [*das neue Land oder Pennsylvanien*] without receiving permission or manumission and leaving behind debts of 100 florins. But Peter Molter possessed from his maternal reservation or inheritance, after payment of the debts [*deductis passivis*] 9 florins, 44 ½ kreuzer. His wife, however, had 194 florins and 16 kreuzer, which had fallen to her share after the death of her father. Her inheritance was in the hands of her brothers and sisters in Niedermiesau. Both partial legacies made together 204 florins and ½ kreuzer. The Oberamt Lautern inquired whether this portion of the inheritance over 204 florins was to be confiscated.

14. According to an extract from the protocols of the Oberamt Zweibrücken dated October 19, 1763, the children of the deceased *Philipp Weber* of Mauschbach by his second marriage, i.e., *Daniel Weber, Georg Weber,* and *Jacob Weber,* had gone to America 13 years previously. On August 10, 1763 the properties of the three children were sold at public auction following an order of May 17, 1763, and 435 florins, 12 batzen and 8 pence were realized from the sale, for which sum the administrator received 27 florins 13 pence, leaving a balance of 408 florins, 7 batzen and 11 pence. The Zweibrücken Government ruled on August 10, 1765, that the mother was to have the usufruct of these 408 florins during her lifetime, but after her death they were then to be confiscated for the treasury. Perhaps *Johann Daniel Weber,* who arrived on the Ship *Isaac* and took the oath of allegiance on September 27, 1749 (Strassburger-Hinke, List 138 C). It is questionable if the *Jacob Weber* who arrived on the Ship *Dragon,* September 26, 1749 (Strassburger-Hinke, List 137 C) was a member of this family, since he was accompanied by *Valentin* and *Johannes Weber,* probably relatives, who are not documented in the above proceedings.

15. By decree of the Zweibrücken Government dated August 4, 1777, the property of *Samuel* and *Friedrich Becker,* sons of *Aaron Becker* of Oberauerbach, which had been confiscated for the treasury because they had gone to America in 1771, was released to *Bernhard Gachot* of Oberauerbach in instalments to be paid over a period of eight years.

16. By decree of September 15, 1767, the Zweibrücken Government made disposal of the property of *Friedrich Conrad* of Baumholder, then established in Virginia. According to this his property, part of it exported, part still in the country, totaled the sum of 1809 florins, 7 batzen and 4 pence, on which the sextile tax was to be paid to the sum of 301 florins, 8 batzen and 18 pence. The balance was however to be confiscated and to be lent out to court-appointed securities. Since the date of emigration is not stated, it is impossible to identify this emigrant with either *Friedrich Conrad* who arrived at Philadelphia in 1749, or with *Johann Friedrich Conrad* who landed in 1751.

17. According to an extract from the Amt Nohfelden protocols of 1738 and a report from Oberamt Nohfelden dated April 29, 1739, the sons of *Johannes Stautt (Staud)* of Wolfersweiler, *Johannes* a hunter lad [*Jägerbursche*] and *Johann Michael* a linenweaver, had gone to America "about 1737-1738 for their trade and their profession" [*um 1737/1738 auf ihrem Handwerck und ihrer Profession*]. The former had nothing, but the latter had taken along 24 reichstaler or 36 florins as trvaeling money.

18. The widow of *Jacob Seibert* of Eitzweiler stated through her son Bernhard, that her son, i.e., Bernhard's brother *Jacob Seibert,* a vassal of the government, who had learned the linenweaver's trade (according to a report of the Amt Nohfelden dated 1738) had gone to America taking with him 50 florins. *Johan Jacob Seibert* took the oath of allegiance in Philadelphia September 9, 1738 (Strassburger-Hinke, List 53 A-C).

19. According to an extract from the Amt Nohfelden protocols of 1739, *Martin Schreyer* had sent his youngest son *Johann Adam Schreyer* to America, without manumission and payment of emigration tax. The emigrant had learned the shoemaker trade and received 50 florins as traveling money.

20. *Jacob Staud (Stautt),* son of *Abraham Staud* of Gimbweiler (Kreis Birkenfeld), had gone to America in 1738 taking along 50 florins as traveling money. The bailiff Hautt received the order that on return of the emigrant manumission and the tithe (tenth penny) were to be paid. Nevertheless the father wanted likewise to go to America.

21. *Matthes Gisch,* stepson of *Andreas Kniebes* of Ausweiler, had likewise gone away (to America) in 1733 and had received from his stepfather 40 florins for the journey. *Mattes Gisch* took the oath of allegiance at Philadelphia, September 18, 1733 (Strassburger-Hinke, List 32 A-C).

22. Likewise *Christian Lauer* of Hirstein, son of *Peter Lauer,* a vassal of the Kellenbach government, a blacksmith by trade, had emigrated to America in 1733, in order to perfect himself in his trade, and he took along 4 reichstaler as traveling money. *Christian Lauer* took the oath of allegiance at Philadelphia, September 18, 1733 (Strassburger-Hinke, List 32 A-C).

From all these cases it follows that not only the permitted but also the clandestine emigration from the Duchy of Zweibrücken must have been unusually large. This can be ascribed as much to the wanderlust of the population as to the bad economic outlook in the area. In Württemberg, which also produced a strong emigration to America in the 18th Century, conditions were similar.

74

Palatine Emigrants to America from the Oppenheim Area, 1742-1749

Translated and Edited by Don Yoder

[The following emigrant list is translated from the article entitled "Amerika-Auswanderer aus dem Oberamt Oppenheim 1742-49," in *Hessische Familienkunde,* XXV (1968), columns 342-345. The towns and villages mentioned can be found on the map South of the City of Mainz, in the area known today as Rheinhessen, part of the present German state of Rheinland-Pfalz.—EDITOR.]

The protocols of the former Electoral Palatine Oberamt of Oppenheim, deposited in the City Archives at Oppenheim on the Rhine, contain some names of em-

igrants from the first half of the 18th Century. They specify, however, only the permission to emigrate, not the emigration itself. Most of those who intended to emigrate and who received permission, did in fact emigrate.[1] There were some who in spite of permission received did not manage to emigrate at the time, as the example of Wendel Runckel of Oberingelheim shows. In view of the scarcity of documentation for

[1] As usual in this series of articles, the names have been checked against the Philadelphia ship lists as given in Strassburger-Hinke, *Pennsylvania German Pioneers* (Norristown, Pennsylvania, 1934).

Oppenheim, from Merian's Topographia Germaniae (.

76

18th Century emigration, a source as important as the Oppenheim Protocols should not be neglected.

The former Electoral Palatine Oberamt of Oppenheim consisted of the city of Oppenheim, the market town of Nierstein, and the villages of Dexheim, Schwabsburg, Ober- and Niederingelheim, Daxweiler, Sauerschwabenheim, Grosswinternheim, Wackernheim, Freiweinheim, Bubenheim, Elsheim, Stadecken, and Essenheim. The very numerous emigrants from Essenheim are not included here, since they have already been published.[2]

EMIGRANTS FROM THE YEAR 1742

1. The Electoral Palatine government granted its subjects in Stadecken *Lorentz Bläss, Peter Westerberger, Johann Kiehl, Friedrich Mengel,* and *Johannes Daum* the permission to emigrate to Pennsylvania, "where they already have relatives living" [*all wo sie schon*

[2]Friedrich Krebs and Milton Rubincam, *Emigrants from the Palatinate to the American Colonies in the 18th Century* (Norristown, Pennsylvania, 1953).

Freunde wohnen haben], and handed over to them the manumission certificates. *Lorentz Place, Johannes Kühl, Johannes Domie, Frietz Mengel,* and *Peter Wasenburger* landed at Philadelphia on the Ship *Loyal Judith,* September 3, 1742 (Strassburger-Hinke, List 93A-C). In List A Bläss is listed as 44 years of age, Westerberger as 30, Kiehl as 29, Mengel as 48, and Daum as 40.

2. With a rescript dated April 17, 1742, *Friedrich Pfeil, Johann Lehn,* and *Jacob Winterheimer,* from Grosswinternheim, received permission to emigrate and landed at Philadelphia on the Ship *Loyal Judith,* September 3, 1742 (Strassburger-Hinke, List 93 A-C). In List A Pfeil is described as 50 years of age, Lehn as 40, and Winterheimer as 40.

3. According to a report from Oberingelheim dating from 1742, four subjects there, *Philips Odernheimer, Peter Weitzel, Ulrich Strassburger,* and the widow of *Nicolas Dörr,* are said to have "sent their grown sons to the New Land, a few weeks ago, and with the knowledge of the entire village gave each one of them 100 florins and various victuals for the trip. These sons were still subject to vassal duties and were even incorporated into the last conscription of young men" [*vor einigen Wochen ihre erwachsene und in Homagialpflichten stehende auch der letzt eingeschickten Conscription der jungen Mannschaft einverleibte Söhne ins neue Landt geschicket und jedem mit Wissen des ganzen Orths 100 fl nebst verschiedenen Victualien mit auff die Reiss gegeben*]. The village mayor of Oberingelheim had on this account to answer for them. Of the sons of the inhabitants named above, *Johannes Odernheimer, Johann Paul Weytzel, Johann Henrich Dörr,* and *Johann Andreas Strassburger* can be found as passengers on the emigrant ship *Loyal Judith,* arriving at Philadelphia, September 3, 1742 (Strassburger-Hinke, List 93 A-C).[3] List A gives Odernheimer's age as 22, Weitzel 26, Dörr 23, and Strassburger 25.

EMIGRANTS FROM THE YEAR 1743

4. On February 25, 1743, *Philips Hardt* of Niederingelheim received permission to emigrate upon payment of the tithe (tenth penny). He landed at Philadelphia on the Ship *Loyal Judith,* September 2, 1743 (Strassburger-Hinke, List 97A-C). List A gives his age as 50.

5. On the same day also *Nicolaus Runckel* and *Nicolaus Keller* of Wackernheim received permission to emigrate. They too appear in the ship lists on the *Loyal Judith,* September 2, 1743 (Strassburger-Hinke, List 97A-C). List A gives Runckel's age as 27, Keller's as 28.

[3]The last-named, who came to America the second time in October 1769 on the Ship *Minerva* (Strassburger-Hinke, List 276 C), was an ancestor of Ralph Beaver Strassburger, later president of the Pennsylvania German Society and responsible for publishing *Pennsylvania German Pioneers* edited by William J. Hinke.

Emigrants from the Year 1748

6. *Friedrich Ploz (Plotz)* and *Adam Imhäusser (Immenhauser)* from Stadecken on February 3, 1748, received permission to leave for the "Island of Pennsylvania" [*Insul Pinsylvaniam*], on payment of 15 and 10 florins respectively for buying out their vassalage and payment of the tithe (tenth penny). They landed at Philadelphia on the Ship *Hampshire* on September 7, 1748 (Strassburger-Hinke, List 118 A-C). List A gives Ploz's age as 36, Imhäusser's as 25.

7. *Franz Graff (Grove)* with wife and two children, *Bartel Krämer* with wife and five children, *Adam Weiss* with his wife, all of Grosswinternheim, and *Wilhelm Laymeister* with wife and children from Schwabenheim, were permitted to emigrate on payment of the tithe (tenth penny), on March 9, 1748. On the same date the propertyless residents *(Beisassen) Wolfgang Wolf* and *Hostermann* (?) of Grosswinternheim, were manumitted gratis. They landed at Philadelphia—*Frantz Grove, Johann Wilhelm Leymeister, Wolffgang Wulff, Hans Jacob Ostermann,* and *Johann Adam Weiss*—on the Ship *Hampshire,* September 7, 1748 (Strassburger-Hinke, List 118 A-C). List A gives Graff's age as 54, Laymeister's as 58, Wolf's as 36, and Ostermann's as 28.

8. *Johann Bischoff* from Grosswinternheim, who because of debt had to sell his propery and was not in condition to support himself, was granted permission to emigrate on March 29, 1748. He landed at Philadelphia with the aforenamed, on the Ship *Hampshire,* September 7, 1748 (Strassburger-Hinke, List 118 A-C). List A gives his age as 34.

9. *Johann Jacob Runckel* and *Friedrich Hammer,* from Wackernheim, were granted permission to emigrate on May 14, 1748. They had to pay 40 and 10 florins respectively for the permission. They landed at Philadelphia on the Ship *Hampshire,* September 7, 1748 (Strassburger-Hinke, List 118 A-C). List A gives Runckel's age as 27, Hammer's as 35.

10. *Christian Ramb* from Elsheim had to pay 43 florins for permission to emigrate, but could not be identified in the ship lists.

Emigrants from the Year 1749

11. *Philipp Haber* from Stadecken with wife and three children paid 54 florins for manumission on March 21, 1749, and 54 florins for the tithe (tenth penny). He landed at Philadelphia on the Ship *Isaac,* September 27, 1749 (Strassburger-Hinke, List 38 C).

12. *Nicolaus Reisinger* from Niederingelheim received permission to emigrate on April 16, 1749, on payment of the tithe (tenth penny), and arrived at Philadelphia on the Ship *Dragon,* September 26, 1749 (Strassburger-Hinke, List 137C).

13. *Adam Dörr, Anton Oster,* and *Wendel Runckel* of Oberingelheim received permission to emigrate on April 29, 1749, Dörr after payment of the tithe (tenth penny), Oster and Runckel gratis, since all three were "without property and of bad conduct" [*ohne Vermögen und schlechten Wandels*]. Dörr landed at Philadelphia on the Ship *St. Andrew,* September 9, 1749 (Strassburger-Hinke, List 128 C), Oster on the Ship *Dragon,* September 26, 1749 (Strassburger-Hinke, List 137 C). Runckel on the contrary did not emigrate and stayed in Oberingelheim, although the Oberamt was in favor of his removal, since he was "dissolute and poor" [*liederlich und arm*].[a]

14. *Friedrich Bohr* from Wackernheim had to pay a supplementary tax of 10 florins, received the permission to emigrate on May 14, 1749, and landed at Philadelphia on the Ship *St. Andrew,* September 9, 1749 (Strassburger-Hinke, List 128 C).

15. *Christian Meckel* from Elsheim, with wife and three children, was permitted to emigrate in return for a supplementary tax of 26 florins. Yet the inheritance of his eldest son, who stayed behind, was first to be secured and established as bearing interest. *Christian Meckel* landed at Philadelphia on the Ship *Isaac,* September 27, 1749 (Strassburger-Hinke, List 138 C).

16. *Philipp Merz,* locksmith in Nierstein, paid the tithe (tenth penny), receiving permission to emigrate on April 29, 1749, and landed at Philadelphia on the Ship *Edinburgh,* September 15, 1749 (Strassburger-Hinke, List 132 C).

17. *Ulrich Jordan (Jordte),* a Mennonite *(Wiedertäufer)* from the Haxthäuserhof near Ingelheim, likewise paid the tithe (tenth penny), and landed at Philadelphia on the Ship *St. Andrew,* September 9, 1749 (Strassburger-Hinke, List 128 C).

18. *Catharina Pfeiffer,* widow, Roman Catholic, from Essenheim, went "secretly" to Pennsylvania, without permission of the authorities, on account of which her assets which remained behind were laid under attachment.

19. *Johann Rooss* and *Abraham Schweickart* from Niederingelheim likewise went "secretly" to the New Land, and their property was confiscated too. One *Johanes Ross* arrived at Philadelphia on the Ship *Dragon,* September 26, 1749; the name following his in the ship list is *Friedrich Schweickhart* (Strassburger-Hinke, List 137 C).

[a] The Reverend John William Runkel (1749-1832), distinguished German Reformed minister who served, among others, the Carlisle, Lebanon, Frederick, Gettysburg, and New York charges, was born at Oberingelheim, April 28, 1749, son of Wendel and Julia Ann (Wertzel) Runkel. Wendel Runkel emigrated with his family in 1764, arriving at Philadelphia on the Ship *Richmond,* October 20, 1764 (Strassburger-Hinke, List 247 C). The son died at Gettysburg, November 5, 1832. He kept a copious journal of his life and ministry which is now unfortunately lost. It was used to prepare the biography in Henry Harbaugh, *The Fathers of the German Reformed Church in Europe and America,* second edition, II (1872), 284-308.—EDITOR.

Emigrants of the 18th Century from the Northern Palatinate

By FRIEDRICH KREBS

Translated and Edited by Don Yoder

[The materials included in this contribution of Dr. Krebs to our knowledge of the 18th Century emigration to America and its German background are translated from the article entitled, "Amerikaauswanderer des 18. Jahrhunderts aus der Nordpfalz," in *Nordpfälzer Geschichtsverein*, XXXV (1955), 63-66. Of particular interest are the many references to Mennonite families (Brubacher, Küntzi, Krebühl, and Ellenberger) who were for the most part "hereditary lessees" *(Erbbeständer)* on the estates of the area—the Münchhof near Albisheim, the Weierhof, the Otterberg estate at Rüssingen, and the Clauserhof near Ramsen. The towns and villages mentioned in the list can be located on the map in the vicinity of Kirchheim-Bolanden, South of Mainz and Northeast of Kaiserslautern.—EDITOR.]

EMIGRANTS FROM MARNHEIM

1. In the release of the property of *Susanne Armknecht,* widow of *Johannes Knauf* of Marnheim (married September 6, 1703, at Marnheim), dated May 2, 1747, it is stated of the sons *Johann Henrich Knauff* and *Anthon Knauff* (the latter born September 17, 1721, at Marnheim), that "both sons . . . went to the New Land or the socalled Pennsylvania four years ago" [*beyde Söhne . . . vor 4 Jahren in das neue Land oder sogenannte Pensylphania gezogen*]. *Johann Hennrich Knauff* and *Anthon Knauff* arrived at Philadelphia on the Ship *St. Andrew,* October 7, 1743 (Strassburger-Hinke, List 103 A-C). List A gives Henrich's age as 30, Anthon's as 20.

2. The inventory of *Maria Magdalena Knauff,* widow of *Lorentz Knauff* of Marnheim, dated November 21, 1777, lists among the sons and heirs *Johann Adam Knauff,* "aged 33 years, living in the New Land" [*alt 33 Jahr im neuen Land sich aufhaltend*]. *Johann Adam Knauff* was born at Marnheim, September 23, 1744.

3. An inventory of *Sophia Sybilla,* wife of *Philipp Debusz,* dated August 18, 1767, names among her sons: *Johann Daniel Debusz,* "who about sixteen years ago went to Pennsylvania in the single state" [*welcher vor ohngefähr 16 Jahren ledigen Standes in Pensylvanien gezogen*], and *Maria Elisabetha Debusz,* "who went out to Pennsylvania twelve years ago in the single state" [*welche aus vor 12 Jahr ledigen Standes in Pensylvanien gezogen*]. *Daniel Debus* arrived at Philadelphia on the Ship *Sandwich,* November 30, 1750 (Strass-

burger-Hinke, List 160 C). Note also that a *Daniel Debus* (aged 28) arrived in company with *Jacob Debus* (aged 26) and *Lodwick Debus* (aged 36) on the Ship *St. Andrew,* October 7, 1743, List 103 A-C; cf. *supra*, No. 1). In the Reformed church register of Marnheim from this period no entries relative to the Debusz family could be located.

EMIGRANTS FROM ALBISHEIM

4. The inventory of *Anna Maria,* widow of *Tobias Trescher* of Albisheim, dated March 2, 1743, lists a daughter *Anna Maria,* "wife of *Jost Diel* who is in Pennsylvania" [*Jost Dielen Ehefrau so in Pensylvanien*]. *Jost Diehl,* son of *Sebastian Diehl* of Offenheim, had married at Albisheim, January 13, 1728, *Anna Maria,* daughter of *Tobias Drescher.* *Jost Diehl* arrived at Philadelphia on the Ship *Robert and Alice,* September 3, 1739 (Strassburger-Hinke, List 71 A-C).

5. The inventory of *Jakob Racke,* inhabitant at Albisheim, dated February 5, 1767, lists two sons of his first marriage, *Johann Philipp Racke* and *Henrich Caspar Racke* as being in Pennsylvania. *Henrich Caspar Racke* was born at Albisheim January 9, 1722, son of *Jakob* and *Anna Margaretha Racke; Johann Philipp* was born there of the same parents, February 12, 1736. *Henrich Caspar Racke* arrived at Philadelphia on the Ship *St. Andrew,* September 9, 1749 (Strassburger-Hinke, List 128 C). *Johann Philipp Racke* arrived on the Ship *Britannia,* September 26, 1764 (Strassburger-Hinke, List 245 C).

6. *Jacob Brubacher,* who has been cited in a previous article as the father of a son *Abraham* who according to an inventory dated 1763 was in Pennsylvania, was hereditary lessee [*Erbbeständer*], under the local government, of the socalled Münchhof near Albisheim. Possibly *Aberham (sic) Brübacher,* who arrived on the Ship *St. Andrew,* September 9, 1749 (Strassburger-Hinke, List 128 C).

EMIGRANTS FROM SIPPERSFELD

7. In an inventory dated October 8, 1793, of *Anna Maria Scholl,* born at Sippersfeld, who died single at Kerzenheim in September 1793, the question comes up of "the sister of the decedent *Margreta,* wife of *Martin Seewald* of Sippersfeld, who had gone to America about 30 years ago and disappeared" [*vor ohngefehr 30 Jahren nach Amerika gezogenen und verschollenen Schwester der Erblasserin Margreta, des Martin Seewalds von Sippersfeld Ehefrau*]. According to the Lutheran church register *Martin Seewald,* son of *Velten Seewald* of Sippersfeld, had married *Maria Margretha,* daughter of *Theobald Scholl* of Sippersfeld on December 22, 1744, at Sippersfeld. *Martin Seewald* arrived at Philadelphia on the Ship *Hero,* October 27, 1764 (Strassburger-Hinke, List 248 C).

8. An inventory dated December 5, 1766, of *Daniel Müller,* widower, who died in 1766 at Sippersfeld, cites among his children a daughter *Catharina,* "who went to Pennsylvania in the year 1764" [*welche anno 1764 in Pensylvanien gezogen*].

EMIGRANTS FROM DANNENFELS

9. A release of the property of *Johann Melchior Ruppert* of Dannenfels, dated February 25, 1766, cites among his children a son *Johann Henrich Ruppert* as being in Pennsylvania. Possibly *Henry Rubert,* who arrived at Philadelphia on the Ship *Jacob,* October 2, 1749 (Strassburger-Hinke, List 140 C).

EMIGRANTS FROM BREUNIGWEILER

10. A guardian's account (1776-1780) "about the property of *Peter Weissmann* of Breunigweiler, who has already been in the New Land some twenty and

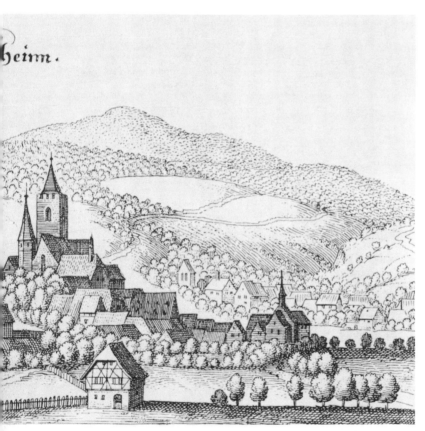

Dürckheim in the Palatinate from Merian's Topographia Germaniae *(1672).*

more years" [*uber des schon ettlich und 20 Jahr im neuen Land sich aufhaltenden Peter Weissmanns Vermögen*], besides a manumission certificate of *Peter Weissmann* dated July 19, 1754, allows us to assume the emigration date at about 1754. This is probably the *Peter Weissmann* who arrived at Philadelphia on the Ship *Edinburgh,* September 30, 1754 (Strassburger-Hinke, List 220 A-C), where his name follows that of *Conrath Enders* (cf. *infra,* No. 11). *Peter Weissmann* was born October 16, 1729, at Sippersfeld, son of the miller *Peter Weissmann* of Breunigweiler.

11. An inventory of *Maria Enders,* widow of *Henrich Enders* of Breunigweiler, dated October 3, 1797, names among the children a *Leonhard Enders,* "at this time in his 33rd year, who long ago journeyed to America, but of whom nothing has been heard for many years" [*dermahlen im 33. Jahr, welcher längst nach Amerika gereist, aber auch in vielen Jahren nichts von sich hören lassen*].

EMIGRANTS FROM WEIERHOF[1]

12. A property list of *Johannes Künzi* of Weierhof, dated August 3, 1785, says of him "that he went to Pennsylvania thirteen years ago" [*dass er vor 13 Jahr nach Pennsilvanien gegangen*]. *Johannes Kintzi* arrived at Philadelphia on the Ship *Crawford,* October 16, 1772 (Strassburger-Hinke, List 296 C). According to an affidavit he died in Autumn 1777 in the Manor [Township] area of Lancaster County, Pennsylvania. He must have been a Mennonite, since the affidavit came from *Christian Hirschy,* preacher [*Lehrer*] of the Manor Mennonite congregation.

13. A property transfer of *Anna,* widow of *Michel Grebühl* of Weierhof, dated October 25, 1752, names among her sons a *Jakob Krebühl* as being in Pennsylvania. He is possibly the *Jakob Crebil* who landed at Philadelphia on the Ship *Mortonhouse,* August 17, 1729 (Strassburger-Hinke, List 9 A-C). Additional material has been published on him in the *Nordpfälzer Geschichtsverein,* XXXIV (1954).

14. A property list of *Elisabetha Krebühl,* daughter of *Johannes Krebühl* of Weierhof, dated April 25, 1739, who died in the single state in the beginning of 1739, names among her brothers and sisters a *Peter Krebühl,* "who went to the New Land four years ago" [*welcher vor 4 Jahren in das neue Land zog*].

[1] Weierhof, near Kirchheim-Bolanden, is an important Palatine Mennonite center. Originally a monastery estate, it was given in hereditary lease in 1682 to Peter Crayenbühl (Krehbiel) under the elector of the Palatinate. According to the lease the lessee and his family were granted the privilege of holding Mennonite worship within the family, but without the right to establish a congregation. In 1706 the area came under the jurisdiction of Nassau-Weilburg and the congregation, which drew together Mennonites from the villages and estates of the area, took on formal character at that time. For the history of the settlement, see Christian G. Neff, "Weierhof," in *The Mennonite Encyclopedia,* IV, 911-913. For a brief history of the Krehbiel (Graybill) family, originally from Grosshöchstetten in Canton Bern, Switzerland, see *The Mennonite Encyclopedia,* III, 235-238.—EDITOR.

EMIGRANTS FROM RAMSEN

15. Of *Conrad Marent,* citizen at Ramsen, it is said in a document dated March 8, 1766, that "with his wife and children, he left here in the year 1764, after receiving manumission, and went to Cayenne in New France" [*mit seiner Frau und Kindern albereits anno 1764 nach erhaltener Manumission von hier ab und nach Cajenne in Neufranckreich gezogen*].

EMIGRANTS FROM RUSSINGEN

16. In a property transfer of the Mennonite *Ulrich Ellenberger,*[2] hereditary lessee of the Otterberg farm property at Rüssingen, to his son *Rudolph Ellenberger,* dated June 9, 1757, and in the estate inventory dated October 7, 1766, it is stated that two sons from his second marriage by the name of *Ullrich* and *Peter Ellenberger* "went to Pennsylvania" [*in Pensylvanien gezogen*]. *Ullrich* and *Peter Ellenberger* arrived at Philadelphia on the Ship *St. Andrew,* September 9, 1749 (Strassburger-Hinke, List 128 C).

EMIGRANTS FROM DREISEN

17. Here there are several documents about the reprimand for debt (i.e., settlement of the debt payment through the crediting of the said persons) of *Adam Siegel,* who went to New England (document dated May 27, 1774); further a document about the reprimand for debt of *Christian Emig* who was going to New England and the debts on his property (document dated May 28, 1774); and a document (reprimand for debt) of the widow of *Ludwig Löwenberg* of Dreisen, who was going to New England (document dated May 28, 1774). A similar document treats of *Daniel Zittel* of Dreisen. *Adam Siegel, Christian Ehmig,* and *Daniel Zittel* all landed at Philadelphia on the Ship *Sally,* October 31, 1774 (Strassburger-Hinke, List 322 C), along with *Peter, Philipp,* and *Friedrich Löwenberg. Philipp* and *Friedrich Löwenberg* are entered in the Reformed church register of Dreisen as children of *Ludwig Löwenberg,* inhabitant at Dreisen, and his wife *Christina. Friedrich Löwenberg* was born September 21, 1740, and *Philipp Löwenberg* was born May 13, 1758, both at Dreisen. With the sons and the widow *Christina* there possibly came other children of hers, *Elias Löwenberg* (born January 10, 1761), *Maria Catharina Sophia Löwenberg* (born February 19, 1763), and *Christoph August Ludwig Löwenberg* (born February 9, 1766), who as minors (under 16 years) do not appear in the ship lists.

EMIGRANTS FROM CLAUSERHOF (NEAR RAMSEN)

18. A property list of the deceased wife, *Anna,* of *Jakob Krebühl,* hereditary lessee of the Clauserhof, dated May 30, 1793, names among her sons a son *Johannes,* "single, 19 years old, being in America" [*ledig, 19 Jahr alt, in America sich aufhaltend*].

[2] Ulrich Ellenberger was the elder (minister) in charge of the Mennonite congregation of Weierhof and vicinity during the middle of the 18th Century. See *The Mennonite Encyclopedia,* IV, 912.—EDITOR.

American Emigration from Baden-Durlach in the Years 1749-1751

By FRIEDRICH KREBS

Translated and Edited by Don Yoder

Along with other areas in Southwest Germany and Switzerland, the Protestant areas of Baden produced significant emigration to the New World in the 18th Century. Among these was the small duchy of Baden-Durlach in the vicinity of Karlsruhe. The Protocols of the Court Council and Revenue Office of Baden-Durlach *(Hofrats- und Rentkammerprotokolle)*, in the Baden State Archives *(Generallandesarchiv Karlsruhe)*, contain many petitions for emigration from which the following list of emigrants to the New World, principally Pennsylvania, has been compiled.

The procedure for emigration was as follows. The petitioner appealed to the Court Council *(Hofrat)* for permission to emigrate, then his appeal was turned over to the Revenue Office *(Rentkammer)*, which worked out the manumission taxes. When these were settled, manumission was proclaimed and the petitioner was free to leave, making his way down the Rhine to Rotterdam, from whence the emigrant ships sailed.

From the standpoint of the social history of the emigration, the reasons cited by the petitioners in Section 2 (1750), mostly bad economic conditions, are particularly valuable. The position taken by the authorities toward the emigration is also graphically portrayed. Allowed to leave were people of modest property, bad reputation, and those from villages already overpopulated. In particular cases even the personal decision of the margrave was invoked.

[The sources for this composite article are (1) "Amerika-Auswanderer aus Baden-Durlach im Jahre 1749," in *Badische Heimat*, XLII (1962), 133-134; and (2) "Studien zur Amerikaauswanderung aus Baden-Durlach für das Jahr 1751," in *Badische Heimat*, XXXVI (1956), 155-156. The emigrant list of 1750 is published here for the first time, although it is also scheduled to appear later this year in *Badische Heimat*. The 1749 list was also published, with some additional names from the Palatinate, in the article "Einige Amerika-Auswanderer des 18. Jahrhunderts," in the *Senftenegger Monatsblatt für Genealogie und Heraldik*, V (1961), cols. 123-126. The 1751 emigrants were also published, without the protocol source references, and unfortunately without umlauts, under the too-inclusive title "Emigrants from Baden-Durlach to Pennsylvania, 1749-1755," in the *National Genealogical Society Quarterly*, XLV (1957), 30-31.

The list of petitioners for emigration in the year 1752 has already been published in the article "Pennsylvania Dutch Pioneers from Baden-Durlach: 1752," in *The Pennsylvania Dutchman*, VIII:4 (Summer-Fall 1957), 48.—EDITOR.]

EMIGRANTS OF THE YEAR 1749

1. *Johannes Bischoff*, citizen and resident of Dietlingen, wanted to emigrate to Pennsylvania. The Oberamt Pforsheim had no objections to his proposal, because there was no lack of citizen residents in Dietlingen. He was therefore manumitted with his wife and two children by the Revenue Office *(Rentkammer)* on payment of 50 florins (Protocol 1319 No. 1185; Protocol 839 No. 724). Perhaps he is identical with the *Johannes Bischoff* who arrived at Philadelphia on the Ship *Duke of Wirtenberg*, October 16, 1751 (Strassburger-Hinke List 176C).

2. *Margarethe Sturm*, widow of *Johannes Sturm*, of Unterwössingen, also was permitted to emigrate to Pennsylvania, with her four children, on payment of 25 florins manumission tax. One *Johannes Storm* landed at Philadelphia on the Ship *Lydia*, October 19, 1749 (Strassburger-Hinke List 142C). Perhaps he is a son of this family, since among the other passengers were Bastian, Bertsch, and Kautz (q.v.).

3. The widow of *Michael Höris*, onetime resident at Stein, was likewise permitted to emigrate to Pennsylvania on payment of the taxes (Pr. 840 No. 910; Pr. 1320 No. 1660).

4. *Michael Bastian*, magistrate *(Beisitzer)* of Berghausen, wanted to go to Pennsylvania; he was manumitted with his wife and two children on payment of seven florins. Further, *Jacob Bertsch*, citizen and shoemaker at Göbrichen, was manumitted gratis on account of his propertyless status (Pr. 840 No. 915, 916; Pr. 1320 Nos. 1792, 1793). *Michael Bastian* and *Jacob Bertsch* took the oath of allegiance October 19, 1749, arriving at Philadelphia on the Ship *Lydia* (Strassburger-Hinke, List 142C).

5. *Ulrich Britz*, tenant of the sawmill at Russheim, wanted also to go to Pennsylvania, and was manumitted with his wife and five children on payment of 20 florins manumission tax (Pr. 1320 No. 1803).

6. *Adam Renker(t)*, of Opfingen, was likewise manumitted with wife and three children on payment of

20 florins (Pr. 1321 No. 2116). Possibly *G. Adam Renecker,* who took the oath of allegiance August 15, 1750, arriving at Philadelphia on the Ship *Royal Union* (Strassburger-Hinke, List 149C).

7. *Anna Maria Saltzer,* wife of the stonemason *Saltzer* of Müllheim, was manumitted with her husband on payment of 12 florins (Pr. 1321 No. 2115).

8. *Georg Adam Gorenflo,* inhabitant of Friedrichstal, with his wife, and *Isaac Friedrich Gorenflo,* and *Philipp Onofre Gorenflo* from Friedrichstal also applied for emigration; their goal was Philadelphia. *Jor Adam Goranslo* (so misread by Hinke) arrived at Philadelphia September 28, 1749, on the Ship *Ann* (Strassburger-Hinke, List 139C).[1]

9. *Adam Bentzlin (Benzle)* of Kleinsteinbach also wanted to go to Pennsylvania with his wife Constantia. Because of their propertyless status he had to pay only six florins emigration tax (Pr. 840 No. 912; Pr. 1320 No. 1790).

10. *Johan Georg Säemann,* subject at Dietenhausen, likewise applied for emigration to Pennsylvania (Pr. 840 No. 913). *Johan Georg Säman* is listed among the passengers on the Ship *Duke of Wirtenberg,* arriving at Philadelphia, October 16, 1751 (Strassburger-Hinke, List 176C).

11. In the case of *Jacob* and *Michael Kautz,* two unmarried brothers from Göbrichen (Pr. 840 No. 1036), there is, it is true, no goal of emigration given, but they are surely identical with the *Jacob* and *Michael Kautz* who landed at Philadelphia on the Ship *Lydia,* taking the oath of allegiance there on October 19, 1749. They were manumitted gratis on payment of doubled expedition taxes (Pr. 1320 No. 1835). In the ship's lists of the port of Philadelphia their names are given incorrectly as *Jacob and Michael Kantz* (Strassburger-Hinke, List 142C).

12. Permission to emigrate to Pennsylvania was also requested by three residents of Blankenloch, *Theobald Nagel, Hans Georg Schauffler,* and *Michael Lehmann* (Pr. 842 No. 2792), who also were manumitted (Pr. 1324 Nos. 4855, 4856, and 4857). *Dewalt Nagel* arrived at Philadelphia on the Ship *Phoenix,* August 28, 1750 (Strassburger-Hinke, List 154C); *Hs. Georg Schauffler* on the *Brotherhood,* November 3, 1750 (Strassburger-Hinke, List 159C); *Michael Lehman* on the *Phoenix,* August 28, 1750 (Strassburger-Hinke, List 154C).

13. *Maria Magdalena,* widow of *Andreas Souz,* inhabitant at Friedrichstal, was permitted finally to go to Pennsylvania, with her seven minor children (Pr. 840 No. 1956). Perhaps *Johan Jacob Sutz,* who arrived on the Ship *Ann,* landing at Philadelphia September 28, 1749 (Strassburger-Hinke, List 139C), was a son of this family.[2]

14. *Caspar Tieffenbach (Diefenbacher),* who was manumitted for his four children, on payment of six florins, was able to emigrate to Pennsylvania. *Caspar Dieffenbacher* arrived at Philadelphia on the Ship *Edinburgh,* August 13, 1750 (Strassburger-Hinke, List 148C), although there was a *Caspar Derffenbecher* who arrived in 1749 (List 139C).[3]

15. *Margaretha Elsser, Barbara Schmied,* and *Catharina Zimmermann,* three widows from Russheim, who wanted urgently to get to Pennsylvania, were quickly dispatched (Pr. 1319 No. 841; Pr. 1320 Nos. 1696, 1697, 1698). While in most ship lists women were not listed, it may be significant that on the Ship *Ann,* arriving at Philadelphia September 28, 1749, there was a *Petter Elser* listed with three *Zimmermans,* and *Gorenflo* and *Souz (Sutz),* q.v. (Strassburger-Hinke, List 139C).

16.. *Johann Michael Jung,* blacksmith by trade, from Dietlingen, was in 1749, by personal decision of the Margrave, graciously repatriated as citizen in his home village of Dietlingen. As a sixteen-year-old youth he had gone in 1744 with his parents *Johann Philipp Jung* and his brothers and sisters to Pennsylvania. On the way he had lost both parents and some of his brothers and sisters and along with the passengers of two ships had fallen into the hands of Spanish pirates. After liberation by the English he was provided with passes and traveling money for Holland. He finally asked to

[1]The Goranflo family is well documented in the volume by Oskar Hornung, *Friedrichstal: Geschichte einer Hugenottengemeinde zur 250-Jahrfeier* (Karlsruhe: C. F. Müller, 1949). The town, a short distance north of Karlsruhe, was founded in 1699 for French Protestant refugees, some of them Walloons from the French-speaking provinces of the Spanish (later Austrian) Netherlands. *Jacques Gorenflo* was the mayor of Friedrichstal, 1699-1710; he was also schoolmaster and the acknowledged leader of the colonists (p. 223). His sons, *Pierre* and *Jacques,* settled about 1710 on the Karlsbacher Hof near the village (p. 222 ff.), returning to Friedrichstal in 1721 (p. 231). *Georg Adam Gorenflo* was born April 12, 1720, son of *Pierre* and *Anna Katharina (Pierrot) Gorenflo,* and grandson of the pioneer Jacques (p. 230). While Georg Adam Gorenflo did emigrate, it appears that the other two members of the family who applied for emigration at the same time, remained in Friedrichstal. *Philipp Onofer Gorenflo* became a citizen in 1754 (p. 157), and in 1785, "old *Isaac Friedrich Gorenflo*" was listed as living in the Hirschgasse in the town (p. 313). The book lists at least twenty-five members of the Gorenflo family who emigrated to America in the 19th Century, from 1834 to 1894 (pp. 215-216). The family name, which has achieved a fantastic number of variant spellings (see p. 194), may derive from the French place-name *Gorenflos,* between Abbeville and Amiens in the Department of the Somme (p. 176).—EDITOR.

[2]*Andres Souz* is listed among the junior citizens *(jeune bourgeois)* of Friedrichstal in 1718 (Hornung, *op. cit.,* p. 156), and as having contributed two gulden toward building the town church in 1725 (p. 88). Five members of the *Sutz* family emigrated to North America in the period 1880-1903, all of them farmers (p. 220).—EDITOR.
[3]The wife of *Caspar Tiefenbach* followed with her children in the year 1752. According to the protocols, they were so poor that the community declared itself ready to advance the travel money (Pr. 853 No. 952, Pr. 1336 No. 1055). See "Pennsylvania Dutch Pioneers from Baden-Durlach: 1752," by Friedrich Krebs, translated by Don Yoder, in *The Pennsylvania Dutchman,* VIII:4 (Summer-Fall 1957), 48.—EDITOR.

84

Air view of Friedrichstal, Huguenot settlement in Baden, from which several families emigrated to Pennsylvania. From Oskar Hornung, "Friedrichstal: Geschichte einer Hugenottengemeinde zur 250-Jahrfeier" (Karlsruhe, 1949).

be taken back in his home village as citizen and to be able to practice his trade. This was granted him in light of the fact that he had followed his parents against their will. Such was one emigrant's fate in the 18th Century (Pr. 842, No. 2740).

EMIGRANTS OF THE YEAR 1750

17. *Johannes Reuschle (Reuschlin)* of Blankenloch, vassal subject, with wife and two children, was permitted to go away to Pennsylvania on payment of a tax of 15 florins (Pr. 845 No. 35, Pr. 1325 No. 208).

18. *Simon Merckle (Mercklin)* with wife and children, *Jacob Merckle (Mercklin)*, and *Jacob Wentz, Jr.*, all of Graben, were permitted to leave for Pennsylvania on payment of a manumission tax of 12, 24, and 14 florins respectively (Pr. 845 No. 268, Pr. 1325 Nos. 723-725). *Jacob Merckle, Simon Merckle,* and *Jacob Wentz* arrived at Philadelphia on the Ship *Edinburgh,* August 13, 1750 (Strassburger-Hinke, List 148C).

19. From the same town (Graben) were also released to go to Pennsylvania *Peter Lind's* two eldest daughters, *Eva Elisabetha Lind* and *Margaretha Lind* (Pr. 845 No. 409, Pr. 1326 No. 1011).

20. Finally also from Graben *Johannes Hafner* (on payment of 25 florins tax), *Michael Heile (Heinle)* (on payment of 25 florins tax), and *Wendel Renninger* (on payment of 34 florins tax). These were, according to a report of the Oberamt "all such, of whom we can well be rid" [*solche insgesambt, deren man wohl entübrigt werden könne*] (Pr. 845 No. 488, Pr. 1326 Nos. 1114-1116). *Johannes Haffner, Wendel Renninger,* and *Michael Heinle* arrived at Philadelphia on the Ship *Edinburgh,* August 13, 1750 (Strassburger-Hinke, List 148C).

21. *Jacob Koch* of Berghausen was manumitted for 17 florins, to go to Pennsylvania (Pr. 845 No. 406, Pr. 1326 No. 1010). He arrived at Philadelphia on the Ship *Edinburgh,* August 13, 1750 (Strassburger-Hinke, List 148C).

22. Of *Georg Ludwig Pallmer,* the single barber *(Bader)* of Linkenheim, who likewise wanted to go to Pennsylvania, and whose request was recommended by Oberamt and Hofrat, I could find nothing either in the Revenue Office Protocols or in the Ship Lists of the Port of Philadelphia.

23. *Michael Krämer,* the 65-year-old citizen of Singen, who wanted to go to Pennsylvania with his 66-year-old wife *Margaretha,* was not manumitted, because he decided to stay in the country (Pr. 845 No. 315, Pr. 1325 No. 701).

24. *Johann Georg Reyling (Raylin)* of Singen, was allowed to go to Pennsylvania with his wife and 17-year-old stepdaughter *Anna Maria Farr,* upon payment of 30 florins manumission tax.

25. *Michael Moll,* inhabitant of Niefern, who was in debt and had not acquired the reputation of a good manager, was able to go to Pennsylvania on payment of the manumission tax of 17 florins (Pr. 845 No. 546, Pr. 1326 No. 1191).

26. In the case of *Matthäus Eurich,* vassal citizen's son of Dürrn, on whose departure the government had agreed, because his property consisted of only 50 florins (Pr. 845 No. 447), I could find nothing on manumission in the Revenue Office Protocols, but he appears to have landed in Philadelphia in 1750 on the Ship *Royal Union* as *Matheas Eyrich* (Strassburger-Hinke, List 149C).

27. *Adam Reichenbacher,* citizen at Söllingen, likewise wanted to go to the "new land" (America); his property amounted to 265 florins after taxes. However, he did not want to leave with his wife, since he lived with her in a constant state of altercation. According to the report of the Oberamt Durlach he was "not of the best house, consequently little benefit is to be expected of him for the Margrave, and still less for the community" [*nicht zum besten Hause, folglich wenig Nutzen vor Serenissimum noch weniger aber vor die Comune von ihm zu hoffen seye*]. After clar-

ification of his marital affairs before the marriage court, and dissolution of the marriage, it was agreed that he could be manumitted on payment of 27 florins (Pr. 845 No. 408, Pr. 1326 No. 1649).

28. There were great difficulties in the case of *Hans Georg Dillmann* and *Florian Brunn*, inhabitants of Deutschneureut, who likewise wanted to leave for Pennsylvania. The authorities were unwilling to let them leave on account of their considerable property. The former wanted to leave in spite of the Oberamt's advice to the contrary, "because he can no longer support himself with his family" [*weil er sich mit seiner Familie nicht mehr nähren könne*]. The latter gave the same reason for emigration, that after yearly duties and payment of shepherds to avert damage from wild game, hardly anything was left over for him to live on. Both requests were finally denied by decision of the Margrave *(resolutio Serenissimi)*, because they had wanted to force emigration through neglect of their economy and partial sale of their properties (Pr. 845 Nos. 542, 568, and 641, Pr. 846 No. 694). Nevertheless *Hans Georg Dillman* landed at Philadelphia on the Ship *Brothers* in 1751, where he took the oath of allegiance on September 16, 1751 (Strassburger-Hinke, List 169C).

29. Also on account of high property valuation the emigration request for Pennsylvania of *Melchior Geiser* of Wolfartsweier was refused to begin with by the Margrave *(resolutio Serenissimi)*. The Oberamt Durlach was in favor of emigration, however, because "as farmer he had already pretty much diminished his considerable property through all kinds of inconsiderate and slovenly transactions" [*als Bauersmann sein considerable anzusehen gewesenes Vermögen bereits durch allerhand unbedachtsame liederliche Händel ziemlich verringert habe*]. The government's conclusion was that "like a member of human society resembling an unfruitful branch, no further hindrance should be laid in his way or indeed in the way of other such members" [*einem unfruchtbaren Ast gleichendes Mitglied der menschlichen Societet ihm oder wohl gar mehreren Membris im Wege nicht länger gelassen werden möchte*]. When in the same year the community of Wolfartsweier presented the petition to permit his emigration, since he was not in condition to support his family—and the fear was expressed that he would, with his wife and children, become a burden to the community after the wasting of his property—he was finally manumitted, on payment of 50 florins (Pr. 845 No. 615, Pr. 846 No. 693, and No. 848, Pr. 1326 No. 1650). He landed at Philadelphia as *Melchior Geissert* on the Ship *Brotherhood*, November 3, 1750 (Strassburger-Hinke, List 159C).[4]

30. *Georg Huber* of Niefern was permitted to leave for Pennsylvania on payment of 19 florins (Pr. 846 No. 778, Pr. 1326 No. 1609). Possibly the *Johann Georg Huber* who arrived at Philadelphia on the Ship *Two Brothers*, August 28, 1750 (Strassburger-Hinke, List 153C).

31. *Anton Hauer* of Blankenloch was permitted to leave for Pennsylvania (Pr. 848 No. 2475, Pr. 1329 No. 4482). Probably *Anthony Hauer,* who arrived at Philadelphia on the Ship *Brothers,* September 16, 1751 (Strassburger-Hinke, List 169C).

32. *Jacob Lehmann* of Blankenloch was permitted to leave for Pennsylvania (Pr. 848 No. 2476, Pr. 1329 No. 4483). *Jacob Lehmann* arrived at Philadelphia on the Ship *Brothers,* September 16, 1751 (Strassburger-Hinke, List 169C).

33. *Friedrich Kloppey,* citizen and cabinetmaker at Weiler near Pforzheim, who according to the report of the Oberamt Pforzheim was a bad manager, on whose departure the village would lose nothing, was permitted to leave for Pennsylvania (Pr. 848 No. 2539, Pr. 1329 No. 4484). *Friedrich Kloppeyn* arrived at Philadelphia on the Ship *Two Brothers,* September 21, 1751 (Strassburger-Hinke, List 170C).

34. *Adam Pfisterer* of Bauschlott, with wife and five children, requested release from vassalage. According to the report of the Oberamt Pforzheim he possessed only 43 florins and "is in the category of those whom we can well do without" [*von der Gattung dererjenigen seye, die man wohl entbehren könne*] (Pr. 846 No. 859). Although his intended goal of emigration is not indicated, and I could find no evidence of manumission, he is probably identical with the *Hans Adam Pfesterer* who landed at Philadelphia in 1750 on the Ship *Two Brothers* (Strassburger-Hinke, List 153C).

35. *Christoph Peter Zechiel* and *Jacob Schwarz* of Auerbach were finally, in spite of their not inconsiderable property, permitted to emigrate to Pennsylvania and that by decision of the Margrave. Even the Oberamt Durlach had no objection, "because the place is already overpopulated anyhow" [*weil der Ort sowieso schon mit Leuten übersetzt sei*] (Pr. 848 Nos. 2575-2576, 2683-2684).

EMIGRANTS OF THE YEAR 1751

36. *Matthäus Hunold,* Reformed, charcoal-burner, from Weiler (near Pforzheim), was permitted to emigrate to Pennsylvania with his wife and child (Pr. 849 No. 26; Pr. 1330 Nos. 432, 690; Pr. 1331 No. 1003). *Mattheis Hunolt,* accompanied by a *Wilhelm Hunolt,* arrived at Philadelphia on the Ship *Two*

[4]It would appear that Melchior Geiser prospered in the new world; at least he achieved centenarian status. The Reverend John William Runkel, Reformed minister in Frederick, Maryland, records in his journal for 1799 "having buried, on the 11th of January, Melchoir Geisser, of Middletown, aged 110 years" (Henry Harbaugh, *The Fathers of the German Reformed Church in Europe and America,* second edition, II (1872), 297.—EDITOR.

Stutensee, hunting castle of the margraves of Baden-Durlach, at Friedrichstal. From Hornung's history of Friedrichstal, 1949.

Brothers, September 21, 1751 (Strassburger-Hinke, List 170C).

37. *Georg Löble* of Wössingen, who was at that time over seventy years old, was also permitted to go to Pennsylvania with his wife, to join his four children who were already living in Pennsylvania (Pr. 849 No. 581; Pr. 1331 No. 1037). Possibly the *Görg Aadam Löble and Wilhelm Löble* who arrived on the Ship *Lydia,* October 19, 1749 (Strassburger-Hinke, List 142C) were sons of his family; others from the vicinity (Unterwössingen) appear among the passengers.

38. *Samuel Winther,* likewise from Wössingen, who also wanted to go to Pennsylvania with wife and children, was permitted to emigrate (Pr. 849 No. 582; Pr. 1331 No. 1036).

39. *Georg Schickle, Jr.,* from Bauschlott, was likewise permitted to emigrate to Pennsylvania, with wife and four children (Pr. 849 No. 583; Pr. 1331 No. 1035).

40. *Gabriel Rössle* of Wössingen was permitted to emigrate to Pennsylvania, with wife and three children (Pr. 849 No. 584; Pr. 1331 No. 1038). *Gabriel Rössler* arrived at Philadelphia on the Ship *Shirley,* September 5, 1751 (Strassburger-Hinke, List 163C).

41. *Johann Georg Dürr,* single, cooper, from Nöttingen, was permitted to emigrate to Pennsylvania (Pr. 849 No. 429; Pr. 1331 No. 1077). *Johan Georg Dürr* arrived at Philadelphia on the Ship *Duke of Wirtenberg,* October 16, 1751 (Strassburger-Hinke, List 176C).

42. *Rudolph Schmelzle, Jacob Wildemann,* and *Hanss Jerg Meyer,* all from Obermutschelbach, the last-named with wife and four children, were manumitted for emigration to Pennsylvania (Pr. 849, Nos. 663, 664, 666, 667; Pr. 1331 Nos. 1386, 1387, 1385). *Johann George Mayer* and *Jacob Wildemann* arrived at Philadelphia on the Ship *Duke of Wirtenberg,* October 16, 1751 (Strassburger-Hinke, List 176C).

43. *Michael Wörlich,* nailsmith, at Stein, was permitted to emigrate to Pennsylvania (Pr. 1331 No. 1384). *Michael Währlich* arrived at Philadelphia on the Ship *Janet,* October 7, 1751 (Strassburger-Hinke, List 175C).

44. *Jacob Heyd* and *Jacob Frantz,* the latter single and a citizen's son, both from Grötzingen, further *Sebastian Nagel* and *Elisabetha Hemperl* of Blankenloch, received permission to emigrate to Pennsylvania (Pr. 849 No. 647; Pr. 1331 Nos. 1402, 1403, 1404, 1405; Pr. 1332 Nos. 1686, 1687). *Sebastian Nagel, Jacob Heit,* and *Jacob Frantz* arrived at Philadelphia on the Ship *Brothers,* September 16, 1751 (Strassburger-Hinke, List 169C).

45. *Jacob Gröner (Kröner), Jr.,* from Bauschlott, was likewise permitted to go to the New Land (Pr. 849 Nos. 734, 585; Pr. 1332 No. 1885).

46. Likewise the four single children of *Abraham Augenstein,* widower, citizen of Auerbach, named *Christian, Anna Maria, Caspar,* and *Hanss Georg Augen-*

87

stein, were permitted to emigrate to Pennsylvania (Pr. 849 No. 428; Pr. 1331 No. 1079). *Caspar Augenstein* arrived at Philadelphia on the Ship *Two Brothers,* September 21, 1751 (Strassburger-Hinke, List 170C); *Hans Georg Augenstein,* with a *Johannes Augenstein,* arrived on the Ship *Duke of Wirtenberg,* October 16, 1751 (Strassburger-Hinke, List 176C).

47. In the case of *Bernhardt* and *Christoph Hauer* of Blankenloch, who likewise were manumitted (Pr. 849 No. 391; Pr. 1331 No. 779), no goal of emigration is given, but they are surely identical with the *Christoph Hauer* and *Bernhart Hawer* who arrived at Philadelphia on the Ship *Brothers,* and took the oath of allegiance there on September 16, 1751 (Strassburger-Hinke, List 169C).

48. In the case of *Mattheus Reich,* citizen of Singen, who likewise was manumitted (Pr. 849 Nos. 488, 767; Pr. 1332 No. 1690), the goal of emigration is given as Pennsylvania. *Mattheus Reich* arrived at Philadelphia on the Ship *Duke of Wirtenberg,* October 16, 1751 (Strassburger-Hinke, List 176C).

49. *Joachim Nagel,* a former grenadier, born at Blankenloch, likewise was granted manumission for himself and his wife, in order to emigrate to Pennsylvania (Pr. 850 No. 819; Pr. 1332 No. 1688; Pr. 1331 No. 1503). *Joachim Nagel* arrived at Philadelphia on the Ship *Brothers,* September 16, 1751 (Strassburger-Hinke, List 169C).

50. *Michael Bossert,* single, citizen's son from Bauschlott, was manumitted to go to Pennsylvania on payment of manumission taxes (Pr. 850 No. 1143, Pr. 1332 No. 1937). *Michael Bossert* arrived at Philadelphia on the Ship *Phoenix,* September 25, 1751 (Strassburger-Hinke, List 173C).

51. *Michael Kaucher,* single, citizen's son from Göbrichen, was manumitted gratis for emigration to America. *Michael Kaucher* arrived at Philadelphia on the Ship *Phoenix,* September 25, 1751 (Strassburger-Hinke, List 173C).

52. *Jacob Kaucher, Jr.,* of Göbrichen, was manumitted with his wife and children to go to Pennsylvania (Pr. 1332 Nos. 1855, 1936). *Jacob Kauher* arrived at Philadelphia on the Ship *Phoenix,* September 25, 1751 (Strassburger-Hinke, List 173C).

53. *Philipp Jacob Wörner,* citizen at Wössingen, who likewise wanted to go to Pennsylvania (Pr. 849 No. 586), is identifiable as *Philipp Jacob Werner,* among the passengers of the Ship *Duke of Wirtenberg* which landed at Philadelphia, October 16, 1751 (Strassburger-Hinke, List 176C).

54. *Michel Hauss* of Knielingen was manumitted with his wife to go to Pennsylvania (Pr. 1331 No. 1561). *Johann Michael Haus* arrived at Philadelphia on the Ship *Brothers,* taking the oath of allegiance on September 16, 1751 (Strassburger-Hinke, List 169C).

55. *Johannes Hauss* of Knielingen, who wanted to emigrate to Pennsylvania with wife and children, is mentioned only in the court council protocols (Pr. 850 No. 972); i.e., there is no proof of manumission. However, a *Johanes House,* accompanied by *Philip House,* arrived at Philadelphia on the Ship *Anderson,* August 25, 1751 (Strassburger-Hinke, List 161C).

56. *Ludwig Schlicker* of Knielingen requested emigration to the New Land with wife and stepson. Permission was recommended by the court council (Pr. 850, Nos. 928, 978). While no indication of manumission could be located, *Lutwig Schlücker* arrived at Philadelphia on the Ship *Brothers,* September 16, 1751 (Strassburger-Hinke, List 169C).

57. *David Mussgnug,* citizen of Grötzingen, requested permission to go to Pennsylvania (Pr. 850 No. 886). While no papers relative to his manumission could be located, *Davit Mussgnug* arrived at Philadelphia on the Ship *Brothers,* September 16, 1751 (Strassburger-Hinke, List 169C).

58. *Johann Jacob Decker,* single, citizen's son of Weissenstein, was permitted to go to America (Pr. 850 No. 814; Pr. 1331 No. 1505). Possibly the *Johann Jacob Decker* who arrived at Philadelphia on the Ship *Ketty,* October 16, 1752 (Strassburger-Hinke, List 189C).

59. *Georg Dillman,* inhabitant at Teutschneureut, and *Martin Meinzer* of Knielingen, were permitted to emigrate to America (Pr. 849 Nos. 773, 790; Pr. 1332, Nos. 1621, 1818). *Hans Georg Dillmann* and *Martin Maintzer* arrived at Philadelphia on the Ship *Brothers,* September 16, 1751 (Strassburger-Hinke, List 169C).

60. *Barbara Graf,* single, subject of Ispringen, was also permitted to emigrate to America (Pr. 850 No. 1047; Pr. 1332 No. 1846).

61. *Johannes Meinzer* of Hagsfelden was permitted to emigrate to America with wife and two children (Pr. 849 No. 375; Pr. 1330 No. 1167). *Johanes Maintzer* arrived on the Ship *Brothers,* September 16, 1751 (Strassburger-Hinke, List 169C).

62. *Matthias Schwarz* of Auerbach, and *Michael Mayer* and *Jacob Binder,* both from Bauschlott, were permitted to emigrate to America (Pr. 849 Nos. 604, 605; Pr. 1331 Nos. 1094, 1093). Schwarz does not appear in Strassburger-Hinke. Two *Michael Mayers* emigrated in 1751 (Lists 173C, 174C); it is impossible to identify this particular emigrant. One *Hans Jacob Binder* emigrated in 1750 (List 157C).

63. *Dieterich Löffler,* non-citizen *(Hintersass)* from from Brötzingen, was permitted to emigrate to America with his wife and children (Pr. 849 Nos. 515, 587; Pr. 1331 No. 1095). *Dietrich Löffler* arrived at Philadelphia on the Ship *Phoenix,* September 25, 1751 (Strassburger-Hinke, List 173C).

Pennsylvania Emigrants from Friedrichstal

Interior view of Reformed Church, Friedrichstal, 1949.

Friedrichstal in Baden is a town founded in the year 1699 by the margrave of Baden-Durlach, specifically for Huguenot refugees. The town history by Oskar Hornung, *Friedrichstal: Geschichte einer Hugenottengemeinde zur 250-Jahrfeier* (Karlsruhe: C.F. Müller, 1949), contains detailed information on most of the founding families. Some of these, like the Gorenflos, are treated in the article by Dr. Friedrich Krebs in this issue. In addition, there came to America from Friedrichstal in the 18th Century the following emigrants: (1) *Philipp Bouquet,* farmer, and family, 1725, to the "New Land"; (2) *Augustin leRoy,* and family, 1725, to North America; (3) *Jacques Bonnet,* farmer, and family, 1734, to the "New Land"; (4) *Jean Corbeau,* farmer, and family, 1738, to Pennsylvania; and (5) *Jean Bonnet,* farmer, and family, 1739, to Pennsylvania. Detailed information on several of these is available in the Strassburger-Hinke ship lists, which begin in 1727. For example, *Jacques (Jacob) Bonnet,* spelled *Bonet* and *Bunett* in the lists, appears in List 30 A-C, on the ship *Elizabeth,* arriving at Philadelphia on August 27, 1733. According to the captain's list (A), *Jacques Bonnet (Jacob Bunett)* was 32 years old, had a wife *Mary* aged 32, and brought four children along: (1) *Margret* (aged 8), (2) *Susanna* (aged 4, listed as dead on the voyage), (3) *Christina* (aged 2, also listed as dead), and (4) *Johan Simon* (aged 9 months). *Jean Corbeau* appears as *Jean Corbo* and *Johan Carbo* on the Ship *Townsend,* arriving at Philadelphia, October 5, 1737, List 48 A-C. Possibly the *Johan Peter Bonnet* who appears in the same list is of the Friedrichstal family as well. - EDITOR.

The original Huguenot Church, 1728. From a sketch in the Baden State Archives at Karlsruhe.

Title page of Friedrichstal History.

Half-timbered village house, Friedrichstal, formerly the Lutheran Schoolhouse.

American Emigration Materials from Pfeddersheim

By ALBERT CAPPEL

Translated and Edited by Don Yoder

An inquiry from the Mennonite Historical Library at Bluffton, Ohio, to the city government of Pfeddersheim concerning the location and contents of documents entitled "Emigration Cases, 1746 ff.," mentioned in W. M. Becker, *Inventare der Gemeindearchive des Kreises Worms* (1937) gave us the occasion of searching for the documents in the city archives. We located a bundle of loose official documents some 15 centimeters thick with the inscription "Abt. XI: Auswanderung ab 1746". It contained chronologically arranged manuscript documents, most of them permissions for emigration or governmental letters concerning emigration affairs, as well as edicts and printed notices from the Electoral Palatine government and after 1816 from the Hessian authorities.

Since in those days any change of residence outside one's home community was included under the word "emigration," there are found in these paper emigrations abroad side by side with removals of individual persons out of Pfeddersheim, for example, for the purpose of marriage in a neighboring village. For a contribution to the migration history of the Palatines it appeared therefore expedient to depart from the chronological organization and to summarize the genealogically interesting documents according to emigration areas and to publish the names of the persons contained under each area in alphabetical order. In order not to extend the work too far, the in-migrations within Germany were noticed only up to the year 1830.[1] Migrations abroad, as far as they are mentioned in these documents, are on the contrary also recorded for later years.[2]

Some emigrants could be ascertained on the basis of official papers citing demands of creditors after a person had emigrated, or documents dealing with suspected secret emigration.

[1.] So it appears from a letter of the mayor and city council of Pfeddersheim, dated January 18, 1790, to Minheer Hermann Hendrick Damen and Company in Amsterdam, that *Wilhelm Gradinger,* citizen and master cartwright at Pfeddersheim, had left his wife *Catharina,* nee *Hees,* as early as March 12, 1787, and contrary to the laws of the land had taken flight. According to a report coming from the man himself he had traveled to Philadelphia on the Ship *New York,*[3] but since then had sent no word. The mayor requested a certified report on "residence, life or death" [*Aufenthalt, Leben oder Tod*]. The answer from Amsterdam was negative. Their advice was to direct the advertisement for the missing person to the "German Commission" [German Society] in Philadelphia.[4]

Johann Wilhelm Gradinger was born April 19, 1748, son of *Henrich Gradinger,* cartwright and resident citizen of Pfeddersheim, and his wife *Anna Barbara,* nee *Wendel.* The emigrant married on February 28, 1786, *Anna Catharina Heess,* daughter of *Christian Heess,* citizen and master blacksmith of Pfeddersheim.

The emigrants to America listed below were not found in the above-mentioned bundle of documents, but among other archival papers. See especially the publication from the Lutheran church register in *Pfälzische Familien- und Wappenkunde,* IV (1963), 359.[5] Also the Reformed church register contains some emigration materials, as follows:

[2.] On Easter 1744 *Jörg Adam Dobeler,* aged 15, and *Johann Peter Dobeler,* aged 14, were confirmed together, "on account of their journey to America" [*wegen ihrer Reisse in America*]. They were sons of *Johann Georg Dobeler,* citizen and master cabinetmaker, and his wife *Catharina Margretha* nee *Hofmann.* The parents were married at Pfeddersheim on April 30, 1727.

---

[1]In this translation we have not included the in-migrations within Germany, 1770-1830.—ED.

[2]The materials on emigration to Hungary (1746-1752), Brazil (1825), Austria (1845), and France (1846) have not been included in our translation.—ED.

[3]The only arrival of the Ship *New York* at the port of Philadelphia listed in Strassburger-Hinke, *Pennsylvania German Pioneers,* was on September 8, 1801 (III, 109).—ED.

[4]The German Society of Pennsylvania, founded in Philadelphia in 1764, was originally an emigrant aid society, such as were founded by other ethnic groups in the colonial period, to protect emigrants from unscrupulous treatment by captains and shipping companies, and in Pennsylvania, by those who hired redemptioners to pay for their passage.—ED.

[5]For additional genealogical data on Pfeddersheim, see Albert Cappel, "Trauungen Ortsfremder im lutherischen Kirchenbuch von Pfeddersheim und Worms-Pfiffligheim," *Pfälzische Familien und Wappenkunde,* XI. Jg. (1962), Bd. 4 Heft 8, 236-237.—ED.

91

Pfeddersheim, from Merian, Topographia Germaniae (1672).

Later the pastor added to this notation: "Nothing came of their trip to America because of the war at that time between the king of Hungary with the French king on the Rhine" [*Auss der Reissen in Amerika ist wegen damaligen Kriegs des Königs in Ungarn mit dem König in Frankreich am Rhein nichts geworden*].

Whether the intentions of emigration later became actuality, cannot be stated for certain.[6] On the contrary the following entry in the burial register of the Reformed congregation of Pfeddersheim contains a documented evidence of two emigrants:

[3.] Died at Pfeddersheim, August 8, 1820, *Anna Maria*, nee *Mayer*, from Dürkheim, widow of *Philipp Köhl*, deceased citizen here, aged 60 years and 4 months, leaving behind three sons, of whom two are in America, and three daughters. One of these sons is very probably identical with *Bastian Koehl*, aged 25, miller, from Pfeddersheim, who arrived at Philadelphia December 3, 1807, on the Ship *William P. Johnson* (Strassburger-Hinke, List 505). He was born about 1782, but his baptismal entry could not be located in the Pfeddersheim church register. Likewise the marriage of his parents was not entered in Pfeddersheim. It was not

until 1792 that *Philipp Jacob Kehl*, flour-handler of Pfeddersheim, and his wife *Anna Maria*, nee *Mayer*, from Dürkheim, had a child baptized here *(Wilhelmina*, born September 10, 1792). The married couple Kehl (Köhl) was named in 1795 as the "current tenant of the New Mill near Leiselheim" [*dermaliger Beständer der Neumühle bei Leiselheim*], when their son *Johann Nikolaus* (born October 21, 1795, died October 10, 1818) was baptized. Besides these we find two baptismal entries in the Reformed church book for (Worms-) Pfiffligheim, of (1) *Eleonora Kehl*, baptized November 7, 1779, and (2) *Johann Konrad Kehl*, baptized February 6, 1781, whose parents, "*Philipp Jacob Kehl* and *Anna Maria*," must be identical with the parents of both emigrants. The last-mentioned *Johann Konrad Kehl* could be the second son mentioned in the above burial entry as being in America. He was named for his grandfather *Konrad Kehl*, citizen and master-baker in Pfeddersheim—born, according to his own statement, at Nierstein in 1718, died at Pfeddersheim December 5, 1800, at the age of 82. *Konrad Kehl* married, before 1752, *Charlotte Weis* of Hochheim, who died at Pfeddersheim February 2, 1802, at the age of 77. The father of both emigrants, *Philipp Jacob Kehl*, was born at Pfeddersheim, September 8, 1758.

From the Pfeddersheim court records [*Pfeddersheimer Gerichtsbuch*] comes another reference to emigration.

On court day, April 4, 1733, it was investigated what real estate of *Peter Cornelius, Balsser Bräunig, Peter Heit,* and *Elias Stricker* had been sold, what had been taken from it, and what of it paid on debts, and final-

---

[6]Neither of these is listed in Strassburger-Hinke. Other Doblers came to America in the 18th Century, however. *Johann Michael Dobler* (1770-1838), a native of Horrheim, Württemberg, came to this country about 1788. After working for his passage three years at Nazareth as a brewer's apprentice, he married near York a daughter of the Mennonite *Friedrich Litz* (d. 1817), and moved to Baltimore. His ancestors were Reformed Toblers from Switzerland, but became Lutheran in Württemberg. His son, *Daniel Dobler* (b. 1804), in his *Tagebuch*, 1819-1844, now in the Historical Society of Pennsylvania, gives details on his ancestry.—ED.

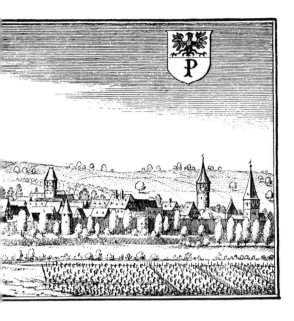

7. *Johann Lorentz Cornelius,* born April 24, 1722. Godparents: *Johann Lorentz Becker* of Kriegsheim and his wife *Anna Elisabetha.*
8. *Veronica Cornelius,* born May 5, 1725. Godparents: *Christophorus Heller* and his wife *Veronica.*
9. *Anna Catharina Cornelius,* born August 1, 1730, died July 29, 1731. Godmother: *Anna Christina Erlebach,* single.
10. *Anna Eva Cornelius,* born March 29, 1733. Godmother: *Anna Eva Finck,* single daughter of *Paul Finck,* Gemeinsmann at Heppenheim/ Wiese.

According to the ship's lists, *Peter Cornelius* (born 1685) arrived in Philadelphia on the Ship *Samuel,* August 17, 1733, with his wife and three children (*Elisabeth,* born 1713; *Lorentz,* born 1722; and *Veronica,* born 1725) (Strassburger-Hinke, List 29 A-C).

[5.] *Elias Stricker,* legitimate son of *Elias Stricker,* deceased citizen at Pfeddersheim, married (1) at Pfeddersheim January 7, 1714 (Reformed churchbook), *Catharina Barbara Ermel* (buried March 16, 1731, at the age of 43), daughter of *Johannes Ermel,* deceased, community resident [*Gemeinsmann*] at Erbes-Büdesheim. *Elias Stricker* married (2), September 4, 1731, *Maria Catharina Dilgen,* single, from Göllheim. Children of the first marriage were the following:

1. *Johann Christophel Stricker,* born October 29, 1714. Godfather: *Johann Christophel Heller,* single.
2. *Johannes Stricker,* born October 3, 1716. Godfather: *Johannes Vollmar* from Niederhessen, serving lad [*Dienstknecht*] under H. Camer-Rath *Trapp* in Pfeddersheim.
3. *Johann Philipp Stricker,* born September 29, 1719. Godparents: *Johann Philip Cörper, Maria Ottilia Carl,* both single.
4. *Johann Adam Stricker,* born October 20, 1722. Godfather: *Johann Adam Jacobi,* son of *Casper Jacobi.*
5. *Johann Henrich Stricker,* born January 23, 1727. Godfather: *Johann Henrich Roth,* farmer [*Hofmann*] in the service of H. Camer-Rath *Trapp.*

There was one child of the second marriage:

6. *Johann Conrad Stricker,* born June 23, 1732. Godparents: *Johann Conrad Christ,* master linenweaver, and his wife *Catharina.*

Elias Stricker was confirmed at Easter 1704 at the age of 16, hence his birth can be set circa 1688. He emigrated with his wife and four children (*Johannes; Philipp,* aged 9; *Adam,* aged 7; and *Henry,* aged 4½) on the Ship *Mary,* landing at Philadelphia on September 29, 1733 (Strassburger-Hinke, List 34 A-C). On his parentage the Council Protocols include the following reference: *Elias Stricker,* cartwright, born about 1639, became citizen of Pfeddersheim in 1663, and was

ly how much was payable to the gracious authorities and to the City for the tithe or additional duty. According to their statement, these four persons wanted to go to America, and it followed from documents cited on the part of each that *Peter Cornelius* had to pay 3 florins 18 kreuzer, *Balsser Bräunig* 1 florin 3 kreuzer 2 pfennig, and *Elias Stricker* 3 florins 30 kreuzer. *Peter Heit's* situation had to be looked into further.

[4.] *Peter Cornelius,* legitimate son of *Johannes Cornelius,* citizen here, married, August 19, 1710, *Anna Elisabetha Fink,* legitimate daughter of the community resident [*Gemeinsmann*] *Paul Fink* at Heppenheim on the Wiese. *Johannes Cornelius* was buried at Pfeddersheim October 20, 1711, aged 60 years. The children, listed in the Reformed church book of Pfeddersheim, are as follows:

1. *Johann Peter Cornelius,* born May 2, 1711. *Godfather: Johann Peter Erlebach,* citizen of Pfeddersheim.
2. *Anna Eva Cornelius,* born August 14, 1712. Godmother: *Anna Eva,* daughter of *Paul Finck* of Heppenheim/Wiese.
3. *Anna Elisabeth Cornelius,* born September 15, 1713. Godmother: *Anna Elisabetha Cornelius,* single.
4. *Johann Andreas Cornelius,* born April 4, 1715. Godfather: *Johann Andreas Lang,* single son of *Wendel Lang.*
5. *Anna Catharina Cornelius,* born August 21, 1716, died April 1, 1718. Godmother: *Anna Catharina,* wife of *Johannes Warch* of Pfeddersheim.
6. *Susanna Catharina,* born August 21, 1719. Godmother: *Susanna Catharina Butterfass,*[†] single.

[†]For this family, see No. 12, below. Perhaps the *Daniel Butterfass* who arrived on the *Winter Galley,* September 5, 1738 (List 52B) was from Pfeddersheim, since on the same ship were the Pfeddersheim emigrant contingent of Derst, Knab, Heller, and possibly Hoffman (see footnote No. 8).—ED.

at that time to produce his birth record [*Geburtsbrief*]. He was twice married, (1) about 1662/1663 to the daughter of Mr. *Marx Vetter,* pastor of Dalsheim, and (2) about 1673. His second wife's name is not known, but she was 26 years old in 1681.

[6.] *Peter Heit [Heyd]* of Holssheim (Holzheim) in the Braunfels government and his wife *Anna Christina Boz* were married September 18, 1725, according to the Reformed church book of Pfeddersheim. Their children were as follows:

1. *Johannes Heit,* born June 9, 1726. Godparents: *Johannes Dauberlein* and wife *Anna Catharina.*
2. *Catharina Margretha Heit,* born September 26, 1727, died May 2, 1729. Godmother: *Catharina Margretha,* daughter of *Michel Boz.*
3. *Anna Christina Heit,* born February 18, 1730. Godmother: the single daughter of *Johann Philipp Hassert,* citizen and master tailor.
4. *Anna Elisabetha Heit,* born March 24, 1731. Godmother: *Anna Elisabetha Heydt,* of Pfifflighem, single.

Peter Heit ("Hite") arrived at Philadelphia on the Ship *Mary,* September 29, 1733, with wife and child (*Anna Elisabeth*) (Strassburger-Hinke, List 34 A-C).

[7.] *Balthasar Breuninger* married *Anna Margretha,* daughter of *Johannes Wagner,* citizen of Pfeddersheim, in November 1712, according to the Lutheran church book of Pfeddersheim. Their children were as follows:

1. *Johann Philipp Breuninger,* born February 8, 1716. Godfather: *Johann Philipp Wagner,* mother's brother.
2. *Jacob Breuninger,* born September 13, 1719. Godfather: *Jacob Jugenheimer,* stepbrother.
3. *Anna Maria Breuninger,* born March 20, 1724. Godmother: *Anna Maria,* wife of *Jacob Jugenheimer.*

Baltzer Breu[n]inger arrived in Philadelphia on the Ship *Mary,* September 29, 1733, with wife and two children (*Hans Jacob,* 13 ½, and *Anna Maria,* 9) (Strassburger-Hinke, List 34 A-C).

According to the property register book [*Schatzungsbuch*], *Baltzer Bräunig* was 4 years old in 1681 and son of *Andreas Bräunig* (41 years old) and his wife *Agnes,* nee *Henrich* (39 years old in 1681). The wife was buried September 10, 1728, according to the Reformed church book, *Andreas Bräunig (Bruning)* became citizen in Pfeddersheim in 1677, after marrying *Agnes Henrich* there in 1675. The above-mentioned godfather, "*Jacob Jugenheimer, der Stiefbruder,*" was an illegitimate son of *Agnes Henrich* to *Julius Jugenheimer.*

[8.] Among the Pfeddersheim Inventories and Estate Divisions [*Inventare und Erbteilungen*], 1740-1759, is a document dated Pfeddersheim July 27, 1740, dividing up the estate of *Adam Hofmann,* who had died eight weeks previously. In it is mentioned the fact that " . . . the one son *Peter Hofmann* went to the New Land in 1738 and took along more than his portion of the inheritance [. . . *der eine Sohn Peter Hofmann ins Neue Land 1738 gezogen und mehr als seine Erbportion hin-*

weg (genommen) habe . . .]. From the Pfeddersheim archival documents the following family tree can be drawn up for this emigrant:

1. *Peter Hofmann,* born April 30, 1710 (Reformed church book, Pfeddersheim).[8]
2. *Johann Adam Hofmann,* citizen and master cabinetmaker, buried June 16, 1740, aged 59 years, 6 months, married September 12, 1702, *Anna Margretha,* legitimate daughter of *Ludwig Peter Wiedersheimer,* citizen and lockmaker of Pfeddersheim. The widow *Anna Margretha* was buried July 19, 1744.
3. *Georg Adam Hofmann,* citizen and cabinetmaker, was 37 years old in 1682, died 1700/1702. He was married before 1671 to (name not given), who was 39 years old in 1682.
4. *Ludwig Peter Widdersheimer,* citizen and lockmaker at Pfeddersheim, was born circa 1654 in Bolanden, became citizen at Pfeddersheim in 1679. His wife was named *Niesenpeter,* born circa 1659, daughter of *Jacob Niesenpeter.*

[9.] Among the same files, Pfeddersheim Inventories and Estate Divisions, 1740-1759, was a document dated Pfeddersheim, February 17, 1751, the inventory of the estate of *Catharina Hofmann,* nee *Gramm,* who died about November 20, 1740, leaving her husband, *Georg Hofmann, Sr.,* and nine children. *Georg Hofmann* married (2) *Anna Margretha,* nee *Küssel (Kusl),* born in Bibelheim. From this marriage there was one son: *Johann Michael Hofmann.* Of the sons of the first marriage there were (1) *Georg Philipp Hofmann,* who is in the New Land [*so im Neuen Land ist*], and (2) *Christian Wilhelm Hofmann,* who went to the New Land [*so ins Neue Land ist*].[9]

The birth-dates of these two emigrants are contained in the Lutheran church book of Pfeddersheim. *Georg Philipp Hofmann* was born May 18, 1716 (godfather: *Georg Philipp Feltfort* (?), miller at Asselheim). *Christian Wilhelm Hofmann* was born February 10, 1726 (godfather: *Christian Wilhelm Chelius,* son of the pastor).

The parents of the emigrants were *Georg Hofmann* and *Anna Christina,* youngest daughter of the deceased *Sebastian Gramm:* they were married before 1706.

[10.] Among the Pfeddersheim Inventories and Estate Divisions for the period 1760-1765, is an inventory dated August 6, 1762, of the estate of *Anna Elisabetha,* nee *Walter,* wife of *Michael Dillinger,* master blacksmith at Pfeddersheim, who died four weeks previously. She left, besides her second husband, three children from her second marriage:

---

[8]While it is difficult to identify this emigrant in the ship lists, because of the commonness of his name, it is possible that he was the *Jan Peter Hoffman,* aged 27, who arrived at Philadelphia on the *Winter Galley,* September 5, 1738 (Strassburger-Hinke, List 52 A-C), with the *Heller* family (q.v.) of Pfeddersheim. With him came a *Jurg Hoffman,* aged 37.—ED.

[9]Without exact dates of emigration, these names are almost impossible to identify in the ship lists. Can readers possibly identify their place of settlement in America?—ED.

94

1. *Abraham Derst,* who at the time was said to be in the New Land [*so dermahlen sich im Neuen Land befinden sollte*].
2. *Jacob Derst,* unknown where he is, was sent to the Netherlands [*ohnwissend wo derselbe sich aufhaltet, (ins Niederland verschickt worden)*].
3. *Maria Magdalena Derst,* married to Adam *Christian Schultz.*

Abraham Derst emigrated in 1743, arriving at Philadelphia on the Ship *Robert & Alice,* September 30, 1743 (Strassburger-Hinke, List 102 C). He was born at Pfeddersheim September 13, 1725, son of *Abraham Jacob Derst* and his wife *Anna Elisabetha,* nee *Walter.* The father was baptized on February 18, 1703, according to the Reformed church book, and was buried on May 5, 1739, aged 36 years, 2 ½ months. The mother was born September 10, 1702.

[11.] In the property accounts [*Vermögensabrechnung*] of the above-mentioned *Michael Dillinger* there is mentioned an additional emigrant. This is the reference: " . . . paid to Mr. *Johannaci* for *Paul Derst* in the New Land, by whom the burial costs of old Mrs. *Derst* were paid, 10 florins, 12 kreuzer" [. . . *an den Herrn Johannaci zahlt wegen Paul Derst im Neuen Land, wovon der alten Derstin ihre Leichkosten bezahlt worden, 10 fl. 12 xer*]. This *Johann Paul Derst* arrived at Philadelphia on the Ship *John and William* on October 17, 1732. He was born at Pfeddersheim April 4, 1713, son of the master blacksmith *Johann Jakob Derst* and his wife *Maria Catharina.* He was therefore an uncle of *Abraham Derst* who emigrated 11 years later. In the same clan possibly belongs *Friedrich Adam Derst,* who arrived at Philadelphia on the Ship *John & Elizabeth,* November 7, 1754 (Strassburger-Hinke, List 231 A-C), although his baptismal entry cannot be found in Pfeddersheim.

The family name Derst appears for the first time in Pfeddersheim in the year 1698 with *Johann Jacob Derst,* citizen and farrier, borń at Neurath near Bacharach, according to the Reformed church book, on November 22, 1674, died at Pfeddersheim July 16, 1723. The name is derived from the place-name Dörscheid near St. Goarshausen. Cf. "Niederderschet" 1605, *Archiv für Sippenforschung,* 1941, p. 60. The name is today still pronounced "Derscht" in the Pfeddersheim dialect.

[12.] An inventory dated September 4, 1760, of the estate of *Balthasar Fontain,* citizen and master baker, who was buried May 17, 1744, at the age of 68, and his wife *Maria Catharina,* nee *Butterfass,* who died one year previously (1759). They left eight children:
1. *Maria Elisabeth,* aged 36.
2. *Anna Barbara,* at that time in Holland.
3. *Johann Peter,* at that time in Holland, and married.
4. *Leonhard,* Pfeddersheim, married.
5. *Catharina Barbara.*
6. *Johann Bernhardt,* at that time in the East Indies.

7. *Theodor Jacob,* in the New Land.
8. *Niclas,* in Holland.

The American emigrant was *Theodor Jacob Fontain,* who arrived at Philadelphia on the Ship *Edinburgh* on September 30, 1754 (Strassburger-Hinke, List 220 A-C). He was born at Pfeddersheim, April 13, 1736, son of the above parents.

The first bearer of the name in Pfeddersheim was the emigrant's grandfather, *Christophel Fontaine,* citizen, master-baker and member of the city council. The birthplace of *Christophel Fontaine* is unknown, but he died at Pfeddersheim 1691/1693, and married circa 1667 *Anna Maria Glatt,* daughter of the master-baker *Hans Philipp Glatt.* She was born at Pfeddersheim in 1650, and died there January 22, 1709.

[13.] In a Letter of the City Council dated July 14, 1787, is the following reference to emigration: " . . . since *Valentin* and *Johannes Becker* left here and went to America some 30 years ago and in reference to their share of their inheritance [the following persons] were summoned by order of the city council" [. . . *Nachdem Valentin und Johannes Becker bereits 30 Jahre von hier weg und nach Amerika gangen und zum Bezug eines jeden Erbanteils . . . von Stadtrats wegen vorgeladen wurden . . .*].[10]

At the division of the inheritance there were present the emigrants' sister, the widow of *Paul Derst,* citizen of Pfeddersheim, and their brother *Johann Adam Becker.*

The family of Becker was Lutheran. The father of both emigrants, *Bernhardt Becker,* married 1705/1706 *Anna Elisabetha,* widow of *Christophel Rothermel.* From 1707 to 1729 they had eleven children baptized, among them (1) *Georg Velten,* baptized March 9, 1712 (godfather: *Georg Velten Becker,* son of the father's brother), and (2) *Johannes,* baptized February 18, 1724 (godfather: the father's brother, *Johannes Becker,* from Steinbach). ·

From the ship's lists and from records in the card catalogue of emigrants at the Heimatstelle Pfalz, Kaiserslautern, Dr. Fritz Braun was able to furnish two additional emigrants from Pfeddersheim, *Simon Heller* and *Michael Knab.* For the former the following family tree can be drawn up, from the Reformed church book and the Council Protocols of Pfeddersheim.

[14.] A. *Simon Heller* was born at Pfeddersheim, June 18, 1721, godfather: Mr. *Simon Wendel,* director of the city council and his wife *Anna Sara,* grandmother. *Simon Heller* arrived in Philadelphia with his father and brothers and sisters on the Ship *Winter Galley,* September 5, 1738 (Strassburger-Hinke, List 52 A-C). He married in 1744, at Tohickon, Bucks County, Penn-

---

[10] One *Vallentin* (XX) *Backer* arrived at Philadelphia on the Ship *St. Andrew,* September 23, 1752 (List 181 C), with a *Philip Backer,* but without further data it is impossible to identify him with the Pfeddersheim emigrant.—ED.

sylvania, *Louisa Dietz* from Milford Township, born 1726. Their children, born at Tohickon, were the following:

1. *Johann Michael Heller,* born January 2, 1757.
2. *Anthony Heller,* born February 1, 1758.
3. *Catharine Heller,* born March 4, 1759.
4. *Anna Maria Heller,* born November 18, 1760.

Simon Heller died May 20, 1783, in Hamilton Township.[11]

B. *Johann Christoph Heller,* born at Pfeddersheim, circa 1689, confirmed at Easter 1708, aged 18. Married before 1718 (not in Pfeddersheim) *Veronica Lavall*[12] from Erbes-Büdesheim. Their children as recorded in the Reformed church book of Pfeddersheim were the following:

1. *Catharina Wilhelmina,* born June 15, 1718, died August 9, 1720. Godmother: *Wilhelmina,* wife of *Johann Jacob Kleeberger* of Nieder Sulzheim.
2. *Simon* (above).
3. *Johann Michael* (is listed among the emigrants), born February 27, 1724; godfather: *Johann Michael Laval* of Erbisbischein (Erbes-Büdesheim), father-in-law.
4. *Daniel,* born July 15, 1726 (godfather: *Johann Daniel Lavall,* inhabitant at Erbes-Büdesheim, brother-in-law).
5. *Johann Ludwig,* born December 31, 1728, godparents: *Johann Ludwig Fress* and wife *Wilhelmina,* married couple and members of the community at Ober Sültzen.
6. *Georg Christoph,* born April 9, 1732, godparents: *Johann Georg Heil* and wife *Anna Margretha.*
7. *Maria Magdalena,* born December 14, 1734. Godparents: Mr. *Johann Adam Strauch*[13] and his wife *Maria Magdalena.*
8. *Ottilia,* born November 8, 1737, died May 11, 1738. Godparents: *Ottilia Schwedes,* daughter of *Johann Georg Schwedes,* master locksmith of Pfeddersheim.

C. *Hans Jacob Heller,* born at Pfeddersheim circa 1662, was received into citizenship there in 1683, as son of the deceased *Conrad Heller;* died after 1689. He married *Anna Sara Stricker* (born circa 1665, buried October 19, 1728, at the age of 63 years 1 month). She was a daughter of *Elias Stricker.* She married for the second time, before 1699, *Simon Wendel,* born at Mörstadt 1658, died at Pfeddersheim August 30, 1721, at the age of 63 years and 4 months, master blacksmith and member of the city council.

D. *Conrad Heller* came from Switzerland, the Zurich area [*aus der Schweiz, Züricher Gebiets*]. He was received into citizenship at Pfeddersheim in 1662, died there 1666/1667. He married at Pfeddersheim in 1662 *Anna Godlieb* (born circa 1644), daughter of Mr. *Adam Schlintwein.* She married for the second time June 25, 1667, Mr. *Hans Conrad Weingartmann,* member of the council at Pfeddersheim (died 1680). She was married for the third time in 1682, to *Samuel Baum* of Göllheim, who was at the time 29 years old.

[15.] On the same ship on which the Heller Family came to America (*Winter Galley,* September 5, 1738, Strassburger-Hinke, List 52 A-C) there was another Pfeddersheim passenger, *Michael Knap (Knabb).*[14] He may be identical with the *Johann Michael Knab,* born August 10, 1716, baptized in the Reformed faith, son of *Johann Nickel Knab* and his wife *Maria Claudina* (godfather: *Johann Michael Bootz,* citizen of Pfeddersheim). His mother *Maria Claudina,* wife of Mr. *Johann Nickel Knab,* citizen and saddler in Pfeddersheim, was buried March 14, 1731, at the age of 42 years. The father, *Johann Niclas Knab,* was buried January 7, 1748, at the age of 63 years. He was first to bear the name in Pfeddersheim (see *Pfälzische Familien- und Wappenkunde,* IV, 360).

[11]This is the family for whom Hellertown in Northampton County, Pennsylvania, is named. *Christopher Heller* the emigrant settled at Seidersville, and his sons *Simon, Michael,* and *Daniel* settled along the Saucon Creek at what is now Hellertown. *Simon Heller* was one of the organizers and first trustee of the Lower Saucon Reformed Church. Moving to Plainfield Township in 1764, he helped to organize the Plainfield Reformed congregation, and laid out the colonial road from Wind Gap to the Wyoming Valley. He died in 1783. *Ludwig Heller* arrived at Philadelphia on the Ship *Eastern Branch,* October 3, 1753 (List 213 A-C); he settled in Bucks County and later in Hamilton Township, now Monroe County, where he died in 1807. *Christopher Heller, Jr.,* arrived at Philadelphia on the Ship *Duke of Bedford,* September 14, 1751 (List 166 C). The Hellers were millers, carpenters, and wheelwrights—and community leaders, church founders, and revolutionary patriots. See *Hellertown Centennial, 1872-1972,* pp. 18-19, for an extended sketch of the original emigrant's family.—ED.

[12]Of the Lavall (Lawall) family, *Daniel* and *Johann Lutwig Lawall* arrived in Philadelphia on the Ship *Phoenix,* November 22, 1752 (List 195 C); *Johann Michel Lawall* on the Ship *Edinburgh,* September 15, 1749 (List 132 C); and *Melchior Lawall* on the Ship *Shirley,* September 5, 1751 (List 163 C). For the Lawalls of Northampton County, Pennsylvania, see A. Stapleton, *Memorials of the Huguenots in America* (Carlisle, 1901), p. 85.—ED.

[13]One *Adam Strauch* arrived at Philadelphia on the Ship *St. Andrew,* September 26, 1737, (List 47 A), his name appearing in the lists next after an *Andreas Heit.*—ED.

[14]In a lengthy sketch of the Knabb family in Morton L. Montgomery, *History of Berks County in Pennsylvania* (Philadelphia: Everts, Peck & Richards, 1886), pp. 401-403, we are told that *Michael Knabb,* born April 17, 1717, at "Pfeldersheim (sic), in Pfalz, a Rhenish province of Bavaria," emigrated to Pennsylvania, "as near as can be ascertained, about the year 1737, in company with his two brothers, John and Peter, and settled in Oley Township". *Michael Knabb* married *Eve Magdalena Seltzer,* daughter of *Jacob* and *Elizabeth Seltzer* of Heidelberg Township, March 11, 1755, and died June 17, 1778, in his 62nd year. He had eight children: *Nicholas, Peter, Jacob, Daniel, Susan, Sarah, Catharine,* and *Mary.* The third son, *Jacob Knabb* (1771-1825), married *Hannah Yoder,* daughter of *Daniel* and *Margaret (Eyster) Yoder.* Their youngest son, *Jacob Knabb* (b. 1817), was a prominent newspaperman in Reading and Harrisburg, remembered particularly for his founding of the *Reading Gazette,* an English weekly, 1840-1843, and his long editorship of the *Berks and Schuylkill Journal,* 1845-1886. In 1869 his firm began publishing the daily *Reading Times and Dispatch.* He was active in local, state and national Whig and Republican politics, an advocate of public schools and city libraries, and an Episcopalian. It would be interesting to know if he visited Pfeddersheim, the Rhineland home of his forefathers, on an extended trip he made to Europe in 1878. The journey produced many travel letters which were published in the Reading newspapers. Montgomery tells us that public interest in them "grew to such an extent that he was invited to issue them in book-form, but he modestly declined to gratify this desire of many friends".—ED.

EMIGRATION MATERIALS FROM LAMBSHEIM IN THE PALATINATE

By HEINRICH REMBE

Translated and Edited by Don Yoder

[We are fortunate to be able to introduce American readers to a new series on West German regional genealogy entitled *Beiträge zur Bevölkerungsgeschichte der Pfalz*—"Contributions to the Population History of the Palatinate". The series is a new project of the Heimatstelle Pfalz in Kaiserslautern, and is edited by Dr. Fritz Braun, director emeritus, and Director Karl Scherer. Volume I in the series is Heinrich Rembe, *Lambsheim: Die Familien von 1547 bis 1800—für Maxdorf bis 1830—mit Angaben aus Weisenheim a.S. Eyersheim und Ormsheim* (Kaiserslautern, 1971). This volume of 297 pages is what German scholarship calls an *Ortssippenbuch*—a lineage book constructed on the basis of archival sources for one municipality, and alphabetized so that one can trace relationships as far back into the past as there is genealogically relevant documentation.

The book begins with a thorough description and history of the town of Lambsheim and its dependencies: Maxdorf, Ormsheim, Eyersheim, and Burghaselbach, describing ecclesiastical, educational, and economic development. There are sections on the local nobility, biographies of prominent citizens, estimates of the work of earlier local historians, and an historical and statistical section on the development of the population. Actual lists of the population at various times, from 1547 to 1652, are included as documents. The largest sections of the book are C: The Families of Lambsheim from 1547 to 1650 (pp. 29-58); and D: The Families from 1650 to circa 1800 for Lambsheim and circa 1830 for Maxdorf (pp. 59-259). Appendices and full family-name and place-name indexes and bibliography conclude the work.

There is a great deal of social history presented in the genealogical section D, giving Americans a good insight into what life must have been like in a small Rhineland town in the period between the Thirty Years War and the 18th Century emigration to America. The town included Reformed, Lutheran, and Catholic families living together and sharing church buildings. For example, the Reformed and the Catholics shared the church building after 1705, in a *simultaneum* arrangement that somewhat resembled the "union church" pattern that was to develop in Pennsylvania between Lutherans and Reformed.

Occupations are listed with most entries and from them we can build up a picture of the economic struc-

ture of a village like Lambsheim. In addition to the professional classes (ministers, schoolmasters), we have the master craftsmen of the various trades (shoemakers, tailors, linenweavers, stockingweavers, wagonmakers, etc.). Innkeepers were important in the social culture of the village and the book includes full materials on the history of all the town's inns. The lower class of workers include day laborers *(Taglöhner, Handfröner)* and even migrant laborers, as for example, harvesters from neighboring areas "who mowed here during the harvest" and had children baptized in the village church during their stay in Lambsheim. In addition to *Oberschultheiss* and *Unterschultheiss*—the top level of village official—the lesser village officialdom was represented in the beadle *(Büttel),* the night watchman *(Nachtwächter),* the field watchman *(Feldschütz),* even the church constable *(Kirchentreiber).* There was a considerable number of herdsmen—*Kuhhirte, Pferdehirte, Ochsenhirte,* performing labor for the community. There were small tradesmen *(Tuchkrämer,* etc.), specialists like the *Sauschnitter* (which needs no translation for a Pennsylvania German), and finally a class of "vagi" or "vagabundi" as the scholarly ministers or town scribes called them—traveling poor people who occasionally are mentioned in the church or town records.

The ethnic makeup of the town's population is interesting. In addition to the old families of Lambsheim that were there before the Thirty Years War, there was considerable migration of other elements, particularly after the Thirty Years War. For example, a large number of French names appear in the records, most of them Huguenots: *Beaufort, Bouquon (Buquin), Bouton, Burree, Burqui, Cajeux, Chabot, Chally, la Combe, Convert (Confer), Deffaa, Defrand, Dupré, Dupont, Grandmange, Hügenell, Levasier, Leveaux, Lojet, de Malade, Strompiers, Voison (Fossé)* and others. From Switzerland migrated many families, among them *Epprich (Epprecht), Geiger, Hauser, Hausswirth, Hollinger, Josy, Maurer,* and *Schowalter.* From the Tirol came some Roman Catholic families, and Protestants from Braband in Belgium and Franconia and other provinces of Germany. Mennonites *(Wiedertäufer)* were represented in Lambsheim in the families of *Fellmann, Finger, Hochermuth, Hirschberger, Neukumeter,* and *Schowalter,* some of them of Swiss origin. Finally a few Jewish families were resident in the town

97

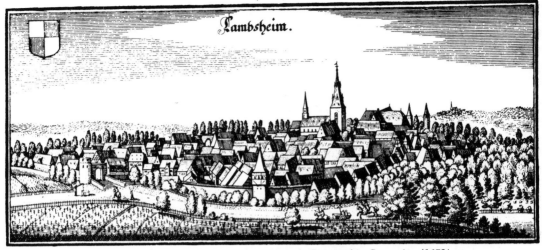

Lambsheim in the Palatinate — from Merian's Topographia Germaniae *(1672).*

after 1700, supporting themselves by trade and merchandising—for example, six families, 34 persons in all, being listed in 1746.

For connections with Pennsylvania history Lambsheim is important particularly for the contributions of two of its emigrants: *Johann Philipp Boehm* and *Matthäus Baumann*. Boehm was the churchman, Baumann the sectarian, and both are remembered in the annals of colonial Pennsylvania. Boehm graduated from schoolmaster status to lay reader to ordained clergyman in Pennsylvania, and is considered the founder of the German Reformed Church in the United States. Baumann was a radical pietist and separatist who got caught in the meshes of the state church machinery in Germany and migrated to Pennsylvania where he was free to propagate his message. In the court case of 1702 in which Baumann was accused of pietism, he testified that he recognized no written confession, but belief in God alone, with whom he had spoken, and who had sent him to call the people to repentance. Furthermore, Baumann declared that the clergy of the state churches preach false doctrine. By 1706 he had converted *Jakob Berg, Jakob Bossert, Philipp Burkhard, George Hört, Valentin Kilian, Philipp Kühlewein* and other members of the Kühlewein family, *Adam Pfarr, Hans Georg Ritter,* and *Johann Traut*. The men were in 1706 imprisoned and sentenced, on bread and water, to clean out the town ditches, on which most of them took the oath. *Andreas Bossert,* who refused to take the oath to the elector, was banished on April 29, 1719 from town and province. *Philipp Kühlewein* left with the Palatine migration of 1709, and *Matthäus Baumann* followed in 1714. In 1719 his brother-in-law *Abraham Zimmermann* and mother-in-law *Dorothea Kühlewein* joined Baumann in Pennsylvania.

The emigration to America from Lambsheim was to increase in the 19th Century. The book estimates a total of 1133 Lambsheimer emigrants to America in the years 1832-1877, or an average of 25 per year. In editing the 18th Century emigration materials we have added the American materials in bracketed sections to each emigrant's sketch as found in the Rembe volume. Will readers who have additional data on these emigrants, particularly information on where they settled in the American colonies, please contact the editor?

We are grateful to Heinrich Rembe, compiler of the book, whose decades of archival research and insistence upon accuracy of transcription are evident on every page, and to Dr. Fritz Braun, director emeritus, and Dr. Karl Scherer, director of the Heimatstelle Pfalz in Kaiserslautern, for permission to make these materials available to our readers. Because of its basic importance as a genealogical aid and as model for similar work in this country, this book—and its successors in the series—should . be in every genealogical library in the United States, as well as every historical society library in the Pennsylvania German counties.— EDITOR.]

1. *Matthäus Baumann* (No. 57), Reformed, "a Pietist and originator of this sect" [*ein Pietist und Urheber dieser Sekte*], 1702. Emigrated to Pennsylvania about 1714, founding there the sect of "Baumannites," and died about 1727. Married 1697, *Katharina Kielewein,* Reformed, single, daughter of *Hans Theobald Kühlewein* (No. 107), Reformed, farmer, field surveyer, almoner, who died before 1697, and his wife *Dorothea,* of Lambsheim, where they had a house in the Hintergasse. *Matthäus* and *Katharina Baumann* had a daughter *Sara,* baptized November 22, 1700; Sponsors: *Johannes Fischer* and wife *Sara*.

[Matthäus Baumann was well known in colonial America. He was a radical pietist who after a conversion experience accompanied by trances in 1701 gathered to himself other believers at Lambsheim. Emigrating to Pennsylvania in 1714 he transplanted his sect to American soil. In the history of religion in America Baumann is recognized as one of the pioneer advocates of the doctrine of perfectionism which in the 19th Century was to flower into the Holiness movement. About 1723 Baumann wrote a volume entitled *Ruf an die Nicht Wiedergeborenen* which was published in Germany in the Pietist work *Die geistliche Fama*. One of the first Reformed ministers in Pennsylvania, Georg Michael Weiss, answered it with the pamphlet *Der in der Amerikanischen Wildnusz unter Menschen von verschiedenen Nationen und Religionen hin und wieder herum wandelte und verschiedentlich angefochtene Prediger* (Philadelphia, 1729). For a translation of his work, which is set as a "conversation" between a "politicus" and a "New Born," see *Penn Germania*, I (1912), 338-361. For Baumann and his conversion, see "Matthias Baumann and the New-Born Sect," in P. C. Croll, *Annals of the Oley Valley in Berks County, Pa.* (Reading, 1926), pp. 17-20. The *Chronicon Ephratense* (1786) describes Baumann as having been "an upright man, and not to have loved the world inordinately; but Kuehlenwein, Jotter and other followers of his were insatiable in their love of the world". This refers to *Philip Kühlewein* (q.v.), brother-in-law of Baumann, and *Hans Joder* (1672-1742), brother-in-law of Philip Kühlewein, who came to America together via London in 1709 and settled in the Oley Valley, where they were joined by Baumann in 1714. For a facsimile of Baumann's will of 1727, see John Joseph Stoudt, *Sunbonnets and Shoofly Pies: A Pennsylvania Dutch Cultural History* (New York, 1973) pp. 187-188.]

2. *Hans Jakob Baumann* (No. 59), "the carpenter," became citizen of Lambsheim 1717, coming from Wallenburg, Canton Basel, Switzerland. Emigrated to Pennsylvania in 1727 on the ship *Adventure,* from Rotterdam via Plymouth.

[*Jacob Bauman* arrived at Philadelphia on the Ship *Adventure,* October 2, 1727 (Strassburger-Hinke, *Pennsylvania German Pioneers,* List 4 A-B), along with *Michel Müller, Johannes Ullerich,* and *Peter Rool (Ruhl),* all of Lambsheim. *Jacob Baumann,* carpenter, was a member of the Reformed Church at Germantown, and one of four trustees who in 1734 planned the erection of a church building. He appears to have been a friend and consultant of the Reverend *Johann Philipp Boehm* (q.v.); see William J. Hinke, ed., *Life and Letters of the Rev. John Philip Boehm, Founder of the Reformed Church in Pennsylvania, 1683-1749* (Philadelphia, 1916), pp. 241-242, 250, 293, 297, 374.

The will of *Jacob Bauman,* carpenter, of Germantown, Philadelphia County, was signed April 30, 1749, and probated May 19, 1749. It mentions his wife *Margaret* and five daughters: *Margaret, Susanah, Elizabeth, Catherine,* and *Sybilla.* Executors were *Dirck Keyser* and *Christopher Meng;* witnesses: *Christopher Sowers, Christ[ian] Lehman,* and *John Dewald End.* It is recorded in the Register of Wills Office, Philadelphia, G, 271.]

3. *Maria Katharina Bechtold* (No. 71) emigrated in 1738 to the "New Land". She was the widow of *Zacharias Bechtold* (No. 70), non-citizen [*Beisass*] of Lambsheim, whom she married January 8, 1730. It appears that she was the widow of *Hans Martin Bentz* of Hessheim; she had a daughter, *Maria Katharina,* from the first marriage, who was eight years of age in 1730. The source for her emigration is the Lambsheim Council Protokol for 1738, p. 92. Her husband *Zacharias Bechtold* was the son of *Hans Stephan Bechtold* (No. 68) and his wife *Anna Elisabetha* of Lambsheim. He had been previously married also. He was buried at Lambsheim January 29, 1734, at the age of 50 years.

[Rembe (p. 22) assumes that *Katharina Bechtold* came to Philadelphia on the Ship *St. Andrew* in 1738, with other Lambsheimers, but since women's names are not given in the lists of passengers on this particular ship, it is impossible to know for sure. Two Bechtold emigrants are listed for 1738 in Strassburger-Hinke.

Town Layout of Lambsheim, showing churches and schoolhouses, inns (the "Hirsch" is No. 6), three town bakehouses, and other details (from Rembe, Lambsheim).

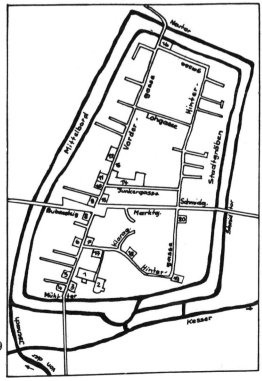

LIFE AND LETTERS

OF THE

REV. JOHN PHILIP BOEHM

FOUNDER OF THE REFORMED CHURCH
IN PENNSYLVANIA

1683-1749

EDITED BY THE

REV. WILLIAM J. HINKE, PH. D., D. D.

PROFESSOR OF SEMITIC LANGUAGES AND RELIGIONS IN AUBURN
THEOLOGICAL SEMINARY

Philadelphia
PUBLICATION AND SUNDAY SCHOOL BOARD OF THE
REFORMED CHURCH IN THE UNITED STATES
1916

The organizer of Pennsylvania's German Reformed churches was a Lambsheim schoolmaster, John Philip Boehm. This is the titlepage of the standard biography of Boehm, by William J. Hinke.

Hennrich Bechdoldt arrived on the Ship *Thistle,* September 19, 1738 (List 57 A-C), and *Veit Bechtoldt,* aged 26, on the Ship *Friendship,* September 20, 1738 (List 58 A-C), the latter in the same list with *Adam Pence,* aged 22, and *Vallentin Benz,* aged 48. Will readers inform the editor if these, or other *Bechtolds (Bechtels)* in the emigrant lists are connected with the Lambsheim family?]

4. *Johannes Bender* (No. 115), blacksmith, of Windecken, was received as citizen of Lambsheim, May 7, 1696. Emigrated to Pennsylvania April 20, 1719. His wife, *Anna Helena,* was living in 1706, died before 1719. His children remained in Lambsheim. One is mentioned: *Anna Dorothea,* who married in 1716 *Veit Dörr* (No. 342), Lutheran, blacksmith, who was received into citizenship at Lambsheim October 22, 1728, was a member of the town council, and died at Lambsheim October 30, 1767. *Anna Dorothea Dörr* was buried at Lambsheim April 11, 1760. Their son *Erhard Dörr* (1715-1752), No. 343, farrier, left descendants in Lambsheim. According to the Lambsheim deed and contract records, *Johannes Bender* on May 7, 1716, sold his smithy to his son-in-law *Veit Dörr* [*Joh. Bender verkauft seine Schmiede seinem Tochtermann Veit Dörr*]. The archival sources for Johannes Bender are the *Bürgerbuch,* the *Rechnungen,* and the *Kauf- und Kontraktbuch.*

[Can readers inform us where *Johannes Bender* settled in America? Of interest is the fact that a later emigrant named *Philip Bender* was born "in the city of Windeck in the County of Hanau," March 28, 1752 *(The Pennsylvania Dutchman,* I:20 [November 1949], 6).]

5. *Johann Philipp Böhm* (No. 187), Reformed, was received as citizen at Lambsheim April 14, 1706. In his earlier years he was innkeeper of the Stag Inn [*Hirschwirt*] at Lambsheim. From 1708-1715 he was Reformed schoolmaster at Worms, 1715-1720 schoolmaster at Lambsheim, emigrated to Pennsylvania in 1720. He was born at Hochstadt, November 25, 1683, and died at Hellertown, Pennsylvania, April 29, 1749. He was the son of *Philipp Ludwig Böhm* and *Maria (Engelhard) Böhm,* of Wachenbuchen. He married, about 1706, *Anna Maria Stehler,* Reformed, daughter of *Hartmann Stähler* (No. 1847), and his wife *Anna Maria,* who on April 17, 1682, bought the Stag Inn [*Herberg zum Hirsch*] from his brother-in-law *Heinrich Ruhl* (No. 1605), and died before 1697. The Widow Stähler married *Johann Philipp Scherer* (No. 1685), q.v.

The children of *Johann Philipp Böhm* were (1) *Anna Maria,* who married *Adam Moser;* (2) *Sabina,* who married *Ludwig Bitting;* (3) *Elisabeth;* (4) *Maria Philippina;* (5) *Johann Philipp;* and (6) *Anton Wilhelm,* born at Worms April 27, 1714, died in Upper Saucon Township, Lehigh County, Pennsylvania.

[The schoolmaster Boehm, on emigrating to Pennsylvania, became a lay reader in the Reformed congregations, and finally at the request of the Pennsylvania congregations was ordained by the Dutch Reformed authorities of New York. The definitive biography is William J. Hinke, ed., *Life and Letters of the Rev. John Philip Boehm, Founder of the Reformed Church in Pennsylvania, 1683-1749* (Philadelphia, 1916), which includes translations of Boehm's annual reports to the Reformed Classis of Amsterdam, and other correspondence and documentation, 1728-1749. It supersedes the biographies by Henry Harbaugh, *Fathers of the Reformed Church,* I, 275-291; and Henry S. Dotterer, *Rev. John Philip Boehm* (Philadelphia, 1890). See also the *Dictionary of American Biography,* II, 404-405. The present publication clears up one point about which Hinke was uncertain. He states (p. 18) that Boehm married a Stehler in Lambsheim but Pennsylvania sources indicate that his wife's father was *Philip Scherer.* He even goes so far as to state (p. 145) that "after leaving Worms Boehm's first wife died and he married again at Lambsheim, Anna Maria Scherer". The mystery is cleared up when we read in the present source that Boehm's mother-in-law, *Anna Maria Stähler,* widow of *Hartmann Stähler,* married as her second husband, *Johann Philipp Scherer* (No. 20, below).

Additional material on Boehm's children can be found in Hinke, Chapter IX, "Boehm's Family and Descendants," pp. 145-151. Of these, the *Bittings* lived in what is now Lower Milford Township, Lehigh

100

County, and the *Mosers* in Philadelphia County. *John Philip Boehm, Jr.*, lived in Whitpain Township, Philadelphia County, before moving to Philadelphia. *Elizabeth Boehm* married *George Shamboh*, weaver, of Upper Milford Township, Bucks County. The youngest daughter, *Maria Philippina*, married *Cornelius Dewees*, cooper, of Whitemarsh Township, Philadelphia County, and later of Gloucester County, New Jersey.]

6. *Jakob Bossert* (No. 213), Reformed, day-laborer, was received as citizen of Lambsheim, May 7, 1696. He was a Pietist, who in 1706, with other adherents of the sect, was punished by having to clean out the town ditches. Emigrated to Pennsylvania on the Ship *Allen* in 1729. He married *Anna Eva Wagenmann*, daughter of *Hans Valentin Wagenmann* (No. 2050), who was received as citizen of Lambsheim December 2, 1663, coming from Hessheim, and his wife *Barbara*. *Jakob* and *Anna Eva (Wagenmann) Bossert* had a daughter *Eva Katharina*, baptized April 26, 1699.

[*Jacob Bosserdt (Possart)* is listed among the passengers of the Ship *Allen,* arriving at Philadelphia September 11, 1729 (List 10 A-C). He was accompanied by *Johannes Possart* (under 15), and *Susanah,* *Marilis,* and *Eve Possart,* in that order. Other Bosserts and Boshearts arrived later. One *Jacob Bossert,* of Berks County, made his will September 12, 1753; it was probated in Philadelphia November 29, 1753. In Egle's *Notes and Queries,* 3d series II (1896), 445-448, there is a lengthy Bible record of another *Jacob Bozart (Bostart)* who was married at the age of 25, on Michaelmas day 1721, to *Esther Mellinger.* "We also left our Fatherland," he writes, "in the year 1726, and betook ourselves upon the journey to Pennsylvania, and through the aid of the Almighty reached our destination on the 8th of November". From its intermarriages *(Mellinger, Denlinger)* this latter family appears to have been Mennonite.]

Andreas Bossert (No. 214), Reformed, from Pfaffenhofen, was received into citizenship at Lambsheim May 7, 1696. He was also a Pietist who in 1719, on refusing to take the oath to the Elector, was banished from the city and the province. His wife, *Katharina Werner,* was still in Lambsheim in 1719. For *Andreas Bossert* and his wife, see Nos. 2172, 2173, and 2174.

[Did this *Andreas Bossert* come to America? Was he, for example, identical with the *Andrew Buzard* who is listed as a taxable in Colebrookdale Township, Philadelphia (now Berks) County, Pennsylvania in 1734 (Morton L. Montgomery, *History of Berks County in Pennsylvania* [Philadelphia, 1883], p. 964)? An emigrant named *Andreeas Bussart* also arrived at Philadelphia on the Ship *Isaac,* September 27, 1749 (List 138 C). Will readers who have information on the Bossert (Boshart, Buzzard) families of Pennsylvania consult us on this identification problem?]

7. *Leonhard Christler* (No. 286) was received as citizen at Lambsheim March 1, 1709, coming from Fussgönheim. His wife's name was *Anna Maria.* He sold his house to Thomas Deffaa (No. 316) and emigrated to Pennsylvania in 1719.

[*Leonard Christoleer* is listed with 200 acres among those who paid quit rents in Franconia Township, Philadelphia County, prior to 1734 (I. Daniel Rupp, *A Collection of Upwards of Thirty Thousand Names of German, Swiss, Dutch, French and Other Immigrants in Pennsylvania from 1727 to 1776* (Philadelphia, 1875), Appendix XVI, p. 471). One *John Jacob Christler,* aged 42, arrived in Philadelphia on the Ship *Harle,* September 1, 1736 (List 41 A-C), with a *Johann Philip Wageman,* aged 23. Were these connected with the Lambsheim families of Christler and Wagenmann?]

8. *Heinrich Grünewald* (No. 643), Reformed, was received as citizen of Lambsheim, October 22, 1728. He married on June 21, 1725, *Anna Maria Ferbert,* Reformed, daughter of *Nikolaus Ferbert* (No. 438), farmer, and his wife *Anna Katharina (Weinheimer) Ferbert,* who lived next to the Stag Inn. *Nikolaus Ferbert* had been received as citizen March 18, 1678, and served as councilman and assistant mayor of Lambsheim, 1706-1711. *Heinrich Grünewald* sold his house and land September 21, 1737, and emigrated to America in 1738. Source: Lambsheim Deed Protocol, 1719-1749.

Heinrich and *Anna Maria (Ferbert) Grünewald* had the following children in Lambsheim: (1) *Maria Katharina,* died January 26, 1729; (2) *Peter,* born 1729; (3) *Johann Adam,* born 1731, died 1732, aged 4 months; (4) *Albert,* born December 3, 1733; and (5) *Sophie,* born January 9, 1737, buried December 2, 1737.

[No Heinrich Grünewald appears in Strassburger-Hinke. Rembe (p. 22) suggests that he may have been identical with the *Johann Henrich Wald* who arrived on the *St. Andrew* in 1738 with Stähler, Hortt and other Lambsheimers, but an examination of the facsimile lists in Volume II rules out this possibility. Can readers identify this emigrant for us? Others of the name arrived later; *Abraham Grünewald* in 1740, aged 40 (List 76 A), and *Jacob Grünewald* in 1741, aged 18 (List 84 A-C). The *Philip Lorentz Greenawalt* who emigrated in 1749 and settled near Ephrata in Lancaster County, was born in 1725, at Hassloch near Böhl in the Palatinate (Egle's *Pennsylvania Genealogies* [Harrisburg, 1896], pp. 303-314).]

9. *Johann Adam Hauck* (No. 685), Reformed, married for the third time August 16, 1733, *Anna Margaretha Bornträger,* Reformed, a native of Hohensülzen. Their children were (1) *Johann Jakob,* born November 11, 1734 (was 30 years old in 1764), and (2) *Anna Maria,* born August 4, 1741 (was 23 years old in 1764). According to documents in the town archives

dated August 1, 1749, and in the state archives at Speyer dated July 28, 1764, both of these children remained in Lambsheim, and did not, like their mother and stepfather, go to America. It appears that *Anna Margaretha (Bornträger) Hauck,* widow, from Hohen-sülzen, married again on July 1, 1749, to *Jakob Hönig* (No. 805), Reformed, son of *Georg Hönig* (No. 801) and his wife *Anna Elisabetha (Ferbert) Hönig* of Lambsheim. Both *Jakob Hönig* and his wife went to Pennsylvania about 1764 (document in Speyer state archives dated July 28, 1764). They had a daughter *Katharina,* born March 10, 1751.

[*Jacob Hönick* arrived at Philadelphia on the Ship *Hero,* October 27, 1764 (List 248 C). It may be significant that on the same passenger list appear the names *Jacob Hauck, Johannes Hauck, Christian Schowalder,* and *Johannes Gress.* Do any of these connect with the Lambsheim families of the same name?]

10. *Georg Adam Hochermuth* (No. 772), Mennonite [*Mennist*], linenweaver, was received into citizenship at Lambsheim February 15, 1709. He was born at Hassel-bach in the Helmstadt dominions [*Helmstättische Herr-schaft*]. He is mentioned in the town records, 1702-1708. His wife's name was *Barbara.* They both emigrated to America in 1709.

The Hochermuth house in the Hintergasse was pur-chased in 1709 by *Bernhard Schowalter* (No. 1770), Mennonite, who is mentioned in the Lambsheim town records, 1704-1719. He was received into citizenship at Lambsheim January 2, 1709, his birthplace being given as Strengelbach in the Aarburg district of Canton Bern, Switzerland [*Strengelbach, Aarburger Amt, Berner Gebiets*]. He was single in 1709; his wife's name was *Magdalena.*

[*George Adam Hoherluth (sic),* aged 45, with wife, sons 12 and 9, and daughters 17 and 14, Baptist (= Anabaptist, i.e., Mennonite), is named among the cloth and linenweavers in the list of "first arrivals" of Pal-atines in London in 1709 with *Philip Kühlewein* ("Lists of Germans from the Palatinate who Came to England in 1709," *The New York Genealogical and Biographical Record,* XL [1909], 53). *Mathias Adam Hogermöd* is listed among those from what is now Berks County, Pennsylvania, who were naturalized between January 9, 1729 and 1730 (*Votes of Assembly,* III, 131, re-produced in I. Daniel Rupp, *A Collection of Upwards of Thirty Thousand Names* [Philadelphia, 1875], Ap-pendix II, p. 435).

For *Showalter (Schowalter)* genealogy, see *The Men-nonite Encyclopedia,* IV, 479-480, 516-517. In 1936 the surname *Schowalter* was the third most common Mennonite name in the Palatinate, after *Krehbiel* and *Stauffer.* Various Schowalter emigrants arrived in Pennsylvania in 1744, 1750, and 1764, branching from there into the Shenandoah Valley of Virginia.]

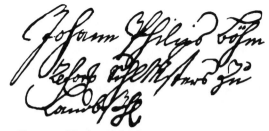

Signature of Boehm while schoolmaster at Lambsheim.

11. *Johannes Hörd* (No. 824), son of *Hans Georg,* Reformed, and *Sara (Wagemann) Hörd,* Reformed, was received into citizenship at Lambsheim January 15, 1734, and emigrated to the New Land in 1738. His father *Hans Georg Hörd* (Nos. 818-819), farmer, who had come from Hesse-Darmstadt territory, had become a citizen of Lambsheim May 7, 1696. He had become a Pietist and in 1706, with others, was penalized by having to clean the town ditches. *Sara Wagemann,* his second wife, was the daughter of *Hans Valentin Wagemann* (No. 2050), who was received as citizen of Lambsheim December 2, 1662, coming from Hess-heim. She died before 1721 and *Hans Georg Hörd,* after a third marriage, died in 1732. Source: Testa-ment of 1732 in the town archives, and other documents.

[*Johannes Hertt,* brother-in-law of *Jacob Bossert* (No. 6, above), arrived at Philadelphia on the Ship *St. Andrew,* October 27, 1738 (List 62 A-C), with *Johann Nickolas Stähler* of Lambsheim (q.v.). In the same list are emigrants named *Behringer, Wisler, Böhm,* and *Messer,* all names found in Lambsheim and vicinity.]

12. *Philipp Kielewein* (No. 1074), Reformed, had become a Pietist, for which in 1706 he was punished, with others, by being forced to clean the town ditches. He was the son of *Hans Theobald Kühlewein* (No. 1071), Reformed, farmer, field surveyor, and almoner, and his wife *Dorothea. Hans Theobald Kühlewein* had been received into citizenship December 2, 1663, and is mentioned in the town archives from 1653 to 1691. In 1673 he is listed as having "five small children". He died before 1697 and his estate was divided by his widow among eight children on February 28, 1707. The children's names were *Sara, Sebastian, Veronika, Albert, Katharina, Anna Maria, Maria Elisabeth,* and *Philipp.* Philipp was still single in 1707. On January 20, 1712, *Abraham Zimmermann* (q.v.) of Lambsheim stated to the town council that *Philipp Kielewein,* his brother-in-law, had, before his departure for the "Island of Pennsylvania," sold him a quarter of an acre of land. Source: Lambsheim Deed Protocols, 1712.

The children of *Hans Theobald* and *Dorothea Kühle-wein* were the following: (1) *Sara,* born circa 1665, buried January 8, 1735, aged 70 years; married *Johannes Fischer* (No. 458), miller, who died before 1717, leaving descendants in Lambsheim; (2) *Sebastian*, (No. 1072), who died before 1723, married *Margareta Weissbecker*, leaving descendants in Lambsheim; (3) *Veronika*, married *Abraham Zimmermann* (No. 2249), q.v.; (4) *Albert* (No. 1073), born circa 1670, died January 6, 1726, aged 56 years; (5) *Katharina*, married *Matthäus Baumann* (No. 57), q.v.; (6) *Anna Maria*, buried at Lambsheim December 16, 1735, married *Johann Valentin Stahl* (No. 1830), born circa 1665, died January 1, 1726, aged 61 years; their son *Johann Jakob Stahl* (No. 1838), q.v., emigrated to Pennsylvania in 1738.

[*Philipp Kühlewein* was an early settler in the Oley Valley in what is now Berks County, Pennsylvania. He came to America in 1709 with *Jean LeDee*, of Eppstein in the Palatinate, near Lambsheim, and *Hans Joder* (1672-1742) (*The New York Genealogical and Biographical Record*, XL [1909], 51-52). Both Joder and Kühlewein married daughters of Jean LeDee. Both also were followers of the New Born sect of Matthäus Baumann (q.v.), who married Kühlewein's sister Katharina. *Philip Kühlwein* is listed among those who paid quit rents on land (200 acres), in Oley Township, Philadelphia County, before 1734 (I. Daniel Rupp, *A Collection of Upwards of Thirty Thousand Names* [Philadelphia, 1875], Appendix XVI, p. 475). He was also naturalized 1729-1730 (Rupp, p. 434). The surname was spelled *Killwaine* and *Coolwine* in early records.]

Dorothea Kühlwein (No. 2327), widow of *Theobald Kühlwein* (No. 1071), requested permission to leave for the "Island of Pennsylvania" on March 8, 1719. Source: Deed protocols of Lambsheim, 1719-1749.

13. *Albrecht Dietrich Marterstock* (No. 1233), born at Lambsheim, married (second) on September 5, 1710, in West Camp, Ulster County, New York, *Elisabetha Rübenich(ts)*, from Sitters (Rockenhausen), widow of *Matthäus Rübenich*. The family had originated in Lambsheim/Frankenthal, and emigrated 1709/1710. The original place of settlement, 1710-1714, was West Camp, Ulster County, New York. Source: the Kocherthal Records in Macwethy's *Book of Names*. Four children were born in West Camp: (1) *Johann Dietrich*, born November 26, 1711; (2) *Johanna Maria*, born December 17, 1714; (3) *Daniel*, born December 23, 1716; and (4) *Maria Christina*, born March 17, 1719. The name *Marterstock* could not be located in the documents in the Lambsheim Archives.

[*Albert Friedrich Marterstock* is listed among the Palatines in Livingston Manor, New York, in the winter of 1710 and the summer of 1711 (I. Daniel Rupp, *A Collection of Upwards of Thirty Thousand Names* [Philadelphia, 1875], Appendix VII, p. 446). *Johannes Marder Steck* and *Johann Martin Martersteck* arrived at Philadelphia on the Ship *Adventure*, from Hamburg, September 25, 1754 (List 217 A-C). Were they connected with the Lambsheim family?]

14. *Christian Merkel* (No. 1296), Reformed, cartwright, married *Katharina Bender* in 1711. Is mentioned in the Lambsheim records beginning with 1704, when his property was valued at 100 florins. On April 19, 1719, he sold his house in the Vordergasse to *Dietrich Roth* and emigrated to America. He died in Pennsylvania in 1766.

Maria Katharina Merkel, daughter of *Christian* and *Katharina (Bender) Merkel*, was baptized at Lambsheim January 21, 1715. She married *Johann Kaspar Stoever* (1707-1779), and emigrated to Pennsylvania in 1728. The sponsor at the baptism of *Maria Katharina Merkel* was *Katharina Ursula Schmidt*. Information from the Reverend Carl T. Smith, 7109 Erdrick Street, Philadelphia, Pennsylvania, February 19, 1958.

[*Christian Merckel* of Philadelphia County made his will April 25, 1749, probated May 22, 1766. It lists his sons *Peter, George, Christian*, and *Casper*, and daughters *Catherine Stover, Frankiena (Franzina?) Rugh, Mary Hill, Anna Maria Cramer*, and *Anna Lena Merckel*. In the Berks County tax lists of 1759, the Merckel family was concentrated in Richmond Township, where they were members of the Moselem Lutheran Church; and in Reading, where *Christian Merckel* had property (Morton L. Montgomery, *History of Berks County in Pennsylvania* [Philadelphia, 1886], pp. 655-656, 1035-1036, 1038). In upstate Pennsylvania the name became *Markle* as reflected in place names (e.g., Marklesville in Perry County, and Marklesburg in Huntingdon County.)

For Pastor Stoever, see John W. Early, "The Two Stoevers: John Caspar Stoever of Virginia and John Caspar Stoever of Pennsylvania," *The Pennsylvania-German*, XI (1910), 267-275. Additional materials can be found in P. C. Croll, *Ancient and Historic Landmarks in the Lebanon Valley* (Philadelphia, 1895), and in the various histories of Pennsylvania Lutheranism.]

15. *Georg Heinrich Mörschheimer (Morsheimer, Mörsheimer)* (No. 1351), Reformed, was received into citizenship at Lambsheim, July 3, 1749. He was born about 1722 (was 21 years old in 1743), son of *Johann Konrad Mörschheimer* (1681-1737), No. 1350, schoolmaster in Grosskarlbach 1718 and in Lambsheim 1728 (received citizenship at Lambsheim October 22, 1738) and his wife *Luisa Eleanora (Müller)*. *Georg Heinrich Mörschheimer* married on January 14, 1749, *Franziska Rhode*, Reformed, daughter of *Johann Georg Rothe (Rode)*, 1699-1735 (No. 1591), master tailor, a native of Frankenthal formerly in Oppau, and his wife *Anna Margareta (Wagner)*, a native of Lambsheim, daughter of *Jakob Wagner* (1675-1735), No. 2056, and his wife *Petronella* (1672-1731).

According to documents in the state archives at Speyer (Kurpfalz No. 1330), *Georg Heinrich Mörschheimer* and his wife were in Pennsylvania in 1770. Their children were the following: (1) *Johann Hein-*

House in which Boehm died, Hellertown, Pennsylvania.

rich, born November 24, 1749; (2) *Johann Philipp,* born January 17, 1751; (3) [a second] *Johann Philipp,* born April 23, 1753 (godfather: *Johann Philipp Roob,* schoolmaster in Hassloch); (4) *Sebastian,* born February 23, 1755; (5) *Anna Margaretha,* born May 22, 1757; (6) *Maria Elisabetha,* born March 26, 1761; and (7) *Johann Heinrich,* born August 2, 1763.

[*Henrich Morschheimer* arrived at Philadelphia on the Ship *Britannia,* September 26, 1764 (List 245 C). *Henry Mershimer* is listed as an inmate in Vincent Township, Chester County, Pennsylvania, in 1771 (*Pennsylvania Archives,* 3d Series, XI, 773).]

16. *Michael Müller* (No. 1371) was born at Steinweiler in the Oberamt Lautern. When he was received into citizenship at Lambsheim, June 4, 1721, it was stated that he was formerly on the farm property at Weilach which belonged to the counts of Leiningen. He arrived at Philadelphia on the Ship *Adventure,* October 2, 1727.

[*Michel Müller* heads. the list of passengers on the Ship *Adventure,* arriving at Philadelphia, October 2, 1727 (List 4 A-B). On the same ship were *Johannes Ullerich, Jacob Bauman,* and *Peeter Rool (Ruhl),* all from Lambsheim.]

17. *Peter Ruhl* (No. 1608), Reformed, was received into citizenship at Lambsheim, November 10, 1721. He was born at Lambsheim, son of *Hans Jakob Ruhl* (No. 1607) and his wife *Anna Barbara.* His occupation was wineloader [*Weinläder*] and night-watchman [*Nachtwächter*], and he was one of three non-hereditary tenants [*Temporalbeständer*] on the Sturmfeder property. He paid his emigration tax in 1727 and emigrated to Pennsylvania on the Ship *Adventure* in 1727. He married, about 1718, *Katharina Stumpf,* Reformed, from Lambsheim, daughter of *Martin Stumpf* (No. 1944) and his wife *Katharina. Martin Stumpf* had been received into citizenship at Lambsheim, May 7, 1696, coming from Bocksberg.

On March 30, 1731, it was reported that *Peter Ruhl* "has sent from Pennsylvania a power of attorney, to auction off the goods inherited from the deceased Margaretha Stumpf" [*hat aus Pensilvanien Vollmacht geschickt, die von der verstorbenen Margaretha Stumpf ererbten Güter zu versteigern*].

[*Peeter Rool* made his mark in the list of passengers on the Ship *Adventure,* arriving at Philadelphia, October 2, 1727 (List 4 A-C), along with *Michel Müller, Johannes Ullerich,* and *Jacob Bauman,* all from Lambsheim. An evidently younger *Peter Rule (Rulle, Rool)* is listed in Rockhill Township, Bucks County, Pennsylvania, 1779-1786; and another in Rapho Township, Lancaster County, 1782 (*Pennsylvania Archives,* 3d Series, XIII, 79, 297, 386, 439, 594, 686; XVII, 787. Will readers help us to identify the emigrant?]

18. *Johann Philipp Scherer* (No. 1685), Reformed, farmer, innkeeper of the Stag Inn [*Hirschwirt*] and city councilor, was received into citizenship at Lambsheim May 7, 1696, from Heuchelheim. He married *Anna Maria Stähler,* widow of *Hartmann Stähler* (No. 1847), circa 1696, and had a son *Hans Peter,* baptized November 10, 1697.

[We have added *Johann Philipp Scherer* as emigrant from the fact that a deed given by the daughters of *John Philip Boehm* to his youngest son *John Philip Boehm, Jr.,* July 1, 1749, mentions "their grandfather Philip Sherer," who is to be supported "with all necessaries during the Term of his natural Life" (Recorder of Deeds Office, Philadelphia, G-12, 450 ff., recorded 1751). The deed was witnessed by *Johann Nicholas Staehler* (No. 20, below). *Philip Sherer* lived at Whitemarsh north of Philadelphia, where he was a deacon of the Reformed Church, 1739-1744 (Hinke, *Boehm,* pp. 148, 284, 292, 316, 340, 363, 395, 476-480).]

19. *Johann Jakob Stahl* (No. 1838), Reformed, farmer, was baptized at Lambsheim January 8, 1697, son of *Johann Valentin Stahl* (1665-1726), No. 1830, Reformed, and his wife *Anna Maria (Kielewein). Johann Jakob Stahl* was received into citizenship at Lambsheim November 10, 1721, and married on January 24, 1736, *Anna Maria Strupp,* Reformed, who was born in Eppstein and appears to be the daughter of *Hans Georg Strupp* of Eppstein. On April 28, 1738, the Stahls sold their entire property for 1201 florins and emigrated to North America (Ratsprotokol 1738, pp. 87, 92). They had two children born in Lambsheim: (1) *Johann Georg,* born August 12, 1736; and (2) *Susanna,* born February 16, 1738.

[*Johann Jacob Stahl,* aged 30, heads the list of passengers on the Ship *Winter Galley,* arriving at Philadelphia on September 5, 1738 (List 52 A-C). Another *Johann Jakob Stahl* arrived in 1739 (List 73 A-C). Various emigrants named *Strub(b)* are listed in Strassburger-Hinke. *Stahl (Stall, Stoll,* etc.) is a not uncommon name in Pennsylvania and it is difficult to identify this emigrant in the tax lists. It would be of interest if he were the *Jacob Stahl* who settled with the *Stählers* in Upper Milford Township, now Lehigh County, where a *Jacob Stahl, Sr.,* is listed in 1772 *(Pennsylvania Archives,* 3d Series, XIX, 11).]

20. *Johann Nikolay Stähler* (No. 1851), son of *Johannes Stähler* (1675-1727), No. 1848, innkeeper of the Stag Inn [*Hirschwirt*], and his wife *Anna Katharina (Ferbert).* *Johann Nikolay Stähler* was the eldest son and married, on December 3, 1730, *Maria Magdalena Maurer,* Reformed. In 1738 *Nikolay Stähler* sold his entire property for 1044 florins and the family emigrated to North America. The Stähler children were (1) *Friedrich,* born October 23, 1731; died 1733; (2) *Johann Georg,* born January 22, 1734; and (3) *Anna Katharina,* born November 11, 1736, buried February 22, 1738. *Johann Nikolay Stähler* was a nephew of *Johann Philipp Böhm* (q.v.).

[*Johann Nickolas Stähler* arrived in Philadelphia on the Ship *St. Andrew,* October 27, 1738 (List 62 A-C), with *Johannes Hertt* of Lambsheim and possibly other Lambsheimers (see above, No. 11). According to the Mathews and Hungerford *History of Lehigh and Carbon Counties, Pennsylvania* (Philadelphia, 1883), pp. 352, 359, 367, *Johann Nicolaus Stähler* settled in Milford (later Upper Milford) Township, Bucks, now Lehigh County, Pennsylvania, about a mile southwest of the village of Zionsville. His name appears in both the Lutheran and Reformed registers of the Upper Milford churches at Zionsville. He made his will September 17, 1794, mentioning six sons: *Anthony* (died 1797), *John Nicholas, Jr., Philip, Ludwig* (executor), *Henry,* and *Peter.* The son Ludwig was Justice of the Peace, 1787-1821, and a grandson, *Daniel Stahler* (1781-1854), established the first hotel in Dillingersville, 1812, and the same year was appointed post-master of the first post office in Upper Milford, Stahler's P.O., later renamed Dillingersville. His nephew *Joshua Stahler* was Register of Wills for Lehigh County, 1851-1854, Coronor 1855, and was elected Associate Judge of Lehigh County, 1856 and reelected 1861. The name is spelled *Stahler* in Lehigh County today.]

21. *Johannes Traut* (No. 1980), Reformed, brewer, accused of Pietism in 1706 and sentenced, with others, to the cleaning of the town ditches. According to the Lambsheim deed registers, he sold his house in the Kirchgasse to *Adam Fauth* in 1709. His wife's name was *Anna Katharina,* Reformed, and they had a son *Johannes,* baptized at Lambsheim, July 5, 1699. *Johannes Traut,* brewer, and his wife *Katharina* were sponsors at the baptism on January 4, 1699, of *Johannes Traut,* son of *Hans Georg* and *Anna Maria Traut* of Lambsheim, both Reformed.

[Among the "first arrivals" of Palatines in London in 1709, along with *Philip Kühlewein* and *Georg*

Adam Hochermuth, appears the name of *John Truat (sic),* aged 40, Reformed, brewer, with wife and two sons aged 10 and 6 respectively ("Lists of Germans from the Palatinate who Came to England in 1709" [*The New York Genealogical and Biographical Record,* XL (1909), 52]).]

22. *Johannes Ullrich* (No. 1996) was received into citizenship at Lambsheim, November 10, 1721. His name appears in the account registers [*Rechnungen*] for 1727 and he may be identical with the *Johannes Ulrich* who emigrated to Pennsylvania with other Lambsheimers on the Ship *Adventure* in that year.

[*Johannes Ullerich* arrived at Philadelphia on the Ship *Adventure,* October 2, 1727 (List 4 A-B), along with *Michel Müller, Jacob Bauman,* and *Peeter Rool (Ruhl),* all of Lambsheim.]

23. *Sebastian Weber* (No. 2092) and his wife *Apollonia (Geyger) Weber* were listed as in Pennsylvania in 1751. She had an inheritance of 270 florins coming to her after the death of her parents (document in the town archives dated May 11, 1751). The wife was a daughter of *Nikolas Geyger (Geiger, Geyer, Geier),* No. 557, Reformed, stonemason, from Dettlingen in Switzerland, who was received into citizenship at Lambsheim February 16, 1701, and his wife *Katharina Müller* (1670-1743), Reformed, a native of Lambsheim, daughter of *Matthäus Müller* (No. 1357), who "came to Lambsheim as a single man from Böhl and married here in 1671" and his wife *Apollonia.*

[*Sebastian Weber* is not listed among the emigrants before 1753 when an emigrant by that name arrived at Philadelphia on the Ship *Rowand,* September 29, 1753 (List 209 A-C). Several *Sebastian Weavers* are listed in the Pennsylvania tax lists. One was a tailor in Exeter Township, Berks County, 1779-1781; there is a *Bastian Weaver* in Reading, 1785; and a *Sebastian Weaver* in Mt. Pleasant Township, York County, in 1783 *(Pennsylvania Archives,* 3d Series, XVIII, 222, 356, 481, 799; XXI, 801). Will readers working on these families inform us if any of these is identical with the Lambsheim emigrant?]

24. *Abraham Zimmermann* (No. 2249), Reformed, town beadle [*Büttel*], is mentioned in the town records from 1704 to 1719. He married *Veronika Kielewein,* Reformed, daughter of *Hans Theobald Kühlewein* (No. 1071) and his wife *Dorothea* (see No. 12, above). The Zimmermanns sold their house and farm fields on April 24, 1719 and emigrated to Pennsylvania.

[*Abraham Zimmermann* settled in what is now Maxatawny Township, Berks County, not too far from the families of his brothers-in-law *Matthäus Baumann* and *Philip Kühlewein.* As *Abraham Timberman* he is listed as among those who paid quit rents on land in Maxatawny prior to 1734 (Rupp, p. 475). His name also appears among those naturalized from Philadelphia County, 1734-1735 (Rupp, p. 435).]

NOTES
and
DOCUMENTS

Edited by DON YODER

The two documents which we have selected for publication in this issue deal with what one may call the "wider world" of the Pennsylvania Farmer in the 19th Century. This world psychologically included much more than his farm and home surroundings on the local scene. In the 18th and early 19th Centuries there was a dwindling orientation toward Europe and the roots of one's family there; in the later 19th Century almost every Pennsylvanian had a partial orientation toward the West—he had relatives who had moved to Ohio, Indiana, Iowa, Kansas, or other areas involved in the great rural diaspora from Pennsylvania.

The first of our documents illustrates the European orientation of the Pennsylvania German farmer—in this case the Bertolet family of Berks County—in the first decades of the 19th Century. The letter was bought at a sale of an Oley Valley Bertolet estate near Pleasantville, Berks County, June 1963. It is written on one sheet of paper and is evidently a contemporary copy (or first draft?) of the original which presumably was sent abroad, in answer to a letter that had come from the Palatinate requesting information on the Bertolets of Pennsylvania. The letter is part of the editor's collection of Pennsylvania manuscript source materials.

The letter is interesting on several counts. The first is the great length of time (80 years) over which pre-emigration family traditions had been preserved in Pennsylvania. Jean Bertolet, of a French-speaking family from Chateau-d'Oex, Canton Vaud, Switzerland, had settled in Minfeld, Germany, and after raising a family, had emigrated to Pennsylvania in 1726, where he died in 1757. This letter, written 1806, documents a continuing, though dwindling, connection kept up between relatives in Continental Europe and Pennsylvania throughout the 18th Century. Secondly, the letter is of interest for its genealogical information, not only for its specific family data but from the fact that, though extremely brief, it is one of Pennsylvania's earliest written genealogies. Thirdly, the letter is important linguistically, as evidence of the level on which the German language—which Pennsylvanians called "High German"—operated in the Pennsylvania German culture.

To our knowledge this document has never before been published. There is no reference to it in Daniel H. Bertolet, *A Genealogical History of the Bertolet Family: The Descendants of Jean Bertolet* (Harrisburg, Pennsylvania, 1914), the official Bertolet history.

The Editor will be pleased to hear from readers who know of other unpublished letters of this sort, either (1) letters *from* Pennsylvanians who corresponded with their relatives in Europe in the 18th and early 19th Centuries, or (2) letters that were sent *from* Europe—from the *Freundschaft*, as Pennsylvanians called the wider relationship to which their family belonged—reporting on news from the home villages —*to* Pennsylvania farmers who had emigrated.

I

A LETTER TO GERMANY (1806)

Mein Herr

Ein Brief von einem reformirten Prediger Nahmens *F. Lorch* aus Wilgartswiesen bei Zweibrücken vom 5ten Juny 1801, ist uns Endes unterschriebenen den 1ten Juny 1806 zu Händen gekomen; in demselben werden Nachrichten verlangt von einer gewissen *Marie Herancourt*, die an einen *Jean Bertolet* verheirathet war, und zugleich gebeten die Antwort darauf an Sie zu addressiren; wir machen Ihnen hie[r]mit also bekant, was wir davon wissen.

Es befindet sich in unsern Händen eine alte französ[is]che Bibel, die im Nachlass des *Jean Bertolet* gefunden worden, in derselben finden wir aufgezeichnet

Abraham Bertolet gebohren den 11ten December 1712
Maria Bertolet gebohren den 12ten July 1715
Johann Bertolet gebohren den 28ten September 1717
Esther Bertolet gebohren den 12ten August 1720
Susanne Bertolet gebohren den 17ten December 1724.

[1] *Abraham Bertolet* war verheirathet zu einem *De Turck*[;] beide sind gestorben un so auch ihre Kinder, ausser einer Tochter, so an einen *Hannes de Turck* verheiratet ist, aber noch viele Kindeskinder von Ihnen am leben.

[2] *Johann Bertolet* war verheirathet an *Catharine Ballie*, beide sind gestorben, von ihren Kindern lebt noch ein Sohn *Hannes Bertolet*, der verheiratet und Kinder hat, und sechs Mädchens die unverheiratet sind.

[3] *Marie Bertolet* war verheirathet an *Stephan Bernet*, beide sind gestorben, und noch fünf ihrer Kinder am leben, nebst Kindeskindern.

[4] *Esther Bertolet* war verheirathet an *Georg de Bannevill*, beide sind gestorben und noch Sechs ihrer Kinder am leben, nebst Kindeskindern.

[5] *Susanne* war verheirathet an *Jacob Frey*[;] beide sind gestorben und noch drey Kinder am leben nebst Kindeskindern.

Weiter können wir Ihnen melden, dass nach der Aussage der ältesten Einwo[h]ner in *Oley,* wie ein anderer Einwo[h]ner daselbst unter dem Nahmen *Bertolet* gewesen, als der alte *Jean Bertolet,* der daselbst mit seiner Frau vor vielen Jahren gestorben mit seinen oben angeführten Kindern und Kindeskindern.

Der alte *Jean Bertolet* hat seinen Kindern oft gesagt, er habe in Europa auf einem *Jesuiter Hoff,* nahe bey *Candel* ohnweit *Landau* gewohnt; seine Kinder wären in der dasigen reformirten Kirche getauft, und habe er drey Schwestern in Deutschland zurückgelassen, wovon eine verheirathet gewesen.

Die noch lebende Verwandte erinnern sich, dass Sie öfters von Ihren Eltern gehört, wie die Briefe von Ihren Freunden aus Deutschland erhalten, auch selbige besonders von *Georg deBannevill,* welches mit der Esther Bertolet verheiratet war, beantwortet worden, allein es können keine desselben mehr gefunden werden.

Im übrigen was die Umstände der hinterlassenen Kindeskinder des *Jean Bertolet* und der *Marie Herancourt* betrift, so sind sie alle in einem blühenden Wohlstand und behaupten den Nahmen rechtschaffener Einwo[h]ner dieses Landes[.] Wir werden und freuen ein gleiches von unsern Freunden in Deutschland zu hören, und sind bereit Ihnen alle Nachrichten unsere Familie betreffend, umständlicher zu geben, wann es verlangt wird. Ihre Briefe werden uns gewiss sicher zu Händen kommen, wann sie addressirt werden, an *John Keim,* Kaufmann in *Reading* im Staat *Pensilvanien*[.] Wir bitten Sie keinen andern Schreiben und Nachrichten von unserer Familie Glauben beizumessen, als die von unserer Hand kommen; indem sich immer Leute finden die durch Betrug suchen Vorteile zu gewinnen.

Wir empfe[h]len Sie alle dem Schutz des Allerhöchsten und verbleiben

> Ihre getreue Freunde
>
> *John Keim,* verheirathet zu einer Tochter des *Georg deBannev*[ill] in *Reading* wohnhaft
>
> *Hannes Bertolet* ein Sohn des *Johan Bertolet* in *Oley* wohnh[aft]
>
> Im Nahmen der Hinterlassenen des *John Bertolet*

An den H[errn] *Professer*

Faber in *Zweibrücken*

Donnersberger *Departement*

in Franckreich

Dieser Herr wird gebeten die hierin enthaltene Nachrichten dem H[errn] Prediger *Lorch* in Wilgartswiesen und dem Schullehrer H[errn] *Cullmann* in *Franckweiler* bei *Landau* bekant zu machen.

TRANSLATION

Dear Sir:

A letter from a Reformed preacher named *F. Lorch* from Wilgartswiesen near Zweibrücken dated 5 June 1801 reached us the undersigned on 1 June 1806. In it information is requested about a certain *Marie Herancourt* who was married to a *Jean Bertolet,* and at the same time an answer to it was ordered, to be addressed to you. We therefore acquaint you herewith with what we know.

There is in our hands an old French Bible, which was found in the estate of *Jean Bertolet.* In it we find recorded:

Abraham Bertolet, born 11 December 1712.

Maria Bertolet, born 12 July 1715.

Johann Bertolet, born 28 September 1717.

Esther Bertolet, born 12 August 1720.

Susanne Bertolet, born 17 December 1724.

[1] *Abraham Bertolet* was married to a *DeTurck;* both are dead and their children are dead too, except a daughter, who is married to a *Hannes deTurck;* but many of their grandchildren are still alive.

[2] *Johann Bertolet* was married to *Catharine Ballie;* both are dead. Of their children a son, *Hannes Bertolet,* is still living, who is married and has children, and six girls who are unmarried.

[3] *Marie Bertolet* was married to *Stephan Bernet.* Both are dead, and there are still five of their children living, besides grandchildren.

[4] *Esther Bertolet* was married to *Georg deBannevill.* Both are dead and there are still six of their children living, besides grandchildren.

[5] *Susanne* was married to *Jacob Frey.* Both are dead and there are still three children living besides grandchildren.

We can further inform you, that according to the statement of the oldest inhabitants in Oley, there was another inhabitant by the name of Bertolet, namely old *Jean Bertolet,* who died there with his wife many years ago, with his above-mentioned children and grandchildren.

Old Jean Bertolet often told his children that he had lived in Europe on a farm owned by the Jesuits, near Candel, not far from Landau, that his children had been baptized in the Reformed Church in that place, and that he left three sisters in Germany, of whom one was married.

The relative[s] who are still living remember that they frequently heard from their parents, how they received letters from their friends [relatives, i.e., *Freundschaft*] in Germany, also that these were answered, particularly by *Georg deBannevill* who was married to *Esther Bertolet,* but none of these letters can be found anymore.

For the rest, as to the particulars of the surviving grandchildren of *Jean Bertolet* and *Marie Herancourt,* they are all in a flourishing state of prosperity and maintain the name of honest inhabitants of this country. We will rejoice to hear the same of our relatives in Germany, and are prepared to give them all more detailed reports concerning our family, when it is requested. Their letters will certainly come safely into our hands, if they are addressed to *John Keim,* merchant, in Reading in the State of Pennsylvania. We ask you to put no faith in any other writings or reports about our family than those that come from our hand, since there are always people who seek to win advantage by deceit.

We commend you all to the protection of the Almighty and remain

> Your true friends,
>
> *John Keim,* married to a daughter of *Georg deBannevill,* resident in Reading.
>
> *Hannes Bertolet,* a son of *John Bertolet,* resident in Oley.
>
> In the name of the survivors of John Bertolet.

To: Professor Faber in Zweibrücken,

Donnersberg Department, in France.

This gentleman is requested to make known the herein contained information to Preacher Lorch in Wilgartswiesen and the schoolmaster Mr. Cullmann in Franckweiler near Landau.

OLD GOSCHENHOPPEN CHURCH, 1858-1915

The Old GOSCHENHOPPEN LUTHERAN BURIAL REGISTER 1752-1772

Translated by CLAUDE W. UNGER

[The records of the Old Goschenhoppen Lutheran Church appeared in *The Perkiomen Region* (Pennsburg, Pennsylvania), I–III (1921–1925). Of the 18th Century Lutheran church registers in existence, the Old Goschenhoppen record is of particular value because of the fullness of its personal data. However, not all the early personalia appear in the printed version. From the Unger-Bassler Collection at Franklin and Marshall College, comes the following missing burial register for the years 1752–1772, valuable for the light it sheds on the life of the times. We are indebted to Prof. Herbert B. Anstaett, Librarian, Fackenthal Library, Franklin and Marshall College, for its use here.

As historical source materials for our study of Pennsylvania folklife, we call attention especially to the many references to the European homeland of emigrants, the frequent mixed marriages (Lutheran-Reformed, Protestant-Catholic), the funeral texts used, the details on the causes of death, the time of death (invariably reported), burial in private burial grounds as well as churchyards, and in one case, mention of a funeral held at sunrise. The translation of the register was done by the late Claude W. Unger of Pottsville, Pennsylvania. —EDITOR.]

THE GOSCHENHOPPEN LUTHERAN BURIAL RECORD, 1752-1772

OF THE DEAD WHO WERE BURIED PUBLICLY

In the year 1752 the following were buried:

1. *Eva Margaretha* [*Kayser*], born March, 1751, died January 31, 1752, buried February 2, in the cemetery in front of the Old Goschenhoppen Church, on Sexagesima Sunday before the public service. Parents: *Johann Jacob Kayser,* Lutheran, and *Anna Marie,* Reformed.

2. *Jacob Eckmann,* aged 65 years, born 1687, from Switzerland, from the Canton of St. Gall, Reformed, from Rumels-

horn. Father: *Ulrich Eckmann.* Left behind only one son, *Jacob* by name, and his widow *Anna.* Died July 3, 1752, and was buried in our cemetery in Old Goschenhoppen, July 4, 1752.

In the year of the Lord 1753, the following were publicly buried:

3. *Johann Jacob Filmann,* died February 14 in morning toward 4 o'clock. Lived in this world of woe 71 years, 1 month, and 18 days. He lived in wedlock almost 50 years. Has 15 children, 19 grandchildren, and 5 great grandchildren. There are still living 2 sons, 1 daughter, 14 grandchildren, and 5 great grandchildren. He was buried in the cemetery at the new stone church in Old Goschenhoppen, February 16, 1753. His funeral text, Micah, 7:20, he chose before his death.

4. *Margaretha Müller,* aged 82 years, 6 months, and 12 days. Died Thursday, July 26, in the afternoon around 4 o'clock, buried July 8, on the Graw place. The funeral text was John 5:28–29. Her husband was *Johannes Müller,* who died in 1735. She was a widow for 15 years. They left no children. She was born near Treschlingen in the district of Gemmingen in Germany and came to America in 1729. Her father was *Martin Sindel,* her mother *Margaretha,* nee *Fischer.*

5. *Peter Schwenk,* aged 62 years, 1 month, 12 days, born September 27, 1690, died November 9, 1753, between 10 and 11 o'clock at noon [*sic*], buried November 11, in Old Goschenhoppen, on the 23rd Sunday after Trinity.

6. *Georg Henrich Bamberger,* aged 1 year, 3 months, born August 22, 1752, died November 22, 1753, at night between 11 and 12 o'clock, buried in the Old Goschenhoppen churchyard, November 24. The funeral text: Luke 7:13, "The sweet word of Jesus Christ," etc. Father: *Lorentz Bamberger,* Reformed; Mother: *Elisabetha,* Lutheran. Sponsors:

Georg Henrich Wiedergrundel and his wife *Catharina*, both Lutheran.

7. *Matthaeus Fetzer*, aged 24 years, 7 months, and 25 days, born April 2, 1728, died November 27, 1753, at night around 10 o'clock, buried November 29 on Martin Deer's place. Text: Revelation 20:12. Father: *Matthaeus Fezer* or *Fetzer* from the Ulm District; Mother: *Anna Agatha;* both of the Evangelical Lutheran religion. He married in 1751, *Anna Barbara Bartholomae,* now the surviving widow. In 1751 came to America. No children.

Died in 1754:

8. *Jacob Bisecker*, born 1687, died March 27, 1754, Friday, in the evening, suddenly; buried in the Old Goschenhoppen cemetery, March 29. Text: Psalm 90:10–12. Father: *Jacob Bisecker* from Manheim, Reformed. In his first marriage he lived 17 years, and had 5 children, of whom only a son survives; in the second marriage he lived 22 years, and had 3 children, who with their mother survive. He came to America in 1733.

9. *Fridrich Moy*, born 1745, around Bartholomew Day, died August 30, at night, buried on Martin Deer's place, September 1, the 12th Sunday after Trinity. Parents: *Simon Moy* and Mother: *Susanna,* born Reformed.

10. *Johann Michel* [*Moy*], born January 21, 1741, died September 1 in evening, buried Tuesday, September 3. Aged 13 years, 7 months, and 10 days. Buried on the Deer place beside his brother *Fridrich Moy.* Text: Judges 11:35. The parents are the above named *Simon Moy* and *Susanna.*

11. *Anna Catharine Kantz*, born May 28, 1723, died November 20, buried November 22 on Matius Reininger's place. The funeral text was Genesis 47:9. Father: *Gerhard Konig* from Eutz, Mother: *Anna Margaretha.* In 1741 she married *Johann Kantz* and lived a married life 13 years and 6 months, and bore 4 children, 1 son and 3 daughters, of whom only one daughter survives. In 1754, the present year, she came into this America. Aged 31 years, 5 months, and 23 days. Was Reformed.

In 1755 the following were publicly buried:

12. *Johannes* [*Bamberger*], born November 15, 1748, died March 10, 1755, in the morning around 5 o'clock, buried March 11. The funeral text was Genesis 22:1–2, preached at the Old Goschenhoppen Church before a befitting gathering. Parents: *Lorenz Bamberger,* Reformed, and *Maria Elisabetha,* Lutheran. Sponsors: *Henrich Bamberger,* Reformed, and *Maria Elisabetha,* Lutheran, the grandparents of the deceased child. Aged 6 years, 3 months, and 25 days.

13. *Anna Margareth* [*Martin*], born December 26, 1711, died July 4, from madness, buried July 6, on Martin Deer's place. Father: *Johannes Teiswalentin* from Rod at the Weil [*sic*] in the District of Asingen, Mother: *Agnese;* baptized December 30, Lutheran. She married 1737, in the month of March, *Jost Martin,* Lutheran. Have 11 children, of which 3 survive. In 1754, they came to America. Aged 43 years, 6 months, and 11 days.

14. *Anna Elizabeth* [*Schwenck*], Lutheran, born December 26, 1732, died November 8, in the afternoon at half past one o'clock, buried November 9, in Old Goschenhoppen. Text: Philippians 1:21. Father: *Peter Schwenck,* deceased, see above, No. 5. Aged 22 years, 10 months, and 13 days.

15. *Margaretha* [*Hornnecker*], Reformed, born 1731, in Spring, died December 25, early, buried December 26, on Jacob Beier's place. Text: Revelation 7:27 ff. Father: *Joseph Eberhardt,* Mother *Catharina,* born Reformed. Married in 1754 *Ulrich Hornnecker,* Reformed. Aged 24 years, died in confinement.

In 1756 the following were buried:

16. *Johann Wilhelm Thaub*, died January 27, in the evening between 4 and 5 o'clock, buried January 29, in our churchyard at Old Goschenhoppen. Text: Psalm 90:10–11.

17. *Anna Maria* [*Schneider*], born March 3, 1756, died April 25, buried April 26 in the Old Goschenhoppen churchyard. Text: 2 Samuel 12:22–23. Father: *Leonhardt Schneider* and *Christina.*

18. *Anna Elisabeth* [*Meperis*], born February 28, 1739, died May 15, around 4 o'clock in afternoon, buried May 16 in Old Goschenhoppen churchyard. Aged 16 years, 2 months, and 16 days. Text Psalm 90:5–7. Father: *Silvanus Meperis* and *Dorothea,* deceased.

19. *Michael Bauman*, widower, Reformed, born 1699. Father: *Henrich Bauman,* Mother: *Maria Barbara,* both deceased; from Alseborn in the Pfalz. In 1742 married *Anna Elisabeth,* who died June 23, 1754, in Pennsylvania. With her he had 8 children, of whom 3 sons and 2 daughters survive. In 1744 he came to America. Died July 26 of this year, around 3 o'clock in morning. Buried on Johannes Zieber's place on July 27; the text was Sirach 41:1; I Samuel 15:32. Aged 57 years.

20. *Maria Dorothea* [*Grau*], born 1749, died May 2, buried May 3, in Old Goschenhoppen churchyard. Parents: *Johann Georg Grau* and *Maria Magdalena.* Aged 7½ years.

21. *Anna Eva Jöckel*, close to 60 years of age. Father: *Wilhelm Klinger* from Pfaffen Beerfurth, in Churpfalz. Had as her first husband *Johann Philip Heist,* from which marriage there remains a grandchild and a daughter living across the Susquehanna. On November 13, 17[-]5, after the death of her first husband, she married *Bernhardt Jöckel,* Catholic, a journeyman mason. In 1751 they came to America, where in that very year Bernhardt Jöckel, her second husband, died, and lies buried on Martin Deer's place. From this second marriage she left behind a son Nicolaus, who is a servant 2 miles from Philadelphia. In her widowhood she stayed in New Goschenhoppen. Was also very sickly until finally her weakness increased so that on October 10, the 17th Sunday after Trinity, she was overcome with an apoplectic stroke on her right side, and immediately lost the power of speech. Finally on November 6, 1756, in the morning somewhere around 2 o'clock she fell peacefully asleep at Simon Moy's place, and on November 7, the 21st Sunday after Trinity, was buried on Martin Deer's place.

In 1757 were buried:

22. *Johann Georg Wagner*, died January 9, 1757, buried the 11th of that month in our churchyard at Old Goschenhoppen. Funeral text: Sirach: 41:3–4. Aged 76 years, 8 months, and 16 days. Was afflicted a few times with apoplexy but recovered, until finally, January 9, he was overcome with hematemesis, or spitting of blood, and as it were suffocated in his own blood.

23. *Fridrich* [*Filler*], born August 17, 1754, died March 2, 1757. Parents: *Balser Filler* and wife *Anna.* Godparents: *Fridrich Gerdi,* single, and *Magdalena,* wife of *Casper Achebacher.* Buried on March 3, on Johann Züber's place. Text Ruth 1:20–21.

24. *Anna Maria* [*Sanders*], 2 years, 6 months, and 8 days old. Died in the Swamp Creek and was found dead on April 29. Buried April 30 at sunrise, on Martin Deer's place. Parents: *Henrich Sanders* and wife *Elisabetha Maria.* Funeral text Amos 3:6, Is there evil in the city.

25. *Johann Jacob* [*Berckheimer*], born October 14, 1753, baptized November 21, died May 13, 1757, from smallpox, buried May 15, in our cemetery. Parents: *Lennert Berck-*

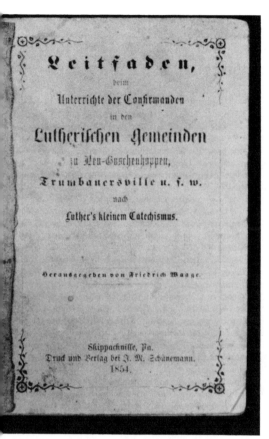

Catechism from New Goschenhoppen, prepared by Friedrich Waage, Lutheran pastor.
Don Yoder Collection

heimer and *Maria Catharina.* Aged 3 years, 6 months, and 30 days.

26. *Maria Elisabeth [Tuchmann]*, born February 23, 1757, died May 14, buried the 15th of same month. Whooping cough cause of death. Aged 2 months and 21 days. Parents: *Christman Tuchmann.* Lies buried on Martin Deer's place.

27. *Johann Jacob Werner*, born June 16, 1754, died June 6, 1757, buried on Johannes Züber's place. Baptized July, 1754. Parents: *Peter Werner* and wife *Anna Maria.* Godparents: *Jacob Issed* and his wife *Anna Maria.* Aged 2 years, 11 months, and 20 days.

28. *Johann Jacob Nuss*, died September 20, 1757, in the morning around 5 o'clock, buried on the 21st of this month in the Old Goschenhoppen churchyard. Reached the age of 41 years, 3 months, and 24 days.

29. *Elisabeth [Wagner]*, born in 1721 in Reichenbach in the Grafschaft of Ehrbach, Father: *Michel Engelhardt,*

Mother: *Elisabetha Catharina.* Lived in union with her first husband, *Balsar Jockel,* who died 1753, 15 years, but with her second husband, *Philip Wagner,* only 5 months. From her first marriage she has 6 children, of whom 2 have died. She died October 26 and was buried October 27 in Old Goschenhoppen. Aged 36 years and 27 days.

1758

30. *Johann Philip [Reith]*, born July 19, 1756. Father: *Philip Reith,* died January 16, buried 17 of this month in Old Goschenhoppen. Text Luke 7:13. Aged 1 year, 5 months, and 27 days.

31. *Jacob Görckes*, born January 14, 1736, died February 2, 1758. Text Ecclesiastes 12:1, Exord[ium] Psalm 119:9. Parents: *Wilhelm Görckes* and *Margreth.* Sponsors, the grandparents: *Jacob Keller* and *Anna Maria,* both deceased. Buried February 4 in the Old Goschenhoppen churchyard. Aged 22 years, 18 days.

32. *Johann Jacob [Detweiler]*, born September 5, 1756, died February 25, buried February 26 on the burial place of Martin Deer, his grandfather. Parents: *Jacob Detweiler* and *Margaretha;* Godparents: *Henrich Keppel* and his wife *Eva Greta.* Died from coughing. Text Proverbs 4:13–14. Aged 1 year, 5 months, and 20 days.

1762

33. *Susanna Gerlach*, born September 18, 1693, died January 15, 1762, in the morning around 3 o'clock. Aged 68 years, 3 months, and 27 days. Buried January 16, in Old Goschenhoppen.

1765

34. *Margretha Frey Vogler*, died January 16, buried January 17, in Mardin Kistner's cemetery in New Goschenhoppen.

35. *Kilian Gaugler*, buried July 26, 1765, church elder at Old Goschenhoppen. Aged 39 years, 10 months, and 2 weeks.

36. *Philip Filman*, buried August 31, 1765. Was a church elder.

37. *Henrich Werner*, died October 13, 1765, buried at Old Goschenhoppen. Aged 70 years.

1766

38. *Nicklas Werckheisser*, died March 16, 1766, buried in Jacob Wentz's cemetery near the new church.

1767

39. *Anna Barbara Grim*, died September 24, 1767, buried on September 26. Aged 1 year, 6 months. Father: *Conrad Grim,* deacon in the Lutheran congregation in Goschenhoppen. Mother: *Anna Barbara.*

40. *Vallentin Nungesser*, died November 1, 1767. Was church elder in the Evangelical [Lutheran] Congregation in Old Goschenhoppen. Aged 49 years, 5 months, and 17 days.

1769

41. *Christina Schneider*, wife of *Lehnhard Schneider,* died March 4, 1769, buried on March 4.

42. *Johannes Grim*, son of *Conrad Grim,* church elder in the Evangelical [Lutheran] Congregation at Old Goschenhoppen. Buried April 1, 1769.

1772

43. *Anna Margaretha [Andreas]*, wife of *Friedrich Andreas,* died April 1, buried on the 3rd. Aged 34 years, 3 months, and 3 weeks.

44. *Anna Christina [Dürr]*, daughter of *Carl Dürr,* died June 29, buried July 1. Aged 3 years, 4 months, and 15 days.

45. *Christina [Eitenmuller]*, daughter of *Johann Nicol[aus] Eitenmuller,* died July 24, buried the following day. Aged 13 years and 6 months.

Personalia from the "Amerikanischer Correspondent" 1826-1828

Edited by DON YODER

[The *"Amerikanischer Correspondent für das In- und Ausland"* (The Domestic and Foreign American Correspondent) was published at Philadelphia from 1826 to 1828 by John George Ritter, printer and publisher and all-round entrepreneur.

From a bound copy of this twice-weekly sheet, from the Editor's Collection, we have culled the following personalia and items of folklife interest. The paper itself was published in an 8 by 10 inch format, with eight pages to each issue. Most of the news was national or international, and the items selected here appeared mostly on the advertising pages. While the locus of the paper was Philadelphia and the readership appears mostly to have been of the urban 19th Century emigrant-German class, the urban "German-American" culture of Philadelphia impinged on the Pennsylvania German culture upstate, and there are many items given here which connect the two cultures.

Especially interesting are the advertisements asking for information on lost emigrants, the patent medicine testimonials, announcements of the German "Fastnacht" Balls, descriptions of German-American taverns and bars and oyster-houses, lists of imported books for sale, European religious prints, Taufscheins for families of fourteen, and other offerings.

In the advertisement pages the Editor, Johann Georg Ritter, appears as an entrepreneur of wide interests. Not only did he publish this newspaper and run a large German and English printshop, but he operated a Lottery Office, a "European-German Forwarding Agency" (*Deutsch-Europäische Spedit. und Commiss. Comptoir*), a "European-German Book and Art Shop" (*Deutsch-Europäische Buch- und Kunsthandlung*), and a German Reading and Lending Library. His book offerings included everything from German almanacs, wholesale and retail, through jokebooks, to Lutheran hymnals and Bibles with large print, for aged and weak-eyed persons.

The paper was printed in two columns to each page, with columns rather than pages numbered continuously in each volume. Thus the numbers preceding each of the items given here refer to the column on which the information is found.

For the *Amerikanischer Correspondent*, see Karl J. R. Arndt and May E. Olson, *German-American Newspapers and Periodicals, 1732-1955*, 2d revised edition (New York: Johnson Reprint Corporation, 1965). The *Correspondent* was published from 1825 to 1829. Apparently the copies abstracted here are unique, since the only library holdings listed are New York Public Library: 1825, Nos. 1-36, 38-52 (January-June 1825), and Historical Society of Pennsylvania: 1829, Nos. 66-104, August-December 1829. —EDITOR.]

No. 43 (May 31, 1826).

686: A letter to Mr. *Christ. Gilliome* in *Kerkrig* Township, Wayne County, Ohio, was sent to us via France and New York, and is to be had on payment of costs and taxes. J.G. Ritter, European-German Forwarding Agency.

687-688: Long list of German books for sale; also Latin. J.G.Ritter.

No. 44 (June 3, 1826).

699: Old bound books for sale in the European-German Book and Art Shop, J.G.Ritter. Subjects: geography, devotion, sermons, plays, medicine, travel, and humor. See also Column 701.

702: *Heinrich Schröder,* innkeeper at the Sign of Wilhelm Tell, change of address. Best choice of drinks, good stabling for 18 to 20 horses. The editors of the *Readinger Adler*, the *Volksfreund* in Lancaster, and the German paper in Baltimore are requested to insert the above advertisement in their respective sheets for a period of three weeks, and send the bill to the office of this newspaper.

702: Ten Dollar Reward for gold watch and chain stolen by a customer, signed by *Gottlieb Schultz,* Clockmaker, 331 N. Second Street.

703: *Johannes Seiser,* tailor business, offers a fine selection of materials, cassimirs, vestings and summer clothing. Needs ten expert tailors immediately.

703: *J.E.Sauter,* cabinetmaker.

703: List of agents of this paper in Baltimore, New York, Allentown, Reading, Lancaster, Hagerstown, and Columbus, Ohio.

704: Advertisement for "Painkilling Spirits" (*Schmerzstillender Spiritus*).

704: Advertisement offering Lutheran Hymnal (*Erbauliche Liedersammlung*).

No. 45 (June 7, 1826).

715: Advertisement for Johann Hübner's *Biblische Historien* [standard devotional work for Pennsylvania Germans in 19th Century]. *Wilhelm Wheit* and *Wilhelm Boyer,* printers, Harrisburg.

718: *Gustav Schulz,* house and pocket-watch maker, 122 N. Third, 4 doors above Race Street.

No. 48 (June 17, 1826).

763: Appeal to the members of the German Lutheran Church of St. Michaels and Zion, on building a new German Lutheran church at Lancaster.

764: Advertisement for Hoyt's Steel Patent Bells, signed by *Lorenz Meyers.*

764: A letter to *Nicolaus Suter,* on Big Pine Creek, Brown Township, Jersey Shore, is available on payment of 50 cents, at the European-German Forwarding Agency.

764: German schoolmaster and his wife, lately arrived from Europe, advertise their services for private instruction to the

The "Amerikanischer Correspondent" was published by Johann Georg Ritter and edited by J. C. Gossler.

educated public. They teach German and French, drawing, piano, and all feminine handiwork.

766: Long list of books for sale by J.G.Ritter, including D.F.Schäffer's *Description de l'Amérique* (Berlin, 1823).

766: Emmenthaler Cheese available at C. G. Ritter's, Confectioner and Distiller, N. Fourth Street, between Cherry and Race.

766: 100 Dollar Reward. According to an advertisement in the *Correspondent* in 1816 the grain-handler *Michael Bär* from Rossbach in Bohemia had died in Pennsylvania several years previously, leaving considerable property, the rightful heirs of which are still living in Germany. Said M.B. according to reports had a significant grain business with England and later hanged himself. Information sought about his death. European-German Forwarding Agency.

766: Two brothers, *Ludwig Maximilian* and *Carl Moritz Sause*, from Bautzen in Oberlausitz in Saxony, went some years ago to America, sending no word since 1822, at which time the former was in Philadelphia and the latter in Heidelberg Township, Lehigh County, Pennsylvania. Their mother, who is very much concerned about them, requests information about them via the Editor of the *Correspondent*.

766: Warning against a pretended merchant who calls himself *J. C. Gerlich,* believed to be a native of the neighborhood of Frankfurt am Main. *Martin Ulmer,* Innkeeper, New York.

768: Philadelphia Market Prices: Butter in barrels, Prime Green Old Java Coffee, Santo Domingo Coffee, Upland Cotton, Tennessee and Alabama Cotton, Louisiana Cotton, Flax, Prime Flour, Rye Flour, Cornmeal, West Anker Gin,

Schiedam Gin, Philadelphia and Domestic Gin, Ginseng, Corn, Wheat, Rye, Oats, Barley, Jersey and Virginia Hams, Foreign Tallow, Domestic Tallow, Domestic Sugar, Yellow Wax, American Iron, Russian Iron, Swedish Iron, Jersey Lard, Pennsylvania Lard, Western Lard, Gypsum, Western Pork, Jersey Pork, Prime Pork, Fresh Rice, Clover Seed, Timothy, Flax.

768: Value of Banknotes: many upstate Pennsylvania banking companies listed.

No. 86 (October 28, 1826).

1365–1366: In the Hagerstown German newspaper we find the following article which might perhaps interest some of our worthy readers: On Sunday the 17th of September a young man came to the Inn of *Daniel Hollinger,* three miles from Chambersburg, and complained of not feeling well. Taking sick, he died on the 22d and was buried on Saturday. From his papers, which were found on him, it appears that his name is *Henry Louis Courvoisier,* and that he was born at Locle not far from Neufchatel in Switzerland, and was baptized in Point de Martel, December 16, 1798. Whoever wishes more detailed information, write to *Daniel Hollinger.*

1367: Report of a "horned" woman in Montgomery County, Pennsylvania, from the *American Medical Review.*

1367–1368: Review of Dr. DeWette's *Die deutsche Theologische Lehranstalt in Nord-Amerika . . .* (Basel, 1826).

1371–1372: Master-Baker *Johann Andreas Koch,* native of Göttingen, has died there with heirs abroad. Official announcement of his property, sent from Göttingen.

1372–1373: List of books for sale by J. G. Ritter.

1373: Family wants news of *Franz Weiss,* clothmaker, born in Riquewyr in the Department of the Upper Rhine in France, son of *Johann Weiss,* official in the Mortgage Bureau in Colmar. F. W. left Hunawyr for the United States June 15, 1819, sailing on the 30th on an American ship from Amsterdam to Philadelphia, and from thence went to Fair View, not far from Washington. His uncle, *Johann Immer,* born in the same place, emigrated eight years later and reported last in a letter from Philadelphia in 1819. According to this letter, Immer is said to have purchased a plantation of 500 acres in [West] Virginia and on October 31, 1819, headed there via Baltimore, Washington, Richmond, Lancaster, Columbia, Little York, Chambersburg, McConnelstown, Bedford, Somerset, Connelsville, Uniontown, Smithfield, and Clarksville. Information wanted by *Mr. Marx,* son of *Mr. Marx,* Collector-General at Colmar. European-German Forwarding Agency.

1373: C. E. Oertelt, N. Sixth Street, offers assortment of silver and other spectacles, made by himself. Takes old gold and silver in exchange. His store is open until 9 P.M.

1375: German Reading and Lending Library opened, Philadelphia.

1375: Appeals relative to power of attorney or requests about inheritance: heirs of *Nikolaus Dihl, Mrs. Wiedersum, Mrs. Eckloff,* a power of attorney to Schwalbach, an Alsheimer and Holzhauser power of attorney. European-German Forwarding Agency.

1375: Letters from Germany are available, upon payment of costs, at the European-German Forwarding Agency, addressed to the following persons in Philadelphia: *Joh. Karsten Granes; Miss Elisabeth Wolfangl,* native of Heimerdingen; *Rosina Barbara Leonhardt,* widow; *Jacob Fried. Mack,* shoemaker, born at Marbach; *Catharina Wolf.* Letters to the following persons in Northampton County: *Joh. Speer,* Forks Township; *Fried. Pet. Loehr,* Mountbethel; *Michael Braun,* Strout [Stroud] Township; *Georg Jak. Körner,* c/o Mr. *M. Braun,* Strout Township. Other areas: *Thomas Deker,* Middle Smithfield Township, Perry County, Pennsylvania; *Anna Barbara Rein,* Pennsylvania; *Jakob Spindler,* from Strassburg, c/o Mr. *Joh. Castor,* merchant in New York; *Peter Jansson,* ship's mate, in the German suburb, New Orleans; *J. Federhaen,* baker, Boston, Massachusetts.

1375: Anton Pfaff and Georg Bermann, N. Fourth Street, advertise all kinds of music boxes, and American, German, and English 8-day and 24-hour clocks.

No. 87 (November 1, 1826).

1383: Article about life in Philadelphia, from *Philadelphia Gazette,* describing slums, Negro section, etc.

1387: Marriage notice, October 30, 1826, Mr. *Wilhelm Pommer* and Miss *Maria Kurtz,* both of Philadelphia, with the following verse:

Still wie eine Nacht im May,
Sanft wie eine Silberwelle,
Fliess' der Legbenstag vorbey,
Immer ruhig, immer helle,
Nicht das kleinste Wölkchen Schmerz
Trübe Eure Jahre;
Reine Freude füll' das Herz,
Bis zur—Todtenbahre!

1387: For sale, a piece of land, Lot No. 9, Canton, Stark County, Ohio, on which stand a dwelling-house, stable and pottery with two ovens, one for stone-ware and the other for red-ware, with the necessary equipment, all in good order. Also wood and pasture land near Canton, with dwelling-house, barn, and young orchard. *John Brauss,* Canton, Ohio.

No. 93 (November 22, 1826).

1483–1484: Advertisements of books for sale by J. G. Ritter.

1485: Maximilian Gümbel announces for Spring, 1827, publication of a book, *Leben und Schicksale eines Nebensohnes des Grafen von L.*

1485: Advertisement by *Joh. Georg Ritter* of his German and English Printery and Book-Publishing Business.

1486: Tin and other toys for sale at the European-German Forwarding Agency.

1486: Letter from Germany to *Johann Philipp Pfeffer* in Emmitsburg, Maryland.

1488: Copyright notice of *Enos Benner's Abhandlung über die Rechenkunst.* [Enos Benner was a German publisher in Sumneytown, Montgomery County, and this book was one of the principal Pennsylvania German "reckoning books" published in the 19th Century.]

No. 90 (November 10, 1827).

1429: Advertisement of "German Ball" (*Deutscher Ball*), next Monday, November 12th; in case of rain, on the 19th. Ladies and Gentlemen are politely invited. *Gottlieb Gundelach.*

1429: Letters for *Friedrich Happold.*

1429: C. F. Hut announces to his friends and patrons that he again has "oysters and other refreshments" for sale at his house, between Fourth and Fifth Streets.

1429: New Augsburg Life-Essence (*Augsburger Lebens-Essenz*) received from Germany, for sale at the European-German Book and Art Shop.

1430: A. Bournonville advertises his services as "Doctor of Medical Scholarship and Obstetrician."

1430: "A German physician, living in a German and English settlement, wishes a German woman as housekeeper who speaks the English language and who, endowed with a cheerful spirit, is prepared to keep a small household in order. He lives in a beautiful region on the Juniata River. He assumes the travel costs and pays wages that the person will be satisfied with. The sooner someone is found, the happier he will be."

1430: German almanacs for sale, wholesale and retail.

1431–1432: Two-column advertisement by *Joh. J. Mayweg,* M.D., of Philadelphia, student of Dr. *Benjamin S. Barton* of the University of Pennsylvania, offering medicines for epilepsy, cramps, St. Vitus Dance, lockjaw, "nerve-balsam," cold fever drops, and a "never-failing worm-powder," with testimonials.

1432: Chr. Friedrich Burkhardt, baker, from Tübingen, who emigrated to Philadelphia in 1803, sent his last letter home in 1805. He would now be about 70 years of age. Property of 1200 florins is available to him in Tübingen.

1432: Christmas and New Year's Presents: "tin toy wares, in the German taste."

1483: J. E. Sauter, cabinet-maker, advertises sideboards, writing desks, bureaus, tables, bedsteads, chairs.

1483: Wilhelm Betz, German hatmaker, advertises children's caps, etc. He has given up his intention to move to Alabama and will remain in Philadelphia.

1483: The relatives, living in Germany, of *Caspar* and *Michael Senghass* and *Martin Simpfendörfer,* who emigrated to America in the previous century, request those Germans living in Pennsylvania who have any news of them to send it, for which a reward is offered. The advertisement quotes the following document: "We *Johann Caspar* and *Michael Senghass,* from *Manthor* [Manor] Township, Lancaster County, in the State of Pennsylvania, sons of [————] in

German-American Shipping Agency, in Post-Civil War Philadelphia. Photograph by Corliss & Ryan, 823 Race Street, who advertised on the reverse: "Views of Homesteads, Public Buildings, Interiors, School Classes and Groups taken to order. Photographing for Business Advertising a Specialty. Negatives saved two weeks."

Don Yoder Collection

Brettach, in the District of Neustadt an der grossen Linde, formerly Duchy, but now Kingdom of Würt[t]emberg, and *Martin Simpfendörfer*, hereby notify all whom it may concern their true will, that our dear sister *Barbara*, resident in the village of Brettach in Germany, shall have the power and authority to appropriate not only the property left to us in Germany, but also our property happily earned in America, and consider it her own. In case this our sister *Barbara Simpfendörfer* should no longer be alive, then we want the rights to pass to her heirs. (Signed): *Caspar Senghass, Michael Senghass, Martin Simpfendörfer.*"

1483: J. G. *Dietrich*, No. 57 Lombard Street, lately arrived from Germany, leather-maker, makes leather trousers, little corsets for children, trusses, and fontanel-bands.

1484: Wilhelm Friedrich Deubel intends to undertake a journey to Germany to bring back his child and his property. Those who wish to send along letters or powers of attorney with him are to leave the same at the meat market of *Gottl. Umahäuser*, in Coates Street, between Fourth and Fifth. Deubel will make his journey via Holland, up the Rhine by way of Mannheim to Heilbronn.

1484: Bibles with quite large print for weak-eyed or aged persons, for sale at the European-German Book and Art Shop.

No. 11 (February 6, 1828).

166: According to reports from 127 practising obstetricians, there were born in the past year in Philadelphia and her liberties 3581 male and 3452 female children.

171: Advertisement for *Jacob Albrecht's* "Columbian Syrup," New Haven, with testimonial from *Joh. Hempstead,* from the *Connecticut Herald.*

172: Mr. *Max* and *Moritz Sause*, from Bautzen in Saxony, the first of whom last sent word from Philadelphia, September 1, 1822, the latter was in 1822 at Heidelberg in Pennsylvania as physician, are requested by their relatives in Europe to notify them of their address.

172: The mother of *Julius von Schlegel,* from Dresden in the Kingdom of Saxony, seeks information on whether her son is still living. He had gone to Philadelphia in 1819, where he served some years as clerk in the business house of *Samuel Canby, Jr.,* but sailed in June, 1823, from Aislingen near Antwerp, on the Ship *Hope de Fortuna* of Amsterdam commanded by *Captain S. K. Siepka,* to Curacao in the West Indies, and from there to Rio de Janeiro and Buenos Aires.

173: Long advertisement on the Union Canal Lottery. *Johann Georg Ritter's* Lottery Office, North 2d Street.

174: New German Drugstore, *Joh. G. Braun,* Northeast corner of *"Wein"* [Vine] and Third Street.

175: Franz Schneider, who arrived here just eight days ago from Europe, lived in Hoheinet [Hoheinöd] in the Canton of Waldfischbach, requests his dear son *Nikolaus Schneider,* who learned the shoemaker trade with *Ferdinand Brändel,* to report his place of residence to his father or to come to him. He wishes to inform his son that master-shoemaker *Brändel* arrived with him. *Nikolaus Schneider* is said to be working in a town five or six miles from Pittsburg[h], with a saddler. Readers are politely requested to give said *Nikolaus Schneider* this happy intelligence. He can inquire of his father and master at the European-German Forwarding Agency.

175: The undersigned has brought along from Alsace two-year-old grapevines of the best sort, with their roots, which he is selling at very reasonable prices. His residence is with Mr. *Heinrich Heuser* in the Black Horse Tavern on the Frankfurt road in Kensington. *Joh. Schelcher.*

175–176: Genuine Blood Purification Pills, by the sole preparer, Druggist *Mörike,* from Neuenstadt. Advertisement signed by *Friedrich Klett,* German Druggist, Second and Callowhill Streets.

No. 12 (February 9, 1828).

187: "Great Ball and Supper" in the Hall, No. 62½ S. Fourth Street. *B. August* has the honor to announce to the

Ladies and Gentlemen of Philadelphia that on the 19th of February, Fastnacht Tuesday, Mardi Gras or Shrove Tuesday, he will give a great Ball, with a good supper and the best wines, liquors and refreshments. A large orchestra is engaged, which will play the newest French cotillions and waltzes, and you can dance as long as the company wishes. Price one dollar, and the subscribers have the privilege of bringing their Ladies free of charge. Price for the supper, 50 cents for a Gentleman and 25 cents for a Lady. Subscription at the above-mentioned place, where the tickets for Ladies are ready. B. A. gives instructions in dancing at the above-mentioned place and in N. Second Street No. 361.

187: Long advertisement about the Rödelsheim Legacy of the Lutheran Church.

188: Sheriff Sale at Handel's Coffeehouse, of wooden dwellings and bakehouses adjoining. Northern Liberties, Philadelphia. *Jacob Strembeck.*

189: New Grocery Store, *Wassermann* and *Osbourn,* adjoining the Red Lion Inn on N. Second Street.

No. 14 (February 16, 1828).

219–220: List of books for sale by *J. G. Ritter.*

220: Gottlieb Gundelach's advertisement for a "German Ball" on Fastnacht Tuesday, February 19. Admission 50 cents, Ladies free. A good supper, costing 25 cents per person, will be ready toward 11 or 12 o'clock. The ball lasts as long as the company desires.

No. 15 (February 20, 1828).

228: Long account of snake in stomach of Schenectady man, from the *Schenectady Cabinet.*

No. 34 (April 26, 1828).

551: William Albrecht, agent for Lancaster County, of *J. Albrecht's* "Columbian Syrup." "On Monday, the 10th of last March Mr. *Josua Blickensdörfer* of Warwick Township, Lancaster County, came to me to get a bottle of Columbian Syrup, and told me he was doing this for a gentleman in Lititz, who had the intention of trying the medicine on his daughter, who was suffering from a white swelling, because three bottles of this medicine had cured his brother, who had suffered for longer than six years with the same ailment, in which time many of the most skilled physicians had tried their art of healing on him in vain. Mr. Blickensdörfer lives with his brother-in-law, Mr. *William Schmick,* in Nazareth, Northampton County . . ." Appended is a testimonial letter from *William Schmick,* Nazareth, dated March 24, 1828; also a testimonial from *Elizabeth Meyers,* Philadelphia, dated February 12, 1828.

552: Jacob Herng advertises his Inn and Cottage Garden on the road to Germantown, with bowling alley.

553: Heinrich Heisser, innkeeper at the Black Horse, on the Frankfurt road in Kensington, announces improvements to his establishment. The garden behind is laid out as a pleasure park, with flowers and plants, footpaths leading to the little summer-house, and a greenhouse with thousands of domestic and foreign plants. His bar is provided with the best wines, liquors, and refreshments.

553: William Henning, Tailor, No. 389 N. Front Street.

553: J. A. Donath, attorney. German, French, and English [*Engländer*] clients served.

554: Letter to Mr. *John Miller,* Jefferson County, [West] Virginia, two miles from Charlestown.

556: List of books for sale by *J. G. Ritter.*

No. 35 (April 30, 1828).

567: Joseph Rickert, German Druggist, Third and Callowhill Streets, advertises Mörike's Blood Purification Pills and the famous Augsburg Life-Essence.

Advertisement for Albrecht's "Columbian Syrup" fro the "Correspondent." Good for the King's Evil, liv ailments, rheumatic pains, dermatological conditior jaundice, and stomach trouble!

568: Universal Remedy to destroy bedbugs, advertised by *Joh. U. Buchler,* with instructions in German and English.

573: C. K. Servos advertises cheap wares, including mirrors, prepared by himself, fireplace instruments, tongs, etc., available cheap to the country merchants.

573–574: List of books for sale by *J. G. Ritter.*

No. 39 (May 14, 1828).

631: Information wanted on *Xaver Suidter* and wife. *Antonia,* nee *Abt* from Riedlingen, who emigrated in 1817 from Schelklingen in the Kingdom of Württemberg. They lived originally with Mrs. Rhun in S. Fifth Street.

631: Long testimonial to Albrecht's "Columbian Syrup" by *Stephen Snare,* Buttonwood Street, Philadelphia.

632–633: Great German Ball announced by *B. August,* to begin at 7 o'clock and lasting until five. Best wines, preferably Rhinewines, available. "Some days ago Mr. August received fifty new waltzes from Europe, which will be played for the first time at his hall."

635–636: List of books for sale by *J. G. Ritter.*

999: Maria Agathe Zimmermann, wife of *Jacob Zimmermann,* barber, an officially approved midwife with the most preferential credentials, offers her services to the public. Her dwelling is in St. John St., No. 158, in the neighborhood of the German Reformed Church.

999: List of books for sale by *J. G. Ritter.*

999: Propertied humanitarian in State of Virginia, advertises for moral emigrants.

1000: J. J. Cohen, Jr., and Brothers, Lottery, Baltimore.

1000: Christian Mühenberg, who emigrated to America in 1803 from the Superior Bailiwick of Frautigen [Frutigen], Canton Berne, Switzerland, has since that time sent no word of himself. His relatives and brothers and sisters, who are longing for news of him, have delegated the undersigned, who also has a letter for him from his sister *Maria,* to initiate inquires about him. *David Buttcher,* Clockmaker, Dundass in Canada.

No. 88 (November 1, 1828)

1413: Stephen Bach not responsible for his wife's debts.

1413: Druggist *Klett* advertises Dr. *Prosche's* unfailing Rheumatism Drops.

1413: The European-German Book and Art Shop has letters for the following persons: Mr. *Adolf Etzler* from Mühlhausen; *Bernard Ferrenbach,* master-shoemaker in Philadelphia, 30 cents; *Peter Schneider,* c/o Mr. *Heinrich Jahraus* in Christian Street No. 18, between Front and Water Streets, Philadelphia, 10 cents; *Jacob Friedrich Huff,* schoolmaster, Philadelphia, 10 cents; *Ludwig Gustav Eggers,* bookbinder in Hagerstown, Maryland, 30 cents; *Valentin Hassinger* in *Blockhaus* [Blockhouse Settlement], Liberty Township, Tioga County, 30 cents; *Johannes Neubrandt,* master-stonemason in Lancaster, 30 cents; *Friedrich Blauer,* Lancaster, 30 cents; *Carl Munder,* baker, in Liberty Street No. 53 in Baltimore, 30 cents; *Joseph Weaver,* living at the new market, Baltimore, 30 cents; *Samuel Hahliger* in Exeter Township, Berks County, Pennsylvania, 30 cents; *Bernhard Huggenberger* from Oberentfeld, with the German-American Mining Union in Mexico; and *Gerhardt Schütz* (2 letters), Mansfield Post Office, Richland County, Ohio, 80 cents.

1414–1415: Advertisement by Druggist *Klett* for the Genuine and Unfailing Rheumatic Pills of Dr. *Laroch* of Paris.

1416: Jacob Trippler and Company, N. Second Street, advertises honey in hogsheads, tierces and barrels; Orleans molasses, Trinidad molasses, Porto Rico molasses, Matanzas Molasses, and Sugarhouse molasses.

1417: Information wanted on *Immanuel Christian Nagel,* born in the year 1756 in the former Imperial City of Esslingen in the Kingdom of Württemberg, later officer at Vienna in the Austrian service, who came to America in 1784. Nothing has been heard from him since his emigration.

1417: Johann Nepomuk Knoblauch in Johnstown: Ritter advertises that he has a letter for this individual from his brother in Immenstadt on the Bodensee, but since there are several Johnstowns, he must advertise before forwarding.

1417: Important news for Mr. *Israel Ellwanger,* who in 1821 was living as butcher in New Berlin, advertised by J. G. Ritter.

1418: F. C. Fischer announces a Great Exhibition, made by himself, to be held in Mälzel Hall, South Fifth Street: Panoramas and Transparent Views of the most beautiful regions in Europe and America.

No. 70 (August 30, 1828).

1125: Sturm Huneck, born at Hünefeld in the region of Fulda, landed at Baltimore in the year 1817. In the year 1822 or 1823 he was in Greencastle, Pennsylvania; from there he traveled to New Orleans. He understood the dyer and blacksmith trades.

1125: Trippler advertisement for coffee, sugar, molasses, etc. Messrs. Hütter in Easton and Allentown, Bär in Lancaster, Ritter in Reading, and Hartmann in Lebanon, are to print this advertisement eight times in their newspapers and send the bill to bookdealer Ritter in Philadelphia.

1125: European lithographs advertised for sale: The wedding of Joseph and Mary; Jesus and Mary and Martha, with Disciples and Lazarus, and the Good Samaritan in the background; Joseph sold by his brethren; battle scenes; death of Napoleon; the cathedrals at Regensburg, Freiburg im Breisgau, and Basel; Swiss towns and landscapes.

1126: Jacob Schwarz, dyer, born at Calw in the Kingdom of Württemberg, is sought by his brother *Philipp Benedikt,* who has recently emigrated.

1126: Joseph Noll, carpenter from Elsass-Zabern, has the clothing of the undersigned, *Lambert Nübert,* taken along from Havre de Grace to Baltimore.

1126: Advertisement by *Ludwig Jörres* on family registers for Bibles. Offers a new printed family register, with space for baptismal and confirmation records of families up to fourteen members. Costs no more than a fine hand-painted *Taufschein.*

No. 71 (September 3, 1828)

1141: C. F. Oertelt advertisement, spectacles and jewelry.

1143: Longer list of Philadelphia market prices.

No. 84 (October 18, 1828)

1349: Letter to *Joh. G. Miller,* native of the Superior Bailiwick of Welzheim, from his homeland, to be had at *Fr. Monninger's* on the Germantown road, at the fourth milestone.

1349: Johannes Spycher repairs all kinds of broken kitchen and other wares, also broken combs.

1349–1350: Joseph Ehrenfried of Lancaster is presently in this city, on his way to Germany. He invites all German friends who wish to entrust powers of attorney to him, to honor him with their trust, which he will serve in honesty and faithfulness. You can ask for him at *J. Albrecht's,* No. 103 Arch Street, or at his own residence in S. Front Street, or c/o the Editor of this paper. The advertisement is addressed: "To European-Germans."

1350–1351: Long advertisement describing *J. G. Ritter's* printery and printing business, which is for sale, available by New Year 1829. It is an English and German business, and the best equipped German printery in the United States.

No. 91 (November 13, 1828).

1460: Johann Georg Geyer, from Vayhingen on the Enz in the Kingdom of Württemberg, is asked to notify his whereabouts to Mr. *Schubert* at Gratztown Post Office in Dauphin County, who has "interesting news" for him.

1460: From *Dorothea Bähr* from Zörbig we have an important letter to her brother, *Joh. Fr. Pollert.*

1460: For *Joh. Galle,* miller, who earlier lived in Lancaster County but is said to have moved to Virginia, we have important letters relative to his property, from the Royal Bavarian Justice of the Peace of Canton Ottenberg.

1460: A new blue silk umbrella was taken, "either intentionally or by mistake," from a house at the corner of Fourth and Callowhill Streets. Kindly return it!

1460: Advertisement by *Z. Howe* of printer's types, inks, etc., for sale.

1460–1461: Announcement of newly arrived novels.

1462: Advertisement of *Sylvanus Lehman's* exchange office, S. Third Street.

117

NOTES and DOCUMENTS:
Eighteenth-Century Letters from Germany

Edited by DON YODER

I.

[The local historian James Y. Heckler (1829-1901) of Montgomery County produced several local historical sketches which present-day Pennsylvania researchers, historians, genealogists, and folklife scholars, find of value. His *History of Lower Salford Township, (Montgomery County), Commencing with a History of Harleysville* (Harleysville, Pennsylvania, 1888) is a 456-page mine of information on early life in the "Dutch end" of Montgomery County. His *History of Franconia Township* which ran in local newspapers, was reprinted in book form in 1960 by the Schlechter Press in Allentown, Pennsylvania.

Another local historian of Montgomery County, whose interests involved particularly church history and genealogy, was Henry S. Dotterer, whose periodical, *The Perkiomen Region, Past and Present,* Volumes I-III (1894-1901), was actually the first regional historical periodical to appear in Pennsylvania. Henry S. Dotterer is remembered also for his researches into Reformed Church history and backgrounds in Pennsylvania; many of his church-historical sketches appeared in the *Reformed Church Messenger* and other church periodicals.

In the *Dotterer Papers,* Volume X, pp. 103, 105 (Collections of the Genealogical Society of Pennsylvania, Volume 319), there is a pencil copy of "An Old Letter from Germany," with the notation: "Mr. James Y. Heckler, of Hatfield, has favored us with a translation of a letter from his unpublished History of the Heckler Family. It will be read with interest by the many members of the Heckler family, as well as by others." The letter was sent from Retschweiler in Lower Alsace, now in France, in 1784, from Michael Hechler to his brother George Hechler, then of Lower Salford Township, Montgomery County, Pennsylvania. No letters had passed between the brothers since 1767, and the European brother tells the family news and asks specifically for the right to dispose of the American brother's property in the home parish. Many similar details can be found in the long series of *Amerikabriefe* that we have published in *Pennsylvania Folklife.*

According to James Y. Heckler's *History of Harleysville* (Harleysville: Benjamin L. Gehman, 1886), pp. 177-183, George Heckler, son of Michael Hechler, was born in Retschweiler, Lower Alsace, April 26, 1736. After learning the tailoring trade at the age of 15, he emigrated to America, arriving in Philadelphia on the *Neptune,* September 30, 1754. After paying for his passage by the very common practise of selling his services for some years as a "redemptioner," he was married in 1764 to Catharine Freed, daughter of Peter Freed, a Mennonite, of Lower Salford. For seventeen years the Hecklers lived near the present town of Blooming Glen in Hilltown Township, Bucks County, then moved back to Lower Salford. The name was originally spelled "Hechler" — the historian blames an Irish stonecutter for changing the spelling to "Heckler" on the emigrant's headstone. George Heckler died August 28, 1816. — EDITOR.]

Ret[s]chweiler, May 3, 1784.
Much beloved brother:

Since the 8th of November, 1767, which was the last date of your writing to us, we have not had any information from you, and of your circumstances. I must presently mention that father and mother have died:—mother about ten years and father about four years; and our sister some twenty-odd years ago.

I, Michael Hechler, your brother am alone left remaining of our family; and you my beloved brother George. It causes me much regret to be at such a distance from you. You can imagine for yourself how sad it is to have an only brother and to be so far from him that it is an impossibility to speak even a few words with him, for which I have wished a thousand times, although I see the impossibility before me. At least mention to me your right address so that I can now and then have a written conversation with you.

The bearer of this is one of our countrymen, a native of Ret[s]chweiler, whose name is Christian Schneider, whom you, as a faithful countryman, may assist as much as you possibly can, that he also may find a home and employment. He leaves here on account of poverty. He has not carried on any unworthy business that he should leave on that account.

Inform me as soon as possible what you wish us to do with your patrimony, which we have kept for you. We can make disposition of it so that our descendants will not come into vexations about it. All people who tell me about you assure me that you have achieved a complete success. If it is so inform me of it.

I will inform you also that I have been married about eighteen years with our neighbor Casper Schneider's daughter, Maria Elizabeth, and with her have had nine children. Of these are living by God's grace, four sons and two daughters, of whom the oldest is a son fifteen years old.

Finding yourself now such a wealthy man please to surrender to my children your share. Please mention

118

*Bergzabern
in the
Palatinate.*

Foto Cramer

to me in what manner it shall be done: although I leave it all to your gracious pleasure (and judgment).

We are, thank God, all healthy and well, hoping and wishing the same may be the case with your family. Salute your dear wife and dear children affectionately for us. Believe and be assured that I am at all times in brotherly love and friendship your sincere and faithful brother.

Michael Hechler.

Beloved brother, I wish you much luck and blessing, and since it is impossible for us to speak together otherwise than by writing, I ask you, beloved brother, to write a letter back to me soon. I send greeting to you, brother George Hechler, and your whole family many thousand times. These few disjointed lines have been written by me, Michael Hechler.

II.

[As a followup to the recent "Mennonite Contacts Across the Atlantic" (*Pennsylvania Folklife*, XIX:1, Autumn 1969, 46-48) the letter of Jacob Rupp of Heppenheim in the Palatinate, dated 1786, and the reply by Rudolph Landes of Deep Run, Bedminster Township, Bucks County, Pennsylvania, dated 1787, are of interest on several counts.

The Jacob Rupp letter is important especially for its explicit reference to the migration of Palatine Mennonites to Eastern Europe. In the same century that the major thrust of German and Swiss emigration was

directed toward the British Colonies, producing the background of the Pennsylvania German culture, a second major migration was taking place into Eastern Europe. Whole areas of Hungary, Poland, and Russia were settled in the 18th Century by German farmers from various states, under the colonization policies of Catharine II and Joseph II. In the 1870's, when the liberal agreements of the colonizing monarchs were abrogated, a counter-migration began, bringing, particularly from Russia, large numbers of German-speaking Mennonites to Canada and the Plains States.

The family details given in the correspondence can be enlarged by reference to *The Mennonite Encyclopedia*. For the Rupp family, including Heinrich Rupp (1760-1800) of Harxheim and Johann Rupp (1747-1787) of Altzey, who emigrated to Galicia in 1784 ff., to Einsiedel and Rosenberg respectively, see IV, 379. For the Landes (Landis) Family in Pennsylvania, see III, 280-282. Background information on the materials in these letters can also be found in the encyclopedia under the headings Heppenheim, Oberflörsheim, Galicia, Einsiedel, and Rosenberg.

The Zimmermann-Hardt migration to Pennsylvania referred to in the correspondence very probably involves two passengers on the Brig Betsey which arrived in Philadelphia in 1771. In the list of the passengers taking the Oath of Allegiance on December 4, 1771 (Strassburger-Hinke, I, 738, List 292 C) there appears a *Jacob Zimmerman* and immediately following, *Jean*

Gaspard Horthe. In addition there are in the same list *Sebastian Harth, Rudy Funck,* and *Martin Funck.*

The Rupp-Landes Correspondence was published in J. S. Hartzler and Daniel Kauffman, *Mennonite Church History* (Scottdale, Pennsylvania: Mennonite Book and Tract Society, 1905), pp. 401-405, without indication of where the authors found the originals. Will Mennonite librarians and archivists please inform us where the original letters, or copies of them, may be found at the present time? — EDITOR.]

Heppenheim, near Altzey,
April 15th, 1786.

Dear Worthy Friends:

I desire to express my heartfelt wish for your true welfare in all pertaining to the thriving of body and soul. The letter from you dear friends, Abraham and Rudolph Landes dated April 12, 1784, we received on the 17th of August, 1784, with great pleasure, and through it ascertained as to your general health. We wish to announce that all who are still living of us are, praise the Lord, in good bodily health. Yet it has pleased the Lord, who alone is Ruler over life and death, to demand from us Elizabeth Burkyen in the month of May as also Christian Schmitt on the 14th of June, 1784. They were called out of this toilsome world and transformed to Eternity, where in accordance with the Christian Faith they will increase the inhabitants of the other world. May the Almighty in his mercy prepare us for a joyful following. I also announce that the youngest daughter, Christina, of Elizabeth Burkyen, deceased, was wedded to Rudolph Forrer also of "Wersheimer Hof," and is in possession of the farm of her father, Jacob Burkyen, deceased. Furthermore I give you without concealment the information that within the past three or four years many of the families from this and other neighborhoods have moved into the kingdom of Poland. This journey of over four hundred hours was made by my brother John, leaving on the 10th of October, 1784, as also my brother Henry, who wedded Catherine Brollin, reformed religion, from Harxheim, on June 13th, 1785, they together with Jacob Muller of Rudelsheim, with his son-in-law, Jacob Bursched of Harxheim. The journey was partly by water, but mostly overland. They went to improve their condition. The country is very fertile and does not belong to the Kingdom of Poland any more. It is called now Mehro-Gallicia, which came into possession of the Roman Empire Majesty Joseph II, during the war times. Through his glorious and more than wise government, many colonists have settled there, as also Estates of Nobility and church. They are furnished with good new homesteads with about fifty acres of land without any cost, also cattle, implements, house utensils, just as farmers need, also several free years without taxation. They have as yet not been assigned to places but hope to shortly. If they haven't been, they will certainly before long as they receive support until they are assigned their land. The favours which these people receive from the wise Joseph, is more than great. Not alone this, he is also a philanthropist whose equal

Title-page of the Franconia Mennonite Hymnal, fifth edition, 1848. Rudolph Landes' acrostic hymn appears in the second appendix, No. 21.

cannot be found among the crowned heads. He permits all religions, which before his time was not permitted. I wrote you a letter which I presume you received in the fall of '84, through my brother-in-law, Jacob Rupp, who visited us from Pennsylvania, at that time, which contained a description of former times. Further I wish to acquaint you with the fact that the year '84 was such a complete failure that the oldest persons remember none such; fruits, vegetables and crops of all kinds were very scarce, causing great hardship at the beginning of '85. The pen cannot describe it at all. Now every thing is again blest and cheaper than in many long years and the growing crops look well with us. We live in hopes of soon getting a letter from you. Information is asked if Casper Hardt, brother of Jacob Hardt, did not come to you about 12 years ago.

Mrs. Landes, her children, I and mine send you many greetings. Remember us in your prayers, we are willing to do likewise with God's sanction. With compliments and under the protection of the Almighty, I am

Your true and sincere friend.

JACOB RUPP.

P. S.—The above greetings include the entire circle of friendship—the Landes family, I must particularly mention Frederick Landes, who is just my age. I would like also to receive a few lines from him some time.

Adieu.

REPLY OF RUDOLPH LANDES.
April 13, 1787, Bucks County.
Bedminster Township at Deep Run.

Worthy Friends:

The Lord be with you through His holy, righteous Spirit, guide you through His sincere grace, love and mercy to the path of love and peace. This I wish you upon your friendly greetings, may the Lord and God of all grace give us and you all, strength to follow Him on the path upon which He preceded us through pure love to our eternal salvation and happiness, and loved not life unto death—His alone be praise, honor and commendation in all eternity. Amen.

Beloved friend and Cousin Rupp, your writing of April 15, 1786, we received and through it perceived that you were in part well, which was very pleasing to us. Also that some of our friends departed this life, and I hope that God in His mercy through Jesus Christ has received and taken them into life eternal, that we may with the wise virgins be prepared, and that our like may be kept burning and our lamps not extinguished; that adorned in the unsoiled wedding robe, we may, like unto mankind, wait for the Lord—that the Friend, the Lord, the Bridegroom may come when He pleases and would not then become alarmed, but would be joyful and enter with Him to the nuptials— may our good Lord help us thereto through Jesus Christ. Amen.

In regard to how we are getting on, we can say as far as bodily health is concerned, we are presumably well, thanks to the Lord, and we have also full and plenty to eat. Nor are we alarmed with war, although they are troubled inland with little warfares. What will come of it, only God knows. It is mostly on account of the money demands. A large portion of the Pennsylvania inhabitants cannot become reconciled to this, and the humbling of the Lord's name does not please many. They have as yet been unaccustomed to it in this country. Yet again there are those who use the name of the Lord to greedily fill their hands and pockets with the farmer's possessions, and as they are no better than others, it causes indignation. Christ's followers have only to give attention to the Lord's commands. He saith, give unto the king whatsoever belongeth to the king, and to God what is his, and to love thine enemies and to plead with the offender, that you may be children of your Father in heaven, says Christ.

It is asked if Casper Hardt had not come to this country. I answer yes, and is still here as much as I know—away up country somewhere. I wrote about him to you last year, about him and Jacob Zimmerman, as they came to this country. Jacob Hardt is still living, as far as I know. He lives thirty hours trip from here. Furthermore you write that your brother had moved into the kingdom of Poland, regarding this I should like to hear more, providing it is not asking too much of you. Regarding the remaining friends, the other letters will inform me. I heard that your brother-in-law, Jacob Rupp, had been in good health this winter. Also the same of the widow and children of Jacob

Landes. I and my housewife and children again send their heartfelt greetings, and to remember one another in prayers is my wish. The beloved God who has brought us this far and aided us will, I hope, help us lay our weary heads into the dust of the earth to rest until the Lord shall awaken us to the glory, comfort and happiness of yonder life. As this goes beyond all thought, may the Lord therefore give us the strength to lead such lives that we may there look upon one another in eternal joy and splendor. This I wish you and us all through Jesus Christ. Amen. I would like to know if Cousin Landes' daughters, Magdalen and Grette, are still living. I send them and theirs hearty greetings, as also all our friends in this writing which has been done in simplicity and love.

From your friend,
RUDOLPH LANDES.*

[P. S.] It has frequently come to my mind that I would like to know if old Christian Weber, William Kramer, Jacob Dahlem and John Haan are still living or any of them or who is in charge of the household of our Mennonite community in Upper Florschheim where I was received in great poverty and ill health and taken up in the congregation of Jesus Christ. Which now being nearly 38 years ago comes to my thoughts that though we wrote to one another from time to time, I fear the time at hand when we mortals will sink or have sunken to sleep and soon to hear "a cry at midnight, and behold the Bridegroom cometh." Now as the one to make the cry is not revealed to us, we should call to one another and be on guard as the enemy is watching and it is said goes about us like a roaring lion to devour us. Oh, that we may withstand him through our belief—though we are strangers by sight I hope that in united belief and united hope and in love, the Lord may strengthen our foundation that we may go on from strength to strength, from might to might, until we reach God in Zion, to this may God help us through Jesus Christ. Amen.

Remember us also in your prayers. I am willing so far as the Lord aids me in my weakness to do likewise. Take this up in love as it is done in love.

To a heartfelt friendly and brotherly greeting in the Lord from

RUDOLPH LANDES.

N. B.—Cousin Rupp, I trust you will execute the wishes expressed, and hope you will write and if we live and the Lord is willing, we will continue our correspondence.

*While reading proof on this article I was visited at the University of Pennsylvania by Ada Kadelbach, a student of Dr. Hans Galinsky's at the University of Mainz who is writing her Ph.D. dissertation in American Studies, on the subject of Mennonite Hymnody in the United States to 1860. I am indebted to her for pointing out the curious acrostic hymn by Rudolph Landes which appeared in print for the first time in the third edition of the Franconia Mennonite hymnal, *Die kleine geistliche Harfe der Kinder Zions* (Germantown, 1820), Zugabe, Nr. 21. The hymn, which begins, "Rath, hülf und trost, o HErr, mein GOtt, Find ich bey dir alleine," was written, according to verse 13, when the author was 65, hence can be dated in 1797. Rudolph Landes died in 1802 and is buried at Deep Run.—EDITOR.

121

SWISS MENNONITE FAMILY NAMES:
An Annotated Checklist
LEO SCHELBERT and SANDRA LUEBKING

Seventeenth-Century View of Andelfingen by Matthäus Merian.

In the decades after 1520 the people of Western Europe experienced a thorough religious transformation. Instead of one Western Christendom centered in Rome a variety of competing interpretations of true Christianity emerged that were able to translate their assumptions into viable and enduring institutions. Among the emerging persuasions one group was unique, however: its members, scornfully called "catabaptists" or "anabaptists" — re-baptizers — by their opponents, rejected the millennia-old idea of the *corpus christianum* which postulates the unity between the ecclesiastical and political domain. For the Brethren, as they called themselves, the secular world was not an aspect of the divinely sanctioned order, but the sphere of anti-Christ. This belief was institutionally expressed not only in a rejection of infant baptism as invalid and blasphemous, but also in an abhorrence of the oath and the bearing of arms as forbidden entanglements with the powers of evil. The true church, they held, was exclusively the gathering of the sanctified who in the acceptance of baptism had submitted irrevocably to divine lordship.

These views led to severe conflicts with the established churches as well as with the authorities of the various states. The three wings of enduring Anabaptism — the Swiss Brethren, the Hutterian Brethren, and the (Dutch) Mennonites — experienced recurrent persecutions, an important reason for their migrations to areas where they were welcome or at least tolerated. The Swiss and Hutterian Brethren

were, furthermore, dedicated to farming as the only God-ordained way of life, a conviction which necessitated successive moves to areas that offered good, but inexpensive farmland.

The Swiss Brethren — the list presented below pertains to them alone — split in the 1690's into two groups. The Swiss minister Jakob Ammann felt that the Brethren had spiritually declined in the second half of the 17th Century. He insisted on a more rigorous observation of discipline (especially in dress and outward appearance), viewed footwashing as an important sacred ritual, and demanded the strict avoidance of those not in unison with the demands of the faith. This split led in the United States to the survival of two sets of religious groups descended from the Swiss Brethren, the "Swiss Mennonites" and the "Amish".

Between 1650 and 1690 persecution and the search for good farm land led many Swiss Brethren to Alsace, the Palatinate, and to adjoining territories like Durlach and Zweibrücken. After 1680 and especially after 1710 the migration to Pennsylvania began which drew its strength not only from Switzerland, but also from Alsace and from South German regions, thus transcending national boundaries. The post - 1680 Swiss Brethren migration has been divided into six phases by the eminent Mennonite historian Harold S. Bender (ME III: 686):

(1) 1683 - 1705: 100 persons, from the Lower Rhine to Germantown, Pennsylvania.

122

(2) 1707 - 1756: 3,000 - 5,000 persons, mostly Mennonite, possibly 300 Amish, from the Palatinate and Swiss regions to Eastern Pennsylvania, especially the Franconia and Lancaster districts.

(3) 1815 - 1880: possibly 3,000 Amish, from Alsace, Bavaria, and Hesse to Ohio, Ontario, Indiana, and Illinois.

(4) 1830 - 1860: possibly 500 Mennonites, from Switzerland to Ohio and Indiana.

(5) 1830 - 1860: possibly 300 Mennonites, from the Palatinate to Ohio, Indiana, and Illinois; (some more immigrants of all three 19th Century groups arrived after 1864 until the end of the century).

(6) 1875 - 1880: about 400 Mennonites, from Galicia, and Volhynia to Kansas and South Dakota.

According to Bender, "a total of possibly 8,000 persons crossed the Atlantic in the two centuries". He estimated their descendants numbered in 1956 "approximately 120,000 or three fifths of the total Mennonite membership" (ibid.).

The following list pertains to these migrations of the Swiss Brethren. It presents the major Swiss Mennonite and Amish family names, their variants, and if known, their Swiss origin as well as the names of successive first migrating family members who had often settled in German areas before moving to North America. Most entries also contain a reference to the general Swiss origin of a given family name which is only seldom exclusively or even principally Mennonite; the earliest known non-Mennonite arrival in Philadelphia of a given family name has also been added. Thus two goals will hopefully be achieved. Genealogical researchers will have a checklist for some 150 family names with a series of bibliographical leads for further investigation. Historians of immigration might find an overview concerning this immigrant group useful, especially in the context of family, religious, and quantitative history; they might also take more extensive note of the impressive scholarly achievements of Mennonite historians.

The compilation is based on the following works (for full citation see the bibliographical note at the end of this article):

BA: Gratz, *Bernese Anabaptists*

F/BR: Faust and Brumbaugh, *Lists of Swiss Emigrants*

HBLS: *Historisch-Biographisches Lexikon der Schweiz* (7 vols. & supplement)

MC: *Mennonite Cyclopedic Dictionary* (4 vols.)

ME: *Mennonite Encyclopedia* (4 vols.)

MQR: *Mennonite Quarterly Review* (since 1927)

PGP: *Pennsylvania German Pioneers* (3 vols.)

Thus the list presents a summary of the research of others; it may also occasionally include their errors. At times a given family name may include in the

variations a non-related family or may be at the same time not only Swiss in origin. The spellings of the names in the lists collected in *Pennsylvania German Pioneers* often vary significantly. In the list given below the spelling was taken whenever possible from the signature of the immigrant, otherwise from the passenger list. The page indicated for *PGP* refers not to the whole list, but only to the page on which the name appears; the ship's name as well as the given date may thus be found on a different page. Readers should also note that names of counties cited without state location refer to Pennsylvania counties.

BIBLIOGRAPHY

Bender, Harold S. (ed. and transl.), "A Trip to Illinois and Iowa in 1872," *Mennonite Quarterly Review,* III (October 1929), 235-242.

————. "Palatinate Mennonite Census Lists, 1664-1774," *Mennonite Quarterly Review,* XIV (January 1940), 5-40; (April 1940), 67-89; (July 1940), 170-186.

Bender, Lynn. "The Yellow Creek Mennonite Settlers: A Study of Land and Family," *Mennonite Quarterly Review,* XLVI (January 1972), 70-83.

Brackbill, Martin H. "New Light on Hans Herr and Martin Kendig," *Historical Papers and Addresses of the Lancaster County Historical Society,* XXXIX (1935), 74-102.

————. "A Communication on the Origins of the Early 18th Century Pennsylvania Mennonite Immigrants," *Mennonite Quarterly Review,* XXVII (January 1953), 78-82.

————. "Origin of the Pequea Settlers (1710)," *Mennonite Quarterly Review,* XLV (January 1971), 84-95.

Braun, Fritz. "Nineteenth Centruy Emigrants from the Mennonite Congregation of Friedelsheim in the Palatinate," Don Yoder, transl., *Mennonite Quarterly Review,* XXX (April 1956), 133-154.

Brunk, H. A. "Bishop Peter Burkholder of Virginia, 1783-1846," *Mennonite Quarterly Review,* XIV (January 1940), 52-56.

Correll, Ernst. "The Value of Family History for Mennonite History," *Mennonite Quarterly Review,* II (January 1928), 66-79; (April 1928), 151-154; (October 1928), 198-204.

Faust, Albert B. and Gaius M. Brumbaugh. *List of Swiss Emigrants in the Eighteenth Century to the American Colonies II.* Washington, D.C.: National Genealogical Society, 1925.

Gingerich, Melvin. "The First Mennonite Settlement in Iowa," *Mennonite Quarterly Review,* XLII (July 1968), 193-202.

Gratz, Delbert L. *Bernese Anabaptists and Their American Descendants.* Scottdale, Pa.: Herald Press, 1953.

Historisch-Biographisches Lexikon der Schweiz. 7 vols. + supplement. Neuenburg: Administration des Historisch-Biographisches Lexikons, 1921-1934.

Kauffman, Daniel (ed). *Mennonite Cyclopedic Dictionary.* Scottdale, Pa.: Mennonite Publishing House, 1937.

Landis, Ira D. "Bishop Peter Eby of Pequea, 1765-1843," *Mennonite Quarterly Review,* XIV (January 1940), 41-51.

————. "Bishop Christian Burkholder of Groffdale, 1746-1809," *Mennonite Quarterly Review,"* XVIII (July 1944), 145-161.

Mennonite Encyclopedia, 4 volumes. Scottdale, Pa.: Mennonite Publishing House, 1952-1957.

Pannabecker, S. F. "The Nineteenth Century Swiss Mennonite Immigrants and Their Adherence to the General Conference Mennonite Church," *Mennonite Quarterly Review,* XXI (April 1947), 64-102.

Pennsylvania German Pioneers. Ralph B. Strassburger and William J. Hinke (eds.), 3 volumes. Norristown, Pa.: Pennsylvania German Society, 1934.

Schelbert, Leo. "Eighteenth Century Migration of Swiss Mennonites to America," *Mennonite Quarterly Review,* XLII (July 1968), 163-183; (October 1968), 285-300.

Wenger, John C. "Brief Notes on the Bernese Wengers," *Mennonite Quarterly Review,* XII (April 1938), 85-97.

————. (ed.) "Documents on the Daniel Brennemann Division," *Mennonite Quarterly Review,* XXXIV (January 1960), 48-64.

Yoder, Don (ed. and transl.) "From the Palatinate to Frontier Ohio: The Risser Letters (1832-1833)," *Mennonite Quarterly Review,* XXX (January 1956), 44-64.

1. ACKERMAN (Achermann, Ackermann, Akermann).
In 1750 two Ackerman families to Lancaster County, (MC 1-2); perhaps *Christoff Ackerman*, on the *Bennet Gally*, August 13, 1750; and *Johan Wendell Ackherman* and *Johann Georg Ackermann*, on the *Osgood*, September 29, 1750 (PGP I:429; 445).

    1. Swiss forms: *Acherman, Ackermann, Akermann;* widely dispersed (HBLS I:88; 90-91).
    2. *Meichel Ackermann*, on the *Alexander and Anne*, September 5, 1730 (PGP I:36).

2. AESCHLIMAN (Aeschiman, Aeschleman, Aeschliman, Ashliman, Eschelmann, Eshelman, Eshleman.).
17th Century Anabaptists Aeschlimann at Rigenen in the Emmental, Ct. Bern (BA 48). 1710 *Margreht Aeschliman* on a Bernese list of Anabaptists (MQR XLV [January 1971] 95).
Daniel Eshelman in Lancaster County, before 1718 (ME II:249).
Johan Eshelman, on the *Britannia*, September 21, 1731 (MC 99; PGP I:47).
Paul R. Aeschliman, b. October 25, 1862 near Brenets, Ct. Neuchâtel; with several family members to Pulaski, Iowa (ME I:20).

    1. Swiss form: *Aeschlimann;* origin in the Emmental and at Grindelwald, Ct. Bern (HBLS I:154).
    2. *Henrich Eschelmann*, on the Mortonhouse, August 24, 1728; *Ulrich Hessleman*, on the *Brothers*, September 30, 1754; *Hans Aeschlimann* and *Peter Eselman*, on the *Phoenix*, October 1, 1754 (PGP I:19; 610; 629, 635).

3. ALBRECHT (Allbrecht, Albright, Allbright).
1629 *Hans Albrecht*, minister in Hungary.
1837 5 brothers and sisters from Bavaria to Bureau County, Illinois (MC 4-5).

    1. Swiss form; *Albrecht;* widely dispersed (HBLS I:217-219).
    2. *Joseph Albrecht*, on the *William and Sarah*, September 21, 1727 (PGP I:9).

4. ALDERFER (Aldorffer, Alldörfer, Altaffer, Altorfer).
Frederick Aldorffer, b. 1715 in Palatinate; on the *Samuel*, August 11, 1732; *Friederich Alldörfer*, age 18, on the *Samuel*, August 17, 1733 (PGP I:60; 112).
Family in Montgomery and Lebanon Counties; Virginia; Williams County, Ohio (ME I:43; MC 5).
    Swiss form: *Altorfer;* in Ct. Zürich since 1331, and in Ct. Schaffhausen (HBLS I:300-301).

5. ALLEBACH (Allenbach, Allebaugh).
Christian Allebach, before 1728 to Pennsylvania, 1739; member of Salford congregation (MC 5; ME I:54).
Family in Bucks and Montgomery Counties (MC 5).

John and *Andrew Allebach*, arrived 1734, no known descendants (ME I:55).
    Swiss form: *Allenbach* (cf. HBLS I:232).

6. AMSTUTZ (am Stutz, Am Stutz, Amstoutz, Amstuz, Stutz, Stutzer).
Mennonite branches from Sigriswil, Lake Thun area, Ct. Bern. 18th Century to Bernese Jura; families at Châtelat, Pruntrut; also at Massevaux, Florimont, and Montbéliard in Alsace (ME I:110-111; BA 91-166, passim).
Migrated in early 19th Century; first arrivals *Johannes Amstutz*, age 18, and sister *Anna*, age 17, in 1818, to Lancaster County; *Johannes* ca. 1821 to Sonnenberg, Wayne County, Ohio (MC 9; MEI:111); concentrated especially in Sonnenberg, Crown Hill, and Bluffton congregations (ME I:111).

    1. Swiss forms: *Amstutz, am Stutz, Stutzer;* primarliy in Ct. Unterwalden and Ct. Schwyz; "one family from Sigriswil, Ct. Bern" (HBLS I:353).
    2. *Anna Stutz*, age 30, on the *Mercury*, May 29, 1735; *Lewis Stutz*, on the *Pallas*, November 25, 1763 (PGP I:148; 688).

7. AUGSBURGER (Augsberger, Augsbourger, Augspurger, Ougspurger, Oxberger).
Mennonite branch from Langnau, Emmental Valley, Ct. Bern; *Johannes Augsburger* (1783-1885) and wife, *Elizabeth Jacob* (m. July 26, 1805), arrived from Amsterdam October 10, 1817; to Liberty, Tioga County; ca. 1829 to Wayne County, Ohio; ca. 1842 to Adams County, Indiana (BA 129-130; ME I:188).
    Swiss forms: *Ougspurger* and *Augsburger, patrician family of city of Bern* (HBLS V:367; I:478).

8. BACHMAN (Bachmann, Bauchman).
Mennonite family 1672 in Bottenstein, Ct. Aargau; to Palatinate; *Andreas Bachman* with other Amish to Pennsylvania, on The *Francis and Elizabeth*, September 21, 1742; especially in Lebanon County. (BA 39, 42, 47, 87 especially on Swiss background; ME I:203; PGP I:329; MC 16).
19th Century: a leading Amish name; from Alsace mainly to Central Illinois (ME I:203).
Other families: to the Palatinate, then to Galicia and after 1875 to prairie states (ME I:204).

    1. Swiss form: *Bachmann*, a widely dispersed named all over Switzerland (HBLS I:513-516).
    2. *Felix, Hans*, and *Heinrich Bachman*, on the *Jamaica*, February 7, 1739 (PGP I:252, 255).

9. BAER (Bähr, Baehr, Bair, Bar, Bare, Barr, Bear, Beare, Beer, Behr, Boehr, Boer, Pare, z'Bären).
Henry Pare, August 24, 1717, to Lancaster County (MQR XLII [October 1968], 287).
Jacob Baer, on the *Molly*, September 30, 1727, one of earliest arrivals (ME I:211; PGP I:13).

1. Swiss forms: *Baer, Beer;* dispersed all over Switzerland; z'Bären from Ct. Unterwalden (HBLS I:533-534).
2. *Samuell Bare,* on the *Molly,* September 30, 1727 (PGP I:12).

10. BASINGER (Basicker, Bösiger, Boesiger),
1759 Mennonite family Bösiger from Attiswil, Ct. Bern, reported in Montbéliard, Alsace (BA 89); other Bosiger families (BA 91-158 passim).
Christian Bösiger, from Rumisberg, Ct. Bern, left Normanvillars, Alsace, aged 23, in New York, June 1819, to Lancaster County; 1825 to Waterloo County, Ontario; 1836 to Putnam County, Ohio (BA 133, 147).
Other families in Ohio 1824 and 1838 (MC 19; BA 145, 156).
Swiss form: *Bösiger* (cf. HBLS, Supplement p. 28).

11. BAUER (Baur, (de) Boer, Bower, Bowers).
17th Century Mennonite family in Oberhofen, Ct. Bern (BA 49).
1711 a Bauer family to Sapperneer, Groningen, Holland (ME I:248).
Hans Bauer (d. 1749) and wife *Anna* (d. 1761), settled between 1711 and 1717 at Hereford, Berks County, near Bally (ME I:248-249).
1. Swiss forms: *Bauer, Baur;* family in Ct. Graubünden (1524); 19th Century in Cts. Bern, Basel, and Neuchâtel (HBLS II:47, Supplement pp. 15-18).
2. *Johann Christoffel Bauer,* on the *Samuel,* August 16, 1731 (PGP I:42).

12. BAUMAN (Baumann, Bouman, Bowman, (de) Buman).
16th Century an Anabaptist Bauman family attested in Bern; to Moravia (BA 14); also in the Palatinate (BA 168).
Wendell Bauman (b. ca. 1689), in 1710 among original settlers of Pequea (ME I:249), most likely of Zürich origin, via the Palatinate to Pennsylvania (BA 168; MQR XLV [January 1917] 98; MC 19).
Jacob Bauman (1722-1770), *Christian,* and *Peter,* ca. 1751 members of Allegheny congregation, Pennsylvania (ME I:55 "Allegheny").
Families in Ohio, Ontario, Missouri, Iowa, Illinois, and Virginia (ME I:249; MC 35-36).
1. Swiss forms: *Baumann (Buman, de Buman)* widely dispersed in Switzerland (HBLS II: 50-52; Supplement p. 18).
2. *Hans Jerrick Bowman,* on the *William and Sarah,* September 18, 1727; *Jacob Baumān,* on the *Adventure,* October 2, 127; 7 *Albert Bowman,* on the *Friendship of Bristoll,* October 16, 1727 (PGP I:7; 15; 16).

13. BAUMGARTNER (Baumgardner, Bomgarner, Pomgarddiner).
First recorded Anabaptist Baumgartner 1608; 1621 several in Langnau, Ct. Bern (ME I:250).
1720's and 1730's Bomgarners listed among settlers in Shenandoah Valley, Virginia (MQR XLII [October 1968] 292).
David Baumgartner (1765-1853); 1835 from the *Jura* to Wayne County, Ohio; 1839 to Wells County, Indiana (BA 135; 153; ME I:250; MC 20); sons *Peter* and *Christian* in September 1838 settled in Wells County, Indiana (BA 153).
1. Swiss forms: *Baumgartner* in most cantons; Liestal family also as *Bongarter, Boumgarter, Bomgartner, Baumgarter* (HBLS II:53-55).
2. *Christopher* and *Ursley Bumgarner,* on the

View of Kyburg by Merian.

125

Mortonhouse, August 17, 1729 (PGP I:24).

14. BEACHEY (Beachy, Beechy, Bitsche, Bitschi, Peachey).
Since 1697 mostly Amish; to the Palatinate; to Pennsylvania.
1767 *Peter Bitsche,* directly from Switzerland to Bedford (now Somerset) County (ME I:254; MC 20-21, 286).

15. BECHTEL (Bachstel, Bachtel, Bachtell, Bächtold, Bechtold, Böchtel, Portel, Vechtel).
Peter Bechtel, 1664 to the Palatinate (ME I:257); others (BA 81).
Hans Jacob Bechtel (d. 1739), wife *Anna* (d. 1761), 1720 to Berks County (MC 21-22).
George Bechtell (d. 1759), arrived in Philadelphia from Mannheim, August 9, 1729; to Berks County (ME I:257).
1. Swiss form: *Baechtold;* origin at Schleitheim, Ct. Schaffhausen (HBLS I:529-530).
2. *Jörg Bechtell,* on the *Mortonhouse,* August 24, 1728 (PGP I:19).

16. BEERY (Beer, Beers, Beire, Beyer, Bieri, Biery).
In 1670's an Anabaptist Bieri family at Kalzbach in the Emmental, Ct. Bern (BA 48).
Abraham Beer (1718-1799) on the *John*, October 19, 1736; to Adams County (MC 22; PGP I:168).
In Shenandoah Valley (MQR XLII [October 1968] 292); in Sonnenberg, Wayne County, Ohio, and in Oregon (BA 165).
1. Swiss form: *Bieri,* especially frequent in the *Emmental,* Ct. Bern, and the Entlebuch Valley, Ct. Luzern; many emigrated to Russia, Germany, and the Americas (HBLS II: 242); perhaps also separate name *Beyer* (ibid., p. 220).
2. *Jacob Beyer,* on the *James Goodwill,* September 11, 1728 (PGP I:21).
Albinus Beyer and *Petter Bier,* on the *Samuel,* August 30, 1737 (PGP I:172, 173).

17. BERGEY (Berge, Berke, Berkey, Berki, Berky, Birkey, Birki, Birky, Borcki, Borcky, Buerckey, Buercki, Buerge, Buergey, Buergi, Buerki, Burckey, Burcky, Burgey, Burkey, Bürki, Bürky, Burky, etc.).
1670's Anabaptist Bürki family at Gibel, Emmental, Ct. Bern (BA 48).
1710 *Hans Bürki,* deacon from Langnau (BA 58).
1737 immigrant *Christian Buercki;* Amish (ME I:278).
Johann Ulrich Bergey, ca. 1719 in Montgomery County (ME I:278-279).
Family besides Pennsylvania in Ontario, Ohio, Illinois, Iowa, Nebraska, Missouri, Kansas, Indiana, New York, Montana (ME I:279; MC 24-25).
1. Swiss forms: *Bürkey,* Cts. of Appenzell and St. Gall, and *Bürki, Bürkli* and *Bürgi* (from Old German *Burghard, Burkhart*) especially

Cts. Bern, Luzern, and Zürich (HBLS II:415-417).
2. *Katherina Birkin,* age 23, on the *Britannia,* September 21, 1731 (PGP I:49).
Jacob Bürckh, on the *Brotherhood,* November 3, 1750 (PGP I:447).
3. Anabaptists *Christen* and *Hans Berger,* also their sisters *Magdalena* and *Anna,* from Signau, Ct. Bern, settled in Pennsylvania; *Christen* paid tax on 80 crowns (F/BR 36; entry for February 4, 1750); a *Hans Bergher,* on the *Bennet Galley,* August 13, 1750 (PGP I:428), but other names do not appear. Name widely dispersed in Switzerland; in Ct. Bern especially in the Emmental (HBLS II:120).

18. BIXEL (Bichsel, Bixler).
Anabaptist family from Eggiwil, Emmental, Ct. Bern; 1670's a Bichsel at Gohl, Emmental (ME I:349; BA 48). others (BA 22, 31, 133, 134, 148).
Andreas Bichsel to the Jura, in 1717 near Corgémont; *Johann* and *Christian Bichsel* ca. 1725 to Pennsylvania; 1821 *Jacob Bichsel* and wife to Sonnenberg, Wayne County, Ohio, brother *Peter Bichsel,* and sister *Verena* 1824 to Holmes County, Ohio (ME I:350; MC 29-30).
Swiss form: *Bichsel,* widely known in Emmental Valley, Ct. Bern (HBLS II: 234).

19. BLANK (Blanck, Plank).
Early 18th Century Anabaptist family Blank in Montbéliard (BA 87).
Hans, Jacob, Nickolas Blanck on the *St. Andrew,* September 23, 1752; to Berks County (MC 30; PGP I:485); later family in Cass County, Missouri (MC 30).
1. Swiss form: *Blank,* origin in Ins and Thun, then to Sigriswil and Steffisburg, Ct. Bern; also in Ct. Schaffhausen since early 16th Century (HBLS II: 264).
2. *Christian Blanck,* age 34, on the *Hope,* August 28, 1733; another *Christian Blanck* on the *Queen of Denmark,* October 4, 1751 (PGP I:116; 473).

20. BLICKENSDOERFER (Blickenstaff, Blickensterffer, Blickenstorffer, Blickersterffer).
Origin Hedingen, Ct. Zürich; some to the Palatinate (MQR XXX [April 1956] 137, 138, 139, 146); *Johannes* and *Ulrich Blickenstörffer,* brothers, 1748 to Pennsylvania, *Christian Blickenstörffer* and two *Josts (Blickersterffer* and *Blickensterffer)* on the *Rowand,* September 29, 1753; settled in Lititz, Lancaster County; none remained in Mennonite Church (ME I:362; PGP I:572).
1. Swiss form: *Blickenstorfer,* in the northern part of district of Affoltern, Ct. Zürich (HBLS II:274).
2. *Jacob Blickenstorfer,* age 25, on the *Patience,* September 16, 1748 (PGP I:386).

126

21. BLOSSER (Bloser, Bläser, Blasser).

In 1670's Anabaptist Blaser at Walistolen, Emmental Valley, Ct. Bern; between 1671 and 1711 Blasers to Alsace (BA 48, 39).

Peter Blaser, on the *Bettsey,* August 27, 1739 (ME I:365; PGP I:257; MC 31-32).

Christian Blaser arrived on August 31, 1750 (ME I:365).

1. Swiss form: *Blaser,* in Cts. Bern (especially Langnau, Emmental) and Schwyz (HBLS II:267).
2. *Christian Blaser* and family (9 people in all), on the *Mary,* September 29, 1733 (PGP I:130-132, names and ages of children).

22. BONTRAGER (Bontreger, Borntraeger, Borntrager, Bornträger, Borntreger).

Martin Bonträger, sons *John, Christian,* and *Andrew,* on the *Sally,* October 5, 1767; Amish; settled at Meyersdale, Somerset County; John in Holmes County, Ohio; Christian in Indiana County; Andrew in Virginia; widely scattered Amish family (ME I: 387; MC 34; PGP I:714).

23. BOSHART (Bosser, Bossert, Buschert, Buzzard).

1706 a Bossert Anabaptist in Mannheim; Amish; in North America, mainly in Ontario, Michigan, Indiana, Iowa, and Nebraska (ME I:392; MC 34-35).

1. Swiss forms: *Bossard, Bossart, Bosshard, Bosshardt, Bosshart;* in Cts. Aargau, Luzern, Schwyz, St. Gallen, Zug, Zürich; in Ct. Freiburg also *Posshart* (HBLS II:319-320).
2. *Jacob Bosserdt,* on the *Allen,* September 11, 1729; a *Peter Bosart,* on the *Samuel and Elizabeth,* September 30, 1740 (PGP I:30; 279).

24. BRACKBILL (Braechtbuehl, Brechbiel, Brechbill, Brechbuehl, Brechbühl, Breckbühl).

Benedict Brechbühl (ca. 1665-1720), at Trachselwald, Ct. Bern; minister and elder, exiled; 1710 deported to Holland; 1717 to Pennsylvania as leader of a large Swiss Mennonite group; founder of Strasburg, Lancaster County, congregation (BA 42, 58f, 63f, 67, 69; ME I:400, 411; MC 37); others (MC 37).

1. Swiss forms: *Brechbühl* (BA 192); also *Brechbühler, Brächbühler,* of Huttwil, Ct. Bern (HBLS II:345).
2. *Johannes Brechbil,* age 19, *Anna Brechbielin, Wendell,* age 24, *Brechbühll,* on the *Samuel,* August 11, 1732; *Benedict Brechbill* and *Hans, Hans Peter,* and *Jacob,* on the *John and William,* October 17, 1732 (PGP I:61, 65; 105).
3. *Abraham Brechtbühler* and family, "very poor Anabaptists," emigrated to Pennsylvania in 1754 (F/BR 30).

25. BRENNEMAN (Branaman, Brannaman, Brenaman, Breneman, Breniman, Brenman, Brennaman, Brennamann, Brenneman, Brennemann, Brinneman, Brönnimann, Penerman).

1671 *Melchior Brönnimann* in the *Palatinate* (BA 191); a *Melchior Brenneman* to Conestoga, Pennsylvania ca. 1717 (ME I:417-418); various 18th Century immigrants (MC 37-39; ME I:417, 418; MQR XXX [April 1956] 146; XXXIV [January 1960] 48).

Daniel Brenneman, on the *Hero,* at Philadelphia, October 27, 1765 (PGP I:697).

26. BRICKER (Brücker, Brügger).

Christian Brigger, leading Anabaptist, from Rohrbach, Ct. Bern, at Zofingen debate in 1532 (BA 17-18); *Jacob Bricker* in 1718 in Lancaster County, married 1719 to *Catherine M[e]ylin;* families of that name in Pennsylvania and in Ontario and Alberta, Canada (MC 40-41).

1. Swiss form: *Brügger;* in Cts. Bern, Graubünden, and Luzern (HBLS II:369-370; Supplement, p. 33).
2. *Peter Biker,* age 32, wife *Christan Bricker,* age 29, and children *Elizabeth Brickerin* and *Anna Barba Bickrer,* on the *Plaisance,* September 21, 1732 (PGP I:79, 80, 81).

27. BRUBACHER (Brubacker, Brubaher, Brubaker, Brupacher, Pupater, Pupather).

From Ct. Zürich, a *Hans Brubacher* ca. 1710 at West Hempfield, Lancaster County; *Abraham* (1731-1811), son; others (ME I:441); August 24, 1717 a *Hans Pupather* to Pennsylvania (ME II:715-716); various individuals listed (MC 42-43).

Aberham Brübacher and *Johanes Brubbacher,* on the *St. Andrew,* September 9, 1749 (PGP I:397).

28. BUCHER (Bogar, Bougher, Bücher, Bugar).

1670's an Anabaptist Bucher at Reichenbach, Bernese Oberland (BA 49).

Martin Boger, married daughter of a *Christian Bomberger,* early 18th Century, in Lancaster County (ME I:461; MC 44); in Ohio (BA 148-167, passim).

1. Swiss form: *Bucher,* widely dispersed in Switzerland, especially Ct. Bern and Unterwalden (HBLS II:388-390).
2. *Niclaus Bucher,* on the *Friendship,* October 10, 1727; a *Martin Boger* (same as above?), on the *Pennsylvania Merchant,* September 10, 1731 (PG I:17; 46).

29. BUCKWALTER (Bookwalter, Boughwalder, Boughwalter, Buckwalder).

A *Louis Boughwalder,* 1723 in Lancaster County; a *Johannes Buckwalter* naturalized in 1730 in Berks County (MC 45; ME I:461).

Swiss form: *Buchwalder* (cf. HBLS II:392).

30. BURKHART (Burckhard, Burckhardt, Burghart, Burkhard, Burkhardt).

1751 a *Joseph Burkhart* in Lancaster County; families in various states (ME I:475; MC 46).

1. Swiss forms: *Burkhard, Burkhardt, Burckhardt;* in many cantons (HBLS II:453-456).

2 *Hans Jerch [Jörg] Burkart,* age 5, and *John Fradrick Burghart,* age 30, on the *Loyal Judith,* September 25, 1732; *Simon Burckhart* and *Johann Georg Burckhardt,* on the *Duke of Bedford,* September 14, 1751; *Jacob Burckhardt,* on the *Phoenix,* September 25, 1751 (PGP I:88, 91; 459; 472).

31. BURKHOLDER (Borcholder, Borcholter, Borck-

Bern (especially Brienz), Luzern, Neuenberg, St. Gallen, and Zürich (HBLS III:769-770).

34. DERSTINE (Derstein, Dierstein, Dirstine, Dürstein, Durstin, Thierstein, Thirstien).

Michael Dirstein (b. ca. 1712-1777), on the *Samuel,* August 11, 1732; settled in Rockhill, Bucks County; families also in Ontario, Canada, and Ohio (ME II: 39; MC 78-79; PGP I:64).

Swiss form: *Tierstein;* from Thunerberg near Boswil, Ct. Bern; origin perhaps from a branch of the princely House of Tierstein (HBLS

View of Aarau by Merian.

holder, Borgholder, Borkholder, Burckhalter, Burckholder, Burgholder, Burgholdter, Burkalter, Burkhalter).

From Langnau and Ruderswyl, Emmental Valley, Ct. Bern; 1670's an Anabaptist *Burkhalter* at Mättenberg, Emmental (BA 48; MQR XVIII [July 1944] 145).

1717 *Abraham Burkholder* in Lancaster (now Dauphin) County; *Hans Burkholder* at Conestoga Creek, Lancaster County; large number of influential leaders among immigrants (ME I:475-478; MC 46-49).

Swiss form: *Burkhalter* (BA 48).

32. BYLER (Beiler, Beyler).

Jacob Beiler, born in Switzerland, on the *Charming Nancy,* October 8, 1737, to Oley Valley, Berks County; Amish; families in Pennsylvania and Ohio (ME I:488; BA 168; MC 23, 49; PGP I:193).

Perhaps Swiss name *Beyeler,* family origin in Guggisberg, Ct. Bern (HBLS II:220).

33. CRESSMAN

Niklos `Nikolaus] Crössman, on the *Friendship of Bristoll,* October 16, 1727, progenitor of families in North America; various prominent men; mostly in Waterloo County, Ontario (since 1807) (ME I:739; MC 71; PGP I:17).

Perhaps Swiss name *Grossmann,* name in Cts.

VI:789-790).

35. DETWEILER (Dätwyler, Dättwyler, Dettweiler, Dettwiler, Detwiler, Dittwiler).

18th Century Mennonite family established especially in Bucks and Montgomery Counties, also in Ontario, Ohio, Indiana, Illinois, Missouri (ME II:40; MC 79-80).

1. Swiss forms: *Dättwyler, Dettwyler, Dettwiler;* in Germany: *Dettweiler;* origin: *Dättwil,* near Baden, Ct. Aargau; in 16th Century in other communes, also in Langenbruck, Ct. Basel (HBLS II:663-664).

2. *Melchior Detwyler,* age 37, on the *Princess Augusta,* September 16, 1736 (PGP I:163).

36. DILLER

1774 An *Abraham Diller* (d. 1783), at Bowmansville, Lancaster County; 1790 family to Cumberland County; also in Ontario, Ohio, Kansas (MC 81).

Perhaps Swiss name *Dillier (Dilger, Tilger);* origin Engelberg, Ct. Unterwalden (HBLS II:723).

37. EBERLY (Eperly).

Lorenz Aeberli from Grünen, executed at Bern, June 3, 1539 (BA 23).

Heinrich Eberle, on the James Goodwill, September 17, 1727, settled in Lancaster County; also *Veronica* (wife?); 6 children; family in Pennsylvania, Ohio, Iowa (MC 89; PGP I:11; cf. also ME I:137).

1. Swiss forms: *Aeberli, Eberle, Eberli, Eberly;* origin on Lake Zürich, known since 14th Century; also in city of Zürich (HBLS I: 115-116).
2. A *[Se]bastian Eb[erle]*,on the *James Goodwill,* September 11, 1728, with 4 others (PGP I:23).

38. EBERSOLE (Aebersold, Ebersohl, Ebersol, Eversole, Eversull).

Abrahm Ebersohl, on the *James Goodwill,* September 27, 1727, 4 in family (PGP I:11); *Johannes, Pedter, Jost Ebersohl,* on the *Robert and Alice,* September 3, 1739 (PGP I:270, 271); *Carl Ebersohl,* age 21, on the *Peggy,* September 24, 1753 (PGP I:550); *Jacob Ebersoll,* on the *Chance,* November 1, 1763 (PGP I:686; ME II:137); 19th Century members (MC 89).

> Swiss forms: *Aebersold, Ebersold;* from district of Konolfingen, Ct. Bern; also Zägiwil and Burgdorf, Ct. Bern (HBLS I:116; II:775).

39. EBY (Aby, Aebi, Aeby, Eaby, Ebee, Ebi, Ebie, Uebi).

Theodorus Eby (1663-1730), 1704 to the *Palatinate;* 1715 to Pennsylvania; settled at Mill Creek, Lancaster County; from Ct. Zürich (ME II:137; 139-140; MC 89-90).

Christian Eby (1698-1756) and family; prominent in Pequea, Lancaster County, especially *Peter* (1765-1843) (MQR XIV [January 1940] 41-51); various prominent leaders (ME II:139-140; MC 90-91).

1. Swiss forms: *Aebi* or *Aeby,* in various Cts. (HBLS I:116-117, 119-120).
2. A *Henrick Ebby,* age 30, on the *Samuel,* August 11, 1732 (PGP I:59; see also entries *Evy, Ewy,* same name?).

40. EGLI (Egle, Egly).

A *Rudolph Egli,* signer of Dordtrecht Confession of Faith, 1632. Immigrant with a group of 1711; to Lancaster County (MC 93).

1839 an *Abraham Egli* to Butler County, Ohio (ME II:163).

1. Swiss form: *Egli:* (in Ct. Baselland also *Eglin, Eggli, Eggelin, Eikelin);* family name widely dispersed (HBLS II:788-790).
2. A *Marx Egli,* on the *Vernon,* August 1747 (PGP I:363).

41. EICHER (Eichert, Eichler, Eycher).

In 1670's an Anabaptist *Eicher* from Schwarzenegg, Thun region, Ct. Bern; between 1671 and 1711 to Alsace, near village of Markirch (Marie-aux-Mines) (BA 49, 38).

Christian Eicher, age 46, and *Johannes,* age 18, on the *Brothers,* September 30, 1754 (ME II:167;

PGP I:612, 613).

19th Century immigrants from Alsace-Lorraine (ME II:167), in Wayne County, Ohio; also in Iowa, Nebraska, Ontario, Indiana, Oregon (MC 94).

1. Swiss form: *Eicher;* Cts. Bern and Luzern (HBLS III:4).
2. *Michael Eichert,* on the *Adventure,* October 2, 1727 (PGP I:15).

42. ELLENBERGER.

Albrecht Ellenberger, on the *St. Andrew,* September 9, 1749 (ME II:189).

Jacob Ellenberger, b. in Germany 1821, in 1847 to Lee County, Iowa (MQR XLII [July 1968] 197, 198, 200).

Christian and *Niclaus Ellenberger,* on the *Robert and Alice,* September 3, 1739; *Ulrich Ellenberger,* on the *St. Andrew,* September 9, 1749 (PGP I:271, 396).

43. ENGEL (Angle, Engle)

1698 a *Paul Engel* at Germantown, Pennsylvania, perhaps a Mennonite.

17th Century to the Palatinate (ME II:214); in 1752 brothers *John* and *Jacob Engle* in Lancaster County (MC 97); in 1755 *Ulrich Engel* at Donegal, Pennsylvania (BA 85); he had emigrated from Sonceboz in the Jura in 1754 and paid an emigration tax of 6 pds., 13 shillings, 3 pence (F/BR 61); *Jacob Engel* (b. 1753); 1754 to America; founder of Brethren in Christ (River Brethren) (ME II:214).

1. Swiss form: *Engel;* families in Ct. Bern, Solothurn, Thurgau, Zürich (HBLS III:36-37).
2. *G[e]org Engel,* on the *Townsend,* October 5, 1737 (PGP I:187).

44. ERB.

Nicholas Erb (1679-1740), from the Emmental Valley, Ct. Bern; via the Palatinate 1722 to Lancaster County (ME II:240-241; MC 98).

1. Swiss origin in Cts. Bern (Thun), Baselland (Orinalingen, Rotenfluh, Rickenbach), St. Gallen (earlier especially Toggenburg), Schwyz, Solothurn, Uri, and Zürich (HBLS III:50-51).
2. A *Christian Erb,* age 46, on the *Harle,* September 1, 1736 (PGP I:158).

45. ESCH (Ashe, Eash, Esh, Oesch).

Jacob Esch, and *Michael,* on the *Duke of Wirtenberg,* October 16, 1751; to Lancaster County (ME II:246-247; MC 87-88, 99; PGP I:477).

1. Swiss forms: *von Aesch,* or *von Esch,* extinct, in city of Solothurn; also in village of Grossaffoltern, Ct. Bern (HBLS I:152) or perhaps *Oesch,* from Amsoldingen, Thun, and Oberlangenegg, Ct. Bern (HBLS V:336).
2. *Christian Est,* on the *St. Andrew,* September 26, 1737 (PGP I:180).

46. EYMANN (Eiman, Eyman).

An Anabaptist family from Ct. Bern to Alsace between 1671 and 1711 (BA 38-39).

A *Jacob Eimann,* on the *St. Andrew,* September 9, 1749 (ME II:282; PGP I:397).

47. FRETZ (Frätz, Fraetz).

1734 a *Christian Fraetz* in Pennsylvania, preceded by *John* and *Christian Fretz,* brothers, between 1710 and 1720; settled at Deep Run, Bucks County; John's son *John* (1730-1826) to Ontario, Canada (ME I:395-396; MC 114-115).

Hanns Martin Fretz, age 22, on the *Billender Thistle,* November 3, 1738 (or October 28, 1738) (PGP I:243).

48. FREY (Frei, Fry).

In 1670's an Anabaptist *Frei* from Hilterfingen, Bernese Oberland (BA 49).

Johannes Frey before 1717 at Skippack, Lancaster County; by 1730 name in Virginia Mennonite settlement; 1839 a *Jacob Frey* from France to Fulton County, Ohio (ME II:396).

1. Swiss forms: *Frey, Frei;* widely dispersed (HBLS II:242-247).
2. Tobias Frey, with four in party, on the *William and Sarah,* September 18, 1727 (PGP I:9).

49. FUNK (Funck).

Johannes Funk, 1710, settled at Pequea, Lancaster County; *Heinrich Funck* (d. 1760), about 1730 in Montgomery County (ME II:420-421; MC 116-118).

1. Swiss form: *Funk,* originally from Mettmenstetten, Ct. Zürich, dispersed throughout the district of Affoltern, spreading to Ct. Bern (HBLS III:360-361).
2. *Hans Funck,* on the *Molly,* September 30, 1727; a *Fritrich Funk,* with 7 week old twins, on the *Mary,* September 29, 1733 (PGP I: 13; 134).

50. GALLE (Galli, Gally).

Peter Gally (Galle) to the Palatinate, most likely from Ct. Bern; son *Peter* at the Geistenmühle in 1734; *Peter (III)* said to have emigrated to Pennsylvania; several Mennonite families with this name in Kansas (ME II:436-437).

1. Swiss forms: *Galli, Galdi* (in Ct. Bern); extinct in city of Bern, but in rural region extant; (in Ct. Tessin, *Galli, Gallo, de Gallis)* (HBLS III:382).
2. *Friederich Galle,* on the *Polly,* September 19, 1764 (PGP I:690).

51. GEHMAN (Gahman, Gaueman, Gäuman, Gäumann, Gayman, Geeman, Geyman).

1759 Bernese family Gäumann from Röthenbach, Ct. Bern in Montbéliard (BA 89).

1732, August 11 on the *Samuel: Christian Geman,* age 24, to Berks County; *Bendich Geman,* age 23, and *Anna Gemanin,* age 20, to Lehigh County (ME II:444-445; MC 122; PGP I:61, 65).

52. GEISER (Geyser, Gyser).

Hans Geiser, 1765 Mennonite minister, in Bishopric of Basel (BA 80); 1823 a family in La Chaux-de-Fonds (BA 125).

Early 1850's a *Geiser* family in Wayne County, Ohio; 1876 *Peter Geiser* to Oregon (BA 165).

1. Swiss form *Geiser,* from Bernese Oberaargau, especially Langenthal and Roggwil, Ct. Bern, and in adjoining regions of Cts. Aargau and Luzern (HBLS III:424-425).
2. *Johanas Gyser,* age 50, *Johanas Petter,* age 17, *Yogha [Johann] Christian,* age 7, *Mariles Pitt [Marie Elsbeth],* age 20, on the *Billender Thistle,* November 3, 1738 (or October 28, 1738); also *Christian,* age 21, and *Kattarina,* age 20, *Gysler* (PGP I:240-242).

53. GERBER (Garber, Gärber, Garver).

Old Mennonite family; *Wälti Gerber* executed July 30, 1566; 1670's Gerber families in the Emmental, Ct. Bern, and at Thun (BA 24, 43, 48, 49); various families (BA, passim).

Gerbers in 1735 in Lancaster County; two families in Shenandoah Valley, Virginia (ME II:478).

1822 *Ulrich, Michael* and *Jacob Gerber* left the Swiss Jura for Sonnenberg, Wayne County, Ohio (BA 133); widely dispersed (ME II:478); various 19th Century individuals (MC 120, 125, 126).

1. Swiss forms: *Gerber, Gerfer, Gerwer,* in Cts. Appenzell, Bern, Freiburg, Graubünden, Luzern, St. Gallen, Solothurn, Uri (HBLS III:478, 479, 493).
2. *Hans Jacob Gerber,* on the *Hope,* August 28, 1733; *Michel,* age 27, *Anna,* age 22, *Anna,* age ½, on the *Hope,* September 23, 1734; *Johannes,* age 32, on the *Harle,* September I, 1736 (PGP I:121, 143, 144, 146).

54. GINGERICH (Gingery, Gingrich, Guengerich, Güngerich).

Originated from Konolfingen, Ct. Bern (1389), name Güngerich; to the Palatinate; 1724 in Conestoga, Lancaster County; wide dispersal (ME II:520-521; MC 128).

55. GOERING (Gehring, Gering, Göring).

In the Emmental, Ct. Bern; Anabaptists of that name in Montbéliard, Galicia; Poland, 1874 to the United States (ME II:535).

1. Swiss forms: *Geering, Gehring, Gering, Gerung, Gehrig, Gerig;* in many cantons (HBLS III:415-416).
2. A *Baltes Gering,* on the *Mortonhouse,* August

56. GRABER (Gräber, Grayber, Greber).

Between 1671 and 1711 Graber Anabaptists family in Alsace (BA 39).

Peter Graber (1741-1805), born in Montbéliard, France, to United States; grandson *Peter*, from Montbéliard to Stark County, Ohio; grandson *Christian* to Washington County, Iowa, in 1856 (ME II:559; MC 135; MQR XLII [July 1968] 201).

1. Swiss form; *Graber;* originated at Langenbruck, Ct. Basel; in Ct. Bern in districts of Thun, Aarwangen, Burgdorf, and Trachselwald; also in Ct. Luzern (HBLS III: 620).

2. A *Leobald Greber*, on the *Robert and Alice*, September 3, 1739 (PGP I:264).

57. GRABILL (Grabiel, Graybill, Grebel, Grebiel, Grebilt, Krabill, Krähenbühl, Kraybill, Krayenbühl, Krebill, Krehbiel, Krehbill, Kreybül, Krienbiel).

Origin Grosshöchstetten, district of Konolfingen, Ct. Bern; early Anabaptist family.

1671 *Jost Krähenbühl* to the Palatinate; 1770 members to Galicia (in 19th Century to New York, Ohio, then Iowa, Kansas).

1719 in Alsace; 1733 name Krähenbuhl at Weaverland, Lancaster County; in Shenandoah Valley as Grabill.

In 1790's *John Graybill*, preacher in Juniata County (MQR XVIII [July 1944] 155).

1831 *Jacob Krehbiel* (1781-1860) from the Pfrimmerhof, Palatinate, to Clarence, N.Y., near Buffalo; bishop in 1839; wide dispersal of family; influential (ME II:559; III:235-237; MC 136-137).

Hans Erick Crable and *Michael Krebiel*, on the *Molly*, September 30, 1727; *Christian Crybile*, on the *Friendship of Bristoll*, October 16, 1727 (PGP I:13-14; 16).

58. GROFF (Graef, Gráf, Grove).

Hans Graf (1661-1746), founded 1717 Groffdale, Lancaster County; 7 sons and 3 daughters; family in Pennsylvania, Illinois, Ontario, and Virginia (ME II: 587; MC 139).

1. Swiss forms: *Graf, Graff;* widely dispersed; also rural Bernese name (HBLS III:624-626).

2. *Sebästian Gräff*, with 3 other persons, on the *William and Sarah*, September 21, 1727; *Johann Christoph Groff* and *Gorg Graff*, on the *James Goodwill*, September 11, 1728 (PGP I:9; 22).

59. GROSS

Jacob Gross (c. 1743-1810), with 2 brothers, to Lancaster County; by 1775 preacher, later bishop; family name in Pennsylvania, Middle West, Canada (ME II:598-599; MC 140).

1. Swiss forms: *Gross, Gros;* widely dispersed

in Switzerland; also in rural Bernese areas like Grindelwald (HBLS III:756-758).

2. *Johannes Gross*, age 36, on the *Plaisance*, September 21, 1732; *Jacob, Johann Anderes, Johann Christian*, on the *Neptune*, October 4, 1752 (PGP I:79; 493-494).

60. HABEGGER (Habecker, Habeger, Hapeger, Hawbecker).

Frist Anabaptist record in 1564; at Trub, Ct. Bern (ME II:619).

In the Bishopric of Basel *Ulrich Habegger* active as minister in 1764 (BA 80).

Hans Jacob Habegger, with others, on the *Charming Nancy*, October 8, 1737 (ME II:619; MC 384; PGP I:188).

Family in Lancaster and Franklin Counties; Adams County, Indiana; and Niagara County, New York (ME II:619).

In 1865 Peter Habegger, minister, from the Jura to Münsterberg congregation, Berne, Indiana (BA 154).

61. HARNISH (Harnisch, Harnist).

Old family name of Schwarzenburg, Ct. Bern (HBLS IV:77).

Before 1718 a *Martin Harnist* in Lancaster County; two families in 1732 (MC 146; ME II:665).

Samuel Harnisch, age 28, and *Anna*, age 28, on the *Plaisance*, September 21, 1732 (PGP I:80, 83).

62. HAURY (Hauri).

17th Century Anabaptist name, in the Bernese Aargau (BA 47).

After 1648 to the Palatinate; in 1745 a *Jacob Haury* there; progeny to Bavaria, later to USA; 19th Century arrivals to Illinois; now mostly in Kansas (ME II: 679-680).

Swiss forms: *Hauri* (Hirschtal, Ct. Aargau), *Hauri* and *Houri* in Ct. Luzern (HBLS IV:90-91).

63. HEGE (Hage, Hagey, Hagy, Hegi, Hegy).

1616 *Hirzel Hägi* sentenced to galley service, in Zürich (MQR XXXIV [July 1960] 201).

Hans Hege, from Zweibrücken, Germany, on the *Goodwill*, September 27, 1727; to Lancaster County. Family in Pennsylvania, Ontario, Canada, Illinois, and Iowa (ME II:687-689; MC 151-152; PGP I:11).

Swiss form: *Hegi;* in Ct. Bern at Roggwil, in 17th Century; also in Ct. Luzern and especially Ct. Zürich (HBLS IV:110-111).

64. HELLER

Very old Swiss name, especially Ct. Zürich; in Ct. Bern at Kirchlindach (HBLS IV:135-136); two families in Lancaster County in 1749 (MC 152).

Rudolf Heeller, on the *Mortonhouse*, August 28, 1728 (PGP I:19).

65. HERR (Hare).

Early Anabaptist family, in Ct. Zürich and the Emmental, Ct. Bern (MQR XXII [July 1948] 188).

Hans Herr (1639-1725] and *Christian,* brothers, on the *Maria Hope,* September 1710; 1717, August 24, brothers *Abraham* and *Emmanuel;* settled in Lancaster County; *Christian,* minister; prominent family; especially in Pennsylvania; 1885 to Oregon (ME II:711-712; MC 154-156); 13,000 descendants estimated from early 18th Century immigrants (ME II:712).

66. HERSHBERGER (Harshbarger, Harshberger, Hersberg, Hersberger, Herscheberger, Hirschberger).

Originating in Ct. Basel, especially Thürneu and Läufelfingen; 1529 Anabaptist members recorded; 1678 to the Palatinate.

Jacob and *Casber Herschberger,* and *Christian Hirschberger,* on the *St. Andrew,* September 9, 1749; to Berks County, members of Amish congregation; widely dispersed in U.S. (ME II:714-715; MC 156; PGP I:396, 397).

67. HERSHEY (Hearsey, Hirschi, Hirsehy).

Origin in district of Schwarzenburg and Trub, Ct. Bern (HBLS IV:229).

Christian Hirschi (d. 1720) and 3 sons, 1717 to Lancaster County; *Christian Hirschi,* on the *Robert and Alice,* September 3, 1739 (ME II:715-716; MC 156-157; PGP I:270).

68. HERTZLER (Hartzler, Herzler).

Jacob Herzler, on the *St. Andrew,* September 9, 1749; first Amish minister and bishop in North America; 1750 settled in Berks County, west of Hamburg, with 3 sons, a daughter; 1749-1761 three other immigrants; prolific; 1952 family history lists 36,548 individuals in 11 generations; 8,757 families; 359 in the ministry (Mennonite and other) (ME II:716-717; MC 157-158; PGP I:396).

69. HESS

Widely dispersed Swiss family name; in Ct. Bern especially Trachselwald and Burgdorf (HBLS IV:207-210).

Hans Hess (d. 1733), early 18th Century, to Lancaster County; families in Pennsylvania, Kansas, California, Iowa, Illinois (ME II:718; MC 158).

Jeremias Hess and two others, on the *Thistle of Glasgow,* August 29, 1730 (PGP I:31, 34).

70. HIESTAND (Heistandt, Heystandt, Histand).

Abraham Hiestand (b. ca. 1703) to Montgomery County; family in Pennsylvania, Canada.

1. Family recorded in 1401 at Richterswil and Hütten, Ct. Zürich (HBLS IV:220; MC 160).
2. *Jacob* and *Johannes Hiestandt,* on the *Friendship of Bristoll,* October 16, 1727 (PGP I:17).

71. HIRSCHLER (Herschler).

Soon after 1700 in the Palatinate; Alsace; to Bavaria; a *Christian Hirschler* in U.S. in 1850's (ME II:746; MQR XXX [April 1956] 140); family in first Mennonite Iowa settlement (MQR XLII [July 1968] 199).

Johann Georg Herschler, on the *Brittania,* September 18, 1773 (PGP I:751).

72. HOFFMAN (Hofmann).

1670's in the Emmental, Anabaptist family *Hofmann* from Affoltern, Ct. Bern (BA 48); in early 18th Century at Groningen, Holland (BA 65); 5 families to Pennsylvania in 1727 (MC 160; ME II:277-278).

1. Swiss forms: *Hofmann, Hoffmann;* widely dispersed (HBLS IV:263-265).
2. *Burckhardt, Hans Lenord, Henerick Hoffmann,* on the *Molly,* September 30, 1727; *Johann Jörg Hoffmann,* on the *Friendship of Bristoll,* October 16, 1727 (PGP I:12, 13; 17).

73. HOFSTETTER (Hoffstetter).

From Langnau, Ct. Bern; 1821, *Peter,* 1824 brothers *Nicolas* and *Christian,* to Sonnenberg, Wayne County, Ohio settlement; today in Ohio, Missouri (MC 161; ME II:785-786).

Swiss forms: *Hofstetter, Hofstettler;* in Cts. Appenzell, Bern, Luzern, St. Gallen (HBLS IV:267-268).

74. HOLDEMAN (Haldeman, Haldenmann, Haldiman, Halteman, Halterman, Holdermann, Holdiman).

1538 first Anabaptist family at Eggiwil, Ct. Bern.

Nicholas, Hans, and *Michael,* brothers, on the *Adventure,* October 2, 1727; to Montgomery County; *Hans* and *Michael* to Chester County; 1827 to Wayne County, Ohio; 1849 Hans's widow and 10 sons to Elkhart County, Indiana; 1873 *David S. Holdeman* to McPherson County, Kansas (ME II:788-789; MC 143, 161; PGP I:15).

Swiss forms: *Haldemann, Haldimann, Haldimand;* family name of Ct. Bern (especially Signau and Konolfingen districts), Cts. Neuenburg and Waadt (HBLS IV:56).

75. HOOVER (Hoober, Hover, Hubbert, Huber, Hubert, Hueber, Huvar).

Ulrich Huber, from Röthenbach, Signau district, Ct. Bern; executed at Bern 1538 (BA 23).

Hans Huber (ca. 1670-1750), between 1710 and 1715 to Pennsylvania, settled at Mill Creek, Lancaster County; *Hoovers* pioneered Haldimand County, Ontario, before 1080 (ME II:809; MC 163-164, 168); *Martin Huber* (ca. 1760-1849), bishop, from Lancaster County 1804 to Markham, Ontario; 1837 to Ohio; 1848 to Indiana (MQR XLVI [January 1972] 73).

1. Swiss form: *Huber;* name known all over Switzerland (HBLS IV:299-305); *Hubert* is listed as a separate name, known in the Cts. of

Freiburg and Wallis (*ibid.*, p. 305).

2. *Hans Jerg* and *Jacob Hüber,* on the *Molly,* September 30, 1727 (PGP I:13, 14); *Johann Heinrich Huber,* linen-weaver of Oberkulm, Ct. Aargau; 1665 to the Palatinate; returned 1674; son *Jonas* (b. 1723), owner of farm in Ellerstadt, Palatinate; 1738 to America with 10 children (HBLS Supplement 86).

76. HOSTETTLER (Hochstetler, Hochstettler, Hostetler, Hostetter).

Origin of Anabaptist family in Guggisberg, Ct. Bern (ME II:818).

1670's a *Hostettler* family in Schwarzenburg region, in 1759 in Montbéliard area (BA 49, 89).

Jacob Hochstettler (1704-1776), on the *Harle,* September 1, 1736; Amish; settled north of Reading, Pennsylvania; others in Lancaster County; also Wayne County, Ohio (ME II:818; MC 166-168; PGP I:155).

1. Swiss form: *Hostettler,* from small settlement Hostett near Schönentannen, Ct. Bern (HBLS Supplement 87).
2. *Oswald Hosteetter,* age 30, with others, on the *Samuel,* August 11, 1732 (PGP I:59-61).

77. HUNSBERGER

Mennonite families in Eastern Pennsylvania and Ontario; *Henry Hunsberger* (1768-1854), bishop (ME II:844; MC 169).

78. HUNSICKER (Honsaker, Hunsecker, Hunsinger, Hunzinger, Hunziker, Unziker).

Of Aargau origin to the Palatinate, Alsace (BA 47).

Valentine Hunsicker (1700-1771), 1717 to Montgomery County, settled at Skippack; families in Pennsylvania, Illinois, Ohio (ME II:844-845; MC 169-170).

1. Swiss form: *Hunziker;* in Cts. Aargau, Bern (Schwarzhäusen, Wynau, Thun), and Luzern (HBLS IV:324).
2. *Elisabeth Hartman,* and six children, named *Huntseker,* on the *Pennsylvania Merchant,* September 10, 1731 (PGP I:43, 44).

79. KAEGE (Kaegi, Kaegy, Kägi, Kaiggey).

First mention 1616; Anabaptist at Wald, Ct. Zürich.

Hans Rudolf Kägy, 1715 to Lancaster County; families in Virginia; never prominent among Mennonite group (ME III:134).

1. Swiss form *Kägi,* in Ct. St. Gallen (Gommiswald) and Ct. Zürich (city, Fischenthal and Bauma) (HBLS IV:432).
2. *Rudolph Kägy,* on the *Hero,* October 27, 1764 (PGP I:698).

80. KANAGY (Genegy, Gnaeg, Gnaegi, Gnagey, Gnagy, Kenagi, Kenege).

1723 *Hans Gnagi* at Montbéliard; 1742 *Johanes Qnäg,* on the *Francis and Elizabeth,* September 21, 1742; 1749 *Barbara Kenege* directly from Switzerland; 1750's *Christian Gnaegi* from Switzerland to Somerset County; descendants in 1950's still there; 1754 *John Kenegy* to America; descendants in Ohio; brother Joseph with 5 sons to Berks County (ME III:143; MC 186, 189; PGP I:329).

Swiss form: *Gnaegi;* Bernese origin, in villages Nidau, Ipsach, Bellmund, Schwadernau, Täuffelen, and Hochstetten (HBLS III:575).

81. KAUFFMAN (Cauffman, Coffman, Kaufman, Kaufmann, Kauffmann).

Between 1671 and 1711 a Bernese family migrated to Alsace (BA 39); Amish; several to Galicia and Volhynia (1803), then to Kansas and South Dakota; *Andreas* and *Isaac Kauffman,* from Steffisburg in Ct. Bern, at Friesenheim, Palatinate, emigrated in 1717 to Pennsylvania; some later to Virginia, name Coffman; in 19th Century, others to Ontario.

Jacob Kauffman, 1754 to Berks County, from the Palatinate; Amish; prominent in that group, especially *Daniel Kauffman* (1865-1944) (ME III:156, 156-157; MC 63, 64, 187-188).

1. Swiss form: *Kaufmann,* in various regions; in Ct. Bern especially in Oberland (HBLS IV: 462).
2. *Heinrich Kaufman,* on the *Molly,* September 30, 1727; *Hanes [Johannes] Kauffman,* on the *Mortonhouse,* August 23, 1728 (PGP I:14, 19).

82. KENDIG (Kindig, Kuendig, Kündig).

Martin Kündig, on the *Maria Hope,* September 1710; to Pequea, Lancaster County; by 1717 more immigrants of that name (MQR XLII [July 1968] 175-181; [October 1968] 289).

First Mennonite in Illinois: *Benjamin Kendig,* from Augusta County, Virginia, in 1833 (BA 170).

1. Swiss form: *Kündig;* name in Cts. Basel, Luzern, Schwyz, Unterwalden, and Zürich (especially villages of Bäretswil and Bauma); earliest mention 1331, village of Kaltbrunn, Ct. St. Gallen (HBLS IV:554).
2. *Martine Kindige,* on the *Molly*, September 30, 1727 (PGP I:13).

83. KENNEL

Peter Kennel (d. 1896), in 1830 to Butler County, Ohio; families now in Pennsylvania, Illinois, Nebraska (ME III:165-166; MC 190-191).

1. Swiss forms: *Kaenel* (in Ct. Bern: Bargen, Kappelen, Schwarzhäussen, Herniswil, Wangenried); *Kaenel,* from Kaenel, Ct. Freiburg; *von Kaenel,* Ct. Bern (Aeschi, Reichenbach, Winomis); *Kennel, Kaennel* in Ct. Schwyz (HBLS IV:434, 476).
2. *Niclaus Kunel,* age 42, and *Katherina Elizabeth Kenel,* age 50, on the *Britannia,* September 21, 1731 (PGP I:49, 53).

84. KIPFER (Küpfer).

Elsbeth Küpfer, from Sumiswald, Ct. Bern, executed at Bern in 1538 (BA 23).

Ulrich Kipfer, Anabaptist leader in the Emmental in 1810; a minister of the same name in 1852 to Adams County, Indiana (d. 1866) (BA 100, 135, 153, 154; ME III:178-179); *Jacob Kuepfer,* b. in Switzerland, May 30, 1798, with two brothers to Waterloo County, Ontario (MC 198).

1. Swiss forms: *Küpfer* (in city of Bern); *Küpfer* and *Kipfer* in Emmental Valley, in the district of Konolfingen, in Bäriswil, Steffisburg, and Wangenried (HBLS IV:557-558).
2. *Rudolf Küpfer,* on the *Countess of Sussex,* October 7, 1765 (PGP I:708).

85. KIRCHHOFFER

David Kirchhofer emigrated 1819 from Sonnenberg in the *Jura,* to Sonnenberg, Wayne County, Ohio (BA 111, 132, 138; MQR XXI [April 1947] 73).

1. Swiss form: *Kirchhofer;* in Cts. St. Gallen, Schaffhausen, and Solothurn (HBLS IV: 498).
2. *Christoph Kirchhoff,* with family of 5, on the *James Goodwill,* September 27, 1727 (PGP I:12).

86. KOENIG

In 1730's Amish *König* family in Berks County. Ca. 1754 family *König* left Courtelary district, Bernese Jura, to Pennsylvania (BA 168, 85).

1. Swiss form: *Koenig:* in various cantons; in Ct. Bern also an old, widely dispersed rural family name (HBLS IV:522-524).
2. *Gabriel Konigh,* on the *Pennsylvania Merchant,* September 11, 1732 (PGP I:69).

87. KOLB (Culp, Kulp).

Early Anabaptist family; between 1671 and 1717 to Palatinate; 1707, *Heinrich, Jacob, Johannes, Dielman,* sons of *Dielman Kolb* (1648-1712), from Wolfsheim, Palatinate, to Germantown, Pennsylvania; 1709 *Martin Kolb,* one of the emigrants, ordained minister. 1717 *Dielman Kolb* (1691-1756), preacher at Salford, Montgomery County (ME III:213-214; MC 194-196, 199).

1. Swiss form: *Kolb;* in Ct. Bern (districts of Burgdorf, Interlaken, Konolfingen, Nidau, and Steffisburg); also in Ct. Thurgau (Güttingen and Lanzenneunform (HBLS IV:527).
2. *Dielman Colb,* and *Judith,* on the *Mortonhouse,* August 17, 1729; *Hans Kaspar Kolb,* on the *Allen,* September 11, 1729 (PGP I: 23, 26; 30).

88. KURTZ

Johannes and *Christian Kurtz,* sons of *Stephen,* from Switzerland to Pennsylvania in 1732, settled in Berks and Lancaster Counties.

A. [*Abraham*] *Kurrtz,* on the *Robert and Alice,* December 3, 1740 (PGP I:289).

David Kurtz, from Germany, early 19th Century to Indiana (MC 199-200; ME III:262).

1. Swiss form: *Kurz;* family name in Cts. Aargau, Basel, Bern, and Luzern (HBLS IV:571).
2. *Johannes Kurtz,* on the *Adventure,* October 2, 1727 (PGP I:15).

89. LANDES (Landis).

Hans Landis, last Anabaptist executed in Ct. Zürich, 1614.

Jacob Landis (1687-1730), with *Benjamin, Felix, Johannes,* 1717 to Pennsylvania from Mannheim; brothers (ME III:280-282; MC 202-203).

Jacob's son Benjamin (1700-1781), minister in Lancaster County; progenitor of Lancaster County Landis line (ME III:281).

1. Old family name of *Horgen* and *Hirzel,* Ct. Zürich (HBLS IV:593).
2. *Rodolf Landish,* on the *Molly,* September 30, 1727 (PGP I:14).

90. LATSCHA (Lachet, Latschar, Latschaw, Leutscher, Lörsch, Lörtscher, Löscher, Lötscher).

Origin at Lafferbach, near Erlenbach in the Bernese Simmental.

1601 hymn by a *Hans Lötscher;* a *Hans Lörsch (Lötscher)* imprisoned 1667 (BA 20, 36); 1714 a *Hans Lötscher* from the Simmental to Alsace; spread to the Palatinate; son *Johannes Franz* to Berks County; other *Lötchers* to Holland, name *Leutscher* (ME III: 297, 329, 400; MC 206).

1. Swiss forms: *Lötscher, Lörtscher;* in Bernese region; spread to other cantons (HBLS IV:704).
2. *Frans Latshow,* on the *Mortonhouse,* August 23, 1728 (PGP I:18).

91. LEHMAN (Layman, Leaman, Leeman, Leemann, Lehmann, Leman).

Early Anabaptist family; 1727 *Hans Leaman (Lehmann),* on the *James Goodwill,* September 27, 1727; preceded by a *Peter Leman,* August 24, 1717; settled in Lancaster County (ME III:313-314; MC 208-210; MQR XLII [October 1968] 287; PGP I:10). Influential Mennonite family (BA 80-168, passim; MC 208-210).

1. Swiss forms: *Lehmann* and *Leemann;* the latter especially of Ct. Zürich origin; in various cantons (HBLS IV:641, 646-647).
2. *Johannes Lemahn,* on the *Adventure,* October 2, 1727; *Peter Leman,* on the *Friendship of Bristoll,* October 16, 1727 (PGP I:15, 16).

92. LICHTI (Leichti, Leichty, Leighty, Lichdi, Lichty, Liechti, Liechty).

Early Anabaptist family; after 1671 in Palatinate; also in Holland; 1750 first family to Lancaster County; later to Ohio, then Indiana (ME III: 335; MC 212).

1754 *Ulrich Liechti* and family, to Pennsylvania, "very poor Anabaptists" (F/BR 31).

In 1850 the *Jacob* and *John Liechty* families settled

View of Aarburg by Merian.

Madison Township, Polk County, Iowa (BA 158, 159).

After 1876, *John* and *Nicklaus Liechty* moved from Sonnenberg, Wayne County, Ohio, to Western Oregon (BA 165).

    1. Swiss forms: *Liechti;* in Ct. Bern (especially districts of Burgdorf, Signau, and Trachselwald); *Lichti* and *Liechti* in Ct. Zürich (HBLS IV:679).

    2. *Christian* and *Catrina Lichtie,* on the *Charming Nancy,* October 8, 1737 (PGP I:188, 190).

93. LITWILLER (Litmiller, Litwiler, Lütwyler).

17th Century Anabaptist family *Lütwyler,* in the Bernese Aargau (BA 47).

From there to Alsace; 1829 *Peter Litwiller* (1809-1878) to Ontario; family also in Ohio, Michigan, Indiana, Illinois (ME III:377; MC 213).

94. LONG (Lang).

In 1728 *John Long,* in Landis Valley, Lancaster County, since ca. 1718; more families in 1730's (MC 214; ME III:282).

    1. Swiss form: *Lang*; family name widely dispersed (HBLS IV:599-600).

    2. *Conrath Long,* age 38, and *Hannah Boble* [*Annababeli*] *Long,* age 28, on the *Adventure,* September 23, 1732; *Hans Adam Lang,* age 30, and family, on the *Samuel,* August 17, 1733; *Johans Lang,* age 45, and family on the *Charming Betty,* October 11, 1733 (PGP I:84, 87; 108, 109, 112; 135, 136).

95. LONGENECKER (Langanacker, Langenecker, Longacre, Longaker, Longinegger).

John Langenegger, ca. 1717 at Pequea, Lancaster County (MQR XLII [October 1968] 289); *Daniel Longenecker* in 1720 (ME III:389; MC 214-215).

    1. Swiss form: *Langenegger,* Ct. Appenzell (HBLS IV:601).

    2. *Christian* and *Anna Barbary Longenacre* on the *Mortonhouse,* August 17, 1729 (PGP I:24).

96. MAST (Maust, Mest, Moist, Moss).

Jacob Mast, with four persons, on the *William and Sarah,* September 18, 1727; to Skippack; *Jacob* and *Barbara Mast,* on the *Charming Nancy,* October 8, 1737; to Lancaster County; *Jacob Mast* (1738-1808), born in Switzerland, with brother, 4 sisters, to Pennsylvania; in 1764 in Berks County; 12 children, all married (ME III:536; PGP I:8, 188, 190).

After 1776; *Abraham Mast,* with brothers *Jacob* and *Christian,* to America (ME III:535; MC 224-225).

1809 Amish *Jacob* and *Joseph Mast* from Somerset County; to Holmes County, Ohio (BA 142).

97. MEILI (Mailen, Meyli, Meylin, Miley, Mylin).

Old Zürich Anabaptist family; *Martin* and *Hans Meili,* on the *Maria Hope,* September 1710; settled at Pequea (MQR XLV [January 1971] 85; ME III: 666; MC 258).

    Swiss forms: *Meile, Meili;* in Cts. St. Gallen, Thurgau, and Zürich; St. Gallen also *Maile, Mayle* (HBLS V:67).

98. METZLER

Jost Metzler, age 45, on the *Glasgow,* September 9, 1738; to Lancaster County; *Valentine Metzler* (1726-1783); arrived 1738 (ME III:659; MC 241-242; PGP I:208).

    Swiss name of Cts. Graubünden and St. Gallen; in the latter also forms of *Maetzler, Mezler* (HBLS V:94).

99. MEYER (Maier, Mayer, Meier, Meyers, Moyer, Moyers, Myer, Myers).

Old Anabaptist name of Switzerland; 1759 also in Montbéliard (BA 15, 47, 89).

In 1719 *Christian Meyer* (d. 1751), settled in Lower

Salford, Montgomery County (ME III:763).

Ca. 1741 a widow *Meyer*, with daughter and four sons from Switzerland to Springfield, Lehigh County (MC 258).

1. Swiss forms: *Meyer, Meier, Mayer, Maier;* in all cantons (HBLS V:96-108).
2. In 1727, various immigrant families *Meyer*, but Swiss origin undetermined (cf. PGP I:7, 9, 10, 12, 14, 17).

100. MILLER (Müller).

1710 *Jacob Miller* to Lancaster County; few descendants.

Name strong in Amish Midwestern congregations (1956, 131 ordained men) (ME III:690-693; MC 244-246).

1. Swiss form: *Müller;* numerous (HBLS V:181-192).
2. Many arrivals, but Swiss origin undetermined (PGP I:8; 11-13; 15; 23; 26).

101. MOSER (Musser).

In 1754 a *Moser* family from Courtelary, Ct. Bern, to Pennsylvania; by 1800 others from there.

1821 *Jacob* and *Barbara Wahli Moser* from Am Stalden in the Jura, Switzerland, to Sonnenberg settlement in Wayne County, Ohio; son *John* (1826-1908), minister, bishop; families in Pennsylvania, Ohio, Oregon (ME III:756; MC 253, 258; BA 85, 133-156, passim).

1. Swiss form: *Moser;* widely dispersed name in Switzerland (HBLS V:169-171).
2. *Christane, Hans,* and *Jost Moser,* on the *Molly,* September 30, 1727 (PGP I:12, 14).

102. MOSIMANN (Moseman, Mosemann, Mosiman).

Origin in the Emmental, Ct. Bern; 1633-1670, 10 cases of *Mosimann* Anabaptists before city council of Bern.

Between 1671 and 1711 to Alsace; 1759 a *Mosimann* family from Sumiswald, Ct. Bern, in Montbéliard (BA 39, 89).

In 1831 *Michael Mosimann* (1820?-1898), from the Lorraine district, France, to United States; 1852, *Jacob* (1795-1876), from Germany to Bowmansville, Lancaster County; families in Pennsylvania, Ohio, Illinois (ME III:757; MC 252-253).

1. Swiss form: *Mosimann*, in Ct. Bern, especially Emmental (HBLS V:171-172).
2. *Andreas Mosemann, Christian Mosiman,* on the *Pennsylvania Merchant,* September 18, 1733 (PGP I:125).

103. NAFZIGER (Naffsinger, Naffzer, Naffziger, Naffzir, Naftiger, Naftsinger, Naftziger, Nafzger, Nafzinger, Noffsinger, Nofsinger, Nofsker, Norfziger).

Ulrich Naffzer, on the *Marlborough,* September 23, 1741 (PGP I:295).

Matheias, Peter Nafsker and *Rudolf Nafzger,* on the *Phoenix,* September 15, 1749 (PGP I:407); others in 1750's "were associated with unmistakably Swiss-Amish Mennonite people" (MQR II [January 1928] 70); origin in Thun, Ct. Bern (*ibid.* [April 1928] 152; and [July 1928], 198; but not in BA!)

Peter Nafziger (1789-1885) from Bavaria.

Christian Nafziger (1819-1892) from France 1831 to Wayne County, Ohio; *Noffsinger* family in first Mennonite settlement in Iowa (MQR XLII [July 1968] 201); families in Ontario, Midwestern states (ME III:806-807; MC 259-260).

104. NEUENSCHWANDER (Neiswander, Neuenswander, Neuschwanger, Newschwanger, Newswanger, Nicewander, Nisewander, Niswander).

Old rural Bernese name in Signau district, also in villages, Niederstocken, Höfen, and Lützelflüh, Ct. Bern (HBLS V:287).

1551 *Mathis Neuenschwander* fled from the Emmental, Ct. Bern.

1729 *Peter Neuenschwander* and family to Cortébert in the Jura; grandson *Michael* to Normanvillars, France, then to Wayne County, Ohio, in 1823; 1849 Michael's son, *John B.* to Polk County, Iowa.

1880's the *Christian Neuenschwander* Mennonite family to Oregon, settled near Silverton (BA 48-165, passim; ME III:847-848; MC 262).

1. Swiss form: *Neuenschwander* (HBLS V:287).
2. *Xtian* [*Christian*] *Newswange,* on the *Mortonhouse,* August 23, 1728 (PGP I:17).

105. NUSBAUM (Nussbaum, Nussbaumer).

16th Century Mennonite family recorded at Ichertswil, Bucheggberg, Ct. Solothurn (BA 43); 1817 *Hans Nussbaum,* author of two emigrant letters from there to Wayne County, Ohio (by 1831 a Mennonite, whether before, uncertain; BA 130, note 8).

Families in Ohio, Indiana, Iowa (ME III:929; MC 270; BA 137-158, passim).

1. Swiss forms: *Nussbaum* from Cts. Bern and Freiburg; *Nussbaumer* from Cts. Zürich and Zug (HBLS V:315-316).
2. *Bendickt* and *Johannes Nusbaum,* on the *Phoenix,* September 30, 1743 (PGP I:346-347).

106. OBERHOLTZER (Oberholzer, Overholser, Overholt, Overholtzer).

1710 *Martin* and *Michael Oberholtzer* from Mannheim, Germany, to Pequea, Lancaster County; of Ct. Zürich origin; families in Pennsylvania (ME IV:12-14; MC 271-272; MQR XLV [January 1971] 85-86).

1. Swiss form: *Oberholzer;* origin Ct. St. Gall, especially village of Goldingen; Ct. Zürich, village of Wald, in neighborhood of Goldingen (HBLS V:322-323).
2. *Jacob Oberholtzer,* age 28, with children *Elizabeth,* age 6, and *Sam*[*uel*], age 3 on

the *Samuel,* August 11, 1732 (PGP I:61, 64).

107. PLANK (Blank).
Early 18th Century Bernese family *Blank* in Alsace (BA 87). 1751 a *Hans* and *Christian Blank* to Pennsylvania.

Melchior Plank (Johann Melchior Blankenberg), 1767, from Holland, of Swiss origin (?) (PGP I:718); to Berks County.

Family in Ohio, Indiana, and other Midwestern states; various bishops (ME IV:185; MC 30; 291-292).
1. Swiss form: *Blank;* Ct. Bern especially at Ins, Thun, Steffisburg, and Sigriswil; also in Cts. Schaffhausen and Uri (HBLS II:264).
2. *Hans, Jacob,* and *Nickolas Blanck,* on the *St. Andrew,* September 23, 1752 (PGP I:485).

108. PLETSCHER (Plätscher, Pletcher).
Ca. 1650 a *Pletscher* family from Schleitheim, Ct. Schaffhausen, to Palatinate; 1757 a widow *Pletcher* and 2 sons in Lancaster County (MC 294).

1833 *Johannes Pletscher* (b. 1780) from Friedelsheim, to USA; wife *Elisabeth Leisi,* with 6 children (MQR XXX [April 1956] 142-151, Nos. 28, 38, 39-41, 50; ME IV:194).
1. Swiss forms: *Pletscher, Bletscher;* Ct. Schaffhausen, especially Schleitheim (HBLS V:455).
2. *Michel Plätscher,* on the *Francis and Elizabeth,* September 21, 1742 (PGP I:328).

109. RABER (Räber, Reber).
Early Mennonite family; 1670 families in the Emmental, Ct. Bern.

1711 *Samuel Reber* deported, escaped at Mannheim (BA 61-62).

1837 *Jacob Raber* and 6 children to Ohio; large progeny; 99 ministers among Amish, other Mennonite groups.

1837 *Christian Raber,* probably brother, to Ohio; later to Lee County, Iowa.

Late 1830's *John Reber* (b. 1820), from Alsace to Elkhart County, Indiana; 1853 to Johnson County, Iowa (ME IV:240-241; MC 302).
1. Swiss forms: *Raeber, Reber,* in Cts. Aargau, Basel, Bern, Luzern (HBLS V:513, 546-547).
2. *Conrad Räber,* on the *Ann Galley,* September 27, 1746 (PGP I:361).

110. RAMSEIER (Ramsayer, Ramseyer).
Mennonite families especially from Eggiwil, Signau and Trub, Ct. Bern.

1710 *Hans Ramseier* among 57 deportees; escaped.

1762 *Peter Ramseier* in the Jura, visiting Palatinate (BA 81, 82).

19th Century, most *Ramseier* Mennonite immigrant families to Ohio; also in Ontario, Central Illinois, and Michigan (ME IV:250; MC 303).
1. Swiss forms: *Ramseyer, Ramseier;* widely dispersed in Ct. Bern (HBLS V:527-528).

2. *Heinrich Ramsauer,* age 30, and *Ann Ramsaurin,* age 32, and *John Ramsaur,* age 9, on the *Samuel,* August 11, 1732 (PGP I:61, 65).

111. REIST
1670 *Reist* Mennonite families at Hinterbrittern and Oberthal, Emmental Valley, Ct. Bern (BA 48).

Peter Reist (d. 1743), ca. 1724 in Lancaster County; families in Pennsylvania; Waterloo County, Ontario; Texas (ME IV:281; MC 307).

Hans Uli Reist, on the *Phoenix,* October 1, 1754 (PGP I:636).

112. RISSER (Reeser, Reesor, Resor, Reuser, Reusser, Rieser, Rüssor).
Bernese Anabaptist family name; between 1671 and 1711 *Reusser* family to Alsace; in 17th Century *Reusser* from Hilterfingen in Thun area (BA 38, 48).

1712 first members to America; 1737 *Peter Risser* (1713-1804) from Switzerland to Lancaster County; 8 children; son *Christian,* 1774 to Markham, Ontario; his son *Jacob* and *Mary,* born *Snyder,* ancestors of *Rissers, Reesors, Reeser* of Lancaster, Dauphin, and Lebanon Counties and Markham, Ontario (ME IV: 340-341; MC 305, 314).

Johannes Risser and *Maria,* his wife, born *Strohm,* in 1832, from Friedelsheim in Palatinate, to Ohio (MQR XXX [January 1956] 45).
1. Swiss forms: *Two* names seem to be involved, perhaps fused:
   a) *Reusser,* in various villages of the district Thun, Ct. Bern (HBLS V:591).
   b) *Ryser,* in many districts of the Ct. of Bern; *Rieser* in Ct. Thurgau; and *Riser* in Ct. Luzern (HBLS V:777-778, 628).
2. *Ulrich Riser* on the *Adventure,* October 2, 1727; *Hans Reser* on the *Friendship of Bristoll,* October 16, 1727; *Hans Jerg* and *Gorg Adam Riser,* on the *Loyal Judith,* September 25, 1732 (PGP I:15, 16; 91).

113. ROTH (Rot).
Early Anabaptist family name; family between 1671 and 1711 to Alsace from Ct. Bern; 1759 a *Roth* from Steffisburg in Montbéliard (BA 39, 89).

1740's a *Roth* had founded Hershey Mennonite Church, York County (ME II:715-716).

Jonas Roth and two brothers from Switzerland 1740 to Pennsylvania, later to Virginia.

Benjamin, Nicholas, and *Joseph Roth,* from Alsace-Lorraine ca. 1820 to Ontario; Benjamin later to Iowa; family name widely dispersed (ME IV:363-364; MC 318; BA 135, 169).

114. RUPP (Ropp).
Early Swiss Anabaptist family in Bernese region. Early 18th Century family from Sigriswil, Ct. Bern, in Montbéliard (BA 87).

1736 *Peter Rupp,* on the *Harle* to Pennsylvania.

1751 *Jonas Rupp,* to Lebanon County, on the *Phoenix,* September 2, 1751 (ME IV:378-379; MC 319; PGP I:156; 471).

> Swiss form: *Rupp,* in Ct. Uri and Bern, especially districts of Burgdorf, Signau, and Thun (HBLS V:758); name should not be fused with *Ruff, Ruf* (Ct. Bern); *Ruf, Ruof, Ruff* (Ct. Schaffhausen), *Ruff, Ruof* (Ct. Wallis), *Ruf, Ruof, Ruff* (Ct. Zürich) (HBLS V:752).

115. RYCHENER

Christian Rychener, b. 1813 in Ct. Bern, ca. 1831 with a Beck family to Wayne County, Ohio (MC 321).

> Swiss forms: *Rychner, Richner;* earlier also: *Ryhines, Rychines, Richines, Richener, Reichnes,* from Ct. Aargau, especially Aarau, Grönichen, Rohr and Ruppenswil (HBLS V:775).

116. SAUDER (Sauter, Souder).

1730 in Weaverland, Lancaster County, a Sauder family (ME IV:905).

1746 two brothers Souder to Montgomery County (MC 324).

In Pennsylvania, Ohio (mostly Amish), Ontario (ME IV:434; MC 324).

1. Swiss forms: *Sauter, Sautter,* in Cts. St. Gallen, Thurgau, and Geneva (since 1696) (HBLS VI:93).

2. *Thomas, Margaretta,* and *Margaretta* (child) *Sauder,* on the *Johnson,* September 18, 1732; *Johann Filb* [*Philipp*] *Sauter* and *Pedter Saudter,* on the *Loyal Judith,* September 25, 1732 (PGP I:73, 74, 77; 92).

117. SCHELLENBERG (Schellenbarg, Schellenberger, Schellingbarg, Schöllenbarg, Shallenberger, Shellenberger).

In 17th Century a Schallenberger family from Erlenbach in Bernese Oberland (BA 49).

Johannes Schellenberger, on the *Pennsylvania Merchant,* September 11, 1732, ancestor of American Mennonite Schellenbergers (ME IV:447-448; MC 338) [no reference to Schellenberger in PGP for that date].

> Swiss form: *Schellenberg,* in Cts. Graubünden, Luzern, Zurich (HBLS VI:156-157). Name also widely native in Southern Germany (ME IV:447).

118. SCHERTZ

After 1664 in the Palatinate.

Johann Henrich Schertz, on the *Francis and Elizabeth,* September 21, 1742.

In 19th Century Amish families to Butler County, Ohio; also to Central Illinois (ME IV:450; MC 325-326; PGP I:329).

> Swiss form: *Scherz,* from Köniz, Aeschi, Reichenbach, and Därligen, Ct. Bern; also in Ct. Aargau (HBLS VI:165).

119. SCHLABACH (Schlabaugh, Schlapbach, Schlappach, Schlaubach, Slaback, Slabaugh).

17th Century a Schlappach family in Thun area, from Oberdiessbach (BA 48).

Johannes Slabach and wife *Maria Elizabeth* and five children on the *Mary,* September 29, 1733 (PGP I:131, 132).

Johannes and *Christian Schlabach,* 1819, in Somerset County.

Daniel Schlabach, ca. 1834, in Fairfield County, Ohio; Pennsylvania; family in various states (ME IV:456-457; MC 328, 344).

> Swiss form: *Schlapbach* (cf. HBLS VI:191).

120. SCHMUTZ

Some of Swiss origin late 18th Century to America, before 1717 to Palatinate (ME IV:468).

1. Swiss form: *Schmutz,* in Cts. Basel, Bern, Freiburg, Thurgau, Zurich (HBLS VI:215).
2. *Abraham Schmutz,* on the *Francis and Elizabeth,* September 21, 1742 (PGP I:329).

121. SCHNEBELE (Schnebel, Schnebeli, Schnebly, Snavely).

Early Mennonite Schnevoli family, Ct. Zurich; 1692 *Christian* and *Daniel Schnebeli* in the Palatine.

1717 *George Snavely* in Lancaster County (MC 347). Ca. 1718 *Johann Jakob Snavely* in Landis Valley, Lancaster County (ME III:282).

1. Swiss forms: *Schnewli;* Ct. Bern also *Schneuwlin;* Ct. Freiburg *Schneuwly, Snewly;* Ct. Glarus also *Schneeli;* Ct. Schaffhausen *Schnewlin, Snewli;* Ct. Zurich also Snewli (1280) (HBLS VI:221-224).
2. *Henrich Schnebli,* on the *Friendship of Bristoll,* October 16, 1727 (PGP I:17).

122. SCHRAG (Schraag, Schrack, Schragg, Schrock, Shrock).

After 1664 in the Palatinate.

1763 *Christen* and *Benedicht Schrag,* from Laumberg near Wymigen, Ct. Bern, living near Court in Münstertal (BA 77).

Jacob, son of *Bendicht Schrag* (b. 1776), 1816 to Pennsylvania; 1817 followed by father; to Wayne County, Ohio.

Family now in many states (ME IV:480; MC 330-331).

1. Swiss form: *Schrag;* native of city of Bern and Wynigen, Ct. Bern (HBLS VI:243).
2. *Hanes Schrag,* on the *Polly,* October 18, 1766 (PGP I:712).

123. SCHUMACHER (Schomacher, Schomecher, Schuhmacher, Shoemaker).

Early Anabaptist family of Safenwyl, Ct. Aargau.

1682 *Jacob Schumacher* with Pastorius to Pennsylvania; 1685 followed by brother Peter; both from Kriegsheim, Palatinate (BA 41; ME IV:501; MC 334).

1. Swiss forms: *Schumacher, Schuhmacher;* widely dispersed in various cantons (HBLS VI:257-258).
2. *Jerich* `Jörg] Schuhmacher* and *Hans Martain Shoomak,* on the *William and Sarah,* September 18, 1727 (PGP I:7, 9).

124. SHANK (Schenck, Schenk, Shenck, Shenk).

Early Anabaptist family; in 1670's a Schänck family

in Mühlebach, Emmental Valley (BA 4) 8; others to the Palatinate.

Michael Schenk, on the *Molly,* September 30, 1727; to Lancaster County; 1729 naturalized; died 1744; son's family 1757 at Millersville, Lancaster County (ME III:963).

> Swiss form: *Schenk;* in Cts. Bern (especially Signau district), Luzern, St. Gallen, Schaffhausen, Waadt, and Zürich (HBLS VI:158).

125. SHANTZ (Jansen, Jantz, Johns, Schantz, Schanz, Shanz, Tschantz, Yantz, Yantzi).

Early Mennonite family; *Hans Tschantz* of Kiesen, Ct. Bern, imprisoned

1737 *Jacob Schantz,* immigrant, in Montgomery County.

1742 *Hans Tschantz* bishop in Lancaster County. Ca. 1768 *Joseph Schantz* (1749-1810), name changed to *Johns;* 1793 to Somerset County; 1810 city of Johnstown founded on his land; descendants to Elkhart County, Indiana; Amish.

1824 *Johannes Tschantz* and son *Abraham* to Sonnenberg, Wayne County, Ohio (ME IV:510-512; MC 181, 325, 375, 336-337).

1. Swiss forms: *Tschanz;* widely known in districts of Konolfingen, Signau and Thun, Ct. Bern (HBLS VII:69).
2. *Jacob Schantz* and family, on the *Charming Nancy,* October 8, 1737; *Jacob,* on the *Townsend,* October 5, 1737; *Johannes,* on the *William,* October 31, 1737 (PGP I:187; 190, 193; 196).

126. SHOWALTER (Schowalter).

From Switzerland to Palatinate; in 19th Century many families there on record (MQR XXX [April 1956], 137, 140, 143).

Jacob Showalter, on the *Brotherhood,* November 3, 1750; to Lancaster County; eight sons: *Christian* (in Lancaster County), *Peter* and *Jacob* (in Bucks County), *John* and *Joseph* (in Chester County), *Daniel, Valentine,* and *Ulrich* (in Rockingham County, Virginia).

1850 *Christian Showalter* (1828-1907) to Hayesville Ohio, then Donnellson, Iowa (ME IV:516-517; MC 330, 342; PGP I:448).

John Shawalter, on the *Muscliffe,* December 22, 1744 (PGP I:359).

127. SHUPE (Shoop).

1718 *John Shoop* to Lancaster County; in Pennsylvania, Middle West (MC 343).

1. Swiss forms: *Schoop, Schop,* in Cts. Schaffhausen and Thurgau (HBLS VI:238-239).
2. *Veronica Shoepin,* on the *St. Andrew,* September 12, 1734, *Johan Jerick* and *Christophal Shope,* on the *Loyal Judith,* September 3, 1739 (PGP I:139; 266).

128. SMUCKER (Schmucker, Smoker, Smooker, Smucker).
18th Century in Switzerland; 1759 a *Schmucker* family from Grindelwald in Montbéliard (BA 98). *Christian Schmucker*, on the *St. Andrew*, September 23, 1752; to Berks County; grandson to Wayne County, Ohio, ca. 1819; 1950's some 8000 descendants in Mennonite communities, especially in Pennsylvania, Ohio, Indiana, Illinois (ME IV:553-554; MC 329, 330; 347; PGP I:485).

1. Swiss forms: *Schmucker, Smuker*, a family from Stein am Rhein (HBLS VI:214).
2. *Johanes Jerg Schmucker*, on the *Elliot*, August 24, 1749 (PGP I:391).

129. SNYDER (Schneider, Schnyder, Snider).
Early Bernese Anabaptist family, *Ulrich Schneider* from Lützelflüh, Ct. Bern, executed in March, 1535 (BA 21); in Alsace after 1671 (BA 39), in 1670's a Schnyder family from Eriz in Thun area, Ct. Bern (BA 4) &

Heinrich Schneider (1272-172), in Lancaster County; perhaps the *Heinrich Schneyder*, on the *Vewrnon*, October 25, 1747; *Hermanus* and *Johannes Schneider* in Juniata County; perhaps *Hermanus Schneider*, on the *Patience*, September 19, 1479; and *Johannes Schneider*, on the *Ranier*, September 26, 1749 (PGP I:363; 408; 411). Families mainly in Lancaster County; Illinois,' Virginia; Nebraska, Ontario (ME IV:556-557; MC330, 348-349).

1. Swiss forms: *Schneider, Schnider, Schnyder;* widely dispersed name in Switzerland (HBLS VI:216-219).
2. *Christian Snyder*, to Germantown, on the *William and Sarah*, September 1, 8 127; 7 *Johannes Snider*, on the *Molly*, September 30, 1727 (PGP I:8, 12).

130. SOMMER (Sommers, Summer, Summers).
Bernese Anabaptist family; after 1671 also in Alsace (BA 39).
Isaac Sommer, from the Jura to Sonnenberg, Wayne County, Ohio, in 1819; same year *Christian* (1811-1891); families in Ohio, Indiana, Illinois, (ME IV:575-576; MC 349-350; BA 132, 133, 138, 144, 155).

1. Swiss forms: *Sommer;* in Ct. Bern also *Summer,* family from Sumiswald; also native of Ct. Zürich (HBLS VI:444).
2. *Adam Sommer*, on the *James Goodwill,* September 11, 127; 8 *Christian* and *Johns Sumer*, on the *Phoenix*, September 15, 1749 (PGP I:22; 407).

131. SPRUNGER
18th Century Mennonite families, native of Sarmenstorf, Ct. Aargau and Oberwangen, Ct. Thurgau.
1741 *Jacob Sprunger* to the Jura; 1852 some 70 from Jura to Adams County, Indiana, nucleus of Berne, Indiana, congregation (ME IV:605-606; BA 154-156; MQR III [April 1929] 235).

132. STAEHLI (Stahley, Stähli, Stahly, Staley, Stehli, Steli).
Early Swiss Anabaptist family; 1670's some to Palatinate.
1711 *Jacob Stähli* (b. ca. 1676), of Hilterfingen, Ct. Bern, to Holland.
1829 first emigrants to America; *Johann* and *Jacob Stähli*, to Ohio; 1839 to Elkhart, Indiana; followed by mother, other children, 1832; families in Ohio, Indiana, Illinois, Canada (ME IV:609; MC 354: BA 44, 49, 68, 126).

1. Widely dispersed Swiss family; Bernese form mainly *Staehli* (in districts of Interlaken, Oberhasle, Schwarzenburg, and Thun); in Basel, *Staechelin,* and *Stehelin;* name also in Cts. Freiburg, Glarus, Schwyz, and Zürich (HBLS VI:489-490, 493, 516-519).
2. *Ulrich,* age 32, and *Anna,* age 27, *Stelley* or *Stalley* with children *Hans Peter Steley* and *Anna Barbra Stelin,* on the *Plaisance,* September 21, 1732 (PGP I:79-81).

133. STAUFFER (Staufer, Stover).
Old Bernese Anabaptist family; 1670's a Stauffer family from Eggiwil in the Emmental (BA 48); also in Alsace (BA 38).
1710 *Hans Stauffer,* expelled from Ct. Bern 1685; to the Palatinate; to Pennsylvania; settled with wife and 5 children in Berks County.
1720's 1730's Stover family in Shenandoah Valley, Virginia.
1727 *Ulrich* and (probably) son *Ulrich* to Pennsylvania; September 27, 1727; from Grosshöchstetten, Ct. Bern; wife, *Lucia,* born *Ramseyer;* 6 children; March 4, 1727, petitioned to emigrate with 1900 pds. property to Pennsylvania; granted (F/BR 72-73).
Families in Pennsylvania, Maryland, Virginia, Ontario, Iowa (ME IV:619-622; MC 355-356; PGP I:11).

Swiss form: *Stauffer,* in Cts. Bern and Luzern (HBLS VI:510-511).

134. STEINER (Stoner [?]).
Old Bernese Anabaptist name; 1670's family Steiner from Diessbach in Thun area and in Ely near Langnau (BA 48, 49).
1711 *Christian Steiner* to Holland; other to the Jura and the Palatinate.
1770 *Hans Steiner* with others to Palatinate (from Switzerland), to settle a dispute (BA 82).
Between 1825 and 1835, brothers of Hans, cousins and grandchildren to Kitchener, Ontario, and Wayne County, Ohio.
1824 *Peter Steiner,* single, from Normanvillars, France, to Virginia. Families in Pennsylvania, Ohio,

Iowa, Virginia, Oregon (ME IV:626-627; MC 357-358; BA 134-178, passim).

1. Swiss form: *Steiner;* name in various cantons, very frequent in all Bernese districts (HBLS VI:533-536).
2. *Ullwrick Styner,* on the *Thistle of Glasgow,* August 29, 1730 (PGP I:31).

135. STROHM (Strahm).

1671 *Ulrich Strohm* to the Palatinate.

1711 *Martin Strahm* in Bernese prison; expelled.

1845 *John Strohm* to Elkhart County, Indiana (MQR XLVI [January 1972].

1852 *Matthias Strahm,* minister, from Emmental Valley to Adams County, Indiana (BA 135, 153).

Johannes Strohm (1781-1852) to Ohio.

(ME IV:646; MQR XXX [April 1956] 144, 149; XLII [July 1968] 199).

Benedice Strome, on the *William and Sarah,* September 18, 1727 (PGP I:17).

136. STUCKEY (Stucki, Stucky).

Old Bernese family; in 1670's a Stucki family from Diemtigen in Bernese Oberland (BA 49).

1830 *Joseph Stuckey* (1825-1902) from Alsace with parents to Butler County, Ohio; 1851 to McLean County, Illinois.

1874 *Jacob Stucky* (1824-1893) from Volhynia to USA (1740, family from Ct. Bern to Volhynia; in 1950's over 1200 descendants in USA (ME IV:647-648; MC 361).

1. Swiss forms: Bernese, *Stucki;* in other cantons, also *Stucky, Stuncky* (HBLS VI:580-581).
3. *Hans Jerg Stucki,* on the *Robert and Alice,* September 30, 1743 (PGP I:347).

137. STUTZMAN (Stutsman, Stutzmann).

In 17th Century a Stutzmann family from Spiez in Bernese Oberland (BA 49).

In 1711 a *Christian Stutzman* to Pennsylvania. *Johann Jacob Stutzman,* on the *Adventure,* October 2, 1727; grandson *Christian,* married *Barbara Hochstedler;* over 15,000 descendants (in 1950's); families in Ohio, Indiana, Nebraska (ME VI:650-651; MC 362; PGP I:15).

138. SUTER (Suder, Sutter, Suttor).

Early Anabaptist family, of Volliken, Ct. Aargau; also in Alsace, Palatinate.

18th Century settlers of that name in Rockingham County, Virginia.

Ca. 1834 *Christian Suter* from Wayne County to Putnam County, Ohio.

In 1848: *Christian Sutter* to neighborhood of Morton, Illinois; also other family members; 1945 over 1000 living descendants.

View of Thun, Canton Bern, by Merian.

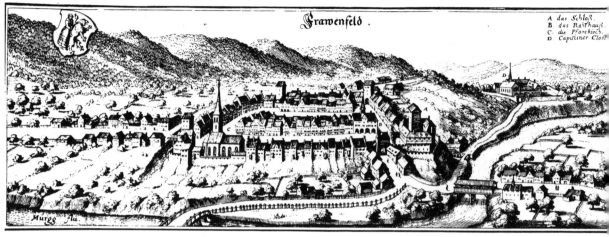

View of Frauenfeld by Merian.

Sutter also in Virginia, Ohio, Nebraska, Iowa, and Michigan (ME IV:664; MC 365; BA 148, 158).

1. Swiss forms: *Suter, Sutter;* Cts. Appenzell, Thurgau, and Zürich; also *Sauter,* Ct. Genf; also *Soutter* (HBLS VI:615-620).

2. *Christian Sooter* and *Nicholas Sauter,* on the *Mary,* September 29, 1733 (PGP I:130).

139. SWARTZ (Schwartz).

Early Anabaptist family, 1527 in Ct. Zürich; 1670's a Schwartz family at Mos in the Emmental, Ct. Bern (BA 48).

18th Century in Alsace.

Abraham Schwartz (Swartz), on the *Friendship,* October 16, 1727; later bishop in Bucks County.

Families in Virginia, Ohio, Ontario (ME IV:666-667; MC 366; PGP I:17).

1. Swiss forms: *Schwarz, Schwartz,* in many cantons; in Bern especially in districts of Konolfingen and Signau (HBLS VI:266-267).

2. *Andreas Schwartz,* on the *Friendship,* October 16, 1727 (PGP I:17).

140. THUT

Aargau Mennonite family name.

1824 from Normanvillars, France, *Peter Thut* and family; to Holmes County, Ohio.

John Thut (1801-1867) from Holmes County to Putnam County, Ohio (MC 371; BA 47, 134, 148, 150, 160, 161).

Swiss name in Cts. Aargau, Glarus, Luzern, and St. Gallen (HBLS VI:786).

141. TROYER (Dreier, Treier, Treyer).

Old Anabaptist family in Ct. Bern; *Hans Dreier* executed in Ct. Bern July 8, 1529.

Ca. 1733 Amish *Treyer* families, now *Troyer,* to Berks County; now in all states with Mennonite congregations (ME IV:750-751; MC 374-375; BA 8, 16, 20, 168).

1. Swiss form: *Treyer,* in Cts. Freiburg and Solothurn (HBLS VII:47).

2. *Frederick Treyer,* age 26, on the *Nancy,* September 30, 1738 (PGP I:226).

142. UMMEL (Umble).

Old Bernese Anabaptist family; 1670's in the Emmental and in Alsace (BA 38; 48); *Christian Ummel,* with wife, five children, to there.

19th Century Amish Ummel families in congregation centered around Les Bressels, near Le Locle (BA 68).

1767, October 5, *Christian Ummel,* to Lancaster County, (ME IV:772 [no Ummel reference in PGP for that date]).

Swiss form: *Hummel* (same family?); Cts. Aargau, Basel, Bern, Schaffhausen, and Unterwalden (HBLS IV:319-320).

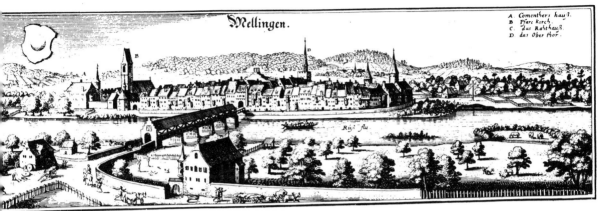

View of Mellingen, now Canton Aargau, by Merian.

143. WEAVER (Weber).

Bernese Anabaptist family Weber in Palatinate, later (ca. 1730) to Pennsylvania, and the Shenandoah Valley, Virginia (BA 168, 169).

Ca. 1733 *Jacob, Henry, George,* and *John Weber* in Weaverland congregation, Lancaster County.

Families in Pennsylvania, Ontario, Kansas, and Iowa (ME IV:903-905; MC 389-391).

1. Swiss forms: *Waeber, Webber;* widely dispersed (HBLS VII:437-444).
2. *Christian Weber,* on the *James Goodwill,* September 27, 1727; *Michael Weber* and *Phillis Wever,* on the *Mortonhouse,* August 17, 1729 (PGP I:11; 24, 26).

144. WELTY (Wälti, Weldy, Welti).

Early Bernese Anabaptist family (BA 22), from Ruderswil by Lauperswil; 1670's in the Palatinate; 1738 in the Jura.

1824 *Ulrich Welty* (1750-1834), of Ruderswil, and *Christian* (b. 1767), to Wayne County, Ohio.

1850's *John Walti,* son of *Niklaus Wälti* (1764-1834) of Lauperswil, in Putnam County, Ohio.

19th Century a Wälti family in Westmoreland County; descendants to Indiana; name now Weldy (ME IV:916; MC 391-392).

1. Swiss forms: *Wallti* in Ct. Luzern; *Welti* in Ct. Aargau, Luzern, Solothurn, Uri, and

Zürich (HBLS VII:347; 469-471).

2. *Johannes Welte,* on the *Neptune,* September 24, 1751 (PGP I:469).

145. WENGER (Wanger, Winger).

In 17th Century a Bernese Anabaptist family from Thierachern in Bernese Oberland, after 1671 in Alsace (BA 39, 49).

Christian Wenger, on the *Molly,* September 30, 1727; to Lancaster County, with wife *Eva Gräbill;* sons settled in Shenandoah Valley, Virginia; family widespread in Mennonite groups (ME IV:916-917; MC 392-394; PGP I:14; MQR XII [April 1938] 85-97).

Swiss form: *Wenger,* in Cts. Bern (especially Thun district), Genf, Waadt, and Wallis (HBLS VII:481).

146. WISLER (Whisler, Whistler, Wissler).

1670's Wisler family in Eyschachen, in the Emmental, Ct. Bern (BA 48).

Before 1830 in Deep Run region, Bucks County.

Christian Wissler, service in the Revolutionary War; died 1830; *Susan Holderman,* wife; 11 children, 3 moved to Columbiana County, Ohio (ME IV:965; MC 397).

1. Swiss forms: *Wissler, Wisler, Wiesler, Wyssler;* old family native to Sumiswald, Ct. Bern (HBLS VII:575).
2. *Henrich Wisler,* on the *St. Andrew,* September

26, 1737 (PGP I:183).

147. WYSE (Weis, Weiss, Weisse, Weisz, Weyss, Wise, Wyss).

Swiss Anabaptist families of that name to Alsace and the Palatinate; *Hans Weiss* there; 3 sons; son *Christian,* ancestor of many Weiss families in the United States.

Jacob Weiss, on the *Albany,* September 4, 1728; perhaps same *Jacob Weisz,* settled in Upper Milford, Lehigh County; 1824 *Peter Wyss* (1800-1856), of Burgdorf, Ct. Bern; to Fulton County, Ohio; ancestor of many (ME IV:999; also IV:913-914; MC 401; PGP I:20).

    1. Swiss forms: *Weiss, Wyss, Wiss;* widely dispersed, in many cantons (HBLS VII:462-464; 574; 607-613).

    2. G. M. Weis, V.D.M., on the *William and Sarah,* September 21, 1727 (PGP I:19).

148. YODER (Ioder, Joder, Jodter, Jotter, Yoeder, Yother, Yothers, Yotter).

A 14th Century Bernese family of Steffisburg, near Thun; 1531 Anabaptist *Heini Joder* in prison at Bern; ca. 1671 family in Alsace; early 18th Century a Ioder family in Montbéliard (BA 39, 87).

1710 Yoder family of the Reformed faith in Berks County; *Barbara Yoder,* widow, with 9 children, settled in Berks County; later married *Christian Beiler;* Amish (BA 168).

1809 *Charles Yoder* family from Somerset County to Holmes County, Ohio (BA 142).

Vast family in U.S., in 1930's over 100,000 members estimated in United States (ME IV:1004-1007; MC 180, 401-405).

    1. Swiss form: *Joder,* of Steffisburg, Ct. Bern (HBLS IV:405).

    2. *Catharina Jotherin,* age 38, on the *Harle,* September 1, 1736; *Christian Jotter* and *Jacob Yoder,* on the *Francis and Elizabeth,* September 21, 1742 (PGP I:157, 329).

149. ZIMMERLI (Zimmerly).

Anabaptist family of the Aargau region; to Alsace, the Palatinate, and North America.

1833 a family Zimmerli from Normanvillars, France, to Wayne County, Ohio.

1893 *Christian Zimmerly,* bishop, organized the Defenseless Swiss Church (BA 47, 148, 152).

    1. Swiss forms: *Zimmerli, Zimmerlin;* in Ct. Aargau (old family of Zofingen) and Ct. Luzern (HBLS VII:660-661).

    2. *Hans Georg Zimerly,* on the *Snow Fox,* October 12, 1738 (PGP I:232).

150. ZIMMERMANN

1698 *Heinrich Zimmermann* from Wädenswil, Ct. Zürich, to Germantown, Pa.; returned; 1706 back in Pennsylvania, settled at Lampeter, Lancaster County; naturalized 1709; Carpenter Mennonite Church named after him; 1717 *Hans Zimmermann* to Cocalico region, Lancaster County. Both ancestors of many Lancaster County Zimmermanns.

Early 19th Century a Zimmermann family in Black Creek Mennonite settlement, Welland County, Ontario (ME IV:521; 1029; MC 408-409).

    1. Swiss form: *Zimmermann* in all regions; in Ct. Bern especially districts of Interlaken, Seftigen and Thun (HBLS VII:661-664).

    2. *Hans Michael Zimmerman* with 7 in party, on the *William and Sarah,* September 18, 1727 (PGP I:9).

151. ZOOK (Zaug, Zaugg, Zougg, Zowg, Zuck, Zug).

Native of Signau, Ct. Bern; 1664 an Anabaptist minister, *Uli Zougg,* recorded (BA 32); 1670's a Zaugg family from Signau in the Emmental (BA 48).

1730's Amish Zaug family in Pennsylvania (BA 168).

Christian, Moritz, and *Johannes Zug,* brothers, on the *Francis and Elizabeth,* September 21, 1742 (PGP I:329); to Chester County.

1817 *John Zook* from Mifflin County, to Holmes County, Ohio (BA 142). (ME IV:1039; MC 410-411 + Addenda).

Peter and Ulrich Zug, on the *James Goodwill,* September 27, 1727 (PGP I:11).

152. ZUERCHER (Zercher, Zerger, Zürcher, Zurger, Zuricher).

Early Anabaptist family; 1649 *Joseph Zurcher* before Bernese court; 1670's Zürcher family from Frutigen (BA 49).

1711 *Hans Zürcher,* age 40, deported.

18th Century many to the Jura, Alsace, and the Palatinate.

1821 *Abraham* and *David Zürcher* from Sonnenberg in the Jura, to Wayne County, Ohio; widespread name there; 1833 *Peter Zürcher* family from the Emmental to region near Whitewater, Butler County, Kansas (BA 157).

    1. Swiss forms: *Zürcher, Züricher.* in Cts. Appenzell, Bern (especially in districts of Burgdorf, Frutigen, Oberhasli, Signau, Obersimmental, Thun, and Trachselwald), Luzern, Uri, and Zug (HBLS VII:690-691).

    2. *Michael* and *Justina Zurchen,* on the *Charming Nancy,* October 8, 1737 (PGP I:188, 190).

153. ZURFLUEH

1852 Abraham Zurflüh from the Bernese Jura to Putman County, Ohio (ME IV:1042).

    1. Swiss form: *Zurfluh,* old family native to Ct. Uri (HBLS VII:766).

    2. *Johannes Zurflie,* on the *Neptune,* October 4, 1752 (PGP I:494).

INDEX TO PERSONAL NAMES

--- A ---

Abt, Antonia 116
Aby, —— 129
Achebacher, Casper 110
    Magdalena 110
Acherman, —— 124
Achermann, —— 124
Ackerman, Christoff 124
Ackermann, Johann Georg 124
    Meichel 124
Ackherman, Johan Wendell 124
Aeberli, Lorenz 128
Aebersold, —— 129
Aebi, —— 12, 129
Aeby, —— 129
Aeschiman, —— 124
Aeschleman, —— 124
Aeschliman, Margreht 124
      Paul R. 124
Aeschlimann, Hans 124
Akermann, —— 124
Albrecht, Hans 124
    J. 116, 117
    Jacob 115
    Joseph 124
    William 116
Albright, —— 124
Alderfer, —— 124
Aldorffer, Frederick 124
Allbrecht, —— 124
Alldörfer, Friederich 124
Allebach, Andrew 124
    Christian 124
    John 124
Allebaugh, —— 124
Allenbach, —— 124
Alt, Simon 47
Altaffer, —— 124
Altorfer, —— 124
Ammann, Jakob 122
Amstoutz, —— 124
Amstutz, Anna 124
    Johannes 124 [2]
Am Stutz, —— 124
am Stutz, —— 124
Amstuz, —— 124
Anders, Elisabetha 110
    Henrich 110
Andreas, Anna Margaretha 111
    Friedrich 111
Angle, —— 129

Antes, Johann Friedrich 56
Anthess, Franz 56
    Friedrich 56
Armknecht, Susanne 80
Arnold, Anna Maria 13
    Anna Ottilia 72
    Catharina 13
    Hans Adam 12
    Johann Georg 12 [3]
    Johann Görg 12
    Maria Barbara 12
    Samuel 13
Artz, Catharina Christina 43
    Johann Philipp 43
    Maria Barbara 43
    Sophia Dorothea 43
Artzt, Johann Philipp 43
    Philipp 44
Ashe, —— 129
Ashliman, —— 124
Astor, John Jacob 65
Augenstein, Abraham 87
    Anna Maria 87
    Caspar 87, 88
    Christian 87
    Hans Georg 88
    Hanss Georg 87
    Johannes 88
Augsberger, —— 124
Augsbourger, —— 124
Augsburger, Johanes 124
Augspurger, —— 124
August, B. 115, 116

--- B ---

Bach, Anna Margreth 58
    Hermann 58
    Michel 44 [2]
    Stephen 117
Bachman, Andreas 124
    Felix 124
    Hans 124
    Heinrich 124
Bachmann, —— 124
Bachstel, —— 126
Bachtel, —— 126
Bachtell, —— 126
Bächtold, —— 126
Backer, Philip 95
    Vallentin 95

Baechtold, —— 126
Baehr, Jacob 124
Baer, —— 125
    Jacob 124
Bähr, —— 21
    Dorothea 117
    Jacob 124
Bair, Jacob 124
Ballie, Catharine 106, 107
Bamberger, Elisabetha 109
    Georg Henrich 109
    Henrich 110
    Johannes 110
    Lorentz 109
    Lorenz 110
    Maria Elisabetha 110 [2]
Bar, Jacob 124
Bär, —— 21, 117
    Anna Catharina 64
    Johann 64
    Johann Georg 64 [2], 65
    Michael 113
Bare, Jacob 124
    Samuell 125
Barr, Jacob 124
Bart, Jacob 37, 39
Barth, Anna Barbara 40
    Georg 39
    Heinrich 39
    Jakob 39, 40
    Maria Catharina 39
    Peter 39
Barther, Anna Elisabetha 11
Bartholomäe, Anna Barbara 110
Barton, Benjamin, S., Dr. 114
Basinger, —— 125
Basler, Andreas 61 [2]
    Henrich 61
Bastian, Michael 83 [2]
Batanfeld, Philip 22
Bathenfeld, Philipp 22
Battefelt, Johannes 22
Battenfeld, Hans Adam 22
    Johann 22
Battesteld, Margaretha 22
Battfeld, Adam 22
    Catharine 22
    Elisabeth 22
Baub, Tobias 44
Bauchman, —— 124
Bauer, Anna 125
    Eva Elisabetha 16
    Hans 125

145

Philipp 16
Baum, Samuel 96
Bauman, Anna Elisabeth 110
    Catherine 99
    Christian 125
    Elizabeth 99
    Henrich 110
    Jacob 99, 104 [2], 105,
      125 [2]
    Margaret 99 [2]
    Maria Barbara 110
    Michael 110
    Peter 125
    Susannah 99
    Sybilla 99
    Wendell 125
Baumann, —— 125
    Hans Jakob 99
    Jacob 99
    Katharina 98
    Matthäus 98 [4], 99, 103 [2],
      105
    Matthias 99
    Sara 98
Baumgardner, —— 125
Baumgarter, —— 125
Baumgartner, Christian 125
    David 125
    Peter 125
Baur, —— 125
Bayer, Elisabetha Catharin 61
Beachey, —— 126
Beachy, —— 126
Bear, Jacob 124
Beare, Jacob 124
Beau, Marie 4, 5
Beaufort, —— 97
Bechdoldt, Hennrich 100
Bechtel, —— 100
    Anna 126
    Hans Jacob 126
Bechtell, George 126
    Jörg 126
Bechtold, —— 126
    Anna Elisabetha 99
    Anna Magdalena 19
    Hans Stephan 99
    Katharina 99
    Maria Katharina 99
    Zacharias 99 [2]
Bechtoldt, Veit 100
Beck, Anna Margaretha 23
    Henrich 23
    Johann Jörg 23
Beckebach, Caspar 23
Beckebag, Adam 23
Beckenbach, ——, Widow 23
    Anna Maria 23
    Georg Leonhardt 23
    Geörg Adam 23
    George 24
    Johann Adam 23
    Johann Georg 23
Beckenbacher, —— 24
Becker, Aaron 74

Anna Elisabetha 93, 95
Bernhardt 95
Friedrich 74
Georg Velten 95 [2]
Johann Adam 95
Johann Lorentz 93
Johannes 95 [4]
Samuel 74
Valentin 95 [2]
Beckly, Henry 23
Beechy, —— 126
Beer, —— 125
    Abraham 126
    Jacob 124
Beers, —— 125
    Abraham 126
    Jacob 124
Beers, —— 126
Beery, —— 126
Behr, Jacob 21 [2], 124
Behringer, —— 102
Beier, Jacob 110
Beiler, Charles 144
    Christian 144
Beire, —— 126
Bender, Anna Dorothea 9, 100
    Anna Helena 100
    Jacob 21 [5]
    Joh. 100
    Johannes 28, 100 [4]
    Katharina 103 [2]
Philip 100
    Susanna 21
Benner, Enos 114 [2]
Benners, Magdalena 51
Benninger, Peter 23
Benter, Catharina 21
    Jacob 21
Bentz, Hans Martin 99
    Maria Katharina 99
Bentzlin, Adam 84
    Constantia 84
Benz, Vallentin 100
Benzle, Adam 84
Ber, Johann Jacob 21
Berckheimer, Johann Jacob 110
    Lennert 110
    Maria Catharina 111
Berckman, Johannes 52
Berckmann, Hermann Christoph
    52
    Johannes 52
Berg, Jakob 98
Berge, —— 126
Berger, Anna 126
    Christen 126 [2]
    Daniel 72 [2]
    Hans 126
    Johann Georg 72
    Johannes 72 [2]
    Magdalena 126
    Maria Catharina 72
    Wilhelm 72
Bergey, Johann Ulrich 126
Bergher, Hans 126

Berke, —— 126
Berkey, —— 126
Berki, —— 126
Berky, —— 126
Bermann, Georg 114
Bernet, Stephan 106, 107
Bernhardt, Agnes Margaretha 5
Bertolet, Abraham 106 [2], 107 [2]
    Esther 106 [3], 107 [3]
    Hannes 106, 107 [3]
    Jean 106 [7], 107 [5]
    Johan 107
    Johann 106 [2], 107 [2]
    John 107 [3]
    Maria 106, 107
    Marie 106, 107
    Susanne 106 [2], 107 [2]
Bertsch, Jacob 83 [2]
Besch, —— 16
    Wilhelm 20 [2]
Bettle, Michel 5 [4]
Betz, Wilhelm 114
Beuerle, Margaretha 56
Beyer, Albinus 126
    Jacob 126
    Susanna 9
Bibickhoffer, Anna Maria 26
    John Jacob 26
    Joseph 26
Bibikhoffer, Anna Delia 26
    John 26
    Nicholas 26
Bichsel, Andreas 126
    Christian 126
    Jacob 126
    Johann 126
    Peter 126
    Verena 126
Bickel, Adam 23
    Johann Adam 23
    Ludwig Adam 23
    Maria Eva 23
Bickle, Adam 23 [2]
    Tobias 23
Bickly, Adam 23
Biehler, Johann Nicolaus 25
    Juliane 25
    Margaretha 9
Bier, Petter 126
Bieri, —— 126
Biery, —— 126
Biker, Peter 127
Binder, Hans Jacob 88
    Jacob 88
Birkey, —— 126
Birki, —— 126
Birkin, Katherina 126
Birky, —— 126
Bischoff, Johann 78
    Johannes 83 [2]
Bisecker, Jacob 110 [2]
Biting, Ludwig 100
Bitsche, Peter 126
Bitschi, —— 126
Bitting, —— 100

Bixel, — 126
Bixler, — 126
Blanck, Christian 126 [2]
    Hans 126, 137
    Jacob 126, 137
    Nickolas 126, 137
Blank, — 126
    Christian 137
    Hans 137
Blankenberg, Johann Melchior
    137
Blaser, Christian 127 [2]
    Peter 127
Bläser, — 127
Bläss, Lorentz 77
Blasser, — 127
Blauer, Friedrich 117
Bletscher, — 137
Bley, Catharina 62 [2]
    Christoph 62 [2]
    Georg 62 [2]
    Johann Adam 62
Blickensdoerfer, — 126
Blickensdörfer, Josua 116
Blickenstaff, — 126
Blickensterffer, Jost 126
Blickenstorfer, Jacob 126
Blickenstorffer, — 126
Blickenstörffer, Christian 126
    Johannes 126
    Ulrich 126
Blickersterffer, Jost 126
Bloser, — 127
Blosser, — 127
Blumer, Abraham 34
Boach, Michel 44
Böchtel, — 126
Boehm, Elizabeth 101
    Johann Philipp 98, 99, 102
    John Philip 100, 104
    John Philip, Jr. 101, 104
    John Philip, Rev. 99,
        100 [2]
    Maria Philippina 101
Boehr, Jacob 124
Boemer, Bernhard 13
Boer, — 125
    Jacob 124
Boesiger, — 125
Boettinger, Anna Catharina 28
Bogar, — 127
Boger, Martin 127 [2]
Böhler, Anna Barbara 9
    Jacob 69
    Johann 9
    Margaretha 9
Böhm, — 102
    Anna Maria 100
    Anton Wilhelm 100
    Elisabeth 100
    Johann Philipp 100 [3], 102,
        105
    Konrad 61
    Maria Philippina 100
    Philipp Ludwig 100

    Sabina 100
Böhmer, Maria Susanna 61
Bohr, Friedrich 78
Bomberger, Christian 127
Bomgarner, — 125
Bomgartner, — 125
Bonet, Jacques 89
Bongarter, — 125
Bonnet, Christina 89
    Jacob 89
    Jacques 89 [3]
    Jean 89
    Johan Peter 89
    Johan Simon 89
    Margret 89
    Mary 89
    Susanna 89
Bontrager, — 127
Bonträger, Andrew 127
    Christian 127
    John 127
    Martin 127
Bontreger, — 127
Bookwalter, — 127
Bootz, Johann Michael 96
Borcholder, — 128
Borcholter, — 128
Borckholder, — 128
Borcki, — 126
Borcky, — 126
Borgholder, — 128
Borkholder, — 128
Borntraeger, — 127
Borntrager, — 127
Bornträger, — 127
    Anna Margaretha 101, 102
Borntreger, — 127
Bosart, Peter 127
Bosch, Anna Maria 43
    Barbara 43
    Jacob 43, 44
    Johann Friedrich 43
    Johann Jacob 43
    Johannes 43
    Joseph 43
    Willhelm 20
Boshart, — 101, 127
Bösiger, Christian 125
Bossard, — 127
Bossart, — 127
Bosser, — 127
Bosserdt, Jacob 101, 127
Bossert, — 127
    Andreas 98, 101 [3]
    Eva Katharina 101
    Jacob 101, 102
    Jakob 98, 101 [2]
    Michael 88 [2]
Bosshard, — 127
Bosshardt, — 127
Bosshart, — 127
Bostart, Jacob 101
Boughwalder, Louis 127
Boughwalter, — 127
Bouman, — 125

Boumgarter, — 125
Bouquet, Philipp 89
Bouquon, — 97
Bournonville, A. 114
Bouton, — 97
Bower, — 125
Bowers, — 125
Bowman, Albert 125
    Hans Jerrick 125
Bowsman, William 6, 13
Boyer, Wilhelm 112
Boz, Anna Christina 94
    Catharina Margretha 94
    Michel 94
Bozart, Jacob 101
Brächbühler, — 127
Brackbill, — 127
Braechtbuehl, — 127
Branaman, — 127
Brändel, Ferdinand 115
Brannaman, — 127
Brastberger, —, Baliff 43
Bräucheler, Theobald 72
Braucheller, Theobald 72
Brauchler, Theobald 72
Braun, Joh. G. 115
    M. 114
    Michael 114
Bräunig, Andreas 94
    Balsser 92, 93
    Baltzer 94
Brauns, Leonhard 40
    Maria Catharina 40
Brauss, Andreas 57 [2]
    John 114
    Peter 57 [2]
Brechbiel, — 127
Brechbielin, Anna 127
Brechbil, Johannes 127
Brechbill, Benedict 127
    Hans 127
    Hans Peter 127
    Jacob 127
Brechbuehl, — 127
Brechbühl, Benedict 127
Brechbühler, — 127
Brechbühll, Wendell 127
Brecht, — 20, 29
    Adam 22
    Anna Maria 4
    Balthasar 4 [2]
    Catharina 4
    Christopher 4
    David 4
    Elizabeth 4
    Johann 4 [3]
    Johann Michael 4 [3]
    Johannes 4 [4]
    John 16
    Michael 4 [2]
    Peter 4
    Stephan 4 [3]
Brechtbühler, Abraham 127
Brechtlen, Barbara 44
    Elisabetha 44

Mattheus 44
Breckbühl, —— 127
Brenaman, —— 127
Brendel, Philip 26
Susanna 26
Brendle, —— 29 [2]
Breneman, —— 127
Breniman, —— 127
Brenman, —— 127
Brennaman, —— 127
Brennamann, —— 127
Brenneisen, Anna Eva 11
Brenneman, Daniel 127
Melchior 127
Brennemann, —— 127
Daniel 123
Brenner, Ann 20 [2]
Catharine 20
Elizabeth 20
Hans Philipp 20
Johann Philipp 20
Maria Catharina 20
Philip 20
Philip, Jr. 20
Philip Adam 20 [2]
Philipp 20 [6]
Philipp Adam 20
Susanna 20
Breuinger, Baltzer 94
Breuninger, Anna Maria 94 [2]
Balthasar 94
Baltzer 94
Hans 94
Jacob 94 [2]
Johann Philipp 94
Bricker, Christan 127
Jacob 127
Brickerin, Elizabeth 127
Brickrer, Anna Barba 127
Brigger, Christian 127
Bright, Johannes 4
John 29
Brinneman, —— 127
Britz, Ulrich 83
Brollin, Catherine 120
Brönnimann, Melchior 127
Brubacher, Abraham 81, 127
Hans 127
Jacob 81
Brübacher, Aberham 81, 127
Brubacker, —— 127
Brubaher, —— 127
Brubaker, —— 127
Brubbacher, Johanes 127
Brücker, —— 127
Brügger, —— 127
Bruner, —— 69
Brunn, Florian 86
Brunner, Anna Barbara 70
Catharina Elisabeth 69
Heinrich Elias 69
Johannes 69 [2]
John Henderick 69
Josef 69, 70 [2], 71
Maria Catharina 69 [2]

Brupacher, —— 127
Bub, Barbara 44
Jerg Friedrich 44
Johannes 44
Sophia Dorothea 44
Tobias 44 [3]
Bubigkoffer, Joseph 26
Bubikofer, Joseph 26
Buby-Kofer, Frantz 26
Joseph 26
Buchacker, Dorothea 16
Bucher, Niclaus 127
Bücher, —— 127
Buchler, Joh. U. 116
Buchmann, Philipp 45 [2]
Buchwalder, —— 127
Bückle, Adam 22
Johann Adam 22, 23 [2]
Susanna Elisabetha 22
Veronica 23
Buckwalder, —— 127
Buckwalter, Johannes 127
Bueckle, Adam 23
George Adam 23
Buerckey, —— 126
Buercki, —— 126
Christian 126
Buerge, —— 126
Buffamoyer, —— 37
Bugar, —— 127
Büller, Margaretha 9
Buman, —— 125
Bumgarner, Christopher 125
Ursley 125
Bunnet, Jacques 89
Bunnett, Jacob 89
Buquin, —— 97
Burckey, —— 126
Bürckh, Jacob 126
Burckhalter, —— 128
Burckhard, —— 127
Burckhardt, —— 127
Jacob 128
Johann Georg 128
Burckhart, Simon 128
Burckholder, —— 128
Burcky, —— 126
Burgey, —— 126
Peter 72
Burghard, —— 126
Burghart, —— 127
John Fradrick 128
Burgholder, —— 128
Burgholdter, —— 128
Bürgi, —— 126
Burkalter, —— 128
Burkart, Hans Jerch (Jörg)
128
Burkey, —— 126
Bürkey, —— 126 [2]
Burkhalter, —— 128
Burkhard, —— 127, 128
Philipp 98
Burkhardt, —— 127, 128
Chr. Friedrich 114

Burkhart, —— 126
Joseph 127
Burkholder, Abraham 128
Christian, Bishop 123
Hans 128
Peter, Bishop 123
Bürki, Hans 126
Burkli, —— 126
Burky, —— 126
Burkyen, Christina 120
Elizabeth 120 [2]
Jacob 120
Burqui, —— 97
Burree, —— 97
Bursched, Jacob 120
Buschert, —— 127
Bussart, Andereas 101
Buttcher, David 117
Butterfass, Daniel 93
Maria Catharina 95
Susanna Catharina 93
Buzard, Andrew 101
Buzzard, —— 101, 127

--- C ---

Cajeux, —— 97
Camp, Daniel 20
Canby, Samuel, Jr. 115
Carbach, Adam 68
Margaretha Gertrutis 68 [2]
Maria Gertruda 68
Carl, Maria Ottilia 93
Casper, Johann Michael 64
Castor, Joh. 114
Cauffman, —— 133
Cetti, Abraham 57
Chabot, —— 97
Chally, —— 97
Chelius, Christian Wilhelm 94
Chembenois, Jacob 61 [2]
Johann Heinrich 61
Chesnebenoist, —— 61
Christ, Catharina 93
Johann Conrad 93
Christler, Anna Maria 101
John Jacob 101
Leonhard 101
Christmann, Anna Margaretha 4
Christoleer, Leonard 101
Clemens, Jacob 53
Clementz, —— 52
Clemenz, Jakob 52 [3]
Clos, Margaretha Catharina 74
Clotter, Johann Paul 3
Susanna 3
Coffman, —— 133
Cohen, J. J., Jr. 117
Colb, Dielman 134
Judith 134
Compter, Adam 40
Salome 40
Confer, —— 97

Conrad, Friedrich 74 [2]
  Johann Friedrich 74
Convert, —— 97
Coolwine, —— 103
Coons, —— 5
Corbeau, Jean 89 [2]
Corbo, Jean 89
Cornelius, Anna Catharina 93 [2]
  Anna Elisabeth 93
  Anna Elisabetha 93
  Anna Eva 93 [2]
  Elisabeth 93
  Johann Andreas 93
  Johann Lorentz 93
  Johann Peter 93
  Johannes 93 [2]
  Lorentz 93
  Peter 92, 93 [3]
  Susanna Catharina 93
  Veronica 93
Cörper, Johann Philip 93
Courvoisier, Henry Louis 113
Crable, Hans Erick 131
Cramer, Anna Maria 103
Crayenbühl, Peter 82
Crebil, Jakob 82
Cressman, —— 128
Creutz, Elisabeth 58
  Hymenäus 58
  Tilman 58
Crössman, Niklos (Nikolaus) 128
Crybile, Christian 131
Cullmann, ——, Mr. 107 [2]
Culp, —— 134
Cunradt, Anna Margaretha 18
  Georg Philipp 18
  Stephan 18 [2]
Cuntz, Jacob 5
  Nick 56
Cunz, Jacob 5 [2], 6

--- D ---

Dahlem, Jacob 121
Dankels, Anna Margaretha 15
Danner, Catharina 15
  Dieter 15 [3]
  Dietrich 15 [4]
  Elisabeth 15
  Eva 15
  Johannes 15
  Michael 15 [5]
  Michel 15 [2]
  Teter 15
Dätiwyler, —— 128
Dätwyler, —— 128
Dauberlein, Anna Catharina 94
  Johannes 94 ·
Daum, Johannes 77
deBannevill, Georg 106
de Bannevill, Georg 106, 107 [5]
de Boer, —— 125
de Buman, —— 125

Debus, Daniel 80 [2]
  Jacob 80
  Lodwick 80
Debusz, Johann Daniel 80
  Maria Elisabetha 80
  Philipp 80
  Sophia Sybilla 80
Decker, Heinrich 42
  Johann Michael 42
  Michael 42
  Wendel 42 [2]
Deer, Martin 110 [6], 111 [2]
Deffaa, —— 97
  Thomas 101
Defrand, —— 97
de Gallis, —— 130
Dehuff, John 4
Deker, Thomas 114
Delp, Margareta 53
de Malade, —— 97
Denlinger, —— 101
Derffenbecher, Caspar 84
Derr, Anna 19
  George 19 [2]
  John 19
  John George 19
  Juliana 19
  Leonard 19
  Mary 19 [2]
Derscht, —— 95
Derst, —— 93
  Abraham 95 [3]
  Abraham Jacob 95
  Friedrich Adam 95
  Jacob 95
  Johann Jacob 95
  Johann Jakob 95
  Johann Paul 95
  Maria Catharina 95
  Maria Magdalena 95
  Paul 95 [3]
Derstein, —— 128
Derstine, —— 128
Dettweiler, —— 128
Dettwiler, —— 128
Dettwyler, —— 128
DeTurck, —— 106, 107
de Turck, Hannes 106, 107
Detweiler, —— 128
  Jacob 111
  Johann Jacob 111
  Margaretha 111
Detwiler, —— 128
Detwyler, Melchior 128
Deubel, Wilhelm Friedrich 115
Dewees, Cornelius 101
DeWette, ——, Dr. 113
Dibbinger, Kilian 17
Diebendoerffer, Johann Alexan-
  der 6
Diebendörffer, Johann Alexander
  6
Diefenbacher, Caspar 84
Diefenderfer, Gertraut 6
Dieffenbacher, Caspar 84

Dieffendoerffer, Alexander 6
Diehl, Adam 5
  Ananias 5
  Daniel 5
  Jacob 5, 53 [3]
  Jakob 5 [2]
  Johann Adam 5
  Johann Michael 5
  Johannes 5, 53 [6]
  Jost 5, 80 [2]
  Michael 5
  Peter 5
  Sebastian 80
  Simon Jacob 5
  Valentin 5
  Wilhelm 5
Diel, Hans Michel 5
  Jost 80
  Michel 5 [3]
Dierstein, —— 128
Dieterich, Maria Philippina 40
Dietrich, J. G. 115
Dietz, Anna Margaretha 29
  Louisa 96
  Martin 26 [2]
Diffenderffer, David 6
Dihl, Nikolaus 114
Dilgen, Maria Catharina 93
Dilger, —— 128
Diller, Abraham 128
Dillinger, Michael 94, 95
Dillman, Georg 88
  Hans Georg 86
Dillmann, Hans Georg 86, 88
Dinges, Filipp 41
  Johann Gerhard 41 [2]
  Johann Philipp 41 [3]
  Philipp 41
Dinnies, John Peter 25
Dirstein, Michael 128
Dirstine, —— 128
Dittwiler, —— 128
Dobeler, Johann Georg 91
  Johann Peter 91
  Jörg Adam 91
Dobler, Daniel 92
  Johann Michael 92
Doerr, George 19
  John Georg 19
Doll, Anna Catharina 9
Domie, Johannes 77
Donath, J. A. 116
Dörr, Adam 78
  Anna Dorothea 100
  Erhard 100
  Johann Henrich 77
  Niclas 77
  Veit 100 [3]
Dory, Dorothea 68 [2]
  Joh. Erdmann 68
  Johann Erdmann 68
Dreher, Andreas 70 [2]
  Anna Margaretha 65
  Appolonia 69, 70
  Catharina 70

Johann Peter 40
Johannes 65 [2]
Maria Anna 70
Maria Eva 70
Martin 69
Petronella 65
Dreier, Hans 142
Drescher, Anna Maria 80
Tobias 80
Drexler, Anna Juditha 43
Dübendorff, John Michael 6
Dübendorffer, Alexander 6
Michael 6
Dübinger, Bernhart 16, 17
Dueffinger, Kilian 17
Duerr, Hans Georg 19
Dupont, — 97
Dupré, — 97
Dürr, Anna Christina 111
Carl 111
Hans Georg 19 [3]
Johan Georg 87
Johann Georg 87
Dürstein, — 128
Durstin, — 128
Duvinger, Kilian 17

--- E ---

Eaby, — 129
Eash, — 129
Eb, Bastian 129
Ebby, Henrick 129
Ebee, — 129
Eberhardt, Catharina 110
Joseph 110
Eberle, Adam 22
Conradt Israel 22
Heinrich 128
Johann Adam 22
Johann Conrad 39 [3], 40
Johann Görg Ludwig 39
Johann Leonhard 19
Leonard 19
Leonhard 19
Sebastian 129
Veronica 128
Eberli, — 129
Eberly, — 128
Ebersohl, Abrahm 129
Carl 129
Johannes 129
Jost 129
Pedter 129
Ebersol, — 129
Ebersold, — 129
Ebersole, — 129
Ebersoll, Jacob 129
Ebi, — 129
Ebie, — 129
Eby, — 12
Christian 129
Peter 129

Peter, Bishop 123
Theodorus 129
Ecker, Johann Jacob 88 [2]
Eckloff, —, Mrs. 114
Eckmann, Anna 109
Jacob 109
Ulrich 109
Edelmann, Johann Peter Melchior 40
Maria Saolome 40 [2]
Edinger, Johann Philipp 66
Philipp 66
Ege, Michael 23
Eggers, Ludwig Gustav 117
Ehmig, Christian 82
Ehrenfried, Joseph 117
Ehret, Elizabeth 21
George 21
John 21
John George 21
Margaret 21
Peter 21 [3]
Eichelberger, Christina 57
Maria Christina 57
Rudolph 57
Eicher Christian 129
Johannes 129
Eichert, Michael 129
Eichler, — 129
Eiman, — 130
Eimann, Jacob 130
Eisenhauer, Adam 24 [3], 25
Anna 24
Anna Elisabeth 24 [4]
Elisabeth 25
Hans Nicolaus 24
Johann Adam 24 [3]
Johann Georg 24
Johann Nicolaus 25 [2]
Johannes 24
Magdalena 24 [2]
Susanna 24
Eisenhower, Dwight D., Pres.
19, 24, 25
Eitemuller, Christina 111
Johann Nicolaus 111
Ellenberger, Albrecht 129
Christian 129
Jacob 129
Niclaus 41, 129
Nicolaus 41
Peter 82 [2]
Rudolph 82
Ullrich 82 [2]
Ulrich 82 [2], 129
Ellich, Andreas 3
Ellwanger, Israel 117
Elser, Petter 84
Elsser, Margaretha 84
Emig, Christian 82
End, John Dewald 99
Enders, Conrath 82
Henrich 82
Leonhard 82
Maria 82

Engel, Georg 129
Gorg 129
Jacob 129
Paul 129
Ulrich 129
Engelhard, Maria 100
Engelhardt, Elisabetha Catharina 111
Michel 111
Engle, Anna 29 [2]
Jacob 129
John 129
Eperly, — 128
Epprecht, — 97
Epprich, — 97
Erb, Christian 129
Nicholas 129
Eret, Peter 21
Erlebach, Anna Christina 93
Johann Peter 93
Ermel, Catharina Barbara 93
Johannes 93
Ernst, Catharina 23
Georg 23
Johann Georg 23
Johann Jürg 23
Ernstorf, Anna Catharin 58
Henrich 58
Erred, Maria Christina 21
Peter 21
Esch, Jacob 129
Michael 129
Eschelmann, Henrich 124
Eselman, Peter 124
Esh, — 129
Eshelman, Daniel 124
Johan 124
Eshleman, — 124
Est, Christian 129
Etschberger, Magdalena 13
Etzler, Adolf 117
Euchenberger, Christina 57
Maria Christina 57
Eulen, Johannes 19
Euler, Johannes 19
Eurich, Matthäus 85
Eversole, — 129
Eversull, — 129
Evy, — 129
Ewig, Christan 12
Christian 12 [2]
Nicholas 12
Ewy, — 129
Christian 12
George 12
Eycher, — 129
Eyler, John 19
Eyman, — 130
Eymann, — 130
Eyrich, Matheas 85
Eyster, Margaret 96

--- F ---

Faber, ——, Professor 107 [2]
Fabian, Anna Catharina 15
  Anna Margreth 15
  Dorothea 15
  Hans 15
  Hans Jacob 14 [2]
  Hans Joseph 14
  Hans Michael 14
  Hanss 15
  Hanss Michel 15
  Johan Caspar 15
  Johann Valentin 14
  Joseph 11, 13 [4], 14 [7], 15
  Michael 14, 15
  Monroe H. 15
Fabion, Joseph 13, 14
  Michael 15
Farr, Anna Maria 85
Fauth, Adam 105
Fauts, Baltus 10
  Jacob 10
Favian, Georg Michel 11, 14
Favon, Jarrick Michr 14
  Michael 14
Federhaen, J. 114
Federolff, Nicolaus 26 [2]
Federwolf, Anna Catharina 27, 64
  Johannes 27, 64
Feil, George 21
Fellmann, —— 97
Feltfort, Georg Philipp 94
Ferbert, Anna Elisabetha 102
  Anna Katharina 105
  Anna Maria 101 [2]
  Nikolaus 101 [2]
Ferrenbach, Bernard 117
Feterholf, Peter 26
Fetzer, Matthaeus 110 [2]
Fezer, Anna Agatha 110
  Matthaeus 110
Filler, —— 21
  Anna 110
  Balser 110
  Fridrich 110
Filman, Philip 111
Filmann, Johann Jacob 109
Finck, Anna Eva 93 [2]
  Paul 93 [2]
Finckbeiner, Anna Maria 43
  Esther 43
  Ludwig Heinrich 43
  Maria Agnes 43
  Philipp Andreas 43
  Tobias 43, 44
Finger, —— 97
Fink, Anna Elisabetha 93
  Paul 93
Fischer, F. C. 117
  Johannes 98, 102
  Margaretha 109
  Sara 98

Fishback, —— 58
Flait, Anna 44 [2]
  Anna Maria 44
  Johannes 44 [3]
  Margaretha 44
Fontain, Anna Barbara 95
  Balthasar 95
  Catharina Barbara 95
  Johann Bernhardt 95
  Johann Peter 95
  Leonhard 95
  Maria Elisabeth 95
  Niclas 95
  Theodor Jacob 95 [2]
Fontaine, Christophel 95 [2]
Fontius, Anna Catharina 64
  Johann Georg 64
  Johannes 64
Forrer, Rudolph 120
Fortunee, Heinrich 20
  Susanna Catarina 20
Fossé, —— 97
Fouts, David 10
Fraetz, Christian 130
Franck, Anna Margarethe 24
Franckh, Michael 70
Frantz, Christian 26
  Jacob 87 [2]
Frätz, —— 130
Freed, Catharine 118
  Peter 118
Frei, —— 130
Fress, Johann Ludwig 96
  Wilhelmina 96
Fretz, Christian 130
  Hanns Martin 130
  John 130 [3]
Frey, Anna Catharina 57
  Anna Margretha 57
  Anna Maria 8
  Catharina Philippina 57
  Conrad 8
  Gottfried 8
  Hans 8
  Henrich 57
  Jacob 20 [6], 106, 107, 130
  Johann Caspar 57
  Johann Henrich 57
  Johann Jacob 20
  Johannes 130
  Margaretha 8
  Margaretha Dorothea 57
  Martin 8 [3]
  Paul 73
  Philipp 73 [2]
  Tobias 7, 8 [5], 130
Frick, Elisabeth 44
Fries, —— 6
Frosch, John George 5
Fry, —— 130
Funck, Hans 130
  Heinrich 130
  Martin 120
  Rudy 120
Funk, Fritrich 130

Johannes 130

--- G ---

Gabel, —— 70
Gachot, Bernhard 74
Gahman, —— 130
Galdi, —— 130
Galle, Friederich 130
  Joh. 117
  Peter 130
Galli, —— 130
Gallo, —— 130
Gally, Peter 130 [2]
  Peter, III 130
Ganshorn, Georg 22 [2]
  Johann Georg 22
  Johann Jacob 22
  Johann Philipp 22
  Susanna Elisabeth 22
Gansshorn, Johann Bartholomäus 22
  Johann Georg 22, 23
  Johann Philippus 22
  Maria Katharina 22
Gantzhorn, Johann Georg 22
  Mateis 22
  Matthias 22
Garber, —— 130
Gärber, —— 130
Garner, Hans Jorg 22
Gärtner, Johann 24
  Johann Georg 24
Garver, —— 130
Gaueman, —— 130
Gaugler, Kilian 111
Gaul, Johann Marthin 52
  Martin 52 [2]
Gäuman, —— 130
Gäumann, —— 130
Gayman, —— 130
Geeman, —— 130
Geering, —— 130
Gehman, —— 130
Gehrig, —— 130
Gehring, —— 130
Geier, Nikolas 105
Geiger, —— 97
  Bernard 22
  Nikolas 105
Geigle, Jacob 43 [3]
  Johann Jacob 43
Geiser, Chris. 15
  Christof 15
  Christoph 15 [2]
  Christopher 15
  Hans 15
  Melchior 86 [2]
  Peter 130
Geisser, Melchior 86
Geissert, Melchior 86
Geister, Christoph 15 [2]
Geman, Bendich 130

Christian 130
Gemanin, Anna 130
Genegy, —— 133
Gengrich, Joseph 26
Gentes, Christina Margaretha 54
    Georg Elias 53
    Juliana Margaretha 53
Gerber, Anna 130 [2]
    Hans Jacob 130
    Jacob 130
    Johannes 130
    Michael 130
    Michel 130
    Ulrich 130
    Walti 130
Gerdi, Fridrich 110
Gerfer, —— 130
Gerhard, Christina 19
    Peter 19
Gerig, —— 130
Gering, Baltes 130
Gerlach, Susanna 111
Gerlich, J. C. 113
Gerner, Anna 22
    Catharine 22
    Eve 22
    Johan Matthes 22
    Johann Mathias 22
    Margaret 22
    Maria 22
    Mathias 22
    Michael 22
    Susan 22
Gernion, Elisabeth 23
Gerung, —— 130
Gerwer, —— 130
Geyer, Johann Georg 117
    Nikolas 105
Geyger, Apollonia 105
    Nikolas 105
Geyman, —— 130
Geyser, —— 130
    Anna Maria 44
    Barbara 44
    Hannss Jerg 44
    Johannes 44
Giezendanner, —— 70
Gilliome, Christ. 112
Gingerich, —— 130
Gingery, —— 130
Gingrich, —— 130
Gisch, Mattes 74
    Matthes 74
Glatt, Anna Maria 95
    Hans Philipp 95
Gnaeg, —— 133
Gnaegi, Christian 133
Gnagey, —— 133
Gnagi, Hans 133
Gnagy, —— 133
Gobel, Anna Catharina 71
    Anna Margaretha 71
    Anna Maria 70 [2]
    Antoni 70

Antonius 70
Barbara 70
Carl Antony 70
Georg Adam 71
Georg Balthasar 70
Hans Georg 70
Hans Jerg 70
Hanss Georg 71
Jerg Adam 70
Magdalena 70
Maria Dorothea 71
Maria Elisabetha 70
Maria Magdalena 71
Göbel, ——, Pastor 58
Gobl, —— 70
Goering, —— 130
Goetschy, ——, Pastor 11
    John Henry, Pastor 15
Goldner, Johanna Henrietta Philippina 52
Göltzer, Johannes 45 [2]
Gooch, William, Lt. Gov. 8
Goranflo, —— 84
Goranslo, Jor Adam 84
Görckes, Jacob 111
    Margreth. 111
    Wilhelm 111
Gorenflo, Georg Adam 84 [3]
    Isaac Friedrich 84 [2]
    Jacques 84 [3]
    Philipp Onofer 84 [2]
    Pierre 84 [2]
Gorenflos, —— 89
Göring, —— 130
Gorner, Elizabeth 20
    John 20
Gorsch, Jacob 28
Götz, Catharina 61
    Christian 69, 70, 71
Götzendanner, Christian 69, 70 [3], 71
Gougher, —— 127
Graber, Christian 131
    Peter 131 [2]
Gräber, —— 131
Grabiel, —— 131
Grabill, —— 131
Gräbill, Eva 143
Gradinger, Henrich 91
    Johann Wilhelm 91
    Wilhelm 91
Graef, —— 131
Graf, Barbara 88
    Friedrich 61
    Hans 131
    Valentin 60
Graff, Franz 78
    Gorg 131
Gräff, Sebästian 131
Gramm, Anna Christina 94
    Catharina 94
    Sebastian 94
Grandmange, —— 97
Granes, Joh. Karsten 114
Grau, Johann Georg 110

    Maria Dorothea 110
    Maria Magdalena 110
Grauss, Jacob 19
Graw, —— 109
Grayber, —— 131
Graybill, —— 82
    John 131
Grebel, —— 131
Greber, Leobald 131
Grebiel, —— 131
Grebilt, —— 131
Grebühl, Michel 82
Greenawalt, Philip Lorentz 101
Grim, Anna Barbara 111 [2]
    Conrad 111 [2]
    Johannes 111
Grimm, Daniel 49
Gring, Anna Catarina 28
Grisemer, Johan Caspar 15
Groff, Johann Christoph 131
Gröner, Jacob, Jr. 87
Gros, —— 131
Gross, Jacob 131 [2]
    Johann Anderes 131
    Johann Christian 131
    Johannes 131
Grossmann, —— 128
Grove, —— 131
    Frantz 78
    Franz 78
Grub, Anna Catharina 66
    Debalt 66
    Eva Catharina 66
    Johann Henrich 66
    Johann Jacob 66
    Johann Michael 66
    Johann Theobald 66 [2]
    Maria Johannetta 66
Grünewald, Abraham 101
    Alebert 101
    Heinrich 101 [4]
    Jacob 101
    Johann Adam 101
    Maria Katharina 101
    Peter 101
    Sophie 101
Gùdelius, Christophel 58
    Tillimany 58
Guengerich, —— 130
Gümbel, Maximilian 114
Gump, Georg 20
    John Georg 20
Gundelach, Gottlieb 114, 116
Güngerich, —— 130
Günther, Anna Dorothea 13
    Christian 13
Gutelius, Johann Peter 58
Guthman, Peter 57
Gutmann, Anna Elisabetha 57
    Johann Peter 57 [2]
    Rudolph 57
Gyser, Johanas 130
    Johanas Petter 130
    Mariles Pitt (Marie Elsbeth) 130

Yogha (Johann) Christian 130
Gysler, Christian 130
Kattarina 130

--- H ---

Haan, John 121
Haass, Benjamin 68 [2]
Habecker, —— 131
Habeger, —— 131
Habegger, Hans Jacob 131
Peter 131
Ulrich 131
Haber, Philipp 78
Haegis, Jacob 7
Judith 7
Haffner, Johannes 85
Hafner, Johannes 85
Hage, —— 131
Hagey, —— 131
Hägi, Hirzel 131
Hagy, —— 131
Hahliger, Samuel 117
Hainel, Jacob 67
Hake, Michael 29
Haldeman, —— 132
Haldemann, —— 132
Haldenmann, —— 132
Haldiman, —— 132
Haldimand, —— 132
Haldimann, —— 132
Halm, Anna Cath(a)rin 58
Johannes 58
Halteman, —— 132
Halterman, —— 132
Hambrecht, Adam 19
Hammer, Friedrich 78
Hamspacher, Margaretha 8
Han, —— 51
Handel, —— 116
Hapeger, —— 131
Happes, Daniel 25
George 25 [2]
Hans Adam 25
Heinrich 25
Jacob 25
Joerg 25
Johann Michael 25 [2]
Johannes 25 [2]
Jörg 25 [2]
Michael, Jr. 25
Happold, Friedrich 114
Hardong, Anna Margretha 57
Johannes 57
Maria Apollonia 57
Hardt, Casper 120, 121
Jacob 120, 121
Philips 77
Hare, —— 132
Harnisch, Anna 131
Samuel 131
Harnish, —— 131

Harnist, Martin 131
Harpel, —— 13
Harshbarger, —— 132
Harshberger, —— 132
Harth, Sebastian 120
Hartman, Elisabeth 133
Hartmann, —— 117
Christoph 61
Johann Christoph 61
Valentin 61 [2]
Hartung, Anna Barbara 37, 39 [4]
Hartzell, —— 2
Hartzler, —— 132
Hasen, Barbara 6
Hassert, Johann Philipp 94
Hassinger, Valentin 117
Hauck, Anna Margaretha 102
Anna Maria 101
Barbara 71
Caspar 15 [2]
Caspar Anton 71
Eva Barbara 21
Georg Peter 71
Jacob 102
Johan Petter 71
Johann Adam 101
Johann Jakob 101
Johann Peter 71
Johann Valatin 71
Johannes 102
Maria Susanna 71
Nicolaus 71
Stephan 21
Wilhelm 71
Hauer, Anthony 86
Anton 86
Bernhardt 88
Christoph 88 [2]
Hauri, —— 131
Haury, Jacob 131
Hauser, —— 97
Hauss, Johann Michael 88
Johannes 88
Michel 88
Hausswirth, —— 97
Hawbecker, —— 131
Hawer, Bernhart 88
Hearsey, —— 132
Hechler, George 118 [2], 119
Michael 118 [3], 119 [2]
Heckler, George 118 [2]
Heckmann, Caspar 24 [3]
Heeb, Johann Adam 24
Heeller, Rudolf 131
Hees, Catharina 91
Heess, Anna Catharina 91
Christian 91
Hefft, Georg 62 [2]
Hege, Hans 131
Hegi, —— 131
Hegy, —— 131
Heidweiler, —— 37
Heil, Anna Margaretha 96
Johann Georg 96
Heile, Michael 85

Heiler, Regina 34
Heilman, John Adam 17
John Adam, Jr. 18
John Jacob 18
Heimlich, Andreas 68 [2]
Anna Margaretha 68
Georg 68
Heinel, Johann Jacob 67
Simon 67
Heinle, Michael 85 [2]
Heinzelmann, Anna Barbara 44
Heisser, Heinrich 116
Heist, Johann Philip 110
Heistandt, —— 132
Heit, Andreas 96
Anna Christina 94
Anna Elisabeth 94
Anna Elisabetha 94
Catharina Margretha 94
Jacob 87
Johannes 94
Peter 92, 93, 94 [2]
Helbig, Andreas 57
Anna Elisabetha 57
Anna Sara 57
Helffenstein, D. M., Rev. 29
Dorothea Margaretha 29
Johann Albert Conrad 29 [2]
Johann Conrad Albert 3
Johann Heinrich 29
Peter, Rev. 29
Helffrich, Donald L., Dr. 29
Johann Heinrich 3, 29 [2]
Johann Peter 29
Johannes 29
Reginald, Rev. 29
William A. 29
Heller, —— 93, 94, 131
Anna Maria 96
Anthony 96
Catharina Wilhelmina 96
Catharine 96
Christopher 96
Christopher, Jr. 96
Christophorus 93
Conrad 96 [2]
Daniel 96 [2]
Georg Christoph 96
Hans Jacob 96
Jacob 10
Johann Christoph 96
Johann Christophel 93
Johann Ludwig 96
Johann Michael 96 [2]
Ludwig 96
Maria Magdalena 96
Michael 96
Ottilia 96
Simon 95 [3], 96 [4]
Veronica 93
Hemperl, Elisabetha 87
Hempstead, Joh. 115
Hennel, Jacob 67
Henning, Jacob 54, 55
William 116

153

Hennop, Friedrich Ludwig 33
  Lucas 33
Henop, Friedrich Ludwig 33
Henrich, Agnes 94 [2]
  Hannah 22
Her, Anna Sybilla 4, 65
Herancourt, Marie 106 [2],
  107 [2]
Herbel, Johann Peter 13
  Johans 13
  Ludwig 13
  Peter 13
Herbst, Johann Nickel 41
Herder, Anna Elisabeth 64
  Johann Valentin 64
Hering, Jacob 116
Herpel, Johann Peter 13
  Johannes 13 [2]
Herr, Abraham 132
  Christian 132 [2]
  Emmanuel 132
  Hans 123, 132
Hersberg, —— 132
Hersberger, —— 132
Herschberger, Casber 132
  Jacob 132
Herscheberger, —— 132
Herschler, Johann Georg 132
Hershberger, —— 132
Hershey, —— 132
Hertt, Johannes 102, 105
Hertzel, George 2
  Hans Georg 2
  Hans Ulrich 2
Hertzler, —— 132
Herzel, Andreas 53
Herzler, Jacob 132
Hesen, Barbara 6
Hess, —— 34
  Hans 132
  Jeremias 132
Hessleman, Ulrich 124
Hetzel, Henry 15
  Jacob 15 [2], 28
Heuser, Heinrich 115
Heyd, Jacob 87
  Peter 94
Heydt, Anna Elisabetha 94
Heyler, Regina 34
Heylmann, Anna Maria 17 [2]
  Regina 17 [2]
Heystandt, —— 132
Hezel, Jacob 15
Hiestand, Abraham 132
Hiestandt, Jacob 132
  Johannes 132
Hiester, Catharine 28
  Joseph, Gov. 29
Hild, Elisabeth 24
Hildenbrand, Conrad 11, 12
  Conrad, Jr. 11 [2]
  Susanna 11
Hildenbrandt, Barbara 12
  Conrad 11 [2]
  Conrad, Jr. 12

Conrad, Sr. 11
Georg Michael 12
Hans Georg 12
Hill, Johann Andreas 6 [2]
  Mary 103
Hillegass, Elisabetha Barbara 11
  Elizabeth Barbara 11
  Frederick 11 [3]
  Georg Peter 11
  John Frederick 11
  Michael 11 [2]
Hillengass, —— 11
Hilligass, Johann Friderich 11 [2]
Hilspach, Friedrich 45
  Georg Friedrich 45
Hirnschael, Tielman 58
Hirnschal, Anna Catharin 58
  Johann Georg 58
  Tillmanus 58
  Tilmanus 58
Hirnschall, Thielman 58
Hirschberger, —— 97
  Christian 132
Hirschi, Christian 132 [2]
Hirschler, Christian 132
Hirschy, —— 132
  Christian 82
Hirtzel, Anna 2
  Clemens 2
  Ulrich 2
Hirzel, —— 134
Histand, —— 132
Hite, —— 8
  Peter 94
Hochermuth, —— 97
  Barbara 102
  Georg Adam 102, 105
Hochstedler, Barbara 141
Hochstedler, —— 133
Hochstettler, Jacob 133
Hoeg, Anna Margaretha 22
Hoerpel, Johannes 13
Hoffman, —— 93, 132
  Jacob 16, 20
  Jan Peter 94
  Johannes 58 [2]
  Jurg 94
Hoffmann, Adam Henrich 24
  Anna Catharina 4
  Anna Maria 28
  Burckhardt 132
  Hans Jost 4
  Hans Lenord 132
  Henerick 132
  Jacob 16 [2]
  Johann Jörg 132
Hoffstaetter, Georg 17
Hoffstätter, Georg 16, 17
Hoffstetter, —— 132
Hofmann, —— 132
  Adam 94
  Anna Margaretha 60
  Catharina 94
  Catharina Margretha 91
  Christian Wilhelm 94 [2]

Georg 94 [2]
Georg, Sr. 94
Georg Adam 94
Georg Philipp 94 [2]
Johann Adam 94
Johann Michael 94
Peter 94 [3]
Hofstetter, Christian 132
  Nicolas 132
  Peter 132
Hofstettler, —— 132
Hogermöd, Mathias Adam 102
Hoherluth, George Adam 102
Holdeman, David S. 132
  Hans 132 [3]
  Michael 132 [2]
  Nicholas 132
Holderman, Susan 143
Holdermann, —— 132
Holdiman, —— 132
Hollinger, —— 97
  Daniel 113 [2]
Honey, George 19
Hönick, Jacob 102
Hönig, Georg 102
  Jakob 102 [2]
  Katharina 102
Honsaker, —— 133
Hoober, —— 132
Hoover, —— 132
  Andrew 10
  Elizabeth 10
  Herbert 10
Hörd, Hans Georg 102 [3]
  Johannes 102
Horgen, —— 134
Höris, Michael 83
Horn, —— 37
Hornnecker, Margaretha 110
  Ulrich 110
Hörpel, Johann Görg 13
  Johannes 13
Hörpell, Jeremias 13
Horsch, Barbara 28
  Jacob 28 [5]
  Joseph 28 [3]
  Peter 28
Hört, George 98
Horthe, Jean Gaspard 120
Hortt, —— 101
Hosteeter, Oswald, 133
Hostermann, —— 78
Hostetler, —— 133
Hostetter, —— 133
  Christian 26
Hostettler, —— 133
Houri, —— 131
House, Johanes 88
  Philip 88
Hover, —— 132
Howe, Z. 117
Hubbert, —— 132
Huber, Andreas 10 [4]
  Christian 10
  Georg 86

Hans 132
Johann Georg 86
Johann Heinrich 133
Johannes 10
Jonas 133
Margaret 10
Maria Salome 23
Martin 132
Ulrich 132
Hüber, Hans Jerg 133
Jacob 133
Hubert, —— 132
Hübner, Johann 112
Hueber, —— 132
Huff, Jacob Friedrich 117
Huffstitter, George 17
Hügenell, —— 97
Huggenberger, Bernhard 117
Humbel, Elisabetha 3
Jerg 3
Hummel, —— 142
Hundsicker, Daniel 72
Elias 72
Jacob 72
Nickel 72
Huneck, Sturm 117
Hungerbieler, Johann Conrad 64
Maria Elisabeth 64
Hunold, Matthäus 86
Hunolt, Mattheis, 86
Wilhelm 86
Hunsberger, Henry 133
Hunsecker, —— 133
Hunsicker, Valentine 133
Hunsinger, —— 133
Huntseker, —— 133
Hunziker, —— 133
Hunzinger, —— 133
Hut, C. F. 114
Hütter, —— 117
Huvar, —— 132

--- I ---

Ibinger, Bernhard 17
Ickes, Ana Johanna 9
Igsin, Ana Johanna 9
Imhäusser, Adam 78
Imhoff, Catharina 62
Hans 62
Immel, Michael 9
Immenhauser, Adam 78
Immer, Johann 114
Impfinger, Anna Elisabeth 65
Ioder, —— 144
Irion, Catharina Regina 37
Franz 37 [2]
J. 34, 37
Johann Philipp 34
Katharine Regina 34
Philipp Jacob 33, 34 [2]
37, 40
Wilhelmine 37

Issed, Anna Maria 111
Jacob 111

--- J ---

Jacob, Elizabeth 124
Jacobi, Casper 93
Johann Adam 93
Jäger, Dietrich 68 [4]
Elisabetha Gertraudta 68 [2]
Jahraus, Heinrich 117
Jansen, —— 139
Jansson, Peter 114
Jantz, —— 139
Jayser, Johann Georg 44
Jentes, Elias 53
Georg Elias 53 [3]
Juliana Margaretha 53 [2]
Job, Georg 54 [2]
George 54
Hanss Görg 54
Michael 54 [2]
Nikolaus 54
Jockel, Balsar 111
Jöckel, Anna Eva 110
Bernhardt 110 [2]
Nicolaus 110
Joder, Hans 99, 103
Heini 144
Jodter, —— 144
Johannaci, ——, Mr. 95 [2]
Johns, Joseph 139
Jop, Georg 54
Margaretha 54 [2]
Michael 54 [2]
Nikolaus 54 [2]
Jopp, Anna Maria 54
Georg 55
Michael 54
Nicklaus 55 [2]
Nikolaus 55
Jordan, Ulrich 78
Jordte, Ulrich 78
Jörres, Ludwig 117
Jost, Daniel 72
Jacob 72 [3]
Josy, —— 97
Jotherin, Catharina 144
Jotter, —— 99
Christian 144
Jouis, Daniel 42 [3]
Jouy, Daniel 42 [4]
David 42
Jue, Daniel 42
Jugenheimer, Anna Maria 94
Jacob 94 [3]
Julius 94
Jung, Anna Margaretha 73
Elisabeth Barbara 56
Friedrich 56
Johann Michael 84
Johann Philipp 84
Johannes 56

Juy, Anna Margretha 42
Daniel 42 [2]
Johannes 42
Ludwig Heinrich 42

--- K ---

Kaege, —— 133
Kaegi, —— 133
Kaegy, —— 133
Kaenel, —— 133
Kaennel, —— 133
Kägi, —— 133
Kägy, Hans Rudolf 133
Rudolph 133
Kaiggey, —— 133
Kaiser, ——, Pastor 63 [2]
Kamerer, Christian 6
Kamm, Anna Barbara 11
Kaspar 11
Kammer, Gertrud 71
Kammerer, Mary Agatha 6
Kamp, Hans Jörg 20
Kanagy, —— 133
Kantz, Anna Catharine 110
Jacob 84
Johann 110
Michael 84
Karg, Anna Margaretha 16
Hans Michel 16
Karsh, Jacob 18
Kaucher, Jacob, Jr. 88
Michael 88 [2]
Kauffman, Andreas 133
Daniel 133
Hanes (Johannes) 133
Hans Adam 19
Isaac 133
Jacob 133
Johann Adam 19
Kauffmann, —— 133
Agatha 44
Anna 44
Bernhard 44 [2]
Hans Adam 19 [2]
Johanna 44
Johannes 44
Kaufman, Heinrich 133
Kaufmann, —— 133
Bernhard 44
Kauher, Jacob 88
Kautz, —— 83
Jacob 84 [2]
Michael 84 [2]
Kayser, Anna Marie 109
Eva Margaretha 109
Johann Jacob 109
Kehl, Anna Maria 92
Eleonora 92
Johann Konrad 92 [2]
Johann Nikolaus 92
Konrad 92 [2]
Philipp Jacob 92 [3]

Keim, John 107 [4]
Keller, —— 53, 66
  Anna Maria 111
  Bastian 12 [2]
  Charles 12 [2]
  Jacob 111
  Johannes 11, 12, 73 [2]
  John 12
  Margaret 12
  Martin 12 [3]
  Mary 12
  Nicolaus 77
Kellermann, Johann Wolffgang
    17 [2]
Kemp, Susanna 5
Kemper, —— 58
Kenagi, —— 133
Kendig, Benjamin 133
  Martin 123
Kenege, Barbara 133
Kenegy, John 133
  Joseph 133
Kenel, Katherina Elizabeth 133
Kenig, Baltzar 25
Kennel, Peter 133
Keppel, Eva Greta 111
  Henrich 111
Keppele, Heinrich 29
Kerber, Anna Walburga 38
Kern, Georg 62
  George 62
  Thomas 54, 55 [2]
Kersh, Jacob 18
Keyser, Dirck 99
Kiefer, Andreas 57
  Elisabetha Margaretha 57
  Maria Margretha 57
Kiehl, Johann 77
Kielewein, Anna Maria 104
  Katharina 98
  Philipp 102 [2]
  Veronika 105
Kiessinger, Jacob 4
Kilian, Valentin 98
Killwaine, —— 103
Kilsenlander, —— 70
Kinder, Christian 13
Kindig, —— 133
Kindige, Martine 133
King, Baltzer 25
Kintzi, Johannes 82
Kipfer, Ulrich 134
Kirchhofer, David 134
Kirchhoff, Christoph 134
Kirchhoffer, —— 134
Kirsch, Conrad 18 [2]
  Georg 18 [3]
  George 18
  Jacob 18
  Johann Jacob 18 [2]
Kissinger, Michael 4
Kistner, Mardin 111
Kitsenlander, —— 70
Kitsintander, —— 70
Klappert, Johannes 58 [2]

Klee, Conrad 46
  Jacob 46
  Michael 46 [2]
  Peter 46 [2]
Kleeberger, Johann Jacob 96
  Wilhelmina 96
Klein, Adam 49, 50
  Anna 49
  Anna Catharina 20, 50
  Anna Clara 50
  Catharina 50, 51 [2]
  Elisabeth 55
  Hans Adam 49, 50, 51 [2]
  Henrich 49, 51 [7]
  Jacob 49, 51 [2]
  Johann Adam 49 [2]
  Johann Henrich 49 [2], 51
  Johann Michael 65
  Johannes 49
  Leonard 27
  Ludwig 50, 51
  Wendel 49 [2], 51 [6]
Klett, —— 117 [2]
  Friedrich 115
Klinger, Wilhelm 110
Kloppey, Friedrich 86
Kloppeyn, Friedrich 86
Knab, —— 93
  Johann Michael 96
  Johann Nickel 96 [2]
  Johann Niclas 96
  Maria Claudina 96 [2]
  Michael 95
Knabb, Catharine 96
  Daniel 96
  Jacob 96 [3]
  John 96
  Mary 96
  Michael 96 [3]
  Nicholas 96
  Peter 96 [2]
  Sarah 96
  Susan 96
Knap, Michael 96
Knauf, Johannes 80
Knauff, Anthon 80 [2]
  Johann Adam 80 [2]
  Johann Hennrich 80
  Johann Henrich 80
  Lorentz 80
  Maria Magdalena 80
Knecht, Henry 19
  Johannes 19 [4]
  John 19
Kneissley, Anthony 19
Kniebes, Andreas 74
Knoblauch, Johann Nepomuk 117
Knöller, Valentin 71
Koberstein, Anna Catharina 22
  Hans Gorg 22
  Johann Georg 22 [2]
Koch, Jacob 85
  Johann Andreas 113
Kocherthal, Joshua 2
Koehl, Bastian 92

Koeller, Martin 12
Koenig, —— 134
  Balthasar 25
Kohl, Philipp 92
Kolb, Andreas 71
  Dielman 134 [3]
  Georg Michael 14
  Hans Kaspar 134
  Heinrich 134 [2]
  Jacob 134
  Johann Andreas 71
  Johannes 134
  Joseph 14
  Martin 134
Konig, Anna Margaretha 110
  Balzar 25
  Gerhard 110
König, —— 134
Konigh, Gabriel 134
Koob, Theobald 42
Koons, —— 5
Körner, Georg Jak. 114
Krabill, —— 131
Krafft, Anna Elisabeth 18
  Hans Georg 18 [2]
Kraft, Johann Friederich 18
Krähenbuhi, —— 131
Krähenbühl, Jost 131
Kramer, William 121
Krämer, Bartel 78
  Margaretha 85
  Michael 85
Kranester, Johannes 15
  Maria Barbara 15
Krause, David, Capt. 27
  John 27
Krauss, Jacob 19 [2]
  Joh. Georg 19
  Johanes 27
  Johannes 27 [2]
  John 27
Kraybill, —— 131
Krayenbühl, —— 131
Krebiel, Heinrich 41
  Michael 41, 131
Krebill, —— 131
Krebühl, Anna 82
  Elisabetha 82
  Jakob 82 [2]
  Johannes 82 [2]
  Peter 82
Krehbiel, —— 102
  Jacob 131
  Peter 82
Krehbill, —— 131
Krehebuehl, Johann Adam 17
Kreybül, —— 131
Krick, Jeremias 61
  Juliana 61 [2]
  Wilhelm 61
Krienbiel, —— 131
Kröbiel, Michael 41
Kröner, Jacob, Jr. 87
Krüger, Anna Margaretha 16 [2]
  Jörg Nickel 16

Kuehlenwein, — 99
Kuemmerling, Johannes 28
Kuendig, — 133
Kuepfer, Jacob 134
Kühl, Johannes 77
Kühlewein, Albert 102, 103
    Anna Maria 102, 103
    Dorothea 98 [2], 102 [2], 105
    Hans Theobald 98, 102 [3], 105
    Katharina 102, 103 [2]
    Maria Elisabeth 102
    Philip 99 [2], 102, 105 [2]
    Philipp 98 [2], 102 [2], 103
    Sara 102 [2]
    Sebastian 102, 103
    Theobald 103
    Veronika 102, 103
Kühlwein, Dorothea 103
    Philip 103
Kuhn, Abraham 72
    Adam Simon 9
    Anna Elisabetha 72
    Johann Wilhelm 72
    Johannes 72 [2]
Kulp, — 134
Kumpff, Georg 20 [2]
Kündig, Martin 133
Kunel, Niclaus 133
Kuntz, Anna 6
    Catharina 6
    Christian 6
    Elizabeth 6
    Francis 6
    George Michael 5
    Jacob 5, 6 [4]
    Jacob, Sr. 6
    Johann Nickel 56
    John 6
    John George 5 [2]
    Margaretta 6
Kunz, Jacob 6
Künzi, Johannes 82
Küpfer, Elsbeth 134
    Rudolf 134
Kurrtz, Abraham 134
Kurtz, Christian 134
    David 134
    Johannes 134 [2]
    Maria 114
    Stephen 134
Kurz, — 134
Kusl, Anna Margretha 94
Kussel, Anna Margretha 94

--- L ---

Labaar, Philip 11
Lachet, — 134
laCombe, — 97
Ladenberger, Catharina Elisa-
    betha Wilhelmina 61
Landes, — 134

Abraham 120
Frederick 120
Grette 121
Jacob 121
Magdalen 121
Rudolph 119, 120 [2], 121 [5]
Landis, — 119
    Benjamin 134 [2]
    Felix 134
    Hans 134
    Jacob 134 [2]
    Johannes 134
Landish, Rodolf 134
Lang, Anna Dorothea 9
    Barbara 17
    Conrad 13, 17 [3]
    Cunradt 17
    Hans Adam 135
    Johann Andreas 93
    Johans 135
    Wendel 51, 93
Langanacker, — 135
Lange, Conrad 17
Langenecker, — 135
Langenegger, John 135
Lantz, George 20
Laroch, —, Dr. 117
Latscha, — 134
Latschar, — 134
Latschaw, — 134
Latshow, Frans 134
Lauer, Christian 74 [2]
    Peter 74
Laval, Johann Michael 96
Lavall, Johann Daniel 96
    Veronica 96
Lawall, Daniel 96
    Johann Lutwig 96
    Johann Michel 96
    Melchior 96
Lay, — 37
    Anna Margaretha 18
Layer, Adam 25
Layman, — 134
Laymeister, Wilhelm 78
Leaman, Hans 134
Lechner, Georg 18 [2]
    Johann Georg 18
LeDee, Jean 103 [2]
Leeman, — 134
Leemann, — 134
Lehman, — 134
    Christian 99
    Michael 84
    Sylvanus 117
Lehmann, Hans 134
    Jacob 86 [2]
    Michael 84
Lehn, Johann 77
Leichti, — 134
Leichty, — 134
Leidig, Gertrude 6
Leier, Jacob 25
    Michael 25
Leighty, — 134

Leisi, Elisabeth 137
Leitner, Magdalena 12
Lemahn, Johannes 134
Leman, Peter 134 [2]
Lenox, — 37
Lentz, George 20
Leonhardt, Rosina Barbara 114
Lerch, Anna Rosina 28
leRoy, Augustin 89
Lessle, Benjamin 22
Leutscher, — 134
LeVan, Daniel 5
Levan, Abraham 5 [2]
    Anna Elisabeth 5
    Barbara 5
    Catharine 5
    Daniel 4 [5], 5 [5]
    Daniel, Jr. 5 [2]
    Isaac 5 [2]
    Jacob 5 [3]
    Joseph 5 [2]
    Magdalena 5
    Margaret 5
    Mary 5 [2]
    Peter 5
    Susanna 5
Levasier, — 97
Leveaux, — 97
leVent, Daniel 4
Lewis, — 8
Leyer, Martin 25
    Peter 25 [3]
    Philipp 27
Leymeister, Johann Wilhelm 78
Lichdi, — 134
Lichter, Anna Dorothea 18
    Georg 18
Lichti, — 134, 135
Lichtie, Catrina 135
    Christian 135
Lichtner, Anna Dorothea 18
    Georg 18
Lichty, — 134
Licker, George 25 [2]
Liechti, — 135
    Ulrich 134
Liechty, Jacob 134
    John 134, 135
    Nicklaus 135
Lind, Eva Elisabetha 85
    Margaretha 85
    Peter 85
Lindemer, Johannes 40
Lindöhmer, Johannes 40
Link, Friedrich 43
Lins, George 20
Lintz, Anna 20
    George 20
    Jerg 20
    John 20 [3]
    Martin 20 [2]
    Sebastian 20
Linz, Georg 20 [3]
Lischy, Jacob 22
Lish, Peter 28

Litmiller, —— 135
Litwiler, —— 135
Litwiller, Peter 135
Litz, Friedrich 92
Löble, Georg 87
  Görg Aadam 87
  Wilhelm 87
Lockmayer, Christina 44
  Hanss Jerg 44
  Hanss Michel 44
  Johann 44
  Johannes 44
  Magdalena 44
Lockmir, Johann 44
Loehr, Fried. Pet. 114
Löffler, Dieterich 88
  Dietrich 88
Lojet, —— 97
Long, Conrad 17
  Conrath 135
  Cunradt 17
  Hannah Boble (Annababeli) 135
  John 135
Longacre, —— 135
Longaker, —— 135
Longenacre, Anna Barbary 135
  Christian 135
Longenecker, Daniel 135
Longinegger, —— 135
Lorch, ——, Preacher 107 [2]
  F. 107
Lorsch, F. 106
Lörsch, Hans 134
Lörtscher, —— 134
Loscher, Petronella 65
Löscher, —— 134
Lötcher, —— 134
Lotschberg, Conrad 61 [2]
  Johann Christoph 61
  Johann Conrad 61 [3]
  Johann Wilhelm 61 [2]
  Johanna Friderica 61
Lötscher, Hans 134 [3]
  Johannes Franz 134
Lotspeich, Johann Christoph 61
  Johann Conrad 61
  William 61
Löwenberg, Christina 82 [2]
  Christoph August Ludwig 82
  Elias 82
  Friedrich 82 [3]
  Ludwig 82 [2]
  Maria Catharina Sophia 82
  Peter 82
  Philipp 82 [3]
Lücker, Jörg 25
Ludwick, George 22
Ludwig, Adam 21 [3]
  Apolonia 55
  Appollonia 54
  George 22
  Hans Adam 21
  Johan George 22
  Johann Georg 22 [2]

  Johannes 54 [2]
  John Adam 21
  Karl 63
  Maria Margaretha 22
  Martin 10
  Philipp 21
Luecker, Anna Johanna 25
  Joerg 25
Lütwyler, —— 135
Lutz, Johann Michael 11

--- M ---

Mack, Jacob Fried. 114
  Rosina 20
Maetzler, —— 135
Maier, —— 135, 136
Maile, —— 135
Mailen, —— 135
Maintzer, Johanes 88
  Martin 88
Marent, Conrad 82
Markle, —— 103
Marquart, Michel 44
Martersteck, Johann Martin 103
  Albert Friedrich 103
  Albrecht Dietrich 103
  Daniel 103
  Johann Dietrich 103
  Johanna Maria 103
  Maria Christina 103
Marthin, Hans Steffan 27
  Joerg 26
Martin, Anna Margareth 110
  Georg 26
  Georg Adam 28
  Johann Stephan 27
  Jost 110
  Stephen 27 [3]
Marx, ——, Mr. 114 [2]
Mast, Abraham 135
  Barbara 135
  Christian 135
  Jacob 135 [5]
  Joseph 135
Mathias, Johann 40
Maurer, —— 97
  Catharina 71
  Friedrich Magnus 57
  Johannes 57
  Maria Magdalena 105
  Maria Philippina 57
Maust, —— 135
Mayer, —— 135, 136
  Anna 7, 16 [2]
  Anna Maria 92 [2]
  Dietrich 7
  Hans Velten 16
  Jacob 7
  Johann George 87
  Margaretha 2
  Michael 88 [2]
  Zacharias 37 [2]

Mayle, —— 135
Mayweg, Joh. J. 114
Meckel, Christian 78 [2]
Meickhart, Peter 71
Meier, —— 135, 136
Meile, —— 135
Meili, Hans 135
  Martin 135
Meinzer, Johannes 88
  Martin 88
Meister, Elisabetha Margaretha 18
  Georg Bernhard 18
  Georg Conrad 18
  Johann Jürg 18
  Veidt 18
  Veit 18 [4]
Meixell, Andreas 11 [3]
Mellinger, Esther 101
Meng, Christopher 99
Mengel, Friedrich 77
  Frietz 77
Meperis, Anna Elisabeth 110
  Dorothea 110
  Silvanus 110
Merckel, Anna Lena 103
  Casper 103
  Catherine 103
  Christian 103 [3]
  George 103
  Peter 103
  Jacob 85 [2]
  Simon 85 [2]
Mercklin, Jacob 85
  Simon 85
Merkel, Christian 103 [2]
  Maria Katharina 103
Mershimer, Henry 104
Merz, Philipp 78
Messemer, Henrich 60
Messer, —— 102
Mest, —— 135
Metzler, Jost 135
  Valentine 135
Meyer, —— 136
  Anna Maria 3
  Christian 29, 135
  Elisabeth 73
  Georg 73 [2]
  George 7
  Hanss Jerg 87
  Johann 71
  Johann Fridrich 3
  John 29
  Julius 71
Meyers, —— 135
  Elizabeth 116
  Lorenz 112
Meyli, —— 135
Meylin, —— 135
  Catherine 127
Mezler, —— 135
Michel, Hans Georg 73
Michenfelder, Johann Caspar 71
Miesemer, Henrich 60

Milch, Johann 71
Miley, — 135
Miller, Adam 8 [5]
   Adam, Jr. 8
   Christian 6
   Christyan 6
   Daniel 71
   Hans Adam 8
   Jacob 8
   Joh. G. 117
   John 116
   John Peter 11
   Michael 13 [3], 14
Millich, Johann 71
Misemer, Henrich 60
Möhl, — 65
Moist, — 135
Moll, Michael 85
Möll, Johann Heinrich 64
   Johann Valentin 64
Molter, Peter 74 [2]
Monninger, Fr. 117
Mörike, — 115, 116
Morschheimer, Georg Heinrich 103
Mörsheimer, Georg Heinrich 103
Moseman, — 136
Mosemann, Andreas 136
Moser, — 101
   Adam 100
   Barbara Wahli 136
   Christane 136
   Hans 136
   Jacob 136
   John 136
   Jost 136
Mosiman, Christian 136
   Jacob 136
   Michael 136
Moss, — 135
Moy, Fridrich 110 [2]
   Johann Michel 110
   Simon 110 [3]
   Susanna 110 [2]
Moyer, — 135
Moyers, — 135
Muck, — 23
Mueller, Christian 6
   David 27
   Dietrich 15
   Jacob 6, 15
   Johann Friedrich 22
   Johann Michel 20
   Philipp Georg 20
Mühenberg, Christian 117
   Maria 117
Mühlefeld, Gerhard 28
   Gerhart 28
   Johann Friederich 28
Muhlenberg, Henry Melchior 3
Mühlenhaüser, Hans Jacob 10
   Ursula 10
Muhlhauser, Jacob 10
Muller, Jacob 120

Müller, — 136
   Adam 73
   Anna Maria 58
   Apollonia 105
   Barbara 20
   Catharina 81
   Christian 5, 6
   Daniel 71, 81
   Dietrich 14, 16
   Filip Gorg 20
   Hanss 51
   Hermanus 58 [2]
   Jacob 6, 73
   Johann Friedrich 58
   Johann Jacob 20
   Johann Michel 20
   Johannes 109
   Katharina 105
   Luisa Eleanora 103
   Margaretha 109
   Maria Dorothea 14 [2]
   Maria Magdalena 73
   Matthäus 105
   Michael 14 [2], 104
   Michel 99, 104 [2], 105
   Nickel 73
   Pips Gorg 20
   Wilhelm 73 [2]
Munder, Carl 117
Munzinger, Conrad 43
Musselman, Abraham 26
   Barbara 26
   Catharina 26
   Christian 26
   Christina 26 [2]
   Elisabeth 26
   Elisabetha 26
   Hans 26
   Jacob 26 [2]
   Johannes 26
   John 26 [3]
   Margaret 26
   Veronica 26
Musselmann, Hans 26
   Johannes 26 [2]
Musser, — 136
Mussgnug, David 88
   Davit 88
Mussier, Catharina 3
   Johann Jacob 3
Muszi, Joseph 40
Myer, — 135
Myers, — 135
Mylin, — 135
   Catherine 127

--- N ---

Naffsinger, — 136
Naffzer, Ulrich 136
Naffziger, — 136
Naffzir, — 136
Nafsker, Matheias 136

   Peter 136
Naftiger, — 136
Naftsinger, — 136
Naftziger, — 136
Nafzger, Rudolf 136
Nafziger, Christian 136
   Peter 136
Nafzinger, — 136
Nagel, Dewalt 84
   Immanuel Christian 117
   Joachim 88 [2]
   Sebastian 87 [2]
   Theobald 84
Neff, Cleophe 9
Neihart, Georg 62
   Jerg Friedrich 62
   Michel 62
Neiswander, — 136
Neu, Anna Margaretha 54
   Georg 54
   Jacob 53
   Johann Otto 54
   Johann Simon 54
   Joseph 54
   Magdalena 53
   Peter 54
   Wilhelm 54
Neubrandt, Johannes 117
Neuenschwander, John B. 136
   Mathis 136
   Michael 136 [2]
   Peter 136
Neuenswander, — 136
Neufer, Salome 67
Neuhard, Adam 62
   Christoph 62
   Elisabeth 62
   Friedrich 62 [2]
   Georg 62
   Hans Georg 62
   Jacob 62
   Michael 62
   Michel 62
Neukumeter, — 97
Neuman, Karl 49
   Margaret 49
Neumann, Carl 49
   Karl 49
Neuschwanger, — 136
Newcomer, John, Jr. 26
Newschwanger, — 136
Newswange, Xtian (Christian) 136
Newswanger, — 136
Nicewander, — 136
Niesenpeter, Jacob 94
Nisewander, — 136
Niswander, — 136
Noffsinger, — 136
Nofsinger, — 136
Nofsker, — 136
Noll, Joseph 117
Norfziger, — 136
Notz, Anna Dorothea 13
   Catharina 13
   Catharine 13

Dorothea 13
Dorothy 13
Elizabeth 13
Jacob 13
Johann Leonhard 13 [2]
John 13
Lenhart 13
Leonard 13 [3]
Margaret 13
Michael 13
Nübert, Lambert 117
Nungesser, Vallentin 111
Nusbaum, Bendickt 136
Johannes 136
Nuss, Johann Jacob 111
Nussbaum, Hans 136
Nussbaumer, —— 136
Nuz, Catharina 15
Friedrich 15

--- O ---

Oberholtzer, Elizabeth 136
Jacob 136
Martin 136
Michael 136
Samuel 136
Oberle, Susanna 65
Odenwälder, Philipp 71 [2]
Odernheimer, Johannes 77
Philips 77
Oehlenberger, Nicolaus 41
Oertelt, C. E. 114
C. F. 117
Oesch, —— 129
Ohr, Henrich 57
Johann Nickel 57
Johann Philipp 57
Maria Elisabeth 57
Osbourn, —— 116
Oster, Anton 78
Ostermann, Hans Jacob 78
Ott, Anna Maria 44
Johann Georg 44 [2]
Johannes 44
Rosina Barbara 44
Otterbein, Philipp Wilhelm 59
Ottinger, Jacob 9, 22
Johanna 22
Ougspurger, —— 124
Overholser, —— 136
Overholt, —— 136
Overholtzer, —— 136
Overholzer, —— 136
Oxberger, —— 124

--- P ---

Pallmer, Georg Ludwig 85
Pare, Jacob 124
Peachey, —— 126

Peckinpah, —— 24
Peischlein, Elsa Rosina 21
John Andrew 21
Pelanus, Cathorina 68
Johann Conrad 68
Simon 68
Pence, Adam 100
Penerman, —— 127
Pesch, Anna Maria 21
John Andrew 21
John William 21
Peter, Anna Barbara 9
Anna Maria 8
Hans, Jr. 12 [2]
Hans Jerg 9
Jerg 9
Rudolph 9
Petri, Johanna 62
Johannes 62 [2]
Petter, Jerg 9
Petzer, Samuel 26
Pfaff, Anna Barbara 39
Anna Maria 39
Anton 114
Isaac 39 [2], 39
Johann Daniel 37 [2], 39 [2]
Joseph 39
Maria Juliana Wilhelmina
39, 40
Maria Juliana Wilhelmine
39
Maria Magdalena 39
Peter 33, 37 [2], 39 [5],
40 [5]
Peter, Jr. 39
Samuel 39
Theobald 39, 40
Pfaffenberger, —— 37
Pfaffenmeier, —— 37
Pfarr, Adam 98
Pfautz, Andreas 10
Anna Barbara 10 [2]
Anna Margaretha 10
David 10
Hans Jacob 10
Hans Michael 10 [5]
Johannes 10
John Michael 10
Margaret 10 [2]
Michael 10 [3]
Pfauz, Andreas 10 [2]
Michael 9 [2], 10
Pfeffer, Johann Philipp 114
Pfefferlen, Johann Friedrich 44
Pfeiffer, Catharina 78
Georg 24
George 24
Johann Georg 24
Pfeil, Anna Margaretha 18
Friedrich 77
Pfesterer, Hans Adam 86
Pfisterer, Adam 86
Pfrang, Anna Maria 28
Georg, Sr. 28
Johann Michael 28 [2]

John Michael 28
Maria Agnes 28
Maria Eva 28
Matthäus, Sr. 28
Phile, George 21
Phouts, David 10
Pierrot, Anna Katharina 84
Pilanus, Catharina 68
Conrad 68
Simon 68 [2]
Pillanus, Anna Catharina 68
Conrad 68 [2]
Maria Margaretha 68 [2]
Simon 68
Simonn 68
Place, Lorentz 77
Planet, Carl Philipp 40
Johann Anton 40
Plank, —— 126
Melchior 137
Plannet, C. Philipp 40
Carl Philipp 40 [2]
Plätscher, Michel 137
Pletcher, —— 137
Pletscher, Johannes 137
Plotz, Friedrich 78
Ploz, Friedrich 78
Poff, —— 37
Poffenberger, —— 37
Poindexter, Sarah 37
Polert, Joh. Fr. 117
Pomgarddiner, —— 125
Pommer, Wilhelm 114
Portel, —— 126
Possart, Eve 101
Jacob 101
Johannes 101
Marilis 101
Posshart, —— 127
Prank, Jacob 28
Johann Georg 28
Prong, George 28
Prosch, —— 117
Prunder, —— 69
Puder, Christina 6
Puffenmoyer, —— 37
Pupater, —— 127
Pupather, Hans 127

--- Q ---

Qnäg, Johanes 133

--- R ---

Raber, Christian 137
Jacob 137
Räber, Conrad 137
Racke, Anna Margaretha 81
Henrich Caspar 81 [3]
Jakob 81 [2]

Johann Philipp 81 [3]
Raeber, — 137
Raitschaff, Johann Paul 3
Ramb, Christian 78
Ramsauer, Heinrich 137
Ramsaur, John 137
Ramsaurin, Ann 137
Ramsayer, — 137
Ramseier, Hans 137
 Peter 137
Ramseyer, — 137
 Lucia 140
Räsh, Michael 27
Raylin, Johann Georg 85
Reb, Eleonore 55 [2]
 Jacob 55 [4]
 Linora 55
Rebell, — 37
Reber, John 137
 Samuel 137
Reeser, — 137
Regula, Johann Peter 55
Rehrer, Gottfried 13
Reich, Georg 55
 Johann 55
 Johann Georg 55
 Mattheus 88 [2]
Reichenbacher, Adam 85
Reicher, Johann 55
Reichert, Jacob 25 [4]
Reichnes, — 138
Reiland, Aberham 47
Rein, Anna Barbara 114
Reinhard, Nicklas 24 [2]
Reinhardt, Johann Leonhard 24
 Margaretha 24
Reininger, Matius 110
Reinsperger, — 64
 Anna Catharina 64
Reisinger, Nicolaus 78
Reist, Hans Uli 137
 Peter 137
Reith, Johann Philip 111
 Philip 111
Renecker, G. Adam 84
Renker, Adam 83
Renkert, Adam 83
Renninger, Wendel 85 [2]
Resch, Anna 27
 Michael 27
Reser, Hans 137
Resor, — 137
Ress, Johannes 102
Reuschle, Johannes 85
Reuschlin, Johannes 85
Reuser, — 137
Reusser, — 137
Reyling, Johann Georg 85
Rhode, Franziska 103
Rhun, —, Mrs. 116
Rich, Michael 27
Richener, — 138
Richines, — 138
Richner, — 138
Rickert, Joseph 116

Riehm, Johann Eberhardt 11
Rieser, — 137
Riess, Christian 55
 Georg 55
 Johann Georg 55
 Ludwig 55
 Melchior 55
Rietz, Christian 55
Riser, Gorg Adam 137
 Hans Jerg 137
 Ulrich 137
Risser, Christian 137
 Jacob 137
 Johannes 137
 Maria 137
 Mary 137
 Peter 137
Ritss, Joseph 14
Ritter, Hans Georg 98
 J. G. 112 [3], 113 [3], 114,
  116 [3], 117 [3]
 Joh. Georg 114
 Johann Georg 112, 115
 John George 112
Rode, Johann Georg 103
Roehrer, — 17
 Johannes 13
Roesch, Johann Michael 27
Röhrer, — 29
 Gottfried 13 [2]
 Johann Gottfried 13
 Johannes 13 [3]
Roht, Cathrin 28
Roland, Aberham 47
 Abraham 46, 47
 Maria Elisabeth 47
Römer, Barbara 62
 Johann Nicolaus 62 [2]
 Wilhelm 62 [2]
Romig, Anna Maria 5
 Johann Adam 5
Roob, Johann Philipp 104
Rool, Peeter 104 [2], 105
 Peter 99, 104
Roop, Christian 18 [2]
Rooss, Johann 78
Ropp, — 137
Rosch, Michael 27
Rösch, Johann Michael 27
Ross, Johanes 78
Rössle, Gabriel 87
Rössler, Gabriel 87
Rost, Matheis 55
Rot, — 137
Roth, Benjamin 137
 Dietrich 103
 Johann Henrich 93
 Jonas 137
 Joseph 137
 Nicholas 137
Rothe, Johann Georg 103
Rothermel, Anna Maria 26
 Christophel 95
 John 27
Rübenich, Elisabetha 103

Matthäus 103
Rübenichts, Elisabetha 103
Rubert, Henry 81
 John 26
Rudesill, Anna Maria 20
 Philip 9
Rudi, Anna Margaretha 9
 Bastian 9
 Dietrich 9 [2]
 Ernst 9
 Hans 9
 Hans Conrad 9 [3]
 Hans Ernst 9 [2]
 Johann Dietrich 9
 Sebastian 9
Rudiesiel, Anna Johanna 9
 Weirich 9
Rudiesile, Philipp 9
Rudisill, —10
 Abraham 9
 Philip 9
Rudisille, Georg Philipp 9 [2]
 Johann Jacob 9
 Philip 9 [3]
 Philipp 9
Rüdisühli, — 9
Rudysil, Catharine 9
 Michael 9
 Philip 9
 Susanna 9 [2]
Ruf, — 138
Ruff, — 138
Rugh, Frankiena 103
 Franzina 103
Ruhl, Anna Barbara 104
 Hans Jakob 104
 Heinrich 100
 Peeter 104, 105
 Peter 99, 104 [2]
Ruland, Catharina 4
Rule, Peter 104
Rulle, Peter 104
Runckel, Johann Jacob 78
 Nicolaus 77
 Wendel 76, 78
Runkel, John William, Rev. 78,
 86
 Wendel 78 [2]
Ruof, — 138
Rupp, Christian 18 [4]
 Heinrich 119
 Henry 120
 Henry Wilson 19
 Israel Daniel 18
 Jacob 119 [2], 120 [2], 121
 Joh. Jonas 18
 Johann 119
 John 18, 120
 John Jonas 18
 Jonas 138
 Peter 137
 William 18
 William J., Rev. 19
Ruppert, Johann Henrich 81
 Johann Melchior 81

Rüssor, — 137
Rust, Michael 27
Rutschly, Philip 9
Rychener, Christian 138
Rychines, — 138
Rychner, — 138
Ryhines, — 138
Ryser, — 137

--- S ---

Sabel, Catharine 22
  Leonard 22
Säemann, Johan Georg 84
Säger, Gabriel 52 [4], 53 [2]
  Johann Balthasar 52
  Margaretha 53
Salade, Johannes 56
  Migel 56
Salathe, Barbara 56
  Johannes 55
  Michael 55
  Niklaus 55
  Nikolaus 56
  Philipp Jacob 55
Salathee, Johann Georg 56
Saltzer, Anna Maria 84
Säman, Johan Georg 84
Sanders, Anna Maria 110
Sauder, Margaretta 138 [2]
  Thomas 138
Saudter, Pedter 138
Sause, Carl Moritz 113
  Ludwig Maximilian 113
  Max 115
  Moritz 115
Sauter, — 142
  Francisca Catharina 12
  J. E. 112, 114
  Johann Filb (Philipp) 138
  Nicholas 142
Sautter, — 138
Schaeffer, — 16, 20
  Alexander 3, 4, 29 [3]
  Anna 29
  Catharine 29 [2]
  Henry 29 [3]
  John 29
  Margaret 29
  Margaretha 4
  Sabina 29
Schafer, Anna Magdalena 40
  Anna Margretha 40
  Catharina 40
  Elisabetha Catharina 40
  Henrich, Jr. 40
  Johann Henrich 40
  Maria Salomea 40
  Susanna 40
Schäfer, — 51
  Catharina 71
  Heinrich 40 [2]
  Johanna Maria 33

Schaffer, Johann 40
  Ludwig 40
Schäffer, Anna Maria 16
  Hans 16
  Hans Heinrich 16 [2]
Schalabaugh, — 138
Schall, Catharina 19
  George 21
  Tobias 19 [4], 21 [2]
Schallenberger, — 138
Schamar, Jakob 47
  Peter 47
Schänck, — 139
Schantz, Jacob 139 [3]
  Johannes 139
  Joseph 139
Schanz, — 139
Schaub, Balthasar 62
  Henrich 62 [3]
  Joha. Henrich 62
Schauer, Magdalena 3
  Michael 3
Schauffler, Hans Georg 84
  Hs. Georg 84
Scheffer, Johann Henrich 40
Scheib, Christian 60 [2]
  Valentin 60
Scheid, Georg 56
  Heinrich 56 [2]
  Johann Leonhard 24
  Peter 62
  Wendel 62
Scheidt, Carl 24
  Catarina 24
  Conrad 56
  Georg 56 [3]
  Georg Henry 56
  Heinrich 56 [2]
Schelcher, Joh. 115
Schellenbarg, — 138 [2]
Schellenberger, Johannes 138
Schellingbarg, — 138
Schenck, — 139
Schenk, Michael 139
Scherer, Anna Maria 100
  Hans Peter 104
  Johann Philipp 100 [2],
    104 [2]
  Philip 100
Scherrer, Christian 73
Schertz, Johann Henrich 138
Scherz, — 138
Schickle, Georg, Jr. 87
Schifferdecker, Jacob 27 [2]
Schilling, Anna Maria 24
  Johann Conrad 24
  Johannes 24 [3]
  Maria Martha 42
Schirmer, Anna Catharina 47 [2]
  Anton 47 [3]
  Georg Jacob 47 [3]
  Jacob 47 [2]
  Johann Jacob 47
  Magdalena 47 [2], 48
  Maria Barbara 47

Peter 47 [4], 48
  Sebastian 47
Schlabach, Christian 138
  Daniel 139
  Johannes 138
Schlapbach, — 138, 139
Schlappach, — 138
Schlatter, Michael 12
Schlaubach, — 138
Schlepp, Anna Barbara 4, 65
Schley, John Thomas 33
Schlicker, Ludwig 88
Schlintwein, Adam 96
  Anna Godlieb 96
Schlosser, Anna Margaretha 40
  Johann Jacob 40
  Johann Peter 40
Schlücker, Lutwig 88
Schmätzlen, Agatha 44
  Barbara 44
  Eva 44
  Jerg 44
  Simon 44
Schmelzle, Rudolph 87
Schmick, William 116 [2]
Schmidt, Agnes 7
  Anna Magdalena 12
  Christian 58
  Elisabeth Catharina 25
  Johann Henrich 58
  Johann Theobald 25
  Katharina Ursula 103
  Margaretha 7
Schmied, Barbara 84
Schmit, Philipp 68 [2]
Schmitt, Christian 120
  Ludwig 47
Schmoll, — 34
Schmucker, Christian 140
  Johanes Jerg 140
Schmutz, Abraham 139
Schnebel, — 139
Schnebele, — 139
Schnebeli, Christian 139
  Daniel 139
Schnebli, Henrich 139
Schnebly, — 139
Schneck, Georg 28
  Hans Georg 28 [2]
  Jacob 28
  Johann Georg 15, 28
Schneeli, — 139
Schneider, Andreas 44
  Anna 44
  Anna Elisabetha 44
  Anna Margreth 58
  Anna Maria 110
  Casper 118
  Christian 118
  Christina 110, 111
  Franz 115
  Georg Friedrich 62
  Hanna 58
  Heinrich 62 [2], 140
  Heinrich Balthasar 62

Henrich 58, 62
Hermanus 140 [2]
Jacob 62 [3]
Johann Henrich 58
Johannes 58 [2], 140 [2]
Lehnhard 111
Leonhardt 110
Maria Catharin 58
Maria Elisabeth 62, 118
Martin 62 [2]
Michael 62 [2]
Nikolaus 115 [3]
Peter 117
Ulrich 140
Schneuwlin, — 139
Schneuwly, — 139
Schnevoli, — 139
Schnewli, — 139
Schnewlin, — 139
Schneyder, Heinrich 140
Schnider, — 140
Schnyder, — 140
Schober, Barbara 48
Georg Peter 48
Hans Peter 48
Isaac 48
Johann Adam 48
Johann Simon 48
Maria 48
Simon 48
Sophia 48
Scholl, Anna Maria 81
Johann Heinrich 65
Maria 81
Maria Barbara 65
Theobald 81
Schöllenbarg, — 138
Schomacher, — 139
Schomecher, — 139
Schoop, — 139
Schop, — 139
Schopf, Anna Maria 9 [4]
Georg Philipp 9 [2]
Schowalder, Christian 102
Schowalter, — 97 [2], 139
Bernhard 102
Magdalena 102
Schowmacker, Peter 47
Schraag, — 139
Schrack, — 139
Schrag, Benedicht 139 [2]
Christen 139
Hanes 139
Jacob 139
Schragg, — 139
Schreiner, Anna Margaretha 39
Schremm, Anna Margaretha 40
Schreyer, Johann Adam 74
Martin 74
Schrock, — 139
Schröder, Heinrich 112
Schubard, Anna Catharina 61
Schubert, — 117
Schuch, Anna 9
Johann Petter 26

Martin 26
Schuck, Abraham 26
Anna Maria 26
Esther 26
John 26 [2]
Joseph 26 [2]
Martin 26 [3]
Salome 26
Susanna 26
Schuhl, Daniel 42
Schuhler, Anna Catharina 68
Johann Michel 68 [2]
Maria Margaretha 68 [2]
Schuhmacher, — 47
Jerich (Jörg)
Schui, Daniel 42 [2]
Schultz, Christian 95
Gottlieb 112
Schulz, Gustav 112
Schulze, David 3
Schumacher, Jacob 139
Schumacher, Peter 139
Schuppert, Anna Catharina 61
Schütz, Gerhardt 117
Schwab, Anna Elisabeth 11
Anna Maria 11
Christina Barbara 44
Dorothea 44
Elisabeth 44
Elisabetha Catharina 44
Georg 10
Hans Georg 10
Hans Georg, Sr. 10
Hans Jörg 10
Jacob Bernhard 44 [3]
Johann Adam 44 [2]
Johann Friedrich 44
Johann Georg 10 [3], 11
Jost 10 [2], 11 [4]
Michael, Colonel 7
Schwann, Abraham 16 [2]
Schwartz, Abraham 142
Andreas 142
Anna Margaretha 53
Georg 53
Hans Georg 73
Hans Jerg 73
Schwarz, — 142
Agnes 44
Catharina 44
Elisabetha 44
Hanss Martin 44
Jacob 44, 86, 117
Maria 44
Matthias 88
Philipp Benedikt 117
Schwe, Daniel 42
Lodawick 42
Margaretta 42
Maria 42
Schwedes, Johann Georg 96
Ottilia 96
Schweickard, Jacob 71
Schweickart, Abraham 78
Schweickhart, Friedrich 78

Schweigert, Samuel 24
Schweikert, Samuel 24
Schwenck, Anna Elizabeth 110
Christoph 62 [2]
Peter 110
Schwenk, Peter 109
Schwob, — 10
Jacob 11
Scott, — 37
Seeger, Anna Elisabetha 52
Gabriel 52, 53
Johann Balthasar 52
Seelbach, Anna Beata 58
Tillmanus 58
Seewald, Margreta 81
Martin 81 [3]
Velten 81
Seibert, Bernhard 74 [2]
Jacob 74 [2]
Johan Jacob 74
Seidebender, Henry 26
Seidenbaender, Henry 26
Seidenbender, George 26
Seiser, Johannes 112
Selbach, Johan Thiel(mann) 58
Seltzer, Elizabeth 96
Eve Magdalena 96
Jacob 96
Senghass, Caspar 114
Johann Caspar 114
Michael 114 [2]
Servos, C. K. 116
Sevic, George 12
Seydenbender, Hennrich 26
Johann Henrich 26
Seyler, Hanss 51
Shaffer, John 16
Shaffner, Caspar 6 [2], 13
Margaretta 6
Shallenberger, — 138
Shamar Peter 47
Shamboh, George 101
Shammer, Peter 47
Shank, — 139
Shantz, — 139
Shanz, — 139
Shawalter, John 139
Shellenberger, — 138
Shenck, — 139
Shenk, — 139
Sherer, Philip 104 [2]
Shiffendecker, Anna Maria 27
Catharina 27
Margaret 27
Maria Catharina 27
Shifferdecker, George 27
Shilling, John 24
Shoemaker, — 139
Shoepin, Veronica 139
Shoomak, Hans Martain 139
Shoop, John 139
Shope, Christophal 139
Johan Jerick 139
Showalter, — 102
Christian 139 [2]

163

Daniel 139
Jacob 139 [2]
John 139
Joseph 139
Peter 139
Ulrich 139
Valentine 139
Shrock, — 139
Shuey, — 42
Shupe, — 139
Shweyart, Hans Samuel 24
Shweyzig, Diterich 13
Shyd, Conrad 56
    Georg 56
    Georg Henry 56
Siegel, Adam 82 [2]
Siegfried, Elisabeth 5
    Johannes 5
    John, Colonel 5
    Joseph 5
    Mary 5
    Susanna 5 [2]
Siepka, S. K., Capt. 115
Sill, Carl 21
Simon, Jacob 67, 73
    Jakob 73
    Johann Jacob 66
Simone, Jacob 4
    Margaret 4 [2]
Simpfendörfer, Barbara 115 [2]
    Martin 114, 115 [2]
Sindel, Martin 109
Sinn, Anna Maria 44
    Barbara 44
    Catharina 44
    Christina 44
    Elisabetha 44
    Eva 44
    Franz Anton 44
    Hanss Jerg
    Jacob 44
    Michel 44
Sinter, Anna 2
    Hans 2
Slabach, Johannes 138
    Maria Elizabeth 138
Slaback, — 138
Slabaugh, — 138
Smoker, — 140
Smooker, — 140
Smucker, — 140
Smyser, Samuel 9
Snare, Stephen 116
Snavely, George 139
    Johann Jakob 139
Snek, Hans Jurg 28
Snewli, — 139
Snewly, — 139
Snider, Johannes 140
Snyder, Christian 140
Soerer, John Cunradt 17
    John Jacob 17
Söller, Johann Adam 3
Söllner, Johann Adam 3
Sommer, Adam 140

Christian 140
Isaac 140
Sommers, — 140
Sonntag, — 52
    Adam 56
    Anna Elisabetha 56
    Brill 56 [3]
    Hann Adam 56
    Hans Adam 56
    Nicklas 56 [2]
    Nikolaus 56
Sontag, — 51
    Adam 56
Sooter, Christian 142
Souder, — 138
Soutter, — 142
Souz, — 84
    Andreas 84
    Andres 84
    Maria Magdalena 84
Sowers, Christopher 99
Spangler, — 10
    Adam 7
    Christopher 7
    Elizabeth 7
    Henry Wilson 7
    Jacob 7
    Michael 7
    Stophel 7
Späth, Anna 44
    Barbara 44
    Catharina 44
    Christian 44
    Eva Margaretha 44
    Hanns Jerg 44
    Hannss Jacob 44
    Hannss Jerg 44
    Hannss Martin 44
    Magdalena 44
Speer, Joh. 114
Spengler, — 11
    Baltzar 12
    Baltzer 7 [2]
    Balzer 12 [3]
    Caspar 7 [3]
    George 7
    Hans Georg 12 [2]
    Hans Rudolf 7 [2]
    Henrich 12 [2]
    Henry 7 [2]
    Jacob 7
    Jerg 12 [3]
    Mary 7
Spindler, Jakob 114
Spohn, Adam 21
    Henry 21
    Peter 21 [2]
    Petter 21
Spon, Michael 21
Spoon, George 21
    Peter 21
Sprunger, Jacob 140
Spycher, Johannes 117
Staechelin, — 140
Staehler, Johann Nicholas 104

Staeli, — 140
Stahl, Jacob 25 [3], 26, 105
    Jacob, Sr. 105
    Johann Georg 104
    Johann Jacob 104
    Johann Jakob 103, 104 [3]
    Johann Valentin 103
    Susanna 104
Stahler, Daniel 105
    Joshua 105
Stähler, — 101
    Anna Katharina 105
    Anna Maria 100 [2], 104
    Anthony 105
    Friedrich 105
    Hartmann 100 [2], 104
    Henry 105
    Johann Georg 105
    Johann Nicklas 102, 105
    Johann Nicolaus 105
    Johann Nikolay 105 [3]
    Johannes 105
    John Nicholas, Jr. 105
    Ludwig 105 [2]
    Nikolay 105
    Peter 105
    Philip 105
Stahley, — 140
Stähli, Jacob 140 [2]
    Johann 140
Stahly, — 140
Staley, — 140
Stall, — 140
Stalley, Anna 140
    Ulrich 140
Stampel, — 34 [3]
Staud, Abraham 74
    Jacob 74
Staufer, — 140
Stauffer, — 102
    Hans 140
Stautt, Jacob 74
    Johann Michael 74
    Johannes 74 [2]
Steck, Johannes Marder 103
Steffen, Johann Adam 28
Steffy, Frederick 28
Steger, John Barnhard 18
    Maria Catharina 18
Stehelin, — 140
Stehler, Anna Maria 100
Stehli, — 140
Stein, Catharina Margretha 28
    Johann Esaias 17
    Wilhelm 24
Steiner, — 140, 141
    Christian 140
    Hans 140 [2]
    Johann 28
    Peter 140
Steinseiffer, Johann Henrich 58
    Tillmanus 58
Steley, Hans Peter 140
Steinseiffer, Johann Henrich 58
    Tillmanus 58

Steley, Hans Peter 140
Steli, — 140
Stelin, Anna Barbra 140
Stelley, Anna 140
   Ulrich 140
Stenger, Adam 19
   Adam, Sr. 19
   Anna Catharina 19
   Christian 19
   Daniel 19
   Jacob 19 [2]
   Johann Adam 19 [2]
   Salomon 19
   Stephan, Adam 28
Stief, Anna Christine 65
   Anna Clara 65
   Anna Margaretha 65
Stöckel, Ulrich 62
Stoever, — 13
   Johann Kaspar 103
   John Caspar 103 [2]
   John Casper, Rev. 3
Stoll, — 104
Stoner, — 140
Stotzmann, Johann Jacob 41
Stover, Catherine 103
   Ulrich 140 [2]
Strahm, Martin 141
   Matthias 141
Strassburger, Johann Andreas 77
   Ulrich 77
Strauch, Adam 96
   Johann Adam 96
   Maria Magdalena 96
Strembeck, Jacob 116
Stricker, Adam 93
   Anna Sara 96
   Elias 92, 93 [6], 96
   Henry 93
   Johanes 93
   Johann Adam 93
   Johann Christophel 93
   Johann Conrad 93
   Johann Henrich 93
   Johann Philipp 93
   Johannes 93
   Philipp 93
Strohm, Johannes 141
   John 141
   Ulrich 141
Strome, Benedice 141
Strompiers, — 97
Strub, — 104
Strubb, — 104
Strupp, Anna Maria 104
   Hans Georg 104
Stuckey, Joseph 141
Stucki, Hans Jerg 141
Stucky, Jacob 141
Stumpf, — 43
   Katharina 104 [2]
   Margaretha 104 [2]
   Martin 104 [2]
Stuncky, — 141

Sturm, Johannes 83
   Margarethe 83
Stutsman, — 141 [2]
Stutz, Anna 124
   Lewis 124
Stutzer, — 124
Stutzman, Christian 141 [2]
   Johann Jacob 141
Stutzmann, — 141
   Jacob 41
   Johann Jacob 41 [3]
   Regina Elisabetha 41
Styner, Ullwrick 141
Suder, — 141
Suidter, Xaver 116
Sumer, Christian 140
   Johns 140
Summer, — 140
Summers, — 140
Süss, Gorg Jacob 48
   Johann Georg 48
   Johann Philipp 48
   Maria Catharina 48
Suter, — 141, 142
   Christian 141
   Nicolaus 112
Sutter, — 142
   Christian 141
Suttor, — 141
Sutz, — 84 [2]
   Johan Jacob 84
Swartz, Abraham 142
Switzig, Bernhart 13
Swoope, Michael, Colonel 7
Swope, — 10, 11
   Edwin 10

--- T ---

Tanner, Michael 15
Teiswalentin, Agnese 110
   Johannes 110
Terr, George 19 [2]
Tesch, Catharina 68 [2]
   Elisabetha 68 [2]
   Johannes 68 [2]
   Wilhelm Henrich 68 [2]
Thaub, Johann Wilhelm 110
Theobald, Friedrich 56 [2]
   Michael 56
Theobalt, Johann Michel 56
Theodor, Karl 63
Thierstein, — 128
Thirstien, — 128
Thomas, Catharina Elisabeth 69
   Michael 71
Thori, Anna Felicitas 68
   Gerhard Johann 68 [2]
   Johann Erdmann 68
Thut, John 142
   Peter 142
Tiebinger, Bernhard 17

Tiefenbach, Caspar 84
Tiefetörfer, Hans Adam 20
Tieffenbach, Caspar 84
Tierstein, — 128
Tilger, — 128
Timberman, Abraham 105
Tobler, — 92
Törr, Hans Georg 19
Tracken, Hans Adam 10
Trapp, H. Camer-Rath 93 [2]
Traut, Anna Katharina 105
   Anna Maria 105
   Hans Georg 105
   Johann 98
   Johannes 105 [4]
   Katharina 105
Trautmann, — 20, 29
   Ann 16
   Anna Maria 17
   Anna Mary 16
   George 16
   Hieronimus 16 [8], 17
   Johannes 16 [4], 17
   Maria Elisabeth 16
   Philipp 16
Trauttman, Hyronimus 16
Trehr, Johannes 65 [2]
Treibel, Martin 21 [3]
Treier, — 142
Trescher, Anna Maria 80 [2]
   Tobias 80
Treyer, Frederick 142
Trible, Martin 21
Trippler, Jacob 117
Troutman, — 17
Troyer, — 142
Truat, John 105
Tschantz, Abraham 139
   Hans 139 [2]
   Johannes 139
Tschanz, — 139
Tübinger, Bernhard 16, 17
   Kilian 17
Tuchmann, Christman 111
   Maria Elisabeth 111
Tuebinger, Bernhard 17

--- U ---

Uber, Johann David 43
   Johann Ludwig 44
   Johannes 43
   Johannes Ludwig 43
   Ludwig 43
   Margaretha Barbara 43
Uebi, — 129
Ullerich, Johannes 99, 104 [2], 105
Ullrich, Johannes 105
Ulm, Catharina 71
   Johann 71
   Margarete 71
   Martin 71
Ulmer, Martin 113

Ulrich, Anna Maria 26
   Johannes 105
   John Jacob 26
Umahäuser, Gottl. 115
Umble, —— 142
Ummel, Christian 142 [2]
Unziker, —— 133

--- V ---

Valentin, ——, Mayor 65
   Susanna Elisabeth 65
Van Stampel, —— 34 [2]
Vechtel, —— 126
Vetter, Marx 94
Vierling, Sophia 55
Vogelgesang, Christian 53
Vogler, Margretha Frey 111
Voison, —— 97
Vollman, Johannes 93
von Aesch, —— 129
von Esch, —— 129
von Kaenel, —— 133
von Schlegel, Julius 115

--- W ---

Waage, Friedrich 111
Waeber, —— 143
Waffenschmidt, Anna Maria 58
   Gerlach 58
Wägelin, Johann Michael 3
Wageman, Johann Philip 101
Wageman, Hans Valentin 102
   Sara 102 [2]
Wagenmann, —— 101
   Anna Eva 101 [2]
   Barbara 101
   Hans Valentin 101
Wagner, Anna Catharina 40
   Anna Margareta 103
   Anna Margretha 94
   Elisabeth 111
   Jacob 68 [2]
   Jakob 103
   Johann Georg 110
   Johann Michel 27
   Johann Philipp 94
   Johannes 25 [4], 94
   Petronella 103
   Philip 111
Währlich, Michael 87
Wald, Johann Henrich 101
Waldhuber, Conrad 71
   Jacob 71
   Johann 71
   Juliana 71
   Maria Eva 71
   Michael 71
Waldmann, Georg Friedrich
   Sam(uel) 56

Georg Jacob 56
Georg Michael 56
Immanuel 56 [2]
Johann David 56
Johann Michael 56
Johann Nicolaus 56
Johann Wilhelm 56
Marianna 56
Wallti, —— 143
Walter, Anna Elisabetha 94, 95
   Christoph 6 [2]
   Henry 6
Walther, Christopher 7
Walti, John 143
Wälti, Niklaus 143
Waltmann, Emanuel 56
   Görg Jacob 56
Waltz, Johann Jakob 65
Wanger, —— 143
Warch, Anna Catharina 93
   Johannes 93
Wasenburger, Peter 77
Wassermann, —— 116
Waydmann, Johann 69, 70, 71
Weaver, —— 143
   Bastian 105
   Joseph 117
   Sebastian 105 [2]
Webber, —— 143
Weber, Anna 62
   Anna Elisabeth Margaretha
     66
   Christian 121, 143
   Daniel 74
   Georg 74
   George 143
   Henry 143
   Jacob 74 [2], 143
   Johann Daniel 74
   Johann Michael 66
   Johannes 40 [2], 74
   John 143
   Magdalena 62
   Maria Margaretha 66
   Michael 71, 143
   Philipp 74
   Sebastian 105 [2]
   Valentin 74
Weberlin, Johannes 40 [2]
   Peter 40
Weberling, Anna Ottilia 40
   Johannes 40 [4]
   Margaretha 40 [2]
Weckerlen, Emanuel Friedrich
     44
   Jeremias Friedrich 44
   Juliana Dorothea 44
   Maria Elisabetha 44
   Sabina Margaretha 44
Weckerlin, Immanuel Friderich
     44
Wedel, Anna Maria 4, 65
   Caspar 12 [2]
   Eva Catharina 4, 64, 65
   Georg 4, 65

Georg Albrecht 4, 65
Johann Peter 4, 65
Maria Catharina 64
Michael 4
Michel 4
Petter 65
Wegman, Christian Friedrich 28
Weidler, Catharine 27
   Elizabeth 27
   Michael 27
Weidman, Georg 58
   Henrich 58
Weidner, Nicolaus 61
Weimer, Jacob 67 [2], 68 [3]
Weingartmann, Hans Conrad 96
Weinheimer, Anna Katharina 101
Weinmüller, Johannes 62 [2]
Weis, Charlotte 92
   G. M. 144
   Michael 27
Weiss, ——, Pastor 2
   Adam 78
   Christian 144
   Franz 114
   Georg Michael 99
   George Michael 2, 27
   Hans 144
   Jacob 144
   Johan Michael 27
   Johann 114
   Johann Adam 78
   Mathias 27
Weissbecker, Margareta 103
Weisse, —— 144
Weisskopf, Carl 68 [2]
   Casper 68 [2]
   Johann Caspar 68
Weissmann, Peter 81, 82 [5]
Weisz, Jacob 144
Weitzel, Peter 77
Welcker, Georg 14, 17 [2]
   John George 17
Weldy, —— 143
Welfling, Henry 60
Welker, ——, Mrs. 17
   George 17
   Hans George 17
Wellecker, Rutolff 8
Weller, Anna Barbara 10
Welte, Johannes 143
Welti, —— 143
Welty, Ulrich 143
Wendel, Andreas 47
   Anna Barbara 91
   Anna Sara 95
   Caspar 12
   Magdalena 47
   Simon 95, 96
Wendell, Caspar 12
Wendle, Caspar 12
Wenger, Christian 143
Wentz, Jacob 85, 111
   Jacob, Jr. 85
Werckheisser, Nicklas 111
Werner, Anna Maria 111

Henrich 111
Johann Jacob 111
Johannes 65
Katharina 101
Peter 111
Philipp Jacob 88
Wertzel, Julia Ann 78
Westerberger, Peter 77
Westlen, Georg Christoph 44 [2]
    Rosina Margaretha 44
Wetstone, Henry 24
Wetzstein, Andreas 24
    Henrich 24
Wever, Phillis 143
Weydner, Henrich 60, 61
    Johann Henrich 60 [2]
    Lenert 61
    Leonhard 60 [2], 61
    Leonhard, Jr. 60 [2]
    Leonhard, Sr. 60
    Philipp Conrad 60
    Susanna Margaretha 60
Weymer, Jacob 68
Weyss, —— 144
Weytzel, Johann Paul 77
Wheit, Wilhelm 112
Whisler, —— 143
Whistler, —— 143
Widdersheimer, Ludwig Peter 94
Wiederer, Anna Margaretha 10
Wiedergrundel, Catharina 110
    Georg Henrich 110
Wiedersheimer, Anna Margretha
    94 [2]
    Ludwig Peter 94
Wiedersum, ——, Mrs. 114
Wiesler, —— 143
Wilcke, Anna Margaretha 8
    Elisabeth 8
    Elisabetha 8
    Johann Georg 8 [2]
    Johann Gottfried 8
    Rudolf 8 [2]
    Rudolph 7, 8 [2]
Wild, Catharina 22 [2]
    Nicholas 22 [4]
    Valentin 22
Wildemann, Jacob 87 [2]
Wildt, Veronica Maria 22
Wilflinger, Henry 60
Will, Anna Maria 6
    Christian 6
    Elizabeth 6
    Michael 6
Willhaut, Frederich 8
    Maria Magdalena 8
Winger, —— 143
Winterheimer, Jacob 77
Winther, Samuel 87
Wise, —— 144
Wisler, —— 102, 143
    Henrich 143
Wiss, —— 144
Wissler, Christian 143
Wistar, Caspar 3, 28 [2], 29 [4]

Caspar, Dr. 28
Caspar, Jr. 29
Catharine 28
John 28
Richard 28
Wister, —— 28
    Sarah 29
Witz, Carl Philipp 49 [2]
    Georg Michael 49
    Johannes 49
    Margaretha 49
Wohlfahrdt, Ludwig 23
Wohlfahrt, Gerhard 22
    Michael 22
Wohlfart, Conrad 23
    Nicholas 22
Wolf, Catharina 114
    Christina 57
    Johannes 57
    John Philip 21
    Maria Margaretha 57
    Nicholas 24
    Wolfgang 78
Wolfahrt, —— 11
Wolfangl, Elisabeth 114
Wolfart, Adam 22
    Catharina 23
    Johan Adam 23
    Joseph 23
    Nicolaus 23
Wolff, Jo. Nicklas 62
    Nickolas 62
    Nicolaus 62
Wolffhart, Anna Catharina 10 [2]
    Hans Jörg 10
Wolffling, Heinrich 60
Wölffling, David 60
    Johann Henrich 60
Wolfhardt, —— 11
Wollfarth, Adam 23
    Johann Adam 23
Wörlich, Michael 87
Wörner, Philipp Jacob 88
Wulff, Wolffgang 78
Wüst, Anna Barbara 48
    Anna Maria 48
    Barbara 48 [2]
    Georg 48 [2]
    Georg, Jr. 48
Wüster, Johann Caspar 28
Wyse, —— 144
Wyss, Peter 144
Wyssler, —— 143

--- Y ---

Yantz, —— 139
Yantzi, —— 139
Yeizer, Jacob 6
Yoder, Barbara 144
    Daniel 96
    Hannah 96
    Jacob 26, 144

Yoeder, —— 144
Yother, —— 144
Yothers, —— 144
Young, Jacob 20

--- Z ---

Zaug, —— 144
Zaugg, —— 144
z'Bären, —— 125
    Jacob 124
Zechiel, Christoph Peter 86
Zercher, —— 144
Zerger, —— 144
Zety, Abraham 57
Zieber, Johannes 110
Ziegeler, Christina 7
    John George 8
Ziegler, —— 10
    Agnes Catharina 44
    Anna 7
    Anna Barbara 8
    Anna Christina 7
    Anna Christine 7
    Anna Magdalena 7
    Anna Maria 8, 44
    Anna Martha 7
    Appolonia 22
    Barbara 7
    Christiana Margaretha 44
    Christoph 8
    Elisabeth 8
    Georg 44 [2]
    Georg Bernhard 44
    Georg Jacob 44
    Georg Philipp 7 [3]
    George 8
    Hans Georg 7, 8
    Hans Jerg 8
    Hans Martin 7, 8
    Jacob 7
    Jacob, Jr. 20
    Jacobina 44
    Johann Georg 7, 8 [2]
    Johann Jacob 7
    Johann Leonhard 23
    Johann Ludwig 8
    Johann Philipp 7 [2]
    John George 8
    John Philip 7
    Judith 20
    Ludwig 7
    Magdalena 44
    Maria 40
    Maria Catharina 7
    Martin 17 [3]
    Philip 7 [3], 8
    Philip, Jr. 7
    Philipp, Jr. 7
    Philipp Jacob 20
    Sarah 7
Zilling, Georg 21
    Michael 22

Michel 21 [2]
Zimerly, Hans Georg 144
Zimmer, Anna C. 15
Zimmerli, —— 144
Zimmerlin, —— 144
Zimmerly, Christian 144
Zimmerman, —— 84
    Abraham 105
    Jacob 119, 121
Zimmermann, Abraham 98,
        102, 103, 105
    Amalia Maria Katharina 6
    Andreas 6 [4]
    Anna Catharina 6
    Anna Elisabeth(a) 6 [2]
    Anna Margaretha 6
    Bernhard 13
    Catharina 27, 84
    Hans 144
    Hans Dietz 6
    Hans Georg 6
    Hans Michael 6, 144

Heinrich 144
Johann Georg 6
Margaretha 6
Maria Agathe 117
Niclas 25 [3]
Sebastian 5
Sybilla 27
Zittel, Daniel 82 [2]
Zook, John 144
Zougg, Uli 144
Zowg, —— 144
Züber, Johann 110
    Johannes 111
Zuck, —— 144
Zuercher, —— 144
Zug, Christian 144
    Johannes 144
    Moritz 144
    Peter 144
    Ulrich 144
Zurchen, Justina 144
    Michael 144

Zurcher, Joseph 144
Zürcher, Abraham 144
    David 144
    Hans 144
    Peter 144
Zurflie, Johannes 144
Zurflueh, —— 144
Zurfluh, —— 144
Zurflüh, Abraham 144
Zurger, —— 144
Zuricher, —— 144
Züricher, —— 144
Zweisig, Valdin 13
    Valentin 13 [2]
Zweissig, Valentin 13
Zweitzig, Bernhard 13
    Marcretha 13
Zweizig, Bernard 13
    Bernhardt 13
Zweysich, Christian 17
    John Cunradt 17
Zwitzig, Bernhard 13

INDEX TO SHIPS

--- A ---

Adolph 40
Adventure 41, 99 [2], 103,
    104 [4], 105 [2], 125,
    129, 132, 134 [2], 135,
    137, 141
Albany 144
Alexander and Anne 13, 124
Allen 69, 70, 101 [2], 127, 134
Anderson 88
Ann 84 [3]
Ann Galley 137
Aurora 58

--- B ---

Bennet Galley 28, 124, 126
Betsey 119
Betsy 19, 45
Bettsey 127
Billender Thistle 130 [2]
Britannia 81, 104, 124, 126, 133
Brittania 132
Brotherhood 84, 86, 126, 139
Brothers 22, 23, 26, 27
    86 [3], 88 [7], 124, 129

--- C ---

Chance 71, 129
Charlotte 22
Charming Betty 135
Charming Nancy 131, 135 [2],
    139, 144
Chesterfield 20, 28
Countess of Sussex 134
Crawford 56, 82

--- D ---

Davy 54
Delphin 68
Dragon 5, 10, 17, 19, 20, 56,
    74, 78 [3]
Duke of Bedford 96, 128

Duke of Wirtenberg 83, 84,
    87 [2], 88 [3], 129
Duke of Wirtenburg 44

--- E ---

Eastern Branch 96
Edinburg 26
Edinburgh 26, 41, 42, 60, 68,
    78, 82, 85 [3], 95, 96
Elizabeth 12, 71, 89
Elliot 140

--- F ---

Fox 144
Francis and Elizabeth 15, 124,
    133, 137, 138, 139,
    144 [2]
Friendship 40, 100, 127, 142 [2]
Friendship of Bristol 125, 128,
    131, 132 [2], 134, 137,
    139

--- G ---

Glasgow 49, 135
Goodwill 131

--- H ---

Halifax 55
Hamilton 48, 70
Hampshire 19, 78 [4]
Harle 101, 129, 130, 133, 137,
    144
Henrietta 27
Hero 4, 65 [2], 81, 102, 127,
    133
Hope 70, 126, 130 [2]
Hope de Fortuna 115

--- I ---

Isaac 74, 78 [2], 101

--- J ---

Jacob 21 [2], 81
Jamaica 124
James Goodwill 6, 126, 128,
    129 [2], 134 [2], 140, 143,
    144
Janet 23, 47, 48, 67, 87
John 126
John & Elizabeth 60, 95
John and William 95, 127
Johnson 138
Johnson Galley 22

--- K ---

Ketty 88
King of Prussia 56

--- L ---

Leslie 46
Little Cherub 71
Loyal Judith 62, 77 [5], 128,
    137, 138, 139
Lydia 57, 83 [2], 84, 87

--- M ---

Maria Hope 132, 133, 135
Marlborough 72, 136
Mary 93, 94 [2], 127, 130, 138,
    142
Mercury 124
Minerva 28, 42, 77
Molly 6, 13 [2], 14, 56, 72, 124,
    125, 130, 131, 132,
    133 [3], 134, 136, 139,
    140, 143
Mortonhouse 10, 82, 126 [2],

130, 131, 133, 134 [2],
135, 136, 143
Muscliffe 139

--- N ---

Nancy 52, 58, 142
Neptune 15, 27, 55, 118, 131,
143, 144
New York 91 [2]

--- O ---

Osgood 22 [2]

--- P ---

Pallas 124
Patience 19, 20 [4], 21 [3], 26,
47, 126, 140
Peggy 129
Pennsylvania Merchant 127,
134, 136, 138
Phoenix 24, 43, 47, 53, 55,
84 [2], 88 [4], 124,
128, 136 [2], 137, 140
Plaisance 9, 127, 131 [2], 140
Pleasant 11, 12 [3], 14
Polly 15, 28, 130, 139
Princess Augusta 58, 128

--- Q ---

Queen of Denmark 25 [4], 126

--- R ---

Ranier 140
Rawley 57
Restauration 18, 19 [3]
Richard and Elizabeth 67
Richard and Mary 66
Richmond 71, 78
Robert and Alice 13, 15 [2], 29,
42, 57, 80, 95, 129 [2],
131, 132, 134, 141
Rosannah 16
Rowand 105, 126
Royal Union 84, 85

--- S ---

St. Andrew 16, 17, 25, 26 [2],
49, 57, 78 [3], 80 [2],
81 [2], 82, 95, 96, 99,
101, 102, 105, 126, 127,
129 [3], 130, 132 [2],
137, 139, 140, 143
St. Andrew Galley 62
Sally 52, 82, 127
Samuel 7, 49, 93, 124, 125, 126,
127, 128, 129, 130, 133

135, 137 [2]
Samuel and Elizabeth 127
Sandwich 67, 80
Sarah 62
Shirley 18 [2], 24, 27, 87, 96
Speedwell 20

--- T ---

Thistle 62, 100
Thistle of Glasgow 71, 132, 141
Townsend 89, 129, 139
Townshend 12
Two Brothers 22, [2], 86 [4], 88
Two Sisters 10, 13

--- V ---

Vewrnon 140

--- W ---

William 139
William and Sarah 2 [4], 4, 5 [3],
7 [2], 8 [4], 9 [3], 10 [2],
11, 124, 125, 130, 131, 135,
139, 141, 144 [2]
William P. Johnson 92
Winter Galley 24, 93, 94, 95,
96, 104